MW01618514

Printed to Perfection

Twentieth-century Japanese Prints from the Robert O. Muller Collection

Joan B. Mirviss
Amy Reigle Newland
Chris Uhlenbeck
Marije Jansen
with Henk Herwig
General Editor Amy Reigle Newland

Arthur M. Sackler Gallery
Smithsonian Institution, Washington, D.C.
IN ASSOCIATION WITH
Hotei Publishing, Amsterdam

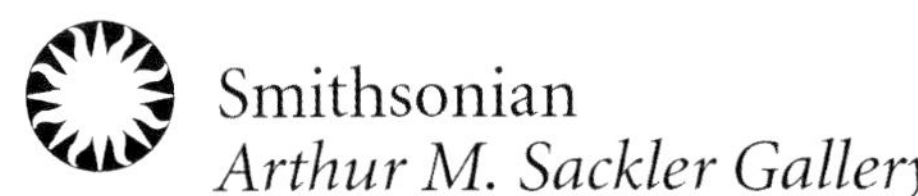

Publishing

Hotei Publishing
Imprint of KIT Publishers
Mauritskade 63
P.O. Box 95001
1090 HA Amsterdam
The Netherlands
www.hotei-publishing.com
www.kit.nl/publishers

ISBN 90-74822-73-8
NUR 642

Publication Coordinator

Chris Uhlenbeck

Design

Robert Schaap
Bergeijk, The Netherlands

Production

Meester & de Jonge
Lochem, The Netherlands

Cover illustration

Kitano Tsunetomi (1880-1947)
"Winter: In Front of a Mirror."
From the series *Seasons of the Pleasure Quarters* (*Kuruwa no shunjū*)
1918; see cat. no. 45
Arthur M. Sackler Gallery; Smithsonian Institution,
Robert O. Muller Collection S2003.8.1087

Contents

Foreword

Robert O. Muller died in April 2003 and bequeathed his collection of nearly 4,500 late nineteenth- and early twentieth-century Japanese prints, paintings and related materials – arguably the finest collection of its kind in the world – to the Arthur M. Sackler Gallery, Smithsonian Institution. The Sackler Gallery and neighboring Freer Gallery of Art together form the national museum of Asian art for the United States.

During the six years prior to his death, Muller conducted an exhaustive investigation of potential repositories for his remarkable holdings. Only after his passing was the destination of the collection made known. The honor and obligation of custodianship for this great resource will be realized in a continuing succession of exhibitions, research projects and publications. Indeed, Muller's prescience as a collector anticipated and provided for our present need to understand the vital visual culture of Japan's most turbulent century.

This publication, featuring a selection from the extensive Muller holdings, is a Sackler Gallery collaboration with Hotei Publishing in Amsterdam. There is a happy sense of predestination in this project. Chris Uhlenbeck, print expert and founder of Hotei Publishing, has been instrumental in introducing the Muller Collection to a European audience. In 1993, Hotei published *The New Wave: Twentieth-century Japanese Prints from the Robert O. Muller Collection*, the first substantial English language examination of Muller's extraordinary collection and an exceptionally informative discussion of the genesis of the modern Japanese print. In subsequent years, Muller prints filled other Hotei publications, most notably productions on the works of Kawase Hasui and Ohara Koson. Uhlenbeck's deep familiarity with Muller and his collection has added to the value of this book, for which he compiled the catalogue entries together with Marije Jansen and Henk Herwig.

The highly personal and instructive essay by Joan Mirviss, long a Muller collaborator and confidant, is equally well informed by a profound knowledge of the collection. Her contribution, built on countless hours of conversation with Muller and study of his archives, effectively establishes Muller's centrality within the world of *Shin-hanga* production, connoisseurship and marketing.

An essay by Amy Reigle Newland, also a veteran of Muller Collection research and the editor of this current project, adds precision and refinement to our understanding of *Shin-hanga*, reminding us of the complexities of artist-publisher alignments and, importantly, placing this print movement within the larger context of the *Nihonga* style of painting, Japan's attempt to give a modern voice to traditional painting styles.

Collaborators for a project of even this modest scale are too numerous to mention. At the Sackler, Amy Lewis served as a highly efficient logistical coordinator. John Tsantes and staff handled all photographic needs. Head Registrar Bruce Young, together with collections management specialists Rocky Korr and George Rogers, were models of patience and perseverance, responding to publication demands while simultaneously integrating this large collection into the museum's data bank. In the Netherlands, thanks are extended to Hotei Publishing's Director Ron Smit and Publisher Arlette Kouwenhoven, Paul Wijsman for his assistance with the annotated bibliography, and Robert Schaap, also a long-time friend of the Muller family and designer of *The New Wave*, for his design of this book. For all involved, the future prospect of immersion into the beauty and complexity of the Muller Collection is enough to insure a continued flow of publications.

James T. Ulak
Deputy Director
Freer Gallery of Art and Arthur M. Sackler Gallery
Smithsonian Institution
Washington, D.C., June 2004

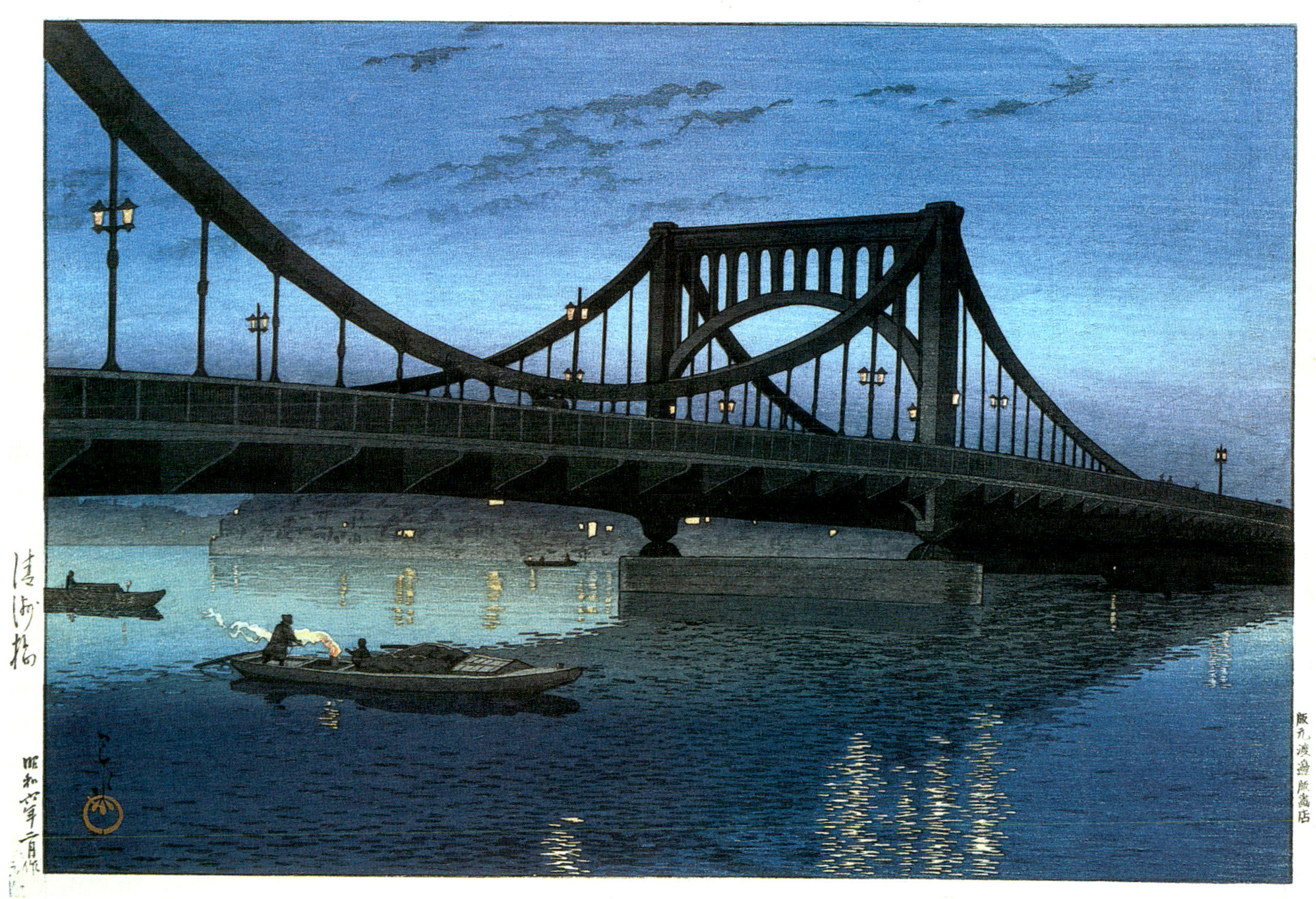

Fig. 1. Kawase Hasui (1883-1957). "Kiyosu Bridge" (*Kiyosubashi*), February 1931. 24.4 x 36.5 cm. Published by Watanabe Shōzaburō. Arthur M. Sackler Gallery, Smithsonian Institution; Robert O. Muller Collection, S2003.8.761.

The Passionate Quest for Perfection

Joan B. Mirviss

Collector, Connoisseur, Dealer
Robert O. Muller and His Unrivaled Collection

Robert O. Muller (1911-2003) spent a lifetime creating a superlative collection of Japanese woodblock prints dating from the late nineteenth to mid-twentieth century, including what is internationally understood as a paramount assemblage of *Shin-hanga*, or "New Prints." While his collection is celebrated for its depth and quality, the man who amassed it was also influential as a collector, connoisseur and dealer. As a collector and connoisseur Robert Muller spent more than seventy years amassing an unparalleled collection, which comprises approximately 4,500 prints, paintings and related materials. As a dealer he affected the course of *Shin-hanga* woodblock printmaking in Japan by placing special orders in great quantity and even commissioning entire editions. His exacting eye required the best that the Japanese publishers could offer. With his acute pragmatism and with a keen intelligence, he turned a personal passion into a thriving business. As he wrote in September 1960 to the widow of the prominent print collector Louis W. Black (1905-58), in reference to Black's connoisseurship: "I know from personal experience that prints of this rarity and quality don't just fly one's way, but demand real devotion and a 'collector's nose' to ferret out." [1] Indeed Robert Muller was blessed with such a "nose" but also displayed a dogged determination and a highly acquisitive nature – a combination destined to drive him towards both collecting and dealing.

His dual hats of collector and dealer enabled him to make important contacts in Japan at the optimal moment in history and to purchase in such significant numbers as to immediately command the attention of the art-publishing world in prewar Japan. His charm, tenacity, and honesty cemented many relationships, particularly in Japan, that endured for generations. This article will focus on the nature of the collection and how these pivotal trade relationships gave him access to tremendous quantity as well as to the rarest examples and finest impressions. It is fortunate that Robert Muller left extensive correspondence and records that enable us to follow his path, most especially the pivotal honeymoon trip to Japan in 1940, which launched his career as a leading dealer of modern Japanese prints.

I first met Bob by chance in 1976 at a Manhattan gallery, where he had consigned an exhibition of forty landscape prints by the then relatively unknown Meiji-era master, Kobayashi Kiyochika (1847-1915). Neatly dressed in a shirt, tie and an unfashionable wool plaid shirt-jacket, this bespectacled gentleman patiently shared with me, a young inexperienced graduate student (and soon-to-be-dealer) in Japanese art history at Columbia University, his insights as to the importance and genius of this unsung artist. He was both truly insightful and unwavering in his refusal to be influenced by popular tastes or current market trends. This chance encounter was the start of a professional relationship and close friendship that lasted until his death.

As one of the first dealers to introduce *Shin-hanga* artists to a broad American audience, Bob readily shared his prints with innumerable visitors and made them available for exhibition and publication. Selections from his collection have been on view at the art museums of Yale and Cornell Universities, Portland Art Museum, Japan Society and the Santa Barbara Museum of Art, among others. In Europe, the show entitled *The New Wave*, the first large exhibition devoted exclusively to his collection (with an accompanying catalogue in English and a later abridged version in French), was mounted in Leiden, Paris and Lausanne. Starting in the late 1980s, as more and more material from his collection was exhibited and published, the collection was actively pursued by museums and dealers from Japan, Europe and the United States. Bob often quipped, the "wolves are constantly at my doorstep." However, he determined that the collection should remain intact and stay in the United States. Acutely aware that it had been Americans who pioneered collecting in this field both before and after the war – the Japanese having come onboard only recently – he insisted that its final home be in an American institution of major standing.

So in 1997, Bob and his trusted advisor and son-in-law, Frederick O. Cowles, turned to me to evaluate the collection and to help Bob consider which institution would be best suited to house and preserve this enormous collection while also fulfilling his dreams for public access and visibility. After countless discussions, consultations and visits – and much soul-searching – Bob decided in 1998 to offer his collection for sale to the Arthur M. Sackler Gallery and the Freer Gallery of Art at the Smithsonian Institution. It was the clear choice since it met his exacting standards for scholarship, research, conservation care, international reputation and exposure. Negotiations for the purchase of the collection by the Freer-Sackler, most prominently with James Ulak, then curator and now deputy director, soon commenced as both parties were eager to see the collection remain intact and secure. However, discussions became protracted and continued even as Bob's health deteriorated dramatically in 2002. Thus, upon his death on April 10, 2003, it was to everyone's surprise to learn that Bob had bequeathed the entire contents of his "core" (personal) collection, library, reference files and related materials to the Museum. Through his generous gift to the nation, Bob Muller's comprehensive collection will enrich the aesthetic and cultural understanding of future generations of students, scholars, collectors and devotees of Japanese art. In order to define and evaluate this remarkable collection, it is essential first to understand just how Bob acquired the prints that comprise it. Especially in the case of the *Shin-hanga*, the fact that he was purchasing "at the source" in huge quantities helps to explain how he was able to form a vast collection of such exceptional quality. Bob's meticulous records and insightful correspondence offer an important resource for future scholars into the context and methods whereby this collection was assembled and how *Shin-hanga* prints, in particular, were created, issued and sold in Japan, then distributed abroad.

The Robert O. Muller Collection at the Freer-Sackler is particularly rich in works by designers who adapted established, "idealized" print subjects – the Kabuki theater, *bijinga* or "pictures of beautiful women," bird-and-flower images and landscape – to modern tastes. The collection can be separated into two major components: Meiji-era (1868-1912) prints by conventional *Ukiyo-e* masters and non-traditional late nineteenth-century interpretations; and the prints and paintings by *Shin-hanga* artists of the first half of the twentieth century. There are more than 250 fine impressions of the major works by the pioneering artist Kobayashi Kiyochika mentioned above, whose innovative techniques and stunning designs are representative of the challenges confronting print artists in the face of a growing demand for photographic imagery in the late nineteenth century. Important works by pivotal Meiji artists include extremely large holdings of works by Tsukioka Yoshitoshi (1839-92), Inoue Yasuji (1864-89), Utagawa Kunichika (1835-1900), Ogata Gekkō (1859-1920) and Shibata Zeshin (1807-91), to name but a few. Of course, the exhaustive collection of prints from the Sino-Japanese (1894-95) and Russo-Japanese (1904-5) Wars are well known through publications and exhibitions.

The collection's *Shin-hanga* holdings include the once extremely popular, romanticized and modernized depictions of traditional Japanese print themes that reflected the rebirth of interest on the part of the Japanese for their own artistic tradition and at the same time catered to a Western (primarily American) taste for nostalgic views of Japan. The publishers of *Shin-hanga* commissioned numerous images expressly for the market abroad. Interestingly, *Sōsaku-hanga*, or "Creative Prints," executed from initial drawing to finished woodblock print by artists like Onchi Kōshirō (1891-1955) or Munakata Shikō (1903-75), held no appeal for Bob. He disparagingly referred to them as "do-it-yourself prints." Like the practitioners of *Shin-hanga*, Bob reveled in the perfection only possible when skillful professional blockcutters and printers executed the production of an artist's design.
No doubt the greatest strength of the collection is the work of Kawase Hasui (1883-1957; cat. nos. 52-63) – possibly Bob's favorite artist throughout his seventy-one years of collecting. With over 500 prints and paintings in superb condition, the holdings in Hasui material are comprehensive. Substantial numbers of fine prints by widely known landscape print designers such as Yoshida Hiroshi (1876-1950; cat. nos. 18-22), Takahashi Hiroaki (Shōtei) (1871-1945; cat. nos. 10-7), Itō Shinsui (1898-1972; cat. nos. 85-101) and Oda Kazuma (1882-1956; cat. nos. 47-51) are also well represented. *Bijinga* constitute another significant area with extensive works by Shinsui with over ninety examples, Hashiguchi Goyō (1880-1921; cat. nos. 36-44) with twenty-one fine impressions, keyblocks and drawings, and Torii Kotondo (1900-76; cat. nos. 105-11), to name but a few. These romanticized images of contemporary women, depicted in somewhat more naturalized poses than their *Ukiyo-e* predecessors, reflect a determined effort on the part of art publishers, especially Watanabe Shōzaburō (1885-1962), to take earlier subject matter as a point of departure for innovative design and to improve upon traditional production techniques.

The collection includes superb examples of the stylized portraits of Kabuki actors in male and female roles with large holdings of exceptional designs by Yoshikawa Kanpō (1894-1979; cat. nos. 78-80), Yamamura Kōka (Toyonari) (1886-1942; cat. nos. 64-71) and Natori Shunsen (1886-1960; cat. nos. 72-5). There are also more than 400 examples by bird-and-flower specialist Ohara Koson (1877-1945; cat. nos. 23-33), many with variant impressions.[2] Altogether, the Muller collection boasts of work by more than 200 Japanese artists, plus considerable holdings of woodblock prints by Westerners living in Japan, such as Elizabeth Keith (1887-1956) and Charles W. Bartlett (1860-1940), another of Bob's personal favorites.[3]

In addition to more than 4,400 woodblock prints, drawings, keyblock prints and paintings, and nearly one hundred related objects, including process-books and woodblocks, Bob's extensive cataloging records, papers, and library are likewise located in the Sackler-Freer. This material will constitute an important archive for research into the history of modern Japanese print movements.[4] Bob's friendships with many of Japan's master print designers and art publishers active between 1940 and the early 1990s are extensively recorded in his papers. From the material in the archives, it is easy to follow his remarkable seventy-one year quest to have the best collection of its type in the world. His unquenchable thirst for the best and earliest impressions, the rarest designs, the hitherto unknown printings and the definitive masterpieces, led him to destinations across the globe – by sea, by plane and even by zeppelin. As late as two months before his death, he was still making additions to his already comprehensive collection.

The Making of a Collector and Connoisseur

Born on October 5, 1911 in Pelham, New York, Bob was first exposed to Japanese prints while a preparatory student at the Gunnery School, in Washington, Connecticut. Although his great-grandfather, Charles Erhart (1821-91), was a co-founder of Pfizer, the international pharmaceutical firm then based in Brooklyn, Bob's childhood was far from idyllic. Due to the divorce of his parents, Gertrude and Robert, when he was just six years old, Bob was shuttled along with his elder brother Erhart between boarding schools and summer holidays in Germany.

Bob made his initial acquisition years later, in 1931, as a twenty-year-old student majoring in history at Harvard University. Walking by the window of the Shima Art Company, located at 16 West 57th Street in Manhattan, Bob was smitten by the print 'Kiyosu Bridge' (*Kiyosubashi*) a night scene designed by Kawase Hasui that had been issued in February of that year (fig. 1). He paid $5 for it, a hefty sum at that time, and it was the first of many thousands of prints in his collection. The owners of the Shima store were Kazue Sumii (1894-1990), who had inherited the business upon the sudden death of her first husband (Earl T.) Torazō Shima (d. 1927), and Hango Sumii (1893-1982), her second husband. They handled both original and reproduction *Ukiyo-e* prints, *Shin-hanga*, as well as commissioning exclusive editions directly from Japanese art publishers that bore their shop seal. The

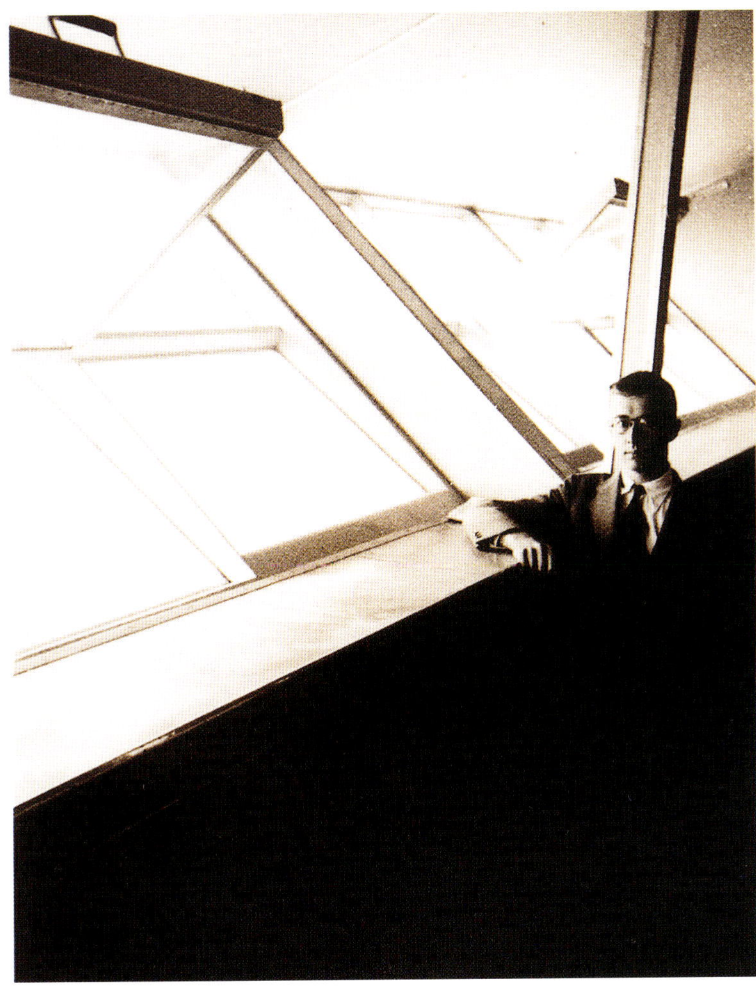

Fig. 2. Bob Muller on the Hindenburg en route from Lakehurst New Jersey to Frankfurt, Germany, August 1936. Robert O. Muller Collection, Freer Gallery of Art and Arthur M. Sackler Gallery Archives, Smithsonian Institution.

style in which their business was run would influence the manner and method in which Bob developed his enterprise a decade later. When the Sumii family was forced to return Japan in June 1942, it was Bob who openly helped them with their belongings and provided desperately needed cash through his purchase of their business. They developed a lasting friendship, and Bob continued to correspond and visit Hango, Kazue and their daughter Noriko on numerous trips to Japan over the subsequent fifty years.[5]

Bob continued to purchase prints through his college years, and a summer job in 1936 at the New York office of Lufthansa enabled Bob to fly to Germany on the infamous zeppelin, the Hindenberg (fig. 2). His ticket receipt shows that he paid the extraordinary sum of $400 for the one-way luxurious voyage to visit his German cousins. On his return trip, he traveled to London expressly to meet with the botanist and Japanese print collector-dealer Thomas Bates Blow (1853-1941) of Welwyn, Hertfordshire, whose acquaintance he may have first made earlier in New York. Long a devotee of woodblock prints of the Meiji era, Blow encouraged Bob to widen his artistic horizons and seek out fine Meiji prints by artists such as Kiyochika and Yasuji. Bob bought many items from Blow. As Bob wrote just a few years before his death, and perhaps referring to this period of his life, "Once bitten by the Modern Print bug [implying *Shin-hanga*] it is incurable, as I can attest from personal experience. And the more you see, the wider the field becomes."

In addition to Blow and the Shima Art Company, various auction houses in New York, Yamanaka and Co. and Tokaido Inc. in Boston, Shintarō Mori in Chicago, The Meiji Store in San Francisco and Kawaguchi & Co. were major sources for Bob in the late 1930s for fine print acquisitions. Prices in America at that time for *Shin-hanga* far outstripped prices in Japan, with prints by Hasui, for example, typically fetching between $10 and $15. While things Japanese were starting to lose their allure for Westerners by the end of the decade, it was Bob's honeymoon trip to Japan in 1940 that was to change his life.

The Making of a Dealer

Days after his marriage on February 3, 1940 to Ingeborg Lee (*b.* 1919), the daughter of Arthur Lee, a Norwegian sculptor and teacher at the Art Student's League in New York City, Bob and his new bride set off on a five-month honeymoon trip to Japan on the ship *Kano Maru* via Los Angeles. Arriving in Tokyo on March 15th, armed with the necessary introductions, the couple met with many of the artists whose works Bob had now been collecting for almost a decade, as well as the leading print dealers and art publishers. Most notable of the latter group were Adachi Toyohisa (1902-82), Nishinomiya Yosaku (1896-?) and Watanabe Shōzaburō. Nearly overwhelmed by the quantity, quality and affordability of the material offered to him, Bob cabled home for additional funds. His mother Gertrude neither supported nor believed in the wisdom of his endeavor; however, she did reluctantly provide the necessary capital for this and future strategic ventures. With this financial assistance he was able to continue purchasing in great quantity.[6] This even drew the attention of the Tokyo press and a story published in the *Japan Times and Mail* on April 19, 1940, headlined "Muller Intends to Introduce Modern Japanese Art in US" quoted Bob as saying: "What attracts me most about Japanese art is the love of nature which is so evident in so great a majority of the prints."

In the *Japan Times and Mail* article Bob and Inge are shown at the Imperial Hotel in Tokyo, admiring Natori Shunsen's print of Nakamura Ganjirō I (fig. 3; *see also* cat. no. 72), which Bob had just acquired for about $7 from Watanabe. While in Japan they were based at the Imperial Hotel, which Bob described in a letter written shortly after their arrival: "We have landed at the World's Most Ugly Hotel – Frank Lloyd Wright's mistake. Such architecture I never hope to see again! Every room on a different level, service is excellent, food unsurpassed. Lots of foreigners of all sorts, and a general aura of international spies."

At this time, Bob was associated with William Lee Comerford, who had been the invaluable manager of the Shima Art Company for fifteen years. It is clear from their correspondence of 1939-40 that Comerford, who seems to have been both colleague and friend as he attended the Muller wedding, supplied Bob with all of the Sumiis' sources and connections. Bob had already set up a business,[7] following their model, of matting and sending out exhibitions of *Shin-hanga* and *Ukiyo-e* reproductions to schools, universities

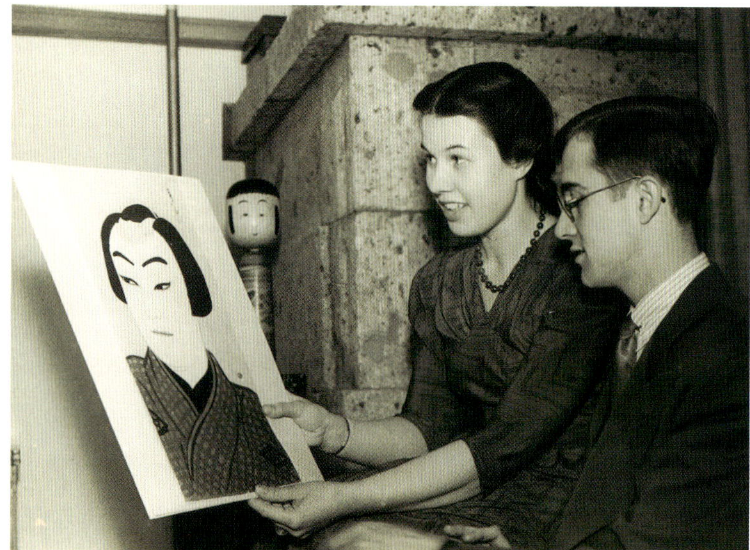

Fig. 3. Bob and Inge Muller at the Imperial Hotel, examining the 1916 print by Natori Shunsen, "The Actor Nakamura Ganjirō I as Kamiya Jihei." Photo: *Japan Times and Mail*, April 19, 1940. Robert O. Muller Collection, Freer Gallery of Art and Arthur M. Sackler Gallery Archives, Smithsonian Institution.

and churches around the world. He also patterned much of his commercial purchasing and placing of special orders after them. At this time, the two men appear to have been renting space on a month-to-month lease from the Sumiis and maintained a friendly working relationship.[8] From January to March alone, they generated as many as thirty traveling print exhibitions to locations as far away as South America, grossing more than $3,000 in sales. In Bob's absence Comerford ran this business as his partner. He kept Bob abreast of their business activities in New York, and Bob in turn wrote him lengthy letters from Japan, chronicling meetings and purchases, and negotiating strategies, constantly asking for advice and support and recounting vivid stories and experiences of life in prewar Japan. Ever the coach and cheerleader, Comerford wrote, as early as February 22nd, "I feel that you will ferret out sources that none of us have ever heard of." In this same letter he warned of threatened trade embargoes but urged Bob to persevere and mentioned that, given the difficult political situation, the Sumiis were considering whether or not to sell them the Shima Art Company and return to Japan.

Working from his base at the Imperial Hotel, Bob met with countless dealers, art publishers, and experts, one connection leading to another as so often happens in Japan. In a letter dated March 28th and written soon after their arrival, Bob described his determination to locate the main publisher of panel prints of bird-and-flower images (*kachōga*) by Ohara Koson, Daikokuya (then under the supervision of Koizumi Shinnosuke), in the Nippori section of Ueno. "It was a difficult chase, believe me – it is like a rabbit warren with dozens of tiny alleyways and flimsy shacks – A policeman led us and himself had to stop 3 times for directions." Greeted by the wife at the door he further observed, "blocks were stacked up head high, so we knew we were in the right place … It was a breezy day and the breezes came straight from the outhouse, which did not seem to be out at all."

Quickly focusing on the task at hand, Bob spent some time piling up his favorite Koson prints. The selected group comprised 634 sheets of fifty-five subjects, including as many as twenty-five impressions of several of the designs. Bob noted further, "All (are) in good condition, and instantly saleable, really hot stuff that will sell itself quickly … He wanted 90 *sen* [21¢] per sheet regardless of quantity. A reduction from ¥576 to ¥500 [$117]." [9]

By now savvy about Japanese wholesale pricing, Bob offered him ¥300. However Koizumi remained adamant, so Bob simply selected the best impressions of forty-six designs, all "sure-fire cracker-jack sellers" and left. Koizumi refused to print further impressions, a common practice in art publishing circles in Japan, even though he appeared to still have the original blocks.

Frustrated that he was unable to do more business with Koizumi, Bob nevertheless wrote Comerford that although few in number, this "fine batch of Kosons makes a good start to a business." Koizumi later sold his business to Nishinomiya and in a letter home dated mid-June, Bob wrote that Nishinomiya boasted that he used to sell 10,000 Koson prints a year to the Shima Art Company alone. He further observed that Nishinomiya had purchased all of the old Koson blocks from Daikokuya and that "they are in fearful state – honeycombed with wormholes. I saw a block on one side of which had been carved part of a Koson design, and on the other side a part of the Kiyochika war triptych."

In another letter addressed to Comerford dated April 5th, Bob tells of his initial meeting with the renowned publisher Adachi Toyohisa. His "work is wonderful-unsurpassable … his [Suzuki] Harunobu's and [Kitagawa] Utamaro's are gold itself. Colors unbeatable, subjects just the ones. He sells to Takamizawa who markets them." And later he recounts, "Adachi is a fine fellow. I like him immensely. He has a thin face, resembles a [Tōshūsai] Sharaku caricature strongly." Adachi became the primary source for *Ukiyo-e* reproductions, and they were to develop a lasting professional relationship in the coming years.

A second visit to Adachi to observe his printing techniques is described in some detail: "By first roughening the paper slightly, he infused a quality in the finished print which others don't get. His paper, workmanship, and colors are far superior to any others. His prices are slightly higher, but worth the small difference." Adachi showed him how the facsimile prints were "aged:" "He wraps a perfect, un-creased print around a bundle of bamboo leaves, and rolls it on the floor, crushing the paper. Then the print gets wrapped around the other way, and the process repeated. After two or more manglings the paper gets dampened and soon it is a fine old print!" It is worth noting that while Bob was purchasing thousands of reproduction traditional *Ukiyo-e* prints to be sold at museum stores, gift shops, resorts, colleges and so on, he was also refining his eye and learning much about the printing process – an education that would prove invaluable to the process of building and refining his "core" collection.

Impressed by Adachi's fastidious printing techniques, Bob requested the publisher produce large editions of thirty Koson designs. Using several of the Daikokuya examples, he commissioned Adachi to create printings for him. However according to his records, only twenty-one were ever completed and shipped to the States.[10] It was quite common for Japanese print publishers to issue contemporary prints bearing the signatures of deceased artists.

Landscape prints interested Bob immensely and were his first love, so it

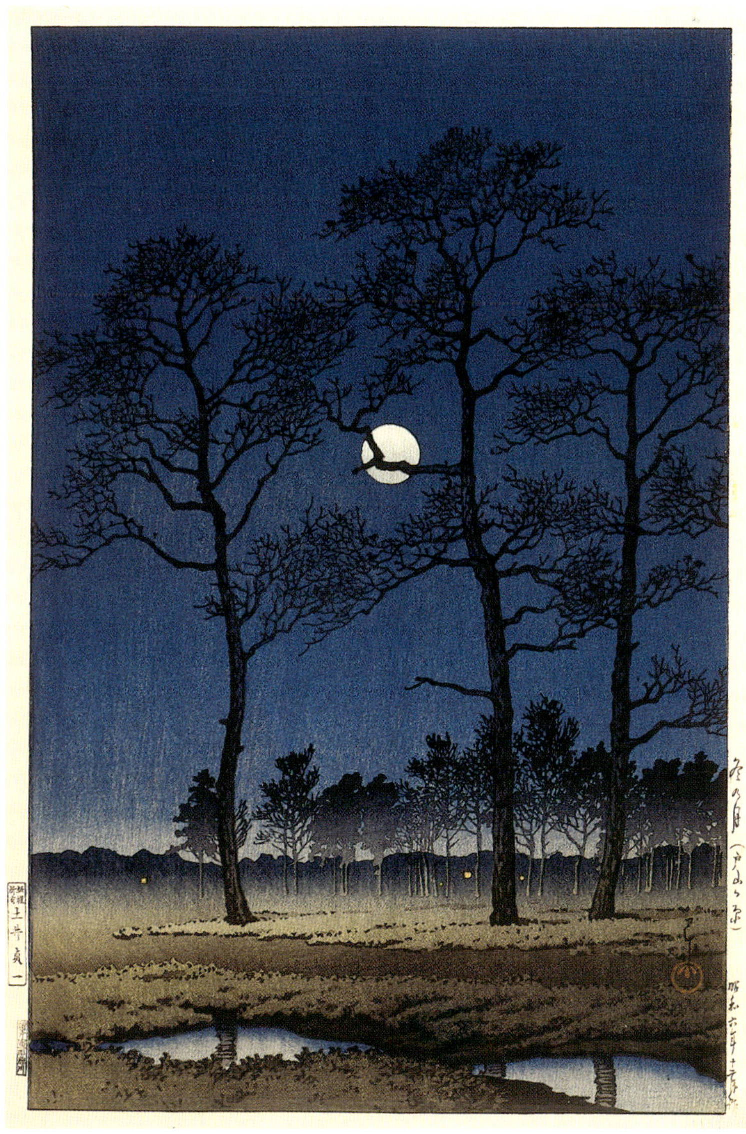

Fig. 4. Kawase Hasui (1883-1957). "Winter Moon over Toyama Plain" (*Fuyu no tsuki [Toyamagahara]*), December 1931. 36.2 x 24 cm. Published by Doi Sadaichi. Arthur M. Sackler Gallery, Smithsonian Institution; Robert O. Muller Collection, S2003.8.743.

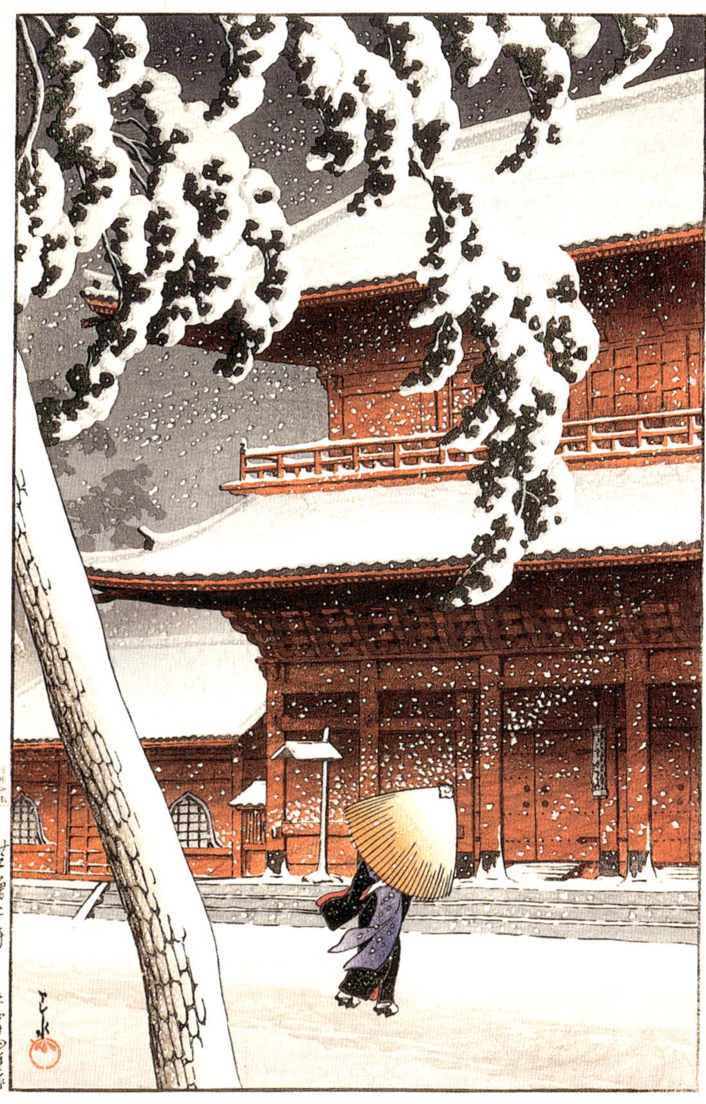

Fig. 5. Kawase Hasui (1883-1957). "Zōzōji Temple, Shiba" (*Shiba Zōzōji*), from the series *Twenty Views of Tokyo* (*Tōkyō nijūkei*), 1925, 36.2 x 23.7 cm. Published by Watanabe Shōzaburō. Arthur M. Sackler Gallery, Smithsonian Institution; Robert O. Muller Collection, S2003.8.643.

was a matter of course that he met with the major artists and publishers in this field. In a twenty-six-page letter dated June 10th, Bob detailed a purchase from the publisher Doi Sadaichi of 190 prints of five landscape designs by Hasui, all ¥2 or 50¢ each. "I think that Toyama Plain [fig. 4] … should be Hasui's very best seller, on a level with Zozoji [fig. 5]. ¥2 is a cheap price and I took all that Doi had." A few days before his departure in mid-July he acquired an additional 150 impressions of this design of the Toyama Plain. By the time of Bob's death over sixty years later only five impressions of this work remained in his "for sale" group.[11] Having been introduced to Hasui at a memorable dinner party at the luxurious home of Itō Shinsui,[12] he frequently met with Hasui's principal publisher, Watanabe Shōzaburō. Judging from the seven-page invoice reflecting five months of acquisitions from this shop, Bob bought a number of his most important treasures and much of the best of his commercial stock from Watanabe. This purchase included thirty Shoson (Ohara Koson) designs totaling nearly 1,500 sheets, sixty-five *ōban* (*c.* 36 x 24 cm) format images by Hasui totaling over 1,400 impressions, 1,880 small *koban* (*c.* 14 x 9 cm) format Hasui landscapes, and numerous prints by Kasamatsu Shirō (1898-1944; cat. nos. 102-4), Oda Kazuma, and even Watanabe himself. Some of the rarer items were purchased as single sheets for his own collection, other prints in groups of as many as 375 impressions of the same design. Bob shrewdly negotiated a substantial 45% discount that brought his cost down to about 55¢ each. Never purely a name buyer, Bob wrote to Comerford on March 20th about a visit to Watanabe's shop, "The new Shinsui landscapes were on the wall – atrocious – I didn't even recognize the artist." Bob is perhaps describing the bright palette of the 1939 series *Eight Views of Izu* (*Izu hakkei*). In the end he did succumb and in later years acquired several images from this set.

Clearly the period that Bob was in Japan was an optimal time for buying prints. For decades, he remained a trusted and loyal customer of Watanabe; the archives contain numerous invoices for additional substantial acquisitions through the 1950s and 1960s. In the following years Bob himself became a major source for Western dealers, collectors and curators.

In early July of 1940, he finally made the acquaintance of Yoshida Hiroshi, the only *Shin-hanga* artist who self-printed his works. "The quality of his work, as you know, is excellent – far superior to Watanabe's … The Yoshida's of course are not for the school trade but rather for store sales and universities – also libraries and museums; and of course the better summer resorts." According to the invoice from Yoshida's studio, Bob purchased four sheets each of fifty designs at ¥5 each and 6 impressions by Yoshida's son, Toshi (1911-95), all for about ¥1,100 (about $460).

One of his closest advisors, guides and sources in Japan was the *Ukiyo-e* dealer Matsuki Kihachirō, Watanabe's associate and proprietor of Shōbisha in the Kanda district of Tokyo. Bob obtained many of his rare prints predating the Great Kantō Earthquake of September 1923 from Matsuki, including superb impressions by Kōka, Shinsui, Kaburagi Kiyokata (1878-1973; cat. nos. 5-7), Kiyochika and Yoshitoshi's celebrated triptych "Fujiwara Yasumasa Plays the Flute by Moonlight" (1883) (for $4), all now housed in the Freer-Sackler.

While Bob did travel to Kyoto in his energetic search for cheaper and better stock, there was (and remains) relatively little print business to be done there. However, he did call on the publishing house Unsodō. This visit initiated a long-term working relationship with Yamada Shigeji that resulted in numerous postwar print commissions of animals based on paintings and book illustrations by the celebrated Kyoto painter, Takeuchi Seihō (1864-1942, *see below* fig. 8). He also secured various early Goyō prints from Unsodō.

During the course of his hard-working honeymoon Bob spent just under $9,000 – a very sizeable sum at that time – on tens of thousands of Japanese prints. This included Meiji prints, *Shin-hanga*, and reproductions of classical *Ukiyo-e*. From Watanabe alone, he acquired nearly 2,500 prints. From Takemura Hideo, the Yokohama publisher whose business was destroyed during World War II, Bob bought 3,800 impressions (at 17¢ each) of sixteen floral compositions bearing the signature Hōdō (Nishimura Hōdō), in addition to another 1,200 prints of six images of animals and 3,000 postcards. And for this sizeable purchase he negotiated the exclusive rights to these floral designs. But while Bob was buying in bulk, stocking up for his business venture in New York, he was simultaneously selecting the best and rarest impressions for himself. In fact, many of the receipts for these 1940 acquisitions relate to single print purchases.

Although Bob and Inge experienced substantial difficulty in securing return passage from economically troubled prewar Japan, they finally set sail on the *Kongō Maru* on July 18, 1940, disembarking in Los Angeles. "We have no less than 40 pieces of baggage (despite having sent scores of packages of prints home). This includes three crates from Watanabe, two crates with postcards, two crates of Yoshida's book, one crate of 4,850 postcards from Shobido, crates of prints books and chinaware … fortunately this ship goes to NY, so that I can leave almost all the baggage on board. It will get to NY a few days before I do."

They were seen off by Takemura Hideo and his son George, Adachi, his wife, younger brother, and young son. Moriyama Tetsutarō (Watanabe's English-speaking assistant) and Watanabe's son, Tadasu, were also in the party (fig. 6): "Because of the delay in sailing, everyone left early, except Moriyama, who stayed until the bitter end, even walked down to the end of the long pier, and continued waving as long as we were visible."

Dealer as Collector/Collector as Dealer

It is important to note that once back in the States, Bob began to keep separate accounting books for those items reserved for his collection and those for the commercial business. Through the years he continued to expand and refine that "core" group destined for his collection, searching for

Fig. 6. Departure from Yokohama, Japan on the *Kongō Maru* on July 18, 1940. Bob and Inge are surrounded by a number of art publishers and their families. Robert O. Muller Collection, Freer Gallery of Art and Arthur M. Sackler Gallery Archives, Smithsonian Institution.

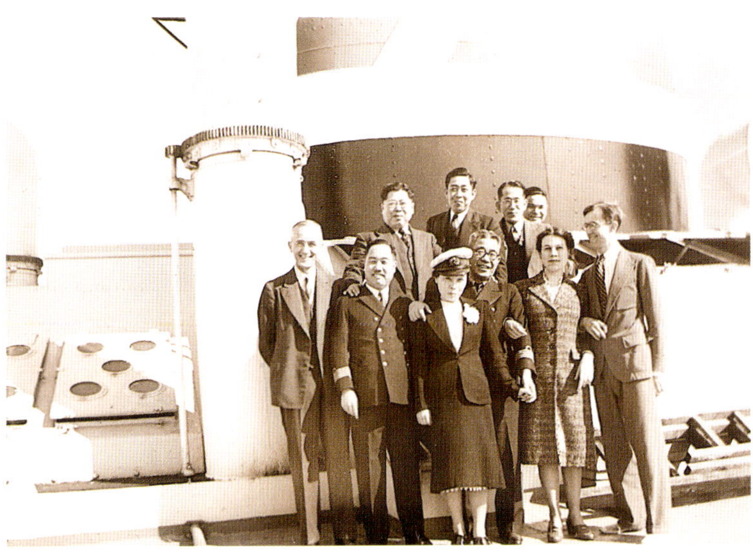

increasingly rare impressions and alternative states. A few months after his return to New York, Bob wrote Watanabe, "the prints I obtained through you this summer are among my greatest treasures, and have made the collection of extraordinary value and interest. I consider the Goyo's to be the finest prints I brought back from Japan … the modern prints are just getting known, largely through my efforts; and therefore I am particularly happy to show my Goyo's. In the spring I hope to have a one-man show in our gallery, showing just the work of Goyo; but for this I have not yet sufficient material."

On the eve of America's involvement in World War II, in September of 1940, Bob purchased the entire assets of the Shima Art Company for $7,500, enabling the owners, the Sumii family, to return to Japan. This purchase gave Bob an enhanced base for his nascent business. On October 21st he opened the Robert Lee Gallery on the second floor of 69 East 57th with a show of works by Kawase Hasui (fig. 7). The gallery's name was derived from Bob's name and that of his partner, William Lee Comerford. Lee was also his wife's maiden name. Just one month earlier Bob wrote to Matsuki, "I have rented a gallery … and hope to open some time next month. There is a great deal to be done to open a business, as you know. The biggest items in a business seem to be the expenses!" The timing could not have been worse, and they were forced to close the gallery after the attack on Pearl Harbor in December 1941. Operations were moved temporarily to 32 West 57th Street. Needless to say, it was more than a decade before things Japanese were again in vogue. Nevertheless, many of Bob's Japanese contacts remained life-long friends, as did their children. Immediately following the war, numerous letters attest to countless care packages that he sent to struggling friends in Japan.

Japan's entrance into World War II effectively brought the Western passion for modern Japanese prints to a temporary end, yet Bob continued collecting in isolation, even after he closed the New York gallery. Undoubtedly frustrated by trade embargoes with Japan, Bob sought out Japanese prints in the West. In 1942, despite trade embargoes he daringly purchased several Shinsui prints from Sotheby's London, including six images from the series *The Eight Views of Ōmi* (*Ōmi hakkei*, 1917-18), numerous Kiyochika images and several Hasui landscape designs. It goes without saying that during the war, prices for these out-of-fashion items hit rock bottom.

Several years later and with the end of the War, in 1946, Bob moved to an early eighteenth-century farmhouse in Newtown, Connecticut, in search of a more rural setting to raise his children. One year later, he re-established his operations there as well. The house, built in 1710, is nestled on eighteen

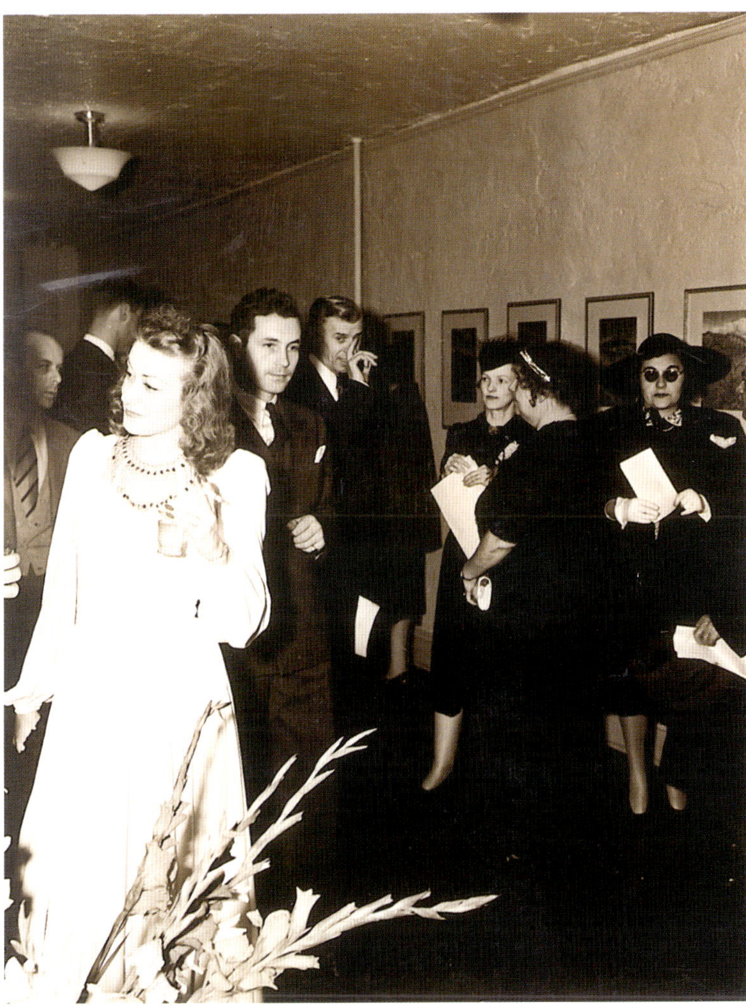

Fig. 7. Opening night of the Kawase Hasui exhibition at the Robert Lee Gallery, 69 East 57th Street, New York City, October 21, 1940. Robert O. Muller Collection, Freer Gallery of Art and Arthur M. Sackler Gallery Archives Smithsonian Institution.

wooded acres, and Bob became an avid farmer. He also continued his print business by assembling sales exhibitions of *Shin-hanga* from his collection of duplicates that traveled to colleges and small galleries throughout the country. In this way, Bob introduced *Shin-hanga* artists to a broad American audience, while at the same time greatly influencing the direction of postwar print production in Japan through his steady orders placed with the Japanese art publishers.

In 1956, a few years after Japan was officially restored to sovereignty, Nishinomiya Yosaku sent him a sample impression of Koson's design of "Pheasants in the Snow." Very much the connoisseur, Bob replied, "I have compared this print with my other copy and find it better in the printing of the trees and in the green of the pheasant's crest, which was probably put on by brush. This is missing from my other copy. However the other copy has a more gentle orange glow in the background sky, which I feel is a little harsh in the copy sent by you. The pheasants is possibly Koson's masterpiece and I am anxious to have it back in perfect condition."

In the mid-1950s, Bob contacted the Kyoto publisher Unsodō about commissioning a print of a bear based on a painting by Takeuchi Seihō, the Kyoto painter mentioned earlier. In December 1956, Yamada Shigeji of Unsodō wrote to say that the "Bear in Snow" would require a laborious printing process of thirty separate steps and hence would be priced at $1.50 per sheet for a minimum order of two hundred. Ever the astute businessman, Bob responded, requesting exclusive rights to this design. Yamada replied: "If you want possession and sole use of its blocks, we hope you (will) pay $50 including postage." Bob commissioned 300 impressions and requested, "I would like to retain sole use of these blocks and have the blocks sent to me when the printing is finished. These blocks might eventually end up in a museum, to illustrate the Japanese craft. So please send me a listing of the order of printing, numbering the blocks accordingly. Also a set of process sheets showing the different stages of printing this subject, would be useful, for which of course I would pay you extra." All of this material is now housed at the Freer-Sackler and is available for further study.

Japanese art was slowly coming back into fashion by the early 1960s. This is most clearly evidenced by the reappearance of Japanese prints at auction and their moderately buoyant sales. Soon it was business as usual. In 1962 Bob purchased Merwin's Art Shop in New Haven, primarily a framing shop situated adjacent to the Yale University campus whose previous owners were Bob's clients. At Merwin's, Bob met many scholars and academics. He also infected many students and teachers with the collecting "bug," selling Japanese prints from the back room. In the same year, 1962, his old Los Angeles friend, author of books on the poet Carl Sandburg and Chinese snuff bottles and fellow Japanese print enthusiast, Lilla S. Perry (1882-1971), introduced Bob to James D. Tobin, a collector in Oregon who was looking for fine quality modern Japanese prints. Bob promptly sent him a list including works by Hasui, Shinsui, Tsuchiya Kōitsu (1870-1949; cat. nos. 8-9), Shirō and Kazuma. According to the archival records, Tobin later purchased numerous prints from Bob. However, in a letter dating to 1964, Tobin wrote of his confusion regarding Bob's dual hats of collector and dealer. Bob responded by writing, "As for my position as a dealer and collector – it is indeed ambiguous. After collecting prints for eight years I practically fell heir to a large collection – the Shima Art Co. of NY – before the war and have been continuing their business ever since. But my heart is still in the collecting – collectors are born – and I keep the two strictly separate. Any overlapping is coincidental ... To eliminate any misunderstanding, my own collection is not for sale, directly or indirectly."

In this letter he also mentioned the wonderful large print of "The Actor Nakamura Ganjirō I as Kamiya Jihei" by Shunsen (*see* fig. 3), and claimed it was his favorite modern actor print, and better than Kōka, whose prints Bob generally preferred over Shunsen. Indeed, this was the print that he had so proudly held for the photo in the *Japan Times and Mail* twenty-four years earlier.

Over the sixty years in which Bob was active as a dealer, he was responsible for the dispersal of tens of thousands of *Shin-hanga* prints throughout the United States and later to Europe and finally back to Japan. There are receipts for purchases of thousands of Hasui landscape prints that he ordered and re-ordered over the years from Watanabe, often numbering several hundred impressions at a time. But he also enjoyed the role of collector/connoisseur. He wrote in a letter to James D. Tobin dated February 25, 1963 about the confusing issue of Watanabe publisher's seals on Hasui prints: "Watanabe changed his copyright from time to time and thereby unconsciously set up a mechanical means by which different printings can be dated roughly ... I have been able to sort out the different seals. Different copies of a subject can often be found with three or even four different seals." Woodblock prints were something that spoke to him directly. In his notes written in the 1960s for a book manuscript on the subject that was never completed, he reveals his highly refined sensibility:

> *A print is considered more valuable than a sketch from which it is made – this is not just due to the mechanics of collection, but to the special woodblock quality – a textural beauty impossible to obtain by any other medium. The flatness and unity imparted by the medium, as well as the special, intensity of color obtained in the "something added" which enhances the original sketch. Any comparison of sketch to print will show this clearly.*

Through the years Bob continued to play a pivotal role in the growing appreciation of Meiji era prints and the *Shin-hanga* tradition. He relished the aesthetic impact he made on others. One Japanese scholar, Professor Haga Tōru, was so moved by his visits with Bob and his collection that he wrote a lengthy article entitled "Ikyō no Nihon bijutsu – Konechikatto no Nihon hanga" (Japanese Art Abroad: Japanese Prints in Connecticut) published in

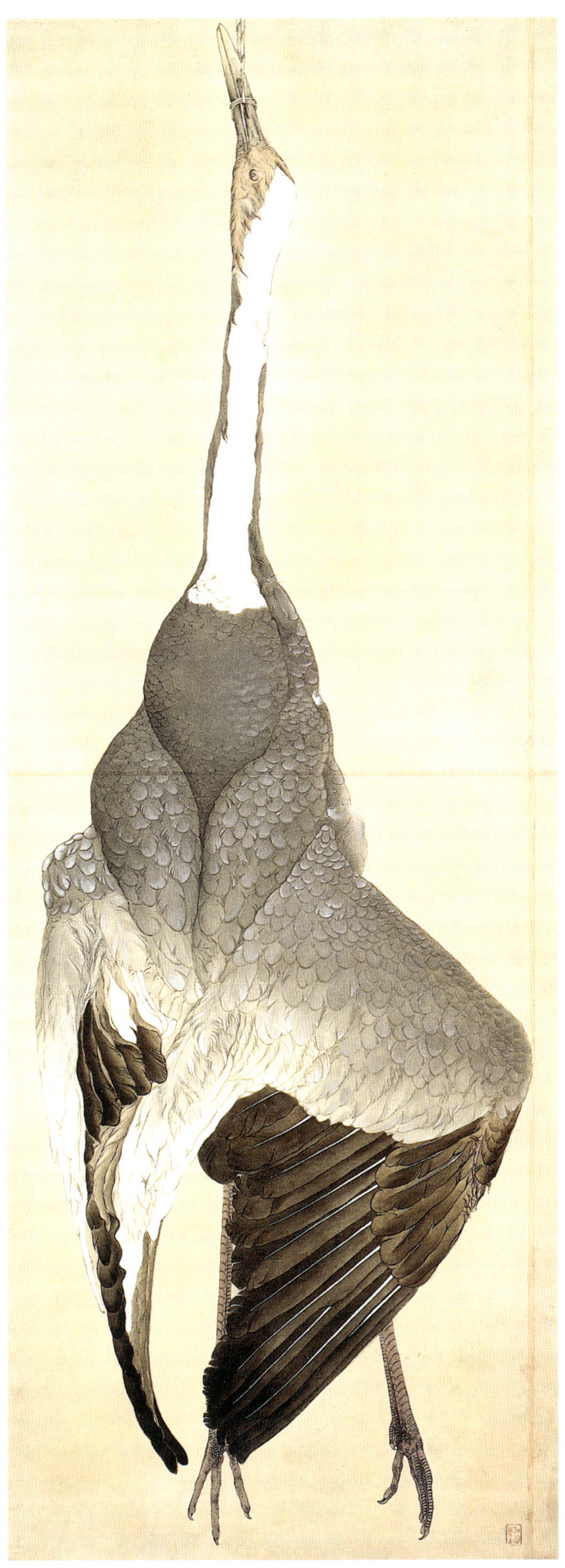

Hikaku bungaku kenkyū (*Studies on Comparative Literature*) at Tokyo University in June 1977. In it he recounted the visits he made while on sabbatical in Washington, first to Merwin's Art Shop and then later to the barn in Newtown. "Mr. Muller took Kiyochika and Shinsui prints out of the drawers (of his shop), but he had no intention of selling them. Far from that. I felt his determination not to part with these favorite prints that he had so rigorously collected. I immediately understood that he was one of the maniacs who you often see among art enthusiasts." Professor Haga obviously passed the grade at their initial meeting and was invited to Newtown. There he noted that this collector's determination to continuously search for ever-better impressions had made this the perfect collection. Bob must have been especially moved and gratified by the lengthy and emotional response that his "treasures" elicited from this respected Japanese scholar.

Bob carefully orchestrated each presentation of paintings or prints to every visitor – hopefully guiding them through the aesthetic experience – to a new-found, shared perception. He always prompted us to see and feel more than we expected. Bob often concluded visits with appreciative guests with the unrolling of Takeuchi Seihō's "Dead Crane" (fig. 8). The painting often brought tears from viewers, as it did for Bob nearly every time he saw it. While Bob possessed a fine collection of paintings, mostly amassed late in his life, his most enduring creation and greatest achievement is his print collection. Future generations will marvel at his foresight and courage to collect in areas unaccepted anywhere else, particularly at a time when Japanese art was unfashionable due to geopolitical events.

In a letter of condolence dated April 11, 1962 to Watanabe Tadasu upon the death of his father, Watanabe Shōzaburō, Bob offered the words: "It has been said that art is a mistress who never betrays one, and I am sure that your father would have agreed with that. Apart from the lifelong personal joy which he derived from prints he contributed to the happiness of countless other people and awakened their eyes to beauty." In hindsight, these words are quite a fitting epitaph for his own life.

Fig. 8. Takeuchi Seihō (1864-1942). "Dead Crane," n.d. Hanging scroll, ink and light color on paper, 154 x 56.8 cm. Ex-collection Robert O. Muller, Collection of Robert and Betsy Feinberg.

Notes

1. All quotes are drawn from the Robert O. Muller archives, now located at the Freer-Sackler. These archives include correspondence relating to Japanese art, detailed accounts of his pivotal honeymoon trip to Japan in 1940, various invoices for purchases as well as sales, account books, related magazine and newspaper clippings, notes for a proposed book and photographs chronicling much of his early career.

2. Many are published in Newland *et al.* (2001).

3. Publications that extensively illustrate works from the Robert O. Muller Collection include: Brown (2003), this publication is dedicated to Bob; Hamanaka and Newland (2000); Stephens (ed.) (1993); Narazaki (1990) and Smith (1988).

4. Fortunately for posterity, Bob kept precise and detailed records. For every item, the relevant data – including the source and date of purchase – was recorded on a large index card that was carefully filed in a large metal filing cabinet by artist and, if relevant, series or format. At the upper right corner of each card he attached a color Polaroid photo. In many cases, he also included notes on exhibition and publication histories. These cards became an indispensable tool for arranging loans to museums, for keeping track of publications, and as references for scholarly comments. Additionally and even more importantly, he painstakingly matted, labeled and stored every print in archival Solander boxes.

5. For a further discussion on the Shima Art Company and the Sumii family, *see* the article by Kotarō Sumii, "The Shima Art Company: The History of My Grandparents' Business," currently posted on the *www.shotei.com* website.

6. This conclusion is based on interviews with numerous family members, including Erhart Muller (Bob's elder brother) and Frederick O. Cowles.

7. While the selection of name, the Robert Lee Gallery, was made shortly after Bob's return from Japan, the title of this prior business remains unknown as there is no letterhead or specific invoices dating to this period in the archives.

8. It is unclear if at this time Comerford was working for the Sumii family and Bob. Unfortunately there is no specific documentation relating to this in the archives; however, it is this author's *impression* that Comerford was working for both.

9. This is based on the then exchange rate of US$1=¥4.30.

10. According to his purchase records for the prints acquired in June 1940, Muller placed an order for thirty Koson *tanzaku* designs, noting however that he only received printings of twenty-one of the selected images and that Adachi took the liberty of adding several of his own choosing. Illustrations of these twenty-one designs may be found in Newland *et al.* (2001): 7.6, 7.10, 7.11, 11.3, 11.10, 11.12, 14.14, 14.23, 28.8, 33.13, 36.9, 38.8, 39.16, 40.6, 41.3, 41.17, 41.21, 43.3, 43.6, and one unidentified image.

11. However, in addition to the Doi version, there was also a pristine copy in the collection of the pre-earthquake "Toyoma Plain" (*Toyama no hara*), from the series *Twelve Scenes of Tokyo* (*Tōkyō jūnidai*) issued by Watanabe in Winter 1920, as well as a watercolor painting dated 1937 with the same title and composition.

12. For a full description of this occasion and a photograph of the participants, *see* Mirviss (2003), 113, fig. 6.

Shin-hanga: *Innovation from Tradition*[1]

Amy Reigle Newland

An artist should use freely whatever materials he pleases. In the case of a woodblock print, he simply goes one step further and employs a block instead of a brush … Some claim that it is not a method of pure art unless it is self-drawn [jiga], *self-carved* [jikoku] *and self-printed* [jizuri], *but in fact it is fine as long as the artist can express himself in the manner he pleases, even if he draws on the strength of another. In short, for the artist to express his ideals, the printer and the blockcutter assist his work as though they were his arms and legs, and this means that the artist himself must have a profound knowledge of the print process.* (Watanabe Shōzaburō, 1916)[2]

Shin-hanga, or "New Prints," are part of a complex art culture that evolved in Japan during the 1910s and 1920s. The economic, social and cultural changes of the Meiji era (1868-1912), which contributed to the decline of the woodblock print as a reprographic medium and the rise of the "art print," as well as a search for cultural "self-identity" that was an undercurrent of the Taishō period (1912-26) coalesced to create *Shin-hanga*. To understand the environment in which *Shin-hanga* evolved, it might be instructive to step back and look briefly at the changes affecting the tradition of woodblock printmaking and art society in the later Meiji and early Taishō periods.

Following the Meiji Restoration of 1868, Japan moved from feudal rule by a succession of Tokugawa shoguns who operated a policy of relative seclusion to a nation returned to imperial rule and open to foreign trade.[3] As the new leaders looked for the means to realize their "Meiji dream," many looked to the West as a model for modernization. The desire for political, economic and technological parity hurried the nascent Meiji government – and its citizens – to embrace all things Western in the first two decades of its rule. "It is as though a bottle has been overturned. Clothing, food and drink, houses, laws, government, customs, even all kinds of crafts and scholarly pursuits – there is nothing which we are not today taking from the West," wrote one government official in 1874.[4] Japanese began to travel to and study in the United States and Europe, and foreigners were employed in Japan as advisors in government programs. The Japanese government also understood the need to exhibit at world expositions, Paris (1867), Vienna (1873), Melbourne (1875) and Philadelphia (1876), to name but a few, while organizing its own *Naikoku Kangyō Hakurankai* (National Industrial Exposition) in Tokyo in 1877.

Technological innovations went hand-in-hand with the changes that besieged Japan at this time. One was an influx of new reprographic techniques that were to challenge the tradition of woodblock printing known as *nishiki-e* ("brocade pictures") or *Ukiyo-e* ("pictures of the floating world") that had been established in the Edo period (1600-1868). Today, we are most familiar with *nishiki-e* as those "popular" images of celebrated Kabuki actors, courtesans and landscapes, oftentimes purchased as mementos of one's favorite theatrical star, celebrated beauty, or a visit to a famous place.[5] However, the role of *Ukiyo-e* prints as mass media graphics during the Meiji era – particularly with the emergence of magazines and newspapers – was superseded by new processes like lithography and copperplate intaglio printing in the 1870s, and later end-grain woodblock printing. According to John Clark, "The oft-lamented decline and passing away of *ukiyo-e* in fact historically masks the entire restructuring of reprographics and printing in general with new techniques from Europe and the United States. This change occurred on such a scale that one may unhesitatingly call it a revolution."[6] Meiji publishers of *nishiki-e* were challenged to seek out new avenues for the woodblock print to supplement existing formats and genres. They did this for a time in the late nineteenth and early twentieth centuries in the form of newspaper illustrations, *kuchi-e* (novel or magazine frontispieces popular from 1890s onward; fig. 1),

Fig. 1. Kajita Hanko (1870-1917). "Plum" (*Ume*), *kuchi-e* or "frontispiece" published in the magazine *Bungei kurabu* 14, no. 3 (1908). 29.9 x 21.9 cm. Arthur M. Sackler Gallery, Smithsonian Institution; Robert O. Muller Collection, S2003.8.436.

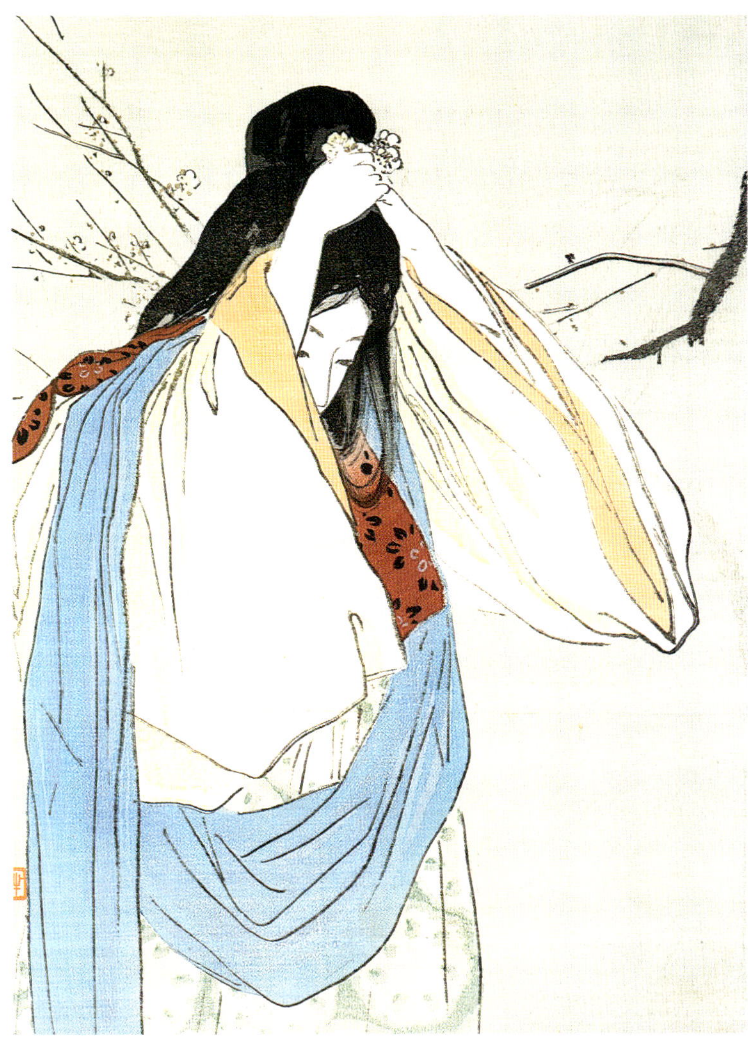

advertisements, art reproduction or as war reportage.[7] But the expansion of the woodblock print away from its role as a reproductive media and popular art to a type of creative "art print" was inevitable for its survival. As will be touched on below, it was this definition of what constituted a *creative print* that was to spark heated debate in the early twentieth century and beyond.

By the 1880s and 1890s the enthusiasm for Western customs and ideologies, so characteristic of the early decades of the Meiji, was met with introspection. It reached a groundswell by the turn of the century and resulted in a contentious debate between those who now questioned the toll that this radically new era and its adoption of Western customs had on Japanese culture and those who advocated total Westernization. This debate over the nature of Japanese identity was equally reflected in the arts, with art society polarized between proponents of Western ideologies and those struggling to define Japan's cultural and moral roots in the modern world. This meant for many artists the dilemma of having to choose between modes oriented toward the traditional (Japanese) and the modern (Western), a distinction that is most clearly seen in *Yōga* ("Western-style painting") and *Nihonga* ("Japanese-style painting"). The division between them became entrenched in art school training programs and in exhibitions which were being established at this time for producers of the "fine arts."[8]

The formation of art schools and the exposure of Japanese artists to styles and ideologies germinated in the West encouraged artists to explore technical and artistic possibilities. This included the discussion of their role in the "creative process," regardless of stylistic or school affiliation. The concept of "artist as creator" would gather strength in the early twentieth century, and was as valid for *Nihonga* as for *Yōga* painters. However, creativity for *Nihonga* artists was channeled through the use of traditional brush techniques and sensibilities while assimilating Western spatial concepts and use of light and color. The very word *Nihonga* or "Japanese-style painting," was to be seen as an assertion of a "Japanese character" (*wakon*) and "from an internal need to preserve and express visual elements that were held to be quintessential to Japan as a culture."[9] *Yōga* artists, who worked in oils and watercolors, were conscious of keeping abreast of new European styles, even though they often did so without grasping fully the underlying polemic. To them creative individualism was paramount.

Parallels exist in the graphic arts, not surprisingly because a number of the artists who produced signature prints in the early twentieth century, that is in *Sōsaku-hanga* and *Shin-hanga*, were trained in *Yōga* and *Nihonga*, respectively.[10] As such, the modern (Western) concept of creativity whereby the artist was in control of all facets of the creative process[11] and *au courant* of international trends (*Sōsaku-hanga*) was played out against the traditional medium of woodblock prints (*Shin-hanga*). A further distinction was forged in the workings of the two groups. *Shin-hanga* were the result of the conventional collaborative and publisher-oriented system involving artist, blockcutter, printer and publisher as known in *Ukiyo-e*. By contrast, *Sōsaku-hanga* artists believed their work embodied the slogan "self-drawn, self-carved and self-printed" (*jiga, jikoku, jizuri*; *cf.* quote at beginning).[12] They derided the group-based *Shin-hanga* as derivative "Neo-*Ukiyo-e*" lacking the artistic qualities necessary to make it creative work and particularly in view of its commercial orientation. But research, especially over the last decade, has demonstrated that on closer inspection, the borders that define and divide *Shin-hanga* and *Sōsaku-hanga* are hardly clear cut. The battle cry of *Sōsaku-hanga* artists that their work was "self-drawn, self-carved and self-printed" and therefore more viable in artistic and creative terms is weakened when we realize that a number of its own defenders at one time relied on the expertise of master blockcutters or printers.[13] We are also aware that they were any number of artists who did not belong to either camp and were artists of a so-called "middle ground," such as Yoshida Hiroshi (1876-1950; cat. nos. 18-22).

It cannot be disputed that by its very nature *Shin-hanga* was a group art, involving a hierarchical relationship and driven by commercial success. These features of the movement and its adoption of traditional themes might appear contrapositive to artistic individualism, giving rise to the criticism leveled at them by their *Sōsaku-hanga* peers. However, as Hollis Goodall-Cristante points out, *Shin-hanga* artists were seeking out integral aspects of their own culture in an effort to define their own identities, and having once gleaned what was needed from Western art, they "returned to the sights around them, seeking the essence of their environment."[14] In the same way that *Nihonga* painters saw their paintings as an assertion of a "Japanese character," so too did the artists who designed *Shin-hanga*. That many of the artists contributing to *Shin-hanga* from the 1910s to the 1930s are *Nihonga* painters and not print designers does not, in this light, seem incongruent. In fact, it is especially illuminating when we realize that Watanabe Shōzaburō (1885-1962) pioneered *Shin-hanga* as a result of viewing paintings – in the main *Nihonga* – and judging them with the eye of a print publisher. It is certainly this connection with *Nihonga* that is vital in a correct "re-interpretation" of *Shin-hanga*.[15]

Innovation from Tradition: Watanabe Shōzaburō, Shin-hanga *until 1923*

Any discussion of *Shin-hanga* inevitably begins with the figure of Watanabe Shōzaburō (fig. 2), without whom the artistic niche culture of "New Prints" would never have come to fruition. The second son of a rural family in the village of Gokamura-Egawa in Ibaraki prefecture, Watanabe Shōzaburō moved to Tokyo as a child.[16] In 1902 he was taken on by the art dealer and publisher Kobayashi Bunshichi (1864-1923) to work at Kobayashi's Yokohama branch, which had been established to export Japanese art to the West. Kobayashi also published reproductions and commissioned prints from contemporary artists like Uehara Konen (1877-1940; cat. nos. 1-4). He was also an instrumental dealer to patrons in the United States in the formation of collections such as those at the Freer Gallery of Art and the Museum of

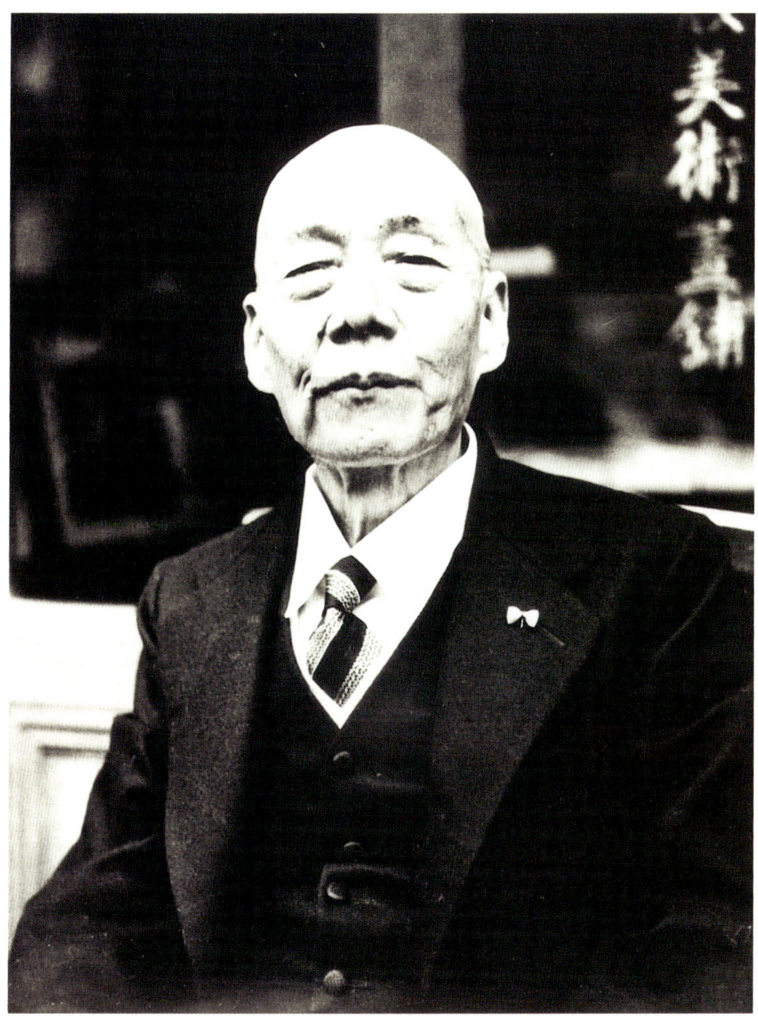

Fig. 2. Photograph of Watanabe Shōzaburō (1885-1962).
Courtesy of Watanabe Tadasu.

Fine Arts, Boston (*see also* text following cat. no. 4).[17] It was at Kobayashi's store that Watanabe first encountered *Ukiyo-e* prints from the Edo to the early Meiji periods. There is no doubt that these early experiences were to shape Watanabe's future path in the creation of *Shin-hanga*, what scholars in the past have conveniently, but in many ways too simplistically, labeled a "revitalization" of the *Ukiyo-e* woodblock tradition.

In 1906, at the age of twenty-six, Watanabe set up his own shop Shōbidō in Tokyo's Nihonbashi district, where he dealt in *Ukiyo-e* and supervised the reprinting of older prints by masters like Suzuki Harunobu (1725?-70). His appetite whetted by the possibilities of print production, he attempted to make his own woodblock prints, especially prints suitable for a foreign market. Around this time, in 1906/1907, he commissioned the little-known artist Takahashi Shōtei (Hiroaki) (1871-1945; cat. nos. 10-7) to design a landscape composition in the print format called *mitsugiriban* (literally, "three-cut size;" three images printed on a single sheet and then cut).[18] Other Shōtei prints by Watanabe were exhibited in 1907 at a friend's shop in the resort town of Karuizawa north of Tokyo, a locale frequented by both Japanese and Western tourists. Sales were good, which must have encouraged Watanabe, whose interest in the potentiality of print production were deepening. In one sense these early prints can be seen as early *Shin-hanga*.

The following year, 1908, witnessed Watanabe's marriage to Chikamatsu Chiyo, the daughter of blockcutter Chikamatsu Otoji, who carved Shōtei's prints for Watanabe. Watanabe's recent marriage and a growing business seems to have prompted a move to the Gorobei-chō in Kyōbashi. He continued to deal in prints, and at the same time engaged artisans to work in his own studio, producing postcards, calendars and Christmas cards, as well as prints in smaller formats.[19] He also commissioned artists other than Shōtei, men such as Itō Sōzan (1884-?), Yauchi Shurei, Shun'yo, Kakei and Fuyō (Narazaki Eishō, 1864-1936), about whom even today we know very little. It is believed, but cannot be fully substantiated, that Sōzan began designing export prints of birds and flowers (*kachōga*), largely in the *mitsugiriban* format, for Watanabe in around 1908/1909. This was the same year that the publisher had formally established his business Watanabe Print Shop (Watanabe Hangaten) in Kyōbashi. Virtually nothing is known about Shurei, Shun'yo or Kakei.

The 1910s dovetailed with Watanabe's increasing success and wealth as a dealer and publisher of graphic art for export. His training at Kobayashi's and his own subsequent experience had instilled Watanabe with an awareness of the value of *Ukiyo-e*, which was increasingly more appreciated abroad than in Japan where it was marginalized in the face of the "fine art" of painting. Perhaps with an entrepreneurial eye, perhaps feeling genuine concern regarding the exodus of Japanese prints abroad (even though he was in part to blame), in the later 1910s Watanabe launched a series of high-quality facsimile sets of the "old masters" of *Ukiyo-e* printmaking – Utagawa Hiroshige (1797-1858), Katsushika Hokusai (1760-1849), Kitagawa Utamaro (1753-1806) and others.[20] Understanding that he could be accused of producing "reproductions" (*fukusei*), Watanabe wrote that "... in no way am I attempting to create reproductions. Rather, I am seeking to 're-create' (*saigen*) original first-edition prints that are free of any defects."[21] Commenting on Watanabe's most ambitious of these projects, *A Collection of Masterpieces of Ukiyo-e Prints* (*Ukiyo-e hanga kessaku shū*, 12 vols., 1916-20), the print designer and painter Hashiguchi Goyō (1880-1921; cat. nos. 36-44) commends the publisher for his efforts in the reproduction of *Ukiyo-e* masterpieces. At the same time he also acknowledges the merits of Watanabe's experiments in producing "creative works" (*sōsaku-teki no mokuhanga*):

> *Most* [Ukiyo-e] *that could be described as masterpieces have already been exported to America and Europe. There are so few left in Japan that students like myself find it very difficult indeed to gain an appreciation of their technical and artistic quality ... Watanabe Shōzaburō, who shares my worries about the declining standards of woodblock printing, has made a notable contribution to the art world by encouraging contemporary painters to design creative, artistic prints which give full expression to their fresh and innovative spirit. For many years he has used his own print workshop to educate blockcutters and printers, and conducted a painstaking programme of research and development, sparing no expense in his tireless and enthusiastic research and experimentation with different types of paper, ink and equipment. Thanks to these efforts the artistic quality of his work improves with every year ...*[22]

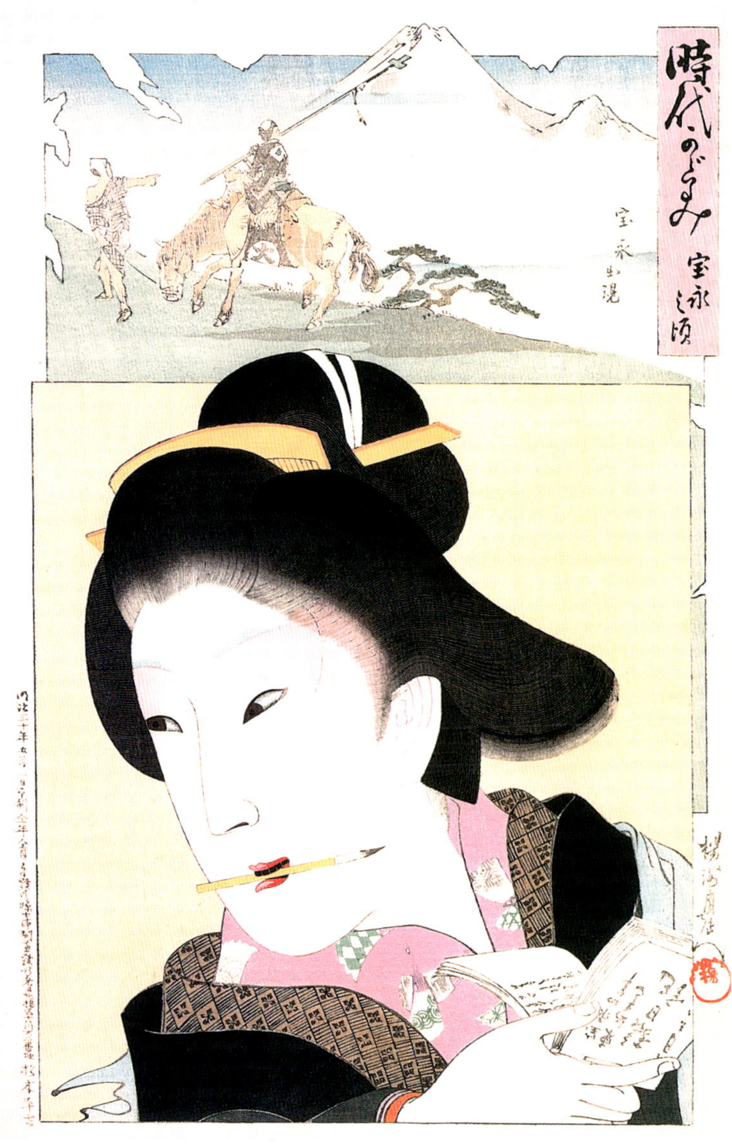

Fig. 3. Yōshū Chikanobu (1838-1912). "Beauty of the Hōei Era (1704-11)," from the series *Mirror of the Ages* (*Jidai kagami*), 1897. 36.7 x 25.1 cm. Published by Matsuki Heikichi. Arthur M. Sackler Gallery, Smithsonian Institution; Robert O. Muller Collection, S2003.8.2586.

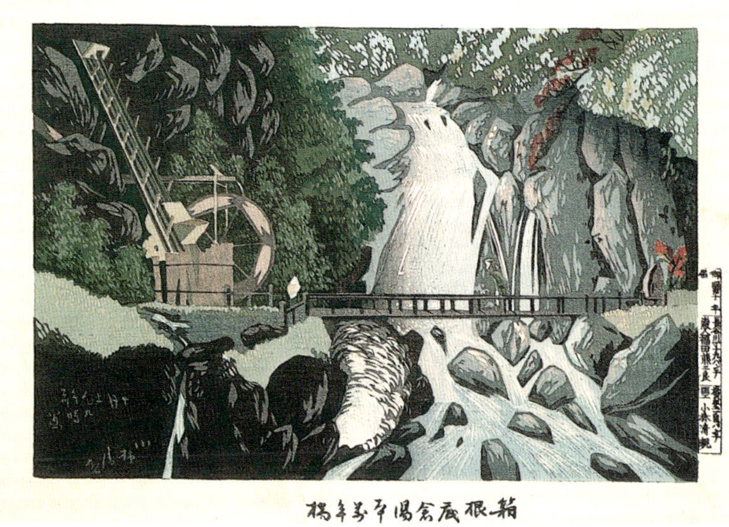

Fig. 4. Kobayashi Kiyochika (1847-1915). "The Mannen Bridge at the Source of the Sokokura Hot Spring, Hakone" (*Hakone Sokokura yumoto Mannenbashi*), 1881. 18.9 x 28.3 cm. Published by Fukuda Kumajirō. Arthur M. Sackler Gallery, Smithsonian Institution; Robert O. Muller Collection, S2003.8.1229.

Goyō's use of the term *sōsaku-teki no mokuhanga* is interesting. Both Goyō and Watanabe employed the term "*sōsaku-hanga*" to refer to their efforts, and it is indicative that *Shin-hanga* artists were committed to the idea that their work was as creative as those produced by *Sōsaku-hanga* artists. Watanabe even labeled his prints *Shinsaku-hanga* or "newly created prints."[23]

Watanabe's words at the beginning of this essay are as close to a statement of "ideology" as we have from the publisher, and it expresses his belief that it was possible to produce prints that were at once traditional – that is, predicated on the traditional "*Ukiyo-e* quartet" between artist, blockcutter, printer and publisher[24] – but at the same time innovative and modern. Moreover, for publishers like Watanabe economic viability was also crucial. On the surface the similarities in the types of subject, medium, commercial orientation, collaborative and publisher-centered system has led to the labeling of *Shin-hanga* as "Neo-*Ukiyo-e*" by Western and Japanese critics alike.[25] But *Shin-hanga* is undeserving of the sobriquet "Neo-*Ukiyo-e*," as if it were merely old wine in new bottles. Moreover, to suggest that *Shin-hanga* is "Neo-*Ukiyo-e*" implies a continuity in style from Edo and Meiji *nishiki-e* traditions, yet one only need compare beauties by Goyō or Itō Shinsui (1898-1972; cat nos. 85-101) with examples by Yōshū Chikanobu (1838-1912; fig. 3) and Kajita Hanko (1870-1917; *see* fig. 1), or a landscape by Shōtei with Kobayashi Kiyochika (1847-1915; fig. 4) and Hiroshige to see that the differences are enormous. These differences are not only restricted to stylistic considerations: *Shin-hanga* print format, paper type and the restriction of edition sizes (the latter is especially important in understanding *Shin-hanga* as "art prints") are also important signifiers of change. During the height of *Shin-hanga* from the 1910s to the 1930s it is characterized by the use of tradition as a springbroad for innovation. Asked whether the production techniques used to produce *Shin-hanga* are the same as those of earlier *nishiki-e*, Watanabe explained that:

> *... the techniques of carving and printing are essentially the same as before, but the sentiments of the artists are entirely different. Shin-hanga does not attempt to be a slave to the "old" style or to be like paintings* [nikuhitsuga]. *Each artist endeavours to create, in a cooperative fashion, an individual work of art.*[26]

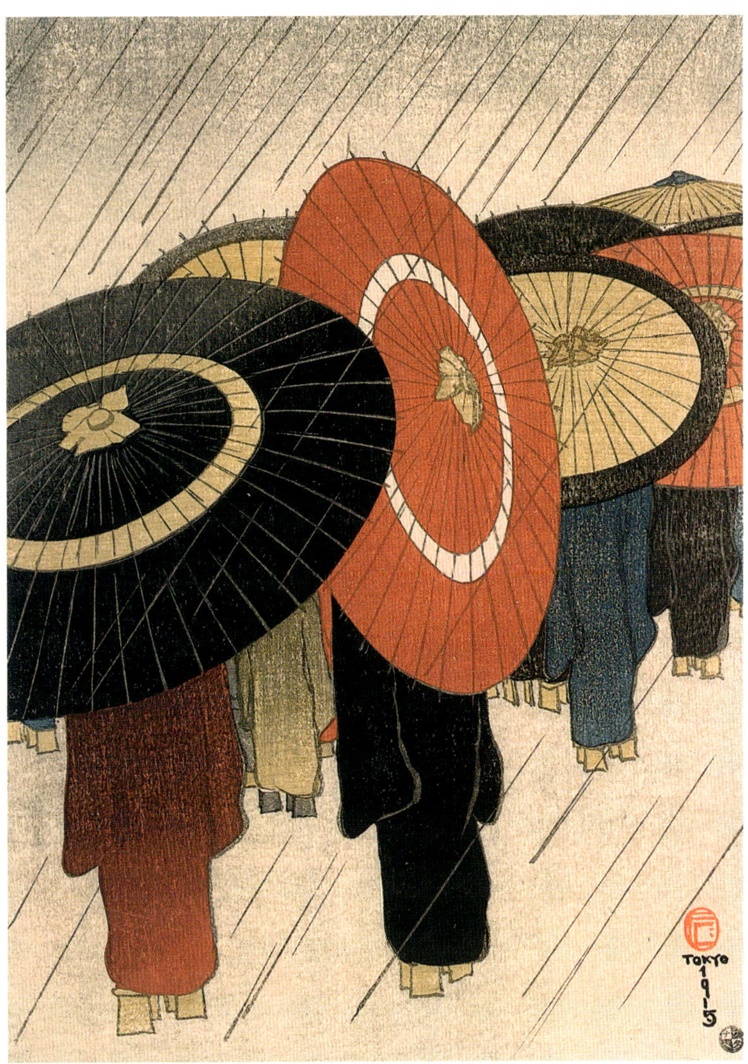

Fig. 5. Fritz Capelari (1884-1950). "Returning Home in the Rain," 1915. 26.7 x 19.7 cm. Published by Watanabe Shōzaburō. Arthur M. Sackler Gallery, Smithsonian Institution; Robert O. Muller Collection, S2003.8.75.

It was the painters of the period who Watanabe thought best represented the cultural ethos of his age and best equipped to realize his graphic vision. But, as Watanabe reminds us above, one must be careful not to define *Shin-hanga* as the reproduction of paintings. The transferral of imagery from successful paintings, such as "Tsukiji Akashi-chō, Kawagishi" (cat. no. 7) by Kaburagi Kiyokata (1878-1973) or the "The Heron Maiden" (cat. no. 46) by Kitano Tsunetomi (1880-1947), should not be interpreted as pure *Shin-hanga*. Instead, the motivation behind such works was as much to make successful images available to a wider audience, as it was to exploit a possible market, but not to generate creative *Shin-hanga*. Watanabe would have understood this dilemma when he chose to work with painters, as did later publishers of *Shin-hanga*, such as the Kyoto-based Satō Shōtarō:

> *Even though publishers here are busy planning for the alluring "revival" prints, there are great difficulties that lie ahead – that is to say, creative prints* [sōsaku-hanga] *have no relation to painting* [nikuhitsuga] ... *they are a completely independent art, and because of this, finding artists who conform is a very serious affair. For a number of years we have been looking for good artists to create prints, and do not wish to produce "reproduction" prints that imitate paintings. It is the mission of prints to pass on contemporary customs and manners and the like to future generations and all told I hope that the "revival" of our unique woodblock print art will transcend any attempts to quench it.*[27]

In his choice of artists it appears that Watanabe was attempting to create a modern aesthetic and international interpretation of Japanese graphic art. It was necessary therefore that the subject matter appeal to a domestic as well as an international audience. Traditional print genres were convenient handmaidens to both, and these formed the basis of the *Shin-hanga* aesthetic: *bijinga* ("pictures of beautiful women"), *fūkeiga* ("landscape pictures"), *kachōga* ("pictures of birds and flowers") and *yakusha-e* ("pictures of actors"). Oddly, the genre of historical prints (including warrior prints or *musha-e*) was not taken up, and perhaps this was due to the description needed to justify such images.[28]

The "birth" of *Shin-hanga* has in some ways become a romanticized tale by Watanabe of his search for suitable artists, with the year 1915 marking its debut. However, we now understand that the undercurrents of *Shin-hanga* were being formulated much earlier, already in the first decade of the twentieth century in the works of Shōtei. Nevertheless, in the usual recounting of events, Watanabe initially approached *Yōga* painters such as Kuroda Seiki (1866-1924), but was turned away. In the Spring of 1915 Watanabe viewed an exhibition of watercolors at a Tokyo department store by the Austrian artist Fritz Capelari (1884-1950). Capelari had studied printmaking in Vienna and was fascinated by *Ukiyo-e*. No doubt impressed by Capelari's composition and use of color Watanabe invited him to his shop. In collaboration with his blockcutters and printers, Capelari's sketches were transformed into what today must be viewed as the early formalized assays at Watanabe's *Shin-hanga* ideal. Perhaps not surprisingly the first Capelari print, "Returning Home in the Rain" (1915; fig. 5), is clearly influenced by figures in snow and rain in *manga* (literally, "random sketches") by Hokusai, and for Watanabe must have represented a harmonious blend of a modern take (by a Western artist) in a traditional Japanese medium. Watanabe later records his obvious delight in participating in this encounter:

> *We tried out a wide variety of different printing techniques with a view to depicting objects in space in a natural way that could not be achieved by conventional painting, and at last perfected a method for capturing an elusive subtlety and grace of expression which had never been possible before.*[29]

Capelari went on to produce twelve more prints in 1915, one in 1918 and a final image in 1920. Well into the 1920s, Watanabe published prints with other foreign artists: the British Charles W. Bartlett (1860-1940) and Elizabeth Keith (1887-1956), and the Americans Cyrus LeRoy Baldridge (1889-1975) and a "Mrs. Raymond." As with Capelari's work, these prints were exotic images of Japan and the Far East that catered to a perception of Japan held by Western audiences as well as by their foreign creators. Possibly one might argue that Watanabe was acutely aware of the balance he needed

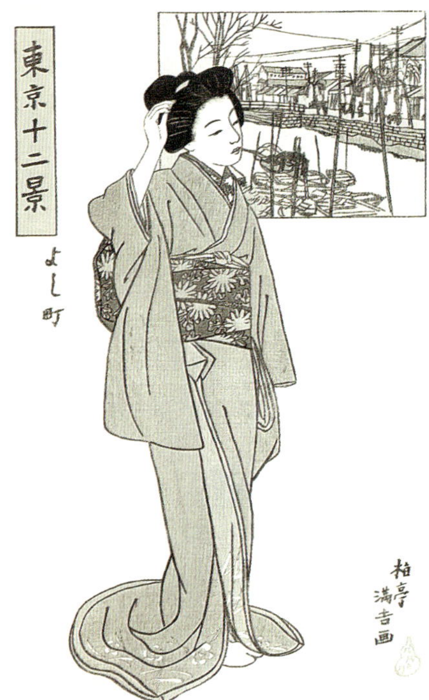

Fig. 6. Ishii Hakutei (1882-1958). "Yoshi-chō," from *Twelve Views of Tokyo* (*Tōkyō jūnikei*), 1910, 1914-16. 39.4 x 25.9 cm. Blockcut by Igami Bonkotsu; published by Watanabe Shōzaburō. Arthur M. Sackler Gallery, Smithsonian Institution; Robert O. Muller Collection, S2003.8.233.

to strike between designing prints that were different, but which nonetheless catered to the stereotypical quaint image of Japan as a distant "Fairyland," even if this image had little to do with reality.[30] Nevertheless, it is an ironic twist that the genre of prints that we so associate with the image of "traditional" Japan was contributed to, in part, by Western artists. Their work would also play no small part in the dissemination of *Shin-hanga* imagery abroad, most notably in the United States.[31]

Undaunted by his rejection by Japanese *Yōga* painters, Watanabe, showed the Capelari prints to Goyō. Although himself a *Yōga* painter, Goyō had a profound interest in *Ukiyo-e*. He amassed his own collection of prints, which he exhibited at Tokyo Imperial University (present-day Tokyo University) in 1916 and in Watanabe's shop in 1918, and he wrote a number of essays relating to his own research. Believing that creative possibilities could be realized when working with the traditional woodblock medium, Goyō supported the collaborative process that historically typified *Ukiyo-e* production – and advocated by Watanabe – in the production of "creative woodblock prints:"

> *I think that that one is able to create works of value that are not inferior to the masterpieces of the past and even able to represent Japan's nature, if a talented print artist endeavors to express one's own art by taking as the raw material research into special characteristics of the art of the woodblock. Yet it does not always follow that the notion of* jiga [self-drawn]/jizuri [self-printed] *holds sway. Instead, working together with the skills of the blockcutter and the printer in the method of blockcutting or printing, I believe that there are many instances when having a "supervisor" is advantageous. The reason is that the technique of blockcutting and printing is highly skilled and by no means easy work, and it can be supposed that the knowledge of a "supervisor" is vitally important. If this type of creative print having artistic merit were able to assume many forms, it would result not only in having wide-ranging educational, popular appeal, but also, I believe, it would pay unparalleled tribute to world art.*[32]

Like Capelari's print, Goyō first and only work with Watanabe, "Woman at the Bath", (1915; cat. no. 36), is a benchmark in *Shin-hanga* history. However, the artist was seemingly dissatisfied with this "experiment" – the work is sealed *shisaku* ("trial work") after the artist's signature. Goyō subsequently broke his collaboration with Watanabe and in 1918 formed his own studio. By the time of his death in 1920 Goyō had completed a further fourteen high-quality prints, including one image of a duck, four landscapes and nine *bijinga*. He also designed covers and illustrations for more than eighty books by contemporary writers like Natsume Sōseki (1867-1916), Tanizaki Jun'ichirō (1886-1965), Izumi Kyōka (1873-1939) and Nagai Kafū (1879-1959).

Goyō's *bijinga* remain still some of the most striking examples of *Shin-hanga* and are exemplary of his age. Harking back to the established genre of *bijinga*, they are nevertheless modern Taishō statements of the female image, in which Goyō's training in Western painting lends a naturalistic, three-dimensionality to his subjects, who seem to have been captured at a moment of secret revelry. They are witness to the extent that the representation of women had broken from the idealized *Ukiyo-e* beauties of the nineteenth century and the "dreamy image of contemporary women"[33] in *kuchi-e* linked with artists like Kaburagi Kiyokata to become a more natural – and in approach more creatively diverse – image of woman in the early twentieth century. The latter is typified by the more classic interpretation by Yamamoto Shōun (1870-1965) in his series *Contemporary Fashions* (*Imasugata*, 1906-9) to a modern take on traditional *mitate* (a type of pictorial trope) *Ukiyo-e* in the series *Twelve Views of Tokyo* (*Tōkyō jūnikei*, 1910, 1914-16; fig. 6) by *Sōsaku-hanga* artist Ishii Hakutei (1882-1958) or the sublime, timeless renditions by Goyō discussed above.[34]

Shin-hanga bijinga can be understood as one vein in the evolution of modern *bijinga* at a time when artists working in the genre, were "struggling to acknowledge 'tradition' and at the same time transcend it."[35] But, "*bijinga* may show continuity, discontinuity or even 'extinction'," argues Hamanaka Shinji, "it is nevertheless closely linked with *Ukiyo-e* and genre painting."[36] It was this inevitable link to the past that led the *Nihonga* artist and essayist Kaburagi Kiyokata to write in defense of the *bijinga* genre and of its universal appeal:

> Bijinga *belongs to a section of genre painting that has been named* Ukiyo-e ... *In the past there was a misconception that it was "vulgar" to reproduce fashionable customs and manners, and the artists who depicted contemporary fashions were limited to* Ukiyo-e ... *Even someone with an afflicted mind or who nurses discontent cannot help but unload his heart of stone before beautiful flowers and charming beauties. The fact that everyone is so attracted*

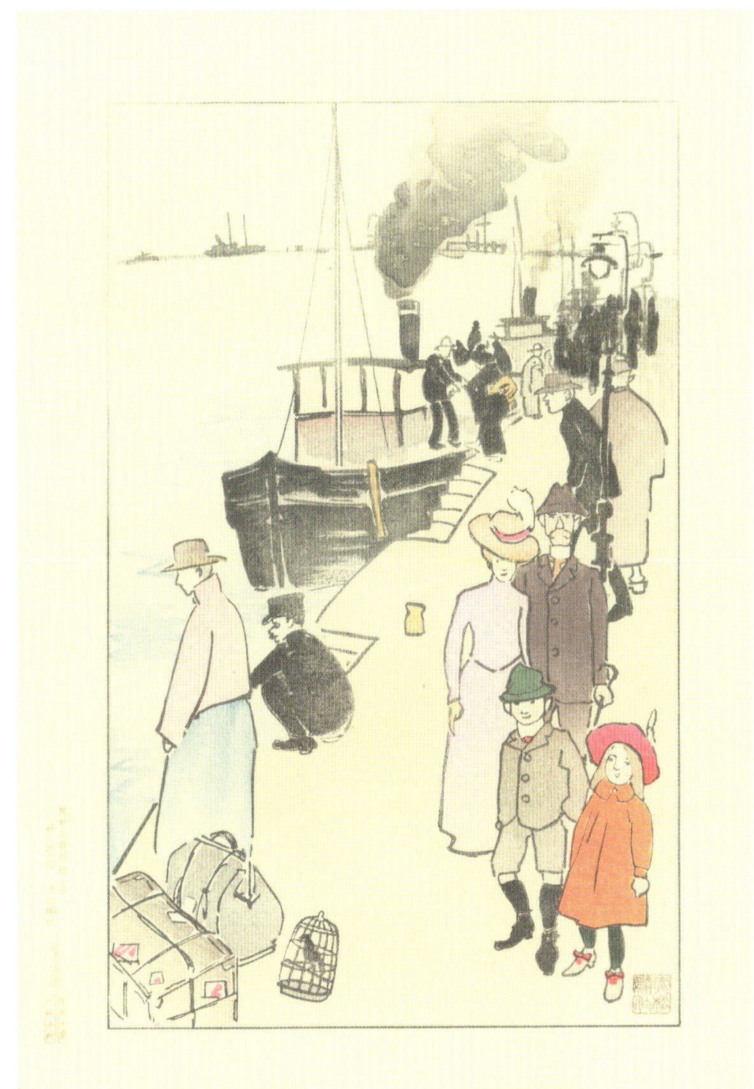

Fig. 7. Akamatsu Rinsaku (1878-1953). "Kobe Wharf," from the series *Views of Famous Places in the Osaka and Kobe Region* (*Hanshin meisho zue*), 1916. 34.6 x 24.5 cm. Published by Kanao Tanejirō. Kees Berbee Collection, The Netherlands.

is the merit of the beauties, in other words, that is the merit of bijinga. *This universality has a conventional side, and I cannot deny the fact that this conventionality sometimes descends into vulgarity. As a result* Ukiyo-e *was looked down upon in olden times. Attractive beauty but not indecency, sweetness is fine but not low-class: the person who paints* bijinga *has to keep this balance very much in mind.*[37]

Kiyokata was not only a staunch defender of *bijinga* in the many essays he wrote, he was also Tokyo's foremost *bijinga* painter and was a recognized contributor to *kuchi-e* illustration (cat. no. 5). He was also pivotal in the evolution of *Shin-hanga*, not as designer but as the teacher of *Shin-hanga* leading lights Shinsui and Kawase Hasui (1883-1957; cat. nos. 52-63). Also included among his students were the equally talented Kobayakawa Kiyoshi (1889-1948; cat. nos. 81-3), Yamakawa Shūhō (1898-1944; cat. no. 84), Kasamatsu Shirō (1898-1991; cat. nos. 102-4) and Torii Kotondo (1900-76; cat. nos. 105-11).

A number of Kiyokata's students joined forces in around 1910 to form the *Kyōdokai* (Homeland Society), which served as a platform for the annual exhibition of their works. In June 1915 Watanabe viewed a painting exhibition of the *Kyōdokai* at the Gahakudō Gallery, near his own shop in Kyōbashi. Taken by the painting of a young woman in a red under-kimono by Shinsui, Watanabe asked the owner dealer Matsui Seishichi for an introduction to Kiyokata. With Kiyokata's blessing and Shinsui's consent, Watanabe converted the design into the print given the title "Before the Mirror" (cat. no. 85). This was soon followed by further *bijinga* prints and in 1917-18 by an expressive set of landscape views, *Eight Views of Ōmi* (*Ōmi hakkei no uchi*; cat. nos. 93-100). This was Watanabe first series. (It is noteworthy that Watanabe never produced multi-artist serial work.) Certainly by the early 1920s, Shinsui had become a "core" artist in Watanabe's growing stable of artists, and would go on to produce some sixty-three *bijinga* prints with Watanabe until 1960. With few exceptions, Shinsui's *bijinga* prints become increasingly conservative and languid views of Japanese womanhood: women at their toilette, women in settings with symbols of season, all of which seem to reinforce an idealized view of "femininity constructed as tradition."[38]

The challenges for early twentieth-century artists to create innovation from tradition as part of their search for a modern identity were no less daunting for landscape artists. In the nineteenth century the woodblock landscape print was dominated by the prints of *Ukiyo-e* artists Hiroshige and Hokusai. However, in the late nineteenth and early twentieth centuries, a new language of landscape form was already emerging in the work of Kobayashi Kiyochika and Takahashi Shōtei (Hiroaki). By the mid-1910s, woodblock printed sketch tour albums *Views of Famous Places in the Osaka and Kobe Region* (*Hanshin meisho zue*; fig. 7) published by Kanao Tanejirō (Bun'endō) in October 1916 or *Prints of Japanese Scenery* (*Nihon fūkei hanga*) issued by Nakajima Jūtarō in 1917-20 were giving a new voice to a time-honored subject.[39]

Views of Famous Places in the Osaka and Kobe Region and *Prints of Japanese Scenery* roughly coincide with Watanabe's own ventures in the landscape genre, and show the vibrancy of the genre at this time. As with *bijinga*, Watanabe's early experiments were divided across tradition and culture, in this case by Shōtei, Shinsui and Charles W. Bartlett. Bartlett had met Watanabe during his Asian tour in 1915. The following year Bartlett collaborated on no less than twenty-two designs from sketches made during his travels in India, Ceylon, Indonesia and China. He published his last print with Watanabe in 1925. In 1916, Shinsui embarked on a new interpretation of the genre by adding modernist fauvre-like expression to a traditional medium with the *Eight Views of Ōmi* mentioned above, its creative impulse not dissimilar to *Views of Famous Places in the Osaka and Kobe Region.* It is not clear why Shinsui produced no further landscape series of this calibre, but his work in *bijinga* would eventually eclipse his output of landscape prints. Perhaps this was hastened by the appearance of another of Kiyokata's students, Kawase Hasui, who in 1917, much taken by Shinsui's *Eight Views* series, approached Watanabe with sketches that he had made at the resort town of Shiobara. In 1918, Watanabe produced three trials prints from his designs. Although Hasui dabbled in other subject manner and on occasion worked with publishers other than Watanabe, he was to become a bedrock of the Watanabe business in landscape and townscape scenes in serial or single-sheet form. In an article Hasui described himself as a "printmaker, pure and simple" – he even went so far as to state that he did not deserve the label "Japan's leading printmaker" but as "Japan's only printmaker,"[40] as he believed he was the only artist to earn a livelihood from his metier. But he also acknowledged the skills of master blockcutters and printers, which were instrumental in the outcome of a print, likening his collaboration with the printer Ono Gintarō (1885-*c.* 1962) to the relationship between *gidayū* chanter and *shamisen* accompanist as they "breathe in perfect unison."[41] The hundreds of Hasui landscape prints do much to reinforce the notion that "every country has its own landscape which deposits itself in layers on the consciousness of its citizens."[42] As such Hasui's prints are products of a cultural sensibility and vision nurtured in the first half of the twentieth century in which mountains, rivers and villages in Japan became emblems of "old Japan,"[43] not only as nostalgic reminders to the Japanese themselves but to audiences abroad who exoticized the country.

The appreciation abroad was an aspect that did much to promote the career of another landscapist, Yoshida Hiroshi. Yoshida was widely traveled and his experiences abroad in America and Europe provided subject matter for his prints, as did the countryside of his own native Japan. They were all very much influenced by his training in oils, watercolors and his own plein-air sketches. Yoshida produced eight prints with Watanabe, the first in an unusual narrow format and entitled "Sacred Garden at Meiji Shrine" (*Meiji jingū no shin'en*, 1920; 126.8 x 30.3 cm).[44] After 1925 he choose to publish prints himself, distancing himself from the ever more conservative approach taken by Watanabe. As a landscape artist and a printmaker, Yoshida believed that traditional printmaking (*Ukiyo-e*) should be emblematic of the era in which it was made.[45] In his early trials for different artists in the landscape genre, Watanabe also approached and issued works by "one-print wonders" like the obscure Kiyokata student Kitagawa Kazuo, as well as other "first-generation" Watanabe artists like Hiroaki and Furuya Taiken (1897-?), who are often side-lined in any discussion of landscape prints in the face of the prodigious figure of Hasui.

Especially deserving of reappraisal, however, is the artist Hiroaki. As mentioned above he first collaborated with Watanabe in the early 1900s under the name *Shōtei*, and by 1921 he had assumed the name *Hiroaki.* Hiroaki's best work – nocturnes, snow scenes and rainscapes – are equipollent with any Hasui or Yoshida in their evocative sensibilities, although in his early career his work is disadvantaged by comparatively poorer quality paper and colorants. Hiroaki broke with Watanabe in around 1926 and subsequently went on to vent full expression to his creativity in landscape and *bijinga* in the late 1920s and 1930s under the supervision of the Tokyo firm of Fusui Gabō (Fusui Art House) established by Kaneko Fusui (Seiji) and Kaneko Seizō in 1924.

Hiroaki is less known for, but was certainly proficient in, animal prints and compositions of "birds and flowers," whose decorative qualities would have guaranteed a broad patron base and therefore ensured their economic viability. Watanabe also commissioned bird-and-flower prints from Itō Sōzan, an artist still little appreciated today. The exact dating of Sōzan's work (fig. 8) remains problematic, but it is thought that his earliest activity with Watanabe may have paralleled that of Ohara Koson (1877-1945; cat. nos. 23-33) when Koson was working with the publisher Matsuki Heikichi (Daikokuya; *see* Koson entry in catalogue). Later, from 1926 onward and under the name *Shōson*, Koson would become the bird-and-flower specialist for Watanabe. Other artists, namely Goyō, Yoshida, and later Oda Kazuma (1882-1956; cat. nos. 47-51) and Kasamatsu Shirō, also published work in this genre, although not necessarily with Watanabe.

When compared to the development of *Shin-hanga bijinga* and landscape prints, actor prints or *yakusha-e* present both differences and similarities. With few exceptions, the genre of actor prints was in effect the depiction of Kabuki actors in role.[46] A theatrical form very specific to Japan, underlying conventions in the illustration of Kabuki actors were very much dictated by tradition. The narrower appeal of the subject matter might also explain why fewer prints were produced in this genre in *Shin-hanga.* Yet artists working in actor portraiture still faced the same questions about how to infuse a traditional medium with innovative expression so as to ensure its vibrancy. Added to this is the idea that while actor portraiture in the nineteenth century had served as a form of popular reportage of theater-goers' favorite stars, by the early twentieth century this role was monopolized by the more modern means of photography and motion pictures. Not unlike *bijinga*, in the genre of actor prints there was a perceived need that it must reinvent itself in order to compete with modern fashions of portraiture.

Like *bijinga*, the transition from traditional *Ukiyo-e* Kabuki prints dating until the late nineteenth century to those in the twentieth century is similarly manifest in the form of illustrations, with the appearance of Kabuki-related *kuchi-e* illustrations in magazines like the *Engei gahō* (*Theater Illustrated*). *Engei gahō* was a monthly publication running from 1906 to 1943 that dealt with Kabuki and other dramatic forms. It commissioned illustrations from a number of artists including Torii Kotondo's predecessor Torii Kiyotada IV (1875-1941), who produced some fine work for the journal in the 1910s. Kiyotada's work was also concurrent with bolder, more radical creative statements proffered in series such as *Stage Sketches* (*Soga butai sugata-e*, 1911) by *Sōsaku-hanga* advocates Sakamoto Hanjirō (1882-1969) and Ishii Hakutei, the "independent" artist Takehisa Yumeji (1884-1934) and artists of the short-lived magazine, *Shin nigao-e* (*New Actor Portraits*), to name but a few.

Shin nigao-e is noteworthy. Appearing in only five issues in 1915, it contained some fifteen woodblock images by ten artists, "preserving the portrait bust compositions and strong lines of traditional *ukiyo-e* actor prints but often adding a greater sense of volume and a rough style of cutting that

Fig. 8. Itō Sōzan (1884-?). "Heron in Flight," c. after 1923. 16.5 x 37.2 cm. Published by Watanabe Shōzaburō. Arthur M. Sackler Gallery, Smithsonian Institution; Robert O. Muller Collection, S2003.8.356.

Fig. 9. Yamamura Kōka (Toyonari) (1886-1942). "Kataoka Nizaemon XI as Ōboshi Yuranosuke," c. 1916. 35.3 x 24.7 cm. Published by Watanabe Shōzaburō. Arthur M. Sackler Gallery, Smithsonian Institution; Robert O. Muller Collection, S2003.8.3440.

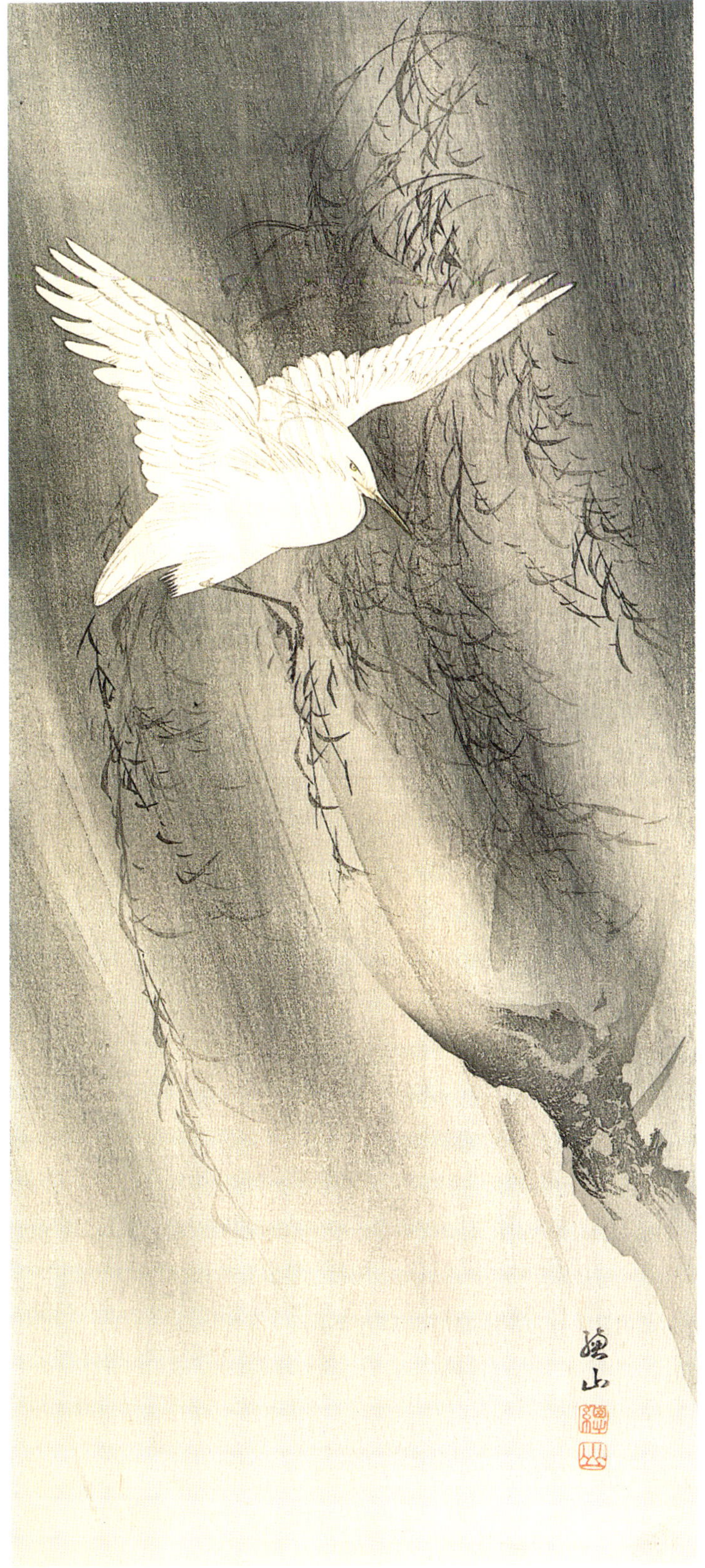

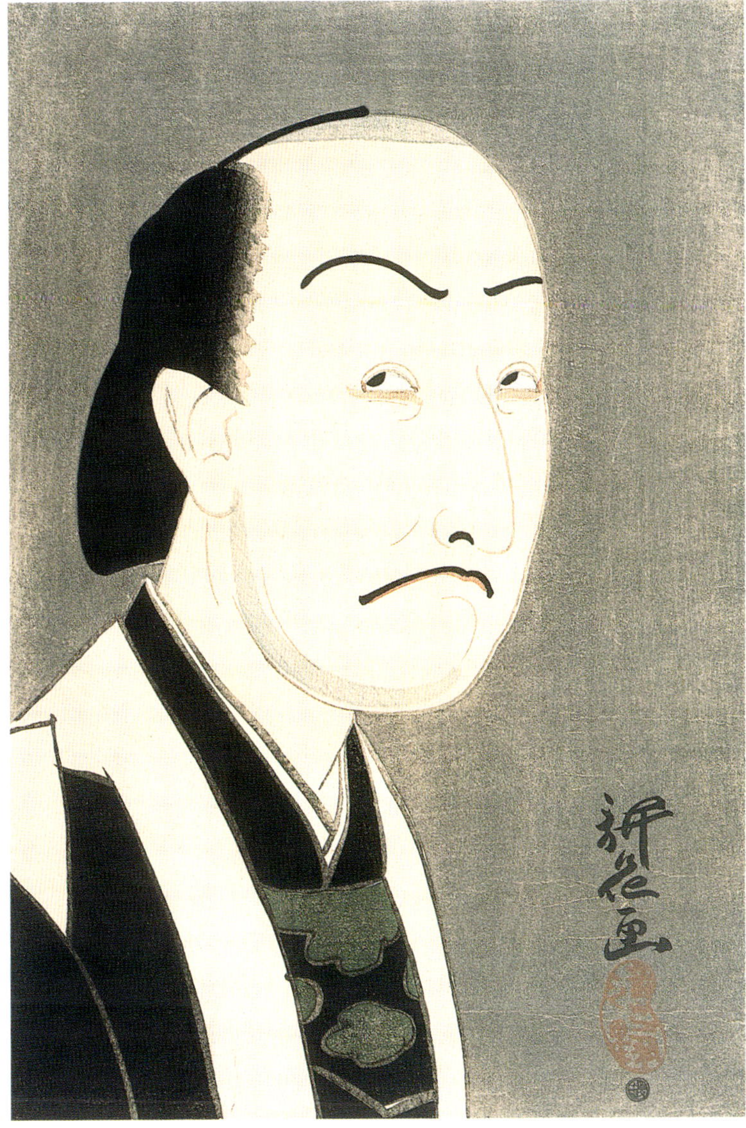

suggest Western sketch tradition."[47] But *Shin nigao-e* is signal as it represents the collaboration between *Sōsaku-hanga* and *Shin-hanga* artists, and as such challenges the preconception that clear-cut boundaries existed between the two camps. The artists involved in *Shin-nigao-e* hoped that their work would fuel interest in actor portraiture in the early Taishō period, for as is stated in the third issue:

> *... in the past there were* nigao-e *by the Torii and Utagawa Schools, but despite the skill in the craft of the print master, in the technique of the printing with the* baren *and the skill of the woodblock master they gradually declined by the end of the Meiji. Other means like lithographic pictures and color photography appears to be spreading the proud face of the times; it is indeed regrettable ...*[48]

Three of the artists who participated in *Shin nigao-e* would later play a role in *Shin-hanga*: Natori Shunsen (1886-1960; cat. nos. 72-5) and Yamamura Kōka (Toyonari) (1886-1942; cat. nos. 64-71) for their work in actor prints with Watanabe, and Torii Kotondo, who would work as a *bijinga* designer with rival publishers, Sakai/Kawaguchi and Ikeda.

Natori's contribution to *Shin nigao-e* was a close-up portrait (*ōkubi-e*) of the actor Sawamura Sōjūrō VII (1875-1949) as Mitsugi. A similar yet more tempered pose was adapted for a painting of the actor Nakamura Ganjirō I (1860-1935) as the paper merchant Kamiya Jihei, which Shunsen exhibited at a show of theatrical pictures at the Gahakudō Gallery in 1916. Watanabe saw the painting, and before long publisher and artist collaborated to issue a print based on it (*see* cat. no. 72). But for reasons not entirely clear Shunsen and Watanabe were to produce only one further print, the actor Onoe Baikō VI (1870-1934) as Otomi in 1917, before a hiatus of eight years.

Around the same time that Watanabe was engaged with the production of the first Shunsen prints he also began work with Yamamura Kōka, a graduate of the *Nihonga* department at the Tokyo Art School. Kōka's debut work with Watanabe, "Kataoka Nizaemon XI (1857-1934) as Ōboshi Yuranosuke"[49] of around 1916 (fig. 9), resulted from the publisher having seen a painting by the artist. Over the next few years Kōka issued a handful of single sheets including a portrait of the actor Onoe Matsusuke IV in the role of Kōmori Yasu, which in actual fact is a reworking of his contribution of the same name to *Shin nigao-e*. Whereas Shunsen's prints have an elegance and an understated prowess, Kōka's portraits possess an intensity that has engendered a convenient comparison with earlier masters like Tōshūsai Sharaku (act. *c.* 1794-95). Certainly Kōka's most accomplished work with Watanabe in the actor genre was a set of twelve prints entitled *Flowers of the Theatrical World* (*Rien no hana*, 1920-22).[50] With completion of *Flowers of the Theatrical World*, Kōka does not appear to have done any further serial work with Watanabe after 1922, and until around 1926 his prints with the publisher focused on the illustration of animal subjects and beauties. Kōka readily acknowledges his debt to the artisans that assisted him with his prints, especially for someone like himself who was first and foremost trained as a painter:

> *If I had to say so, painters being painters create splendid pictures, and if print masters being print masters convert these faithfully into prints, I think it can be said that these are entirely "creative works"* [sōsaku-hanga]. *However, if an artist cannot be satisfied with his own work, they should create just the keyblock and color blocks themselves and then leave them in the hands of the specialist blockcutters and printers. I believe that this end result is a creative work. And then, if all is under strict supervision, I feel that in the end it is generally a creative print when done in this manner. Even I at one time tried to "self-draw, self-carve and self-print," but I recognized that the technique was crude, and these days I have stopped doing this altogether … in order to create* Shin-hanga *I meet with artisans and while talking it through with blockcutters and printers, I rely on their technique and work diligently with them to produce prints.*[51]

By 1921, having gathered together a group of artists and a body of work, Watanabe had concretized his *Shin-hanga* vision. In June 1921 he mounted his debut *Shinsaku-hanga Tenrankai* (New Creative Print Exhibition) at the Shirokiya Department Store in the Nihonbashi district of Tokyo; a total of 150 works by ten artists was included. Further shows were organized in May 1922 and April 1923 at the Shirokiya. With the obvious success of Watanabe's *Shin-hanga* in early Taishō, and especially following his debut exhibitions in 1921 at the Shirokiya, Watanabe's *Shin-hanga* was in some ways at its creative peak in the early 1920s.

The Impact of the Great Kantō Earthquake, 1923 and Beyond

September 1923 is often considered a turning point in the Watanabe's investment in *Shin-hanga*. At midday 1 September the Kantō region was shook by the massive "Great Kantō Earthquake," with hundreds of aftershocks over four days that created "a red desert here and there a crematory" filling rivers and canals with tens of thousands of "the floating dead."[52] Tokyo was engulfed in flames that raged for two days, with one observer likening "the relentless roar of flames" to the sounds of heavy surf, with "frequent crashes of thunder."[53] Watanabe's shop and business was destroyed, and with it years of work – woodblocks for prints and facsimile productions, and innumerable print impressions. Artists like Kōka and Yoshida lost their work at Watanabe's, others like Hasui were doubly affected with the destruction of stock at Watanabe's as well as his home and numerous sketchbooks.

It would be difficult to speculate how *Shin-hanga* would have evolved had Watanabe's shop not been damaged, and if the idealism that powered Watanabe up to this point would have continued through the 1920s and 1930s. Certainly in the post-earthquake period Watanabe's print reproduction projects were indeed less ambitious than those before 1923. Instead, Watanabe focused his energies on individual *Shin-hanga* prints and series. He enlisted pre-earthquake artists, and perhaps in hopes of boosting production and his profits, or perhaps due to a dissatisfaction with what was being produced, he additionally sought out new artists in the various genres. (These "new" designers have been conveniently labeled as *Shin-hanga* artists of the "second generation.") In birds and flowers, Watanabe's production of Sōzan's prints cease after 1923 and from 1926 the lacuna was filled by Ohara Koson. Koson's move to the Watanabe firm might have been occasioned by the decline in the Daikokuya in the years up until 1930. From the 1930s onward Koson also designed works under the name *Hoson* for the joint publications of Sakai/Kawaguchi.

In landscape, Watanabe experimented with the work of Oda Kazuma,

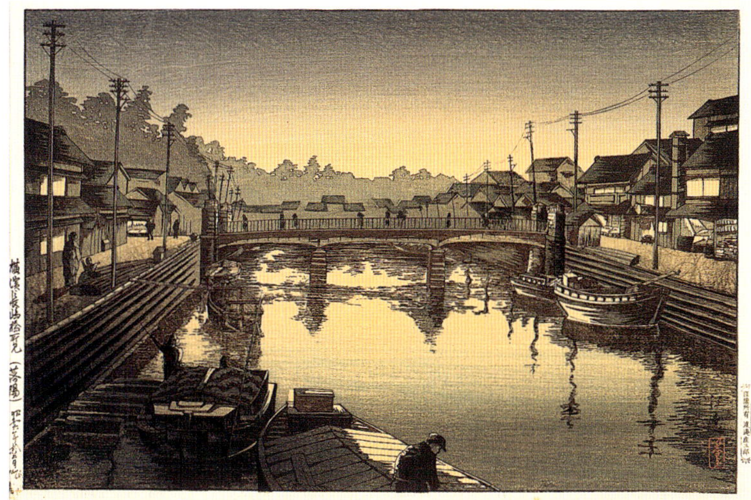

Fig. 10. Ishiwata Kōitsu (1897-1987). "Setting Sun at the Nagashima Bridge, Yokohama" (*Yokohama Nagashimabashi shoken [rakuyō]*), 1931. 23.8 x 36.1 cm. Published by Watanabe Shōzaburō. Arthur M. Sackler Gallery, Smithsonian Institution; Robert O. Muller Collection, S2003.8.240.

Itō Takashi (1894-1982; cat. nos. 76-7), Kasamitsu Shirō and Ishiwata Kōitsu (1897-1987; fig. 10). Itō Takashi and Kasamitsu Shirō were both students of Kiyokata. Itō produced some of his best prints in the late 1920s and early 1930s, while Oda Kazuma attempted a handful of atmospheric landscapes (and flowers) prints with Watanabe in 1924 before returning to his more familiar medium of lithography. In this regard he belongs to the number of artists, such as Goyō, Yoshida and Kōka, who attempted *Shin-hanga* with Watanabe but found that for whatever reasons (Watanabe's growing aesthetic conservatism and parsimonious treatment of artists?) that their aesthetic sensibilities were better served through self-publication, either as *Sōsaku-hanga* artists or as *Shin-hanga* independents, through work with other publishers, or as in Kazuma's case in a completely different medium. In the post-earthquake era, too, artists like Shōtei may have shifted their loyalties to other publishers because of a dispute with Watanabe over royalties.

In the years following the earthquake and leading up to the Second World War, *Shin-hanga* witnessed a coming of age which, according to Kendall H. Brown, included a rejection of "… the powerful emotive and explicitly creative character of pre-1923 works in favour of a serenity in mood and a nuanced variety in form that found a receptive audience."[54] What was important about this "receptive audience" is that it now extended beyond the domestic market to the international scene. Certainly in Japan itself there were an increased number of publishers, some who had been in operation since the Edo and/or Meiji periods, issuing *Shin-hanga* in the 1920s and 1930s. In Tokyo these included, among others, the firms of Nishinomiya Yosaku, Isetatsu, Doi Sadaichi (also read Teiichi), Adachi Toyohisa, Katō Junji, Takamizawa Enji, the Bijutsusha, Fusui Gabō, Sakai/Kawaguchi and Ikeda. These publishers were commissioning designs from new artists or were engaging those already with an established record with Watanabe.

Hasui and Koson – core artists for Watanabe – also worked for the joint firm of Sakai/Kawaguchi. The Sakai/Kawaguchi partnership additionally released meticulously printed works of Torii Kotondo, who is unusual in this exhibition as one of only two men whose artistic lineage is directly rooted in *nishiki-e* precedents (the other being the landscapist and Kiyochika student Tsuchiya Kōitsu [1870-1949]; cat. nos. 8-9). Kotondo eventually became the head of the Torii School, which had monopolized the genre of Kabuki theater prints as far back as the eighteenth century. But if anything, Kotondo was a thoroughly modern artist. A talented student of Kaburagi Kiyokata, his oeuvre is divided between his theater-related works and *Nihonga*-inspired *bijinga*. Kotondo's prints – all of which are *bijinga* – were published by Sakai/Kawaguchi (and later Kawaguchi alone) and by the less distinguished firm of Ikeda.

In Japan, *Shin-hanga* publishing was centered in Tokyo, but the capital was not its exclusive domain. There were also publishers in the Kansai or *Kamigata* region (around Kyoto/Osaka/Nara), including Satō Shōtarō, Nezu Seitarō, the Uchida Bijutsu Shoshi (Uchida Art Publishers) and the Kyōto Hangain (Kyoto Print Institute). Of these, Satō Shotarō is usually cited as promoting a distinct image of *Kamigata*-based *Shin-hanga*, although his activity as a *Shin-hanga* publisher appears to have been limited to the mid-1920s to the 1930s. His publication of the six sheets of *Kanpō's Creative Prints, First Series* (*Kanpō sōsaku-hanga shū daiisshū*) by Kyotoite Yoshikawa Kanpō (1894-1979; cat. nos. 78-80) is an arresting rejoinder to the actor prints by Tokyo-based artists Yamamura Kōka or Natori Shunsen.

Satō's forays into *bijinga* and picturesque landscape views showcasing beauties are manifest in the some fourteen prints by *Nihonga* painter Miki Suizan (1887-1957).[55] Suizan's *bijin* compositions can border on the staid, cluttered or saccharine and pale against the refinement of Tokyo-based *bijinga* specialists Goyō, Shinsui, or even Hirano Hakuhō (1879-1957; cat. nos. 34-5). By contrast, the solemn ephemerality of the aforementioned "The Heron Maiden" by Kitano Tsunetomi, issued by the Osaka publisher Nezu Seitarō, is an exceptional treatment of a theme that was popular at this time in paintings and prints.[56] Interestingly, Satō also issued a print of the subject in 1918 by Taniguchi Kōkyō (1864-1915).

Of vital importance to *Shin-hanga* publishing at this time was the growing appreciation of it in the West, namely the United States, and the opening up of a foreign market must have been something of a boon for *Shin-hanga* publishers. Exhibitions of *Shin-hanga* were beginning to be mounted abroad in the 1920s, and articles on *Shin-hanga* were appearing in art journals like *The International Studio*, *The Studio*, *The Art News* and *The Art Digest*, to name but a few.[57] But undisputedly the greatest stimulus to a Western appreciation of *Shin-hanga* was provided by two sale exhibits held at the Toledo Museum of Art in the state of Ohio in 1930 and 1936. Their realization was largely due to the efforts of Yoshida Hiroshi, and the Museum's curators, Dorothy Lillian Blair, herself a Yoshida student, and J. Arthur MacLean. Not surprisingly, in the first show approximately one-third of the 336 prints on display were by Yoshida, with the majority of the remaining pieces Watanabe publications.[58] The show was favorably received by American audiences, so much so that it was proposed that a similar show be staged around every five years. A second exhibit followed in 1936 and contained 289 prints.[59] It is fair to say that this exhibition too was dominated by Yoshida's work and Watanabe's publication.

It would indeed be interesting to question whether this increased activity in the West spawned, in part, the increased publishing activity in Japan, especially vis-à-vis a collector-dealer like Robert O. Muller. It is certainly an area that merits further research. Equally intriguing to speculate is to what extent the imagery and "serenity in mood" of *Shin-hanga* is influenced by the fact that its publishers saw the West as a potential market. (That they sought to cater to a foreign clientele is evinced by the number of catalogues published in English.) As noted earlier, Watanabe and others strove to create images that conformed to Western preconceptions of the country, while at the same time stressing the essential "Japaneseness" of its people and its land.

As the dialogue about the nature of *Shin-hanga* was shifting in Japan, so too were writers in the United States re-evaluating *Shin-hanga* in the years between its first major exhibition in 1930 and the second six years later. A comparison of reviews of the first and second Toledo shows reveals that at least in America perceptions of *Shin-hanga* were moving toward its acceptance as a viable form of modern art. Writing in 1930, Blair and MacLean, seem hesitant to view *Shin-hanga* as a thoroughly modern movement, one open to influences from modern aesthetics: "Ultra modern tendencies have caused Occidental pictorial effects to creep into the work of many of the modern print designers, which some of us may lament. But it is inevitable."[60] In referring to the 1936 exhibition, however, Blair is quoted as saying that it is "a refreshing exposition of a modern phase of activity," while another critic maintained that it was "a very interesting exhibition in the field of modern Oriental art" and that it continues "the Museum's survey of modern trends in one of the significant phases of present day pictorial art in Japan."[61]

The rising demand for *Shin-hanga* may well have continued into the 1940s had not historical realities come into play. But with Japan's actions in China in the late 1930s and the outbreak of the Pacific War in 1941 a once intrigued public began to "look upon exotic views of *torii* gates and geisha with less enchanted eyes."[62] Against this background, plans for a third Toledo show in 1940-41 were quashed.

Shin-hanga sales were again buoyant during the Allied Occupation forces, due to the availability of prints by artists like Hasui at military personnel post-exchanges, and beyond into the 1950s and early 1960s as suggested by the release of English-language catalogues by publishers like Watanabe. The Watanabe catalogues also demonstrate that many artists from the prewar period continued to collaborate with him. Although it is generally true that by this time *Shin-hanga* was out of pace with new developments in the print world, artists like Hasui produced some commendable designs, as did Shunsen with his twenty-four set *New Prints of Actors on the Stage* (*Shin han butai no sugata-e*) dating from 1951 to 1954.

In the preface to the Toledo catalogue of 1936 Dorothy Blair remarked that five years previously there was no particular demand for modern Japanese prints. "Such a statement," she wrote, almost prophetically, "is no longer true. Museum collections are being formed and many a private collector finds them as interesting as the more expensive prints of former times ..."[63]

Notes

1. As a brief overview of *Shin-hanga* history, this essay does not aim to present new material and has drawn from the numerous scholarly writings on *Shin-hanga* and Watanabe Shōzaburō that have appeared in the last decade and a half. For the best summaries in English, see the forthcoming essays on Watanabe Shōzaburō by Setsuko Abe and on *Shin-hanga* by Kendall H. Brown in Amy Reigle Newland (ed.), *Hotei Dictionary of Japanese Prints* (working title, forthcoming, 2005), Kendall H. Brown (*Visions of Japan. Kawase Hasui's Masterpieces*, Hotei Publishing, 2004), Hamanaka and Newland (2000), Brown (1996), Brown and Goodall-Cristante (1996), Merritt and Yamada (1992), Smith (1994), Stephens (ed.) (1993), Merritt (1990) and Smith (1983). The author would also like to extend her heartfelt thanks to James Ulak and Chris Uhlenbeck for reading this essay and for their valuable comments.

2. Watanabe Shōzaburō, "Ukiyo-e hanga kenkyū shōwa" (A Chat About Research on *Ukiyo*-e Prints) (1916), reprinted in Inoue Kazuo and Watanabe Shōzaburō (eds.) (1931), 240-41; English translation appears in Okamoto Hiromi and Henry D. Smith II, "*Ukiyo-e* for Modern Japan: The Legacy of Watanabe Shōzaburō," 32-3, in Stephens (ed.) (1993), 27-39.

3. Although the Tokugawa shogunate enforced a policy of seclusion (*sakoku* or "closed country"), Japan was not completely isolated from or ignorant of other countries. From the Dutch station at Nagasaki it had access to both European products and European information, and it had regular, albeit limited, contact with China and Korea. With the restoration of imperial power in 1868, however, and the subsequent opening of its borders to foreign trade, the country was to set out on its path of "modernisation" – in the words of pro-Western Japanese thinker Fukuzawa Yukichi (1835-1901) "examining history we [the Japanese] see that life has been dark and closed and that it advances in the direction of civilization and enlightenment [*bunmei kaikai*]" (from his *Seiyō jijō* (Conditions in the West, 1867-1870), see Seidensticker (1983), 35).

4. MacClain (2002), 181.

5. This definition and discussion does not include specialized or privately published prints such as *surimono*.

6. Other technologies introduced in the later nineteenth century included planometric aluminium and zincplate lithography, photographic collotypes and chromolithography; see John Clark, "Indices of Modernity, Changes in Popular Reprographic Representation," 25-49, in Tipton and Clark (eds.) (2000), 27-8.

7. This is not to say that woodblock prints disappeared overnight in the Meiji. It is true to say that late nineteenth-century *nishiki-e* artists were forced to diversify when confronted with the competition from other types of reprographic materials. Open to them were opportunities to design individual prints – by and large in adherence to the conventional genres of landscape, beautiful women and actors, but also for a short while exploiting the sensationalism of an opened country with *Yokohama-e* and catering to newspaper illustrations and war reportage with the Sino-Japanese (1894-95) and Russo-Japanese (1904-5) Wars, etc.. The woodblock print industry did remain buoyant until the turn of the century, although it carried with it the perception of being pictorial journalism/"popular art." As part of this and with the call for modernization in the Meiji, Japanese "art society" was splintered between artists of the "fine arts," and the artists of what would have been seen as the anachronistic *Ukiyo-e* school were relegated to the notion of popular illustrators in mass graphics, in short, "popular artists."

8. *See* Paul Berry, "The Transformation of Traditional Painting Practices in Nineteenth- and Twentieth-century Japan," 185-201, in Rotondo-McCord (ed.) (2002), 188-90, for a brief discussion of exhibition practices; for further reading in *Nihonga*, *see also* Conant *et al.* (1995).

9. *Ibid.*, 190.

10. Clark (2000), 33, attempts to delineate the rather complex nature of the types of graphic artists since the 1890s.

11. And as part of this, *Sōsaku-hanga* pioneer Yamamoto Kanae (1882-1946) emphasized the importance of making a distinction between prevailing practices of illustration and reproduction from his own work, which he described as "non-utilitarian, artistic prints." This description was a "conceptual definition of the 'print as art,' put forward by a producer of art by consciously imbuing the work with artistic value;" *see* Chiaki Ajioka, "*Hanga*: Japanese Creative Prints," 9-13, in Ajioka *et al.* (2000), 9.

12. Interestingly, however, scholar Kōno Minoru explains that *Sōsaku-hanga* artists included *Ukiyo-e* prints of the Edo period as "Creative Prints" because of the close cooperation between print designer and artisans, as it was felt that they incorporated their own interpretation into a work; quoted in Ajioka *et al.* (2000), 10, fn. 5.

13. Most famously the series *Twelve Views of Tokyo* (*Tōkyo jūnikei*, 1910, 1914-16) by artist and critic Ishii Hakutei (1882-1958), which was carved by Igami Bonkotsu (1875-1933).

14. Hollis Goodall-Cristante, "*Shin-hanga*, Traditional Prints in a New World," 11-33, in Brown and Goodall-Cristante (1996), 15.

15. The connection of *Shin-hanga* to *Nihonga* artists should not be overlooked. It should be noted that in the late nineteenth and early twentieth centuries *Nihonga* was especially promoted by historian-idealogue Okakura Tenshin (Kakuzō, 1862-1913) and Ernest Fenollosa (1853-1908). Okakura and Fenollosa formed the *Kangakai* (Painting Appreciation Society) in 1884 as part of their promotion of *Nihonga* as a type of Japanese painting that combined traditional themes and brush techniques with stylistic elements from the West. The curriculum proposed by Okakura, Fenollosa and the *Kangakai* later became the model for the curriculum of the *Tōkyō Bijutsu Gakkō* (Tokyo School of Fine Arts), est. 1887, of which Okakura was the director. Okakura broke with the school in 1898 to form the *Nihon Bijutsuin* (Japan Art Institute; *see* glossary), which has come to embody the ideals of *Nihonga*. Okakura eventually left Japan and joined the staff of the Museum of Fine Arts in Boston, where Fenollosa had been curator. Closely allied with Okakura was the painter Yokoyama Taikan (1868-1958); *see also* fn. 59 below.

16. Setsuko Abe, "Watanabe Shōzaburō and the *Shin-hanga* Movement: Its Beginnings until the 1930s," in Newland (ed.) (2005).

17. For further reading on the formation of significant American collections of Japanese prints, see Meech (2003).

18. Abe, in Newland (ed.) (2005); apparently this work was "Night on the Banks of the Sumida River" (*Sumida tsutsumi no yoru*), but its existence has yet to be confirmed.

19. Okamoto and Smith, in Stephens (ed.) (1993), 29.

20. They included *A Collection of Prints by the Great Masters of Ukiyo-e* (*Ukiyo-e taika gashū*, 1915); *A Collection of Masterpieces of Ukiyo-e Prints* (*Ukiyo-e hanga kessaku shū*, 12 vols., 1916–20); *An Ukiyo-e compendium* (*Ukiyo-e taikan*, 1917); *Catalogue of an Exhibition held to mark the Sixtieth Anniversary of Hiroshige's Death* (*Hiroshige rokujūkaiki tsuizen kinen isaku tenrankai mokuroku*, 1917); *Fifty-three Stations on the Tōkaidō Series* (*Tōkaidō gojūsan eki zokuga*, 1918); *Eight Views of the Eastern Capital* (*Tōto hakkei*, 1926); and *Lives of the Ukiyo-e Masters* (*Ukiyo-eshi den*, 1931). For descriptions of these, see Abe, in Newland (ed.) (2005).

21. Watanabe Shōzaburō, "Ukiyo-e hanga kenkyū shōwa," in Inoue and Watanabe (eds.) (1931), 241; English translation in Okamoto and Smith, in Stephens (ed.) (1993), 30.

22. From Inoue and Watanabe (eds.) (1931); English translation in Abe, in Newland (ed.) (2005).

23. Okamoto and Smith, in Stephens (ed.) (1993), 32. Goyō's observation relating to contemporary painters creating artistic prints is indeed prophetic, for in this formative period of *Shin-hanga* history neither Goyō nor Watanabe could have known the impact *Shin-hanga* would have had on the future map of twentieth-century Japanese graphic arts.

24. Volker (1949).

25. *Sōsaku-hanga* artist Onchi Kōshirō (1891-1955) so loathed *Shin-hanga* that he called them "semi-prints" or "Neo-*Ukiyo-e*;" see Okamoto and Smith, in Stephens (ed.) (1993), 33. Western writers like Richard Lane leveled the same criticism (see Lane (1978), 196-99), and they were similarly described by Lawrence Smith (see Smith (1983), 16).

26. A transcription of the interview with Watanabe appears in Itabashi Ward Museum of Art (1988), 100; *see also* Amy Reigle Newland, "The Appreciation of *Shin hanga* in the West: The Interwar years, 1915-40," 24-30, in Hamanaka and Newland (2000), 25.

27. Iwakiri Shin'ichirō. "1920 nendai no Nihon no hanga – Taishō kara Shōwa-e" (Japanese Prints of the 1920s – Taishō to Shōwa), 10-5, Chiba City Museum of Art (2001), 10-1. English translation by author.

28. It is perhaps conceivable that by their very nature they might have attracted attention from the Taishō-government authorities. By comparison, then, perhaps the four categories of women, landscapes, actors and birds and flowers were seen as relatively "safe," but this is an aspect that needs further research to be substantiated.

29. Watanabe (1936).

30. If the term "Neo-*Ukiyo-e*" were to be applied to *Shin-hanga* it could only ever be in the sense that *Shin-hanga* was an escape of realities in the Taishō period, in an analogous fashion that *Ukiyo-e* were "pictures of a floating (transient) world."

31. This perception in the West was further fueled by the "Oriental" prints blockcut and printed by Japanese craftsmen already being produced by American artists Helen Hyde (1863-1919) and Bertha Lum (1879-1954); *see also* Brown, in Newland (ed.) (2005).

32. Cited in Chiba City Museum of Art (1999), 158; originally from Goyō's "Nihon no hanga" (Japanese Prints), *Shin shōsetsu* 20:9 (September 1915). English translation by author.

33. Brown, in Newland (ed.) (2005).

34. Not included in this discussion are the depictions of nudes inspired by Western tradition, as we are speaking about a "Japanese" aesthetic.

35. This is particularly true when we realize that the majority of artists who designed *Shin-hanga bijinga* were *Nihonga* painters (Goyō was an anomaly in this regard).

36. Hamanaka Shinji, "*Bijinga*: The Portrayal of Beauties in Modern Japan," 10-6, in Hamanaka and Newland (2000), 14.

37. *Ibid.*, 14. Originally cited in "Bijinga kōgi" (Discourse on *Bijinga*), in *Shin bijutsu kōza, Nihongaka* (New Art Lectures: Japanese Artists), vol. 1 (Tokyo: Chūō Bijutsusha, n.d.).

38. Brown and Minichiello (2002), 60.

39. C. H. Mitchell maintained that *Views of Famous Places in the Osaka and Kobe Region* was the first in *Shin-hanga* landscape, but this does not take into account Hiroaki and foreign artists; see Mitchell (1982). The thirty prints in this series were by Noda Kyūho (1879-1971), Akamatsu Rinsaku (1878-1953), Mizushima Nihofu (1884-?), Hata Tsuneharu (1883-?) and Nagai Hyōsai (Eizō).

40. Quoted in Okamoto and Smith, in Stephens (ed.) (1993), 37.

41. *Ibid.*, 38; originally cited in Hasui, 'Hangasō zuihitsu' (Miscellaneous Thoughts by Hangasō), *Ukiyo-e geijutsu* 4:3 (March 1935), 64. Moreover, Hasui's prints and the poetics of *Shin-hanga* landscape imagery have been the subject of a recent study and *catalogue raisonné* of the artist's work; see Brown *et al.* (2003).

42. Taken from a truly antipodean novel (in an unrelated context) by Murray Bail entitled *Eucalyptus* (Melbourne: Text Publishing, 1998), 23.

43. Brown *et al.* (2003), 20.

44. Illustrated in Ogura *et al.* (1987), no. 1, page 33.

45. Chiba City Museum of Art (2001), 176; originally cited in the article "Hanga ni tsuite" (Regarding Prints), *Ukiyo-e kai* 7 (September 1936). English translation by author.

46. One noticeable exception is *One Hundred Noh Dramas* (*Nōgaku hyakuban*, 1901-5) by Tsukioka Kōgyo (1869-1927).

47. Kendall H. Brown, "Modernity and Memory: *Shin-hanga* and Taisho Culture," 35-89, in Brown and Goodall-Cristante (1996), 49.

Shin nigao-e was published by the Tokyo firm Nigaodō. It was blockcut by Igami Bonkotsu (1875-1933); the printer is unknown. The artists were Ishii Hakutei, Ishizuka Kan, Koito Gentarō (1887-1978), Kondō Kōichirō (1884-1962), Matsuda Seifū (1880-1978), Natori Shunsen, Ogawa Hyōe, Terasawa Kōtarō, Torii Kotondo and Yamamura Toyonari.

48. Cited in Chiba City Museum of Art (1999), 174. English translation by author.

49. In the past the actor in this print has been misidentified as Nakamura Ganjirō I.

50. The term *rien* or "pear tree garden" was derived from the Chinese and relates to the dubbing of imperial entertainers as "children of the pear garden;" in the Edo period it was applied to Kabuki. The images in the Kōka series include (from 1920): Nakamura Ganjirō I as Akane Hanshichi, Ichikawa Shōchō II (1886-1940) as Oman, Onoe Matsusuke (?IV, 1843-1928) as Gorōji, Kataoka Nizaemon XI as Kakiemon, Matsumoto Kōshirō VII (1870-1949) as Sukeroku; and (from 1921): Ichimura Uzaemon XV (1874-1945) as the Gardener Kichigorō, Morita Kanya XIII (1885-1932) as Jean Valjean, (??) Kichiiemon as Hoshikage Tsuchiemon, Nakamura Utaemon V (1865-1940) as Owasa, 1921, Ichikawa Ennosuke II (1886-1963) as Hayami no Tōta; and (from 1922): Sawamura Sōnosuke I as Umegawa and Bandō Mitsugoro VII (1882-1961) as the Mute in "Sannin-Katawa."

51. Chiba City Museum of Art (1999), 161. English translation by author.

52. McClain (2002), 389. The seven prefectures affected: Tokyo, Kanagawa, Shizuoka, Chiba, Saitama, Yamanashi and Ibaraki.

53. Recorded by a O. M. Poole, who had fled with his family to a yacht anchored in the harbor at Yokohama; see the informative website of NISEE, National Information Service for Earthquake Engineering University of California, Berkeley (http://nisee.berkeley.edu/kanto/yokohama.html).

54. Brown, in Newland (ed.) (2005).

55. Represented in the two series: *Select Views of Kyoto, First Series* (*Shinsen Kyōto meisho daiisshū*; six vertical prints, 1925) includes "Snow on Higashiyama" (*Higashiyama no yuki*), "Flower Viewing Boat on the Ōi River" (*Ōigawa no hanamibune*), "Presenting Tea at the Miyako Festival" (*Miyako-odori no tencha*), "Moon on Nijō Castle" (*Nijōjō no tsuki*), "Visiting Kiyomizu" (*Kiyomizu mōde*) and "The Daimonji Illumination at Kiya" (*Daimonji no yoru no Kiya-chō*). The series *Select Views of Kyoto, Second Series* (*Shinsen Kyōto meisho dainishū*; eight horizontal prints, 1925) includes "Kiyomizu on a Spring Night" (*Haru no yoru no Kiyomizu*), "Early Summer on the Hōzu River" (*Shoka no Hōzugawa*), "Evening Shower on the Kamogawa" (*Kamogawa no yūdachi*), "Snow at the Kinkaku Temple" (*Kinkakuji no yuki*), "Spring on Arashiyama" (*Haru no Arashiyama*), "Cherry Blossoms at Omuro" (*Omuro no sakura*), "Snowy Dawn over the Imperial Gardens, Kyoto" (*Gyoen nai yuki no akatsuki*) and "Autumn at the Tsūten Bridge" (*Tsūtenkyō no aki*).

56. The theme of the Heron Maiden (*sagi musume*) is drawn from the dance drama of the same name first performed in 1762. For a brief discussion of the subject, see Brown and Minichiello (2001), 104-9.

57. For further reading, see Newland, in Hamanaka and Newland (2000).

58. The ten artists represented were Goyō, Shinsui, Hasui, Suizan, Shunsen, Oda, Shōson, Kōka, Yoshida and Kanpō. It should be noted that the 1930 exhibit was not the first Japanese print show at the Toledo Museum of Art, for example, one was held in late 1928; see MacLean and Blair (1929), 98.

59. The ten artists in this show were Hakuhō, Hasui, Kiyoshi, Kotondo, Shinsui, Shirō, Shōson, Shunsen, Hiroshi and Nomura Yoshimitsu. It is also important to point out that due to its exhibitions in 1930 and 1936 Toledo was not only a nexus for *Shin-hanga* in the West, but also for *Nihonga*. An article in the *Toledo Blade Pictorial* suggests that Dorothy Blair, co-curator of both prints exhibits, was involved in a show at Toledo of *Nihonga* in 1931, and it states clearly that she was a friend of artist Yokoyama Taikan, who in turn was closely alied to the *Nihon Bijutsuin* and its later forms. See Aline Jean Treanor, "Oriental Art Expert – By Chance," *Toledo Blade Pictorial* of (16 March 1952); a Taikan painting is illustrated alongside prints by Goyō, Shinsui, Hasui, Kazuma and Yoshida.

60. MacLean and Blair (1930), 443.

61. Anonymous reporter, "Toledo Museum of Art Shows Modern Japanese Prints," *The Art News* 34:16 (18 January 1936), 3. The critical reception of Watanabe's *Shin-hanga* prints in Europe is demonstrated on a smaller scale in the four works each by Shinsui, Hasui, Shunsen, Shōson (Koson) and Hasegawa Kiyoshi (1891-1980), then living in Paris, in the International Print Exhibition in Warsaw, Poland, which included 698 works from twenty-three countries. Exhibitions and recognition of the artists working with Watanabe also continued in Japan throughout the 1930s, most noteworthy, the 1932 exhibition of modern woodblock prints held at Mitsukoshi Departure Store in Tokyo's Shinjuku district.

62. Merritt (1990), 67.

63. Blair (1936), un-paginated preface.

Notes to the Catalogue

All prints illustrated in this catalogue section are housed in the Arthur M. Sackler Gallery, Smithsonian Institution; Robert O. Muller Collection. Accession numbers are included for the reader's reference.

Japanese names and terms have been transliterated in accordance with the modified Hepburn system of romanization. Japanese names are generally given in traditional order – surname preceding first name – unless otherwise known in the West. Dates of individuals are only given when known. Personal names, place and era designations appear in their original accented form, unless they have entered into common English usage (e.g., Tokyo, not Tōkyō) or if they are cited as part of an original title, name, etc. in Japanese. Titles of literary works, names of newspapers, exhibitions and institutions are introduced by the original Japanese, followed by its translated English form, for example, *Tōkyō Bijutsu Gakkō* (Tokyo School of Fine Arts).

Image and/or series titles of prints are listed in both English translation and the original Japanese, if the title is included on the print or on the series wrapper. Where no title is found on a print, only the given English title is given. (Works in other media, such as paintings, generally include both English and Japanese titles, as it was not always possible to view the original piece.) Artists' signatures are sometimes followed by the single characters *hitsu* ("from the brush of"), *ga* ("drawn by") or *saku* ("work of"), therefore a signature like *Shinsui saku* (cat. no. 87) would be read "Work of Shinsui."

Dates given on prints are indicated as such; the Japanese era equivalent is included when that form appears on the work. When a work is not dated, an approximate date has generally been supplied.

Sizes are given in centimeters, height before width, and all sizes are approximate.

Select terms used regularly throughout the book are explained in the Glossary, and most bibliographical references are cited throughout in abbreviated form. Complete citations are found in the Bibliography.

Uehara Konen (1877-1940)

Uehara Konen was born Uehara Sennosuke in the Asakusa district of Tokyo. In 1893 he became the pupil of the painter Kajita Hanko (1870-1917) and of the well-known artist and uncle to Takahashi Hiroaki (1871-1945; cat. nos. 10-7), Matsumoto Fūko (1840-1923). From 1896 he studied at the *Nihon Bijutsuin* (Japan Art Institute) and was requested by the Tokyo Prefectural Office to act as a painting judge. He also offered services to the Imperial Household and the Foreign Office. Konen participated in several exhibitions, such as the *Bunten* and that of the *Nihon Kaiga Kyōkai* (Japan Painting Society), as well as being the recipient of numerous awards. It seems that his first woodblock prints were published by Kobayashi Bunshichi (1864-1923). However, with the destruction of Kobayashi's shop in the Great Kantō Earthquake of September 1923 and the publisher's own death that same year, Kobayashi's former employee Watanabe Shōzaburō (1885-1962) assumed the publication of Konen's prints.

REFERENCES Watanabe Shōzaburō (1936), 107; Merritt and Yamada (1992), 161; Stephens (ed.) (1993), 102-3; Yui (1998), 56

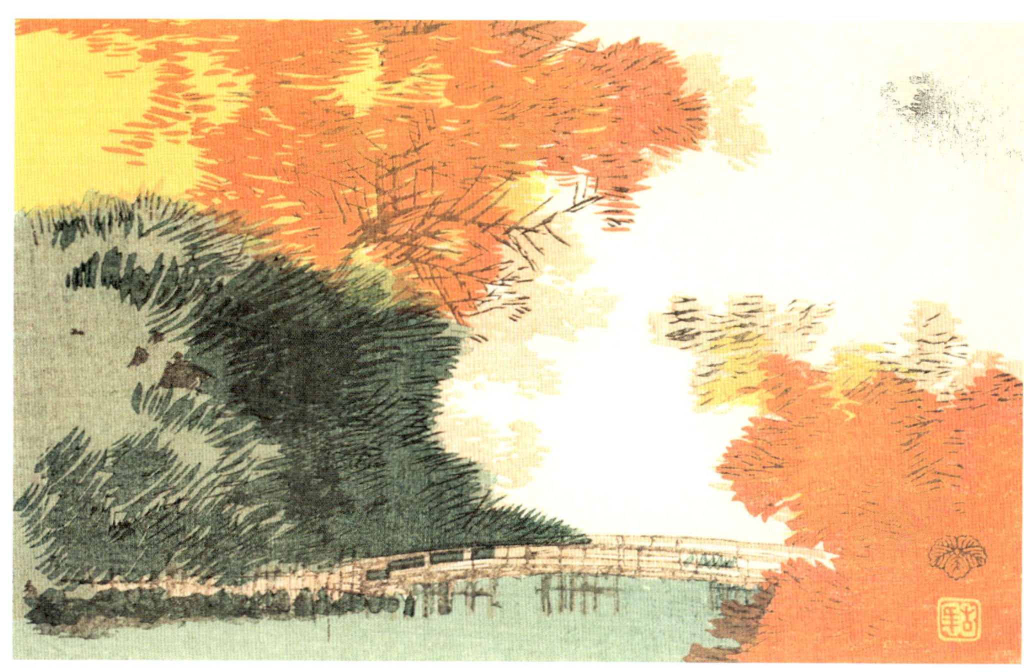

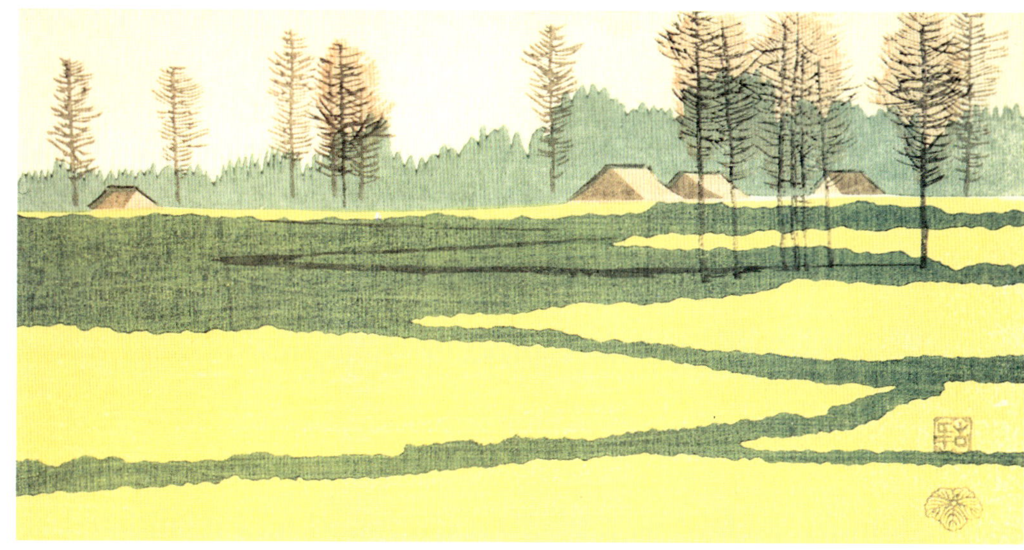

1
"Bridge"

DATE Undated, *c.* pre-1923
SIGNATURE Unsigned
ARTIST'S SEAL *Konen*
PUBLISHER Kobayashi Bunshichi
SIZE 8.6 x 13.7 cm
PROVENANCE Shima Art Co., New York, 1940
ACCESSION NUMBER S2003.8.3137

2
"Early Summer, Fields with Pine Trees"

DATE Undated, *c.* pre-1923
SIGNATURE Unsigned
ARTIST'S SEAL *Konen*
PUBLISHER Kobayashi Bunshichi
SIZE 7.0 x 13.7 cm
PROVENANCE Shima Art Co., New York, 1940
ACCESSION NUMBER S2003.8.3136

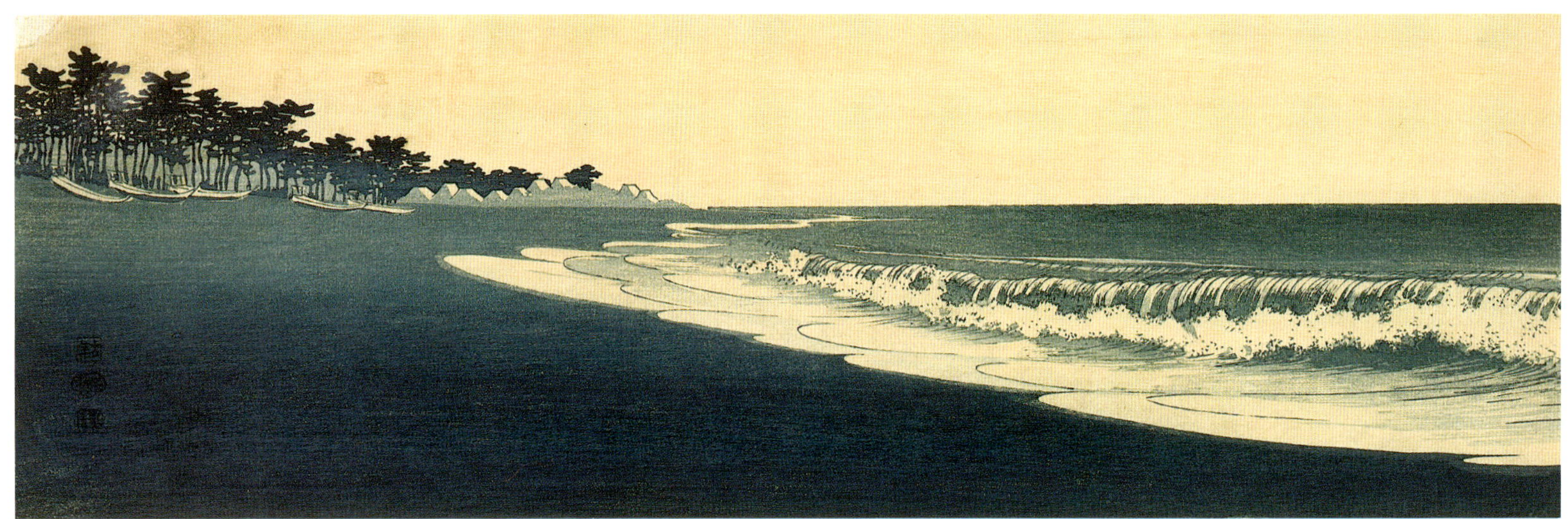

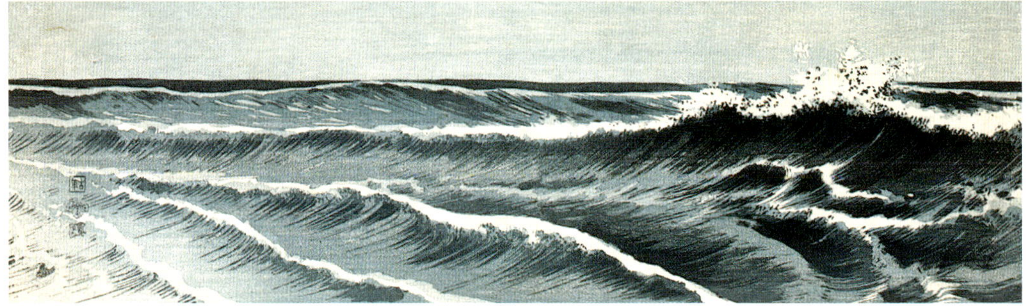

3

"Waves Along the Shore"

DATE Undated, c. pre-1923
SIGNATURE Unsigned
ARTIST'S SEAL *Konen*
PUBLISHER Kobayashi Bunshichi
PUBLISHER'S STOCK NUMBER 433 (on front)
SIZE 11.4 x 36.1 cm
PROVENANCE Shima Art Co., New York, 1940
ACCESSION NUMBER S2003.8.3111

4

"Ocean Wave"

DATE Undated, c. pre-1923
SIGNATURE Unsigned
ARTIST'S SEAL *Konen*
PUBLISHER Kobayashi Bunshichi
PUBLISHER'S STOCK NUMBER 429 (on front)
SIZE 10.6 x 36.1 cm
PROVENANCE Shima Art Co., New York, 1940
ACCESSION NUMBER S2003.8.3103

These four works belong to a group of approximately forty prints issued in various formats that were designed by Konen for the publisher Kobayashi Bunshichi. Robert O. Muller coined the term "Sumida River School" to refer to these prints, because they often illustrate water scenes. Some are of identifiable locations, other are anonymous.

Kobayashi was an extremely influential figure in the world of late nineteenth- and early twentieth-century Japanese woodblocks prints, not only for his position as a collector and dealer, but also as a publisher (principally of facsimiles) and a promoter of Japanese prints. Together with Ernest Fenollosa (1853-1908), Curator of Japanese Art at the Museum of Fine Arts, Boston from 1890 to 1895 and himself an important collector of Japanese art, Kobayashi organized the first exhibition of *Ukiyo-e* in Tokyo's Ueno Park in 1898. In his role as a dealer Kobayashi supplied the Paris-based Japanese art handler Hayashi Tadamasa (1853-1906) with artworks. Kobayashi's own collection of Japanese prints was generally recognized as one of the finest in the world. Sadly, it was consumed by the conflagration following the Great Kantō Earthquake of 1 September 1923.

It seems that Konen's prints for Kobayashi were made for the export market. The majority of his forty prints have only the artist's seal *Konen* and Kobayashi's distinctive ivy-shaped publisher's seal. All of these works roughly pre-date the earthquake, when the Kobayashi premises, including stock and woodblocks, were destroyed. A great many Konen prints found their way into the Muller collection with his acquisition of the Shima Art Company in 1940.

The publisher Watanabe Shōzaburō became acquainted with Konen's work during his employment from 1902 to 1906 at the Yokohama branch of the Kobayashi firm. In his 1936 English sales catalogue, Watanabe refers briefly to Konen's early work for Kobayashi: "Over thirty years ago he had an experience to produce small color-prints intended for the United States."[1] Watanabe suggests that Konen was introduced to him after 1926 through the artist Ohara Koson (1877-1945; cat. nos. 23-33),[2] but the artist was to produce only two prints for Watanabe.

1. Watanabe Shōzaburō (1936), 107.
2. *Ibid.* For more on Uehara Konen, see Stephens (ed.) (1993), 102-3.

Kaburagi Kiyokata (1878-1973)

Kaburagi Kiyokata was born Kaburagi Kenichi in the Kanda district of Tokyo. His father Jōno Saigiku (1832-1902) was a novelist and founder of the *Tōkyō Nichinichi Shinbun* (*Tokyo Daily News*) and *Yamato Shinbun* (*Yamato Newspaper*). He received drawing lessons at a very young age from Shibata Shinsai (1858-95), the second son of Shibata Zeshin (1807-91). In 1891 he became a student of Mizuno Toshikata (1866-1908), a staff member at the *Yamato Shinbun* as well as a painter and printmaker of historical themes and beautiful women. It was from Toshikata that he received his artist's name *Kiyokata*. Kiyokata worked as an illustrator for several newspapers from 1894, including those owned by his father and, together with Kajita Hanko (1870-1917), for the *Yomiuri Shinbun*. He became a well-known designer of *kuchi-e* for novels by authors such as Ozaki Kōyō (1869-1903) and Izumi Kyōka (1873-1939), while also building his reputation as a *Nihonga* painter working in a polished, refined style. In 1901 he initiated the founding of the *Ugōkai* (Cormorant Society), a group formed by students of Toshikata and Ogata Gekkō (1859-1920). He frequently showed his paintings at the official exhibitions *Bunten* and *Teiten*, and won several prizes. In 1929 he became a member of the *Teikoku Bijutsuin* (Imperial Fine Arts Academy) and in 1954 he received the *Bunka Kunshō* (Order of Cultural Merit). A number of his pupils designed *Shin-hanga* prints, including Kawase Hasui (1883-1957; cat. nos. 52-63), Itō Shinsui (1898-1972; cat. nos. 85-101), Yamakawa Shūhō (1898-1944; cat. no. 84), Kasamatsu Shirō (1898-1991; cat. nos. 102-4) and Kobayakawa Kiyoshi (1899-1948; cat. nos. 81-3).

REFERENCES Merritt and Yamada (1992), 50-1; Stephens (ed.) (1993), 106-8; National Museum of Modern Art (ed.) (1999); Hamanaka and Newland (2000), 95, 209; Merritt and Yamada (2000), 198-201

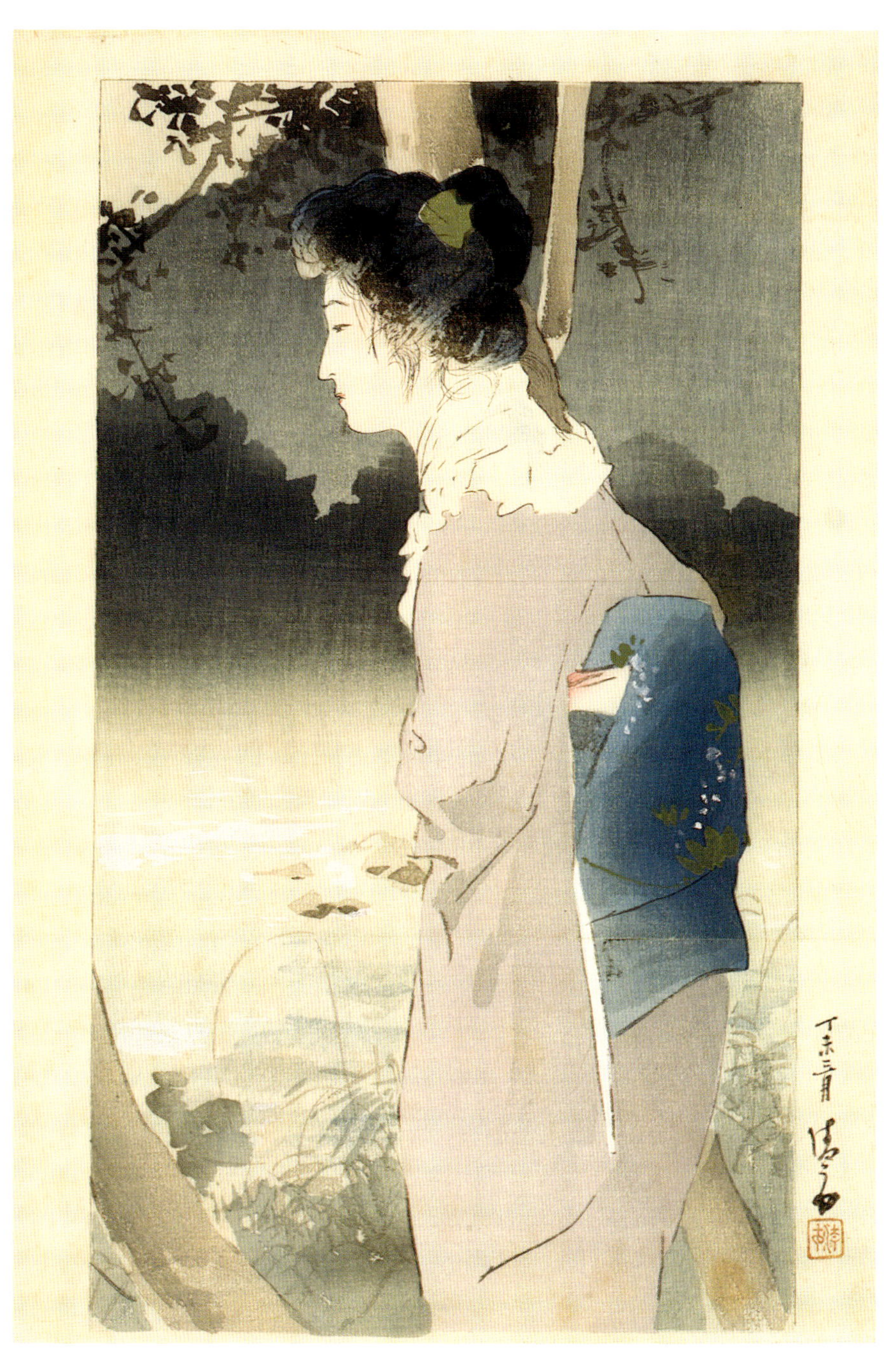

5

Kuchi-e* for the novel *Yomegafuchi

DATE 1907 [Year of the Goat], March
SIGNATURE *Kiyokata*
SIZE 29.9 x 17.6 cm
PROVENANCE Yamada Shoten, Tokyo, June 1986
ACCESSION NUMBER S2003.8.403
REFERENCE Stephens (ed.) (1993), cat. no. 79

The seemingly slow start to Kiyokata's artistic career is generally explained by his dedication to his father's newspaper *Yamato Shinbun*, which was to suffer financial setbacks in around 1894. Thanks to his association with the author Izumi Kyōka from 1901, however, it appears that Kiyokata began to design *sashi-e* (inserted illustrations) and *kuchi-e* for Kyōka's novels. In 1907, he designed the *kuchi-e* illustrated here for the novel *Yomegafuchi*, which was written by the little-known author of romances, Ogasawara Hakuya. The importance of Kiyokata vis-à-vis the development of the *Shin-hanga* movement cannot be underestimated. His mark was made not so much for his body of printed work as for his role of teacher to many artists who designed *Shin-hanga*.

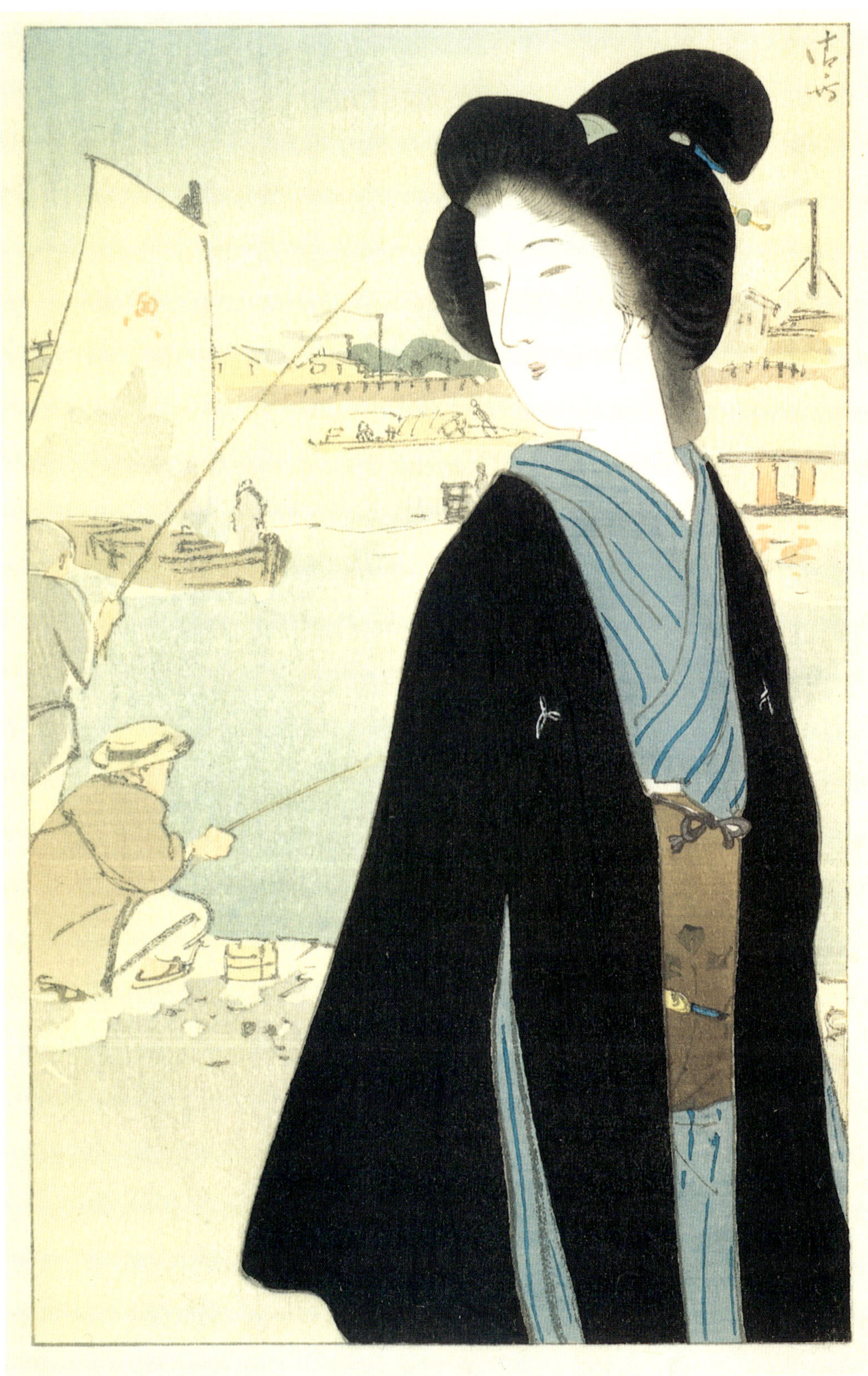

6

"Autumn at Hama-chō: Riverside"

FROM *Album of Beauties by Kiyokata (Kiyokata bijin gafu)*
DATE 1914 (Taishō 3)
SIGNATURE *Kiyokata*
SIZE 17.4 x 11.7 cm
ACCESSION NUMBER S2003.8.399
REFERENCE Stephens (ed.) (1993), cat. no. 80

This design is from a small album that contains four woodblock and eight mechanically printed images of contemporary beauties, a table of contents and explanatory text. The combination of reprographic techniques is typical of the late Meiji and Taishō periods.

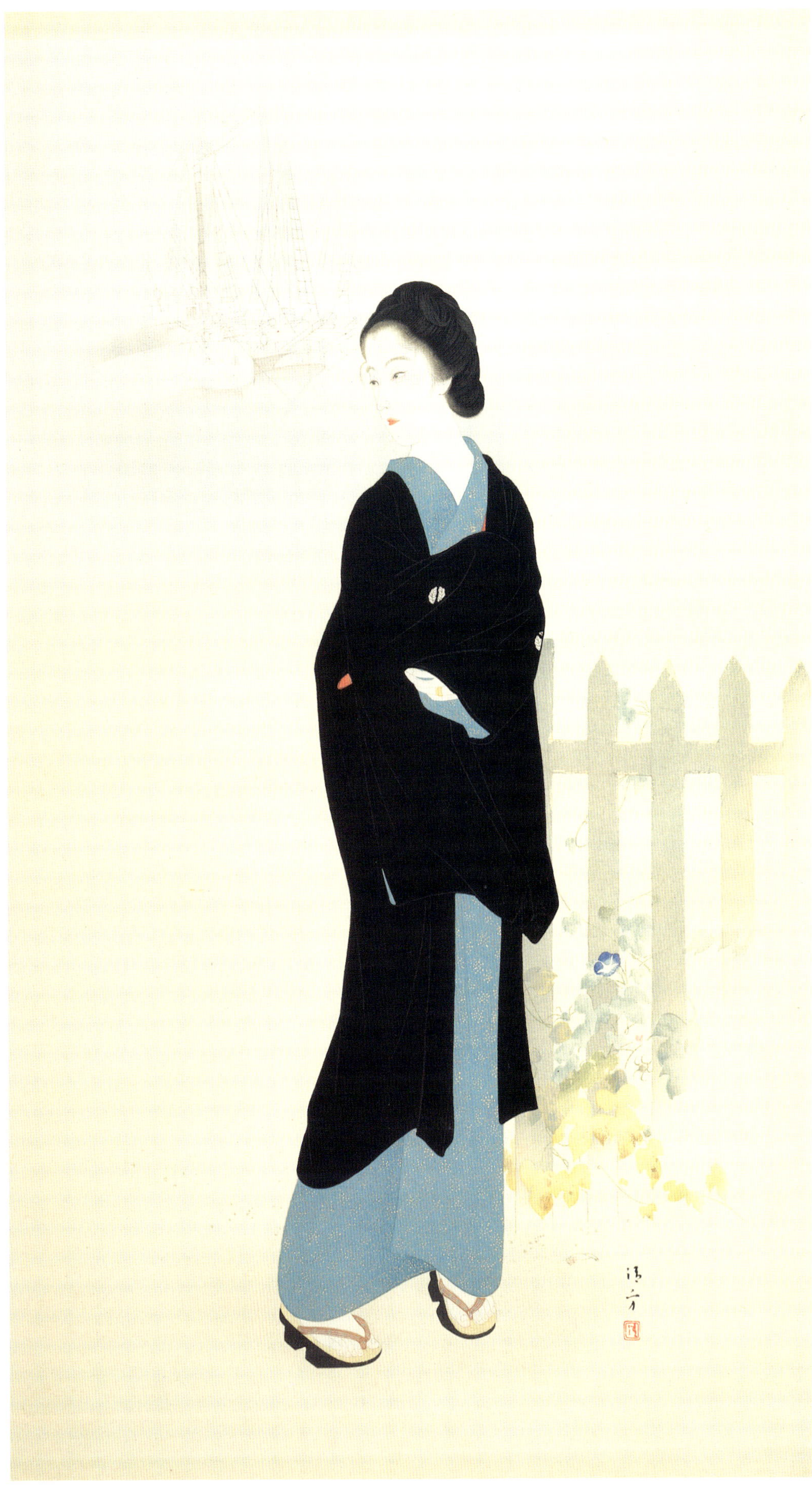

7
"Tsukiji Akashi-chō, Kawagishi"

DATE Undated, c. 1928
SIGNATURE *Kiyokata*
ARTIST'S SEAL *Kiyo*
SIZE 59.1 × 34.8 cm
PROVENANCE Shōbisha (Matsuki Kihachirō), Tokyo, April 1940
ACCESSION NUMBER S2003.8.396
REFERENCE Stephens (ed.) (1993), cat. no. 82

Undoubtedly Kiyokata's most famous print, this deluxe work was based on a painting on silk of the same theme exhibited at the eighth *Teiten* in 1927. In composition it varies only slightly from the original painting and thus demonstrates the trend to convert popular paintings into woodblock prints. (Another example is seen in the work of Kitano Tsunetomi; cat. nos. 45-6.) The unusually large size and the absence of publisher's information on this piece distinguishes it from other more characteristic *Shin-hanga* produced by Kiyokata's numerous pupils, which were intended from the outset as graphic art. By contrast, in conception this particular work was not intended as such.

Publishers were instrumental in shaping the face of *Shin-hanga*. Admittedly, some artists decided to self-publish (e.g., Hashiguchi Goyō and Yoshida Hiroshi), but the seal of a publisher like Watanabe Shōzaburō was important in defining a print as "*Shin-hanga*." From the presence of a Watanabe seal we know much about edition size (large), price (generally low) and the extent of its target audience (generally widespread). In other words, the underlying conceit of *Shin-hanga* had to do not only with design and stylistic considerations, but also with the division of labor and the role of the publisher.

Tsuchiya Kōitsu (1870-1949)

Tsuchiya Kōitsu was born Tsuchiya Kōichi in Hamamatsu, Shizuoka Prefecture, and at the age of fifteen he moved to Tokyo. According to the publisher Watanabe Shōzaburō (1885-1962), Kōitsu studied with a blockcutter named Matsuzaki who worked for print designer Kobayashi Kiyochika (1847-1915). Kōitsu is said to have later become a pupil of Kiyochika and to have resided with him for nineteen years. Kōitsu produced woodblock prints of the Sino-Japanese War (1894-95) and was active as a lithographer. He met Watanabe in 1931 at a Kiyochika memorial exhibition, and their acquaintance led to the publication of a number of landscape prints – Kōitsu's speciality. He likewise worked with the publishers Doi Sadaichi (also read Teiichi) and Sakai/Kawaguchi, in total designing some 200 prints.

REFERENCES Watanabe Shōzaburō (1936), 116; Merritt and Yamada (1992), 156; Stephens (ed.) (1993), 110; Chigasaki City Art Museum (ed.) (1999); *www.koitsu.com*

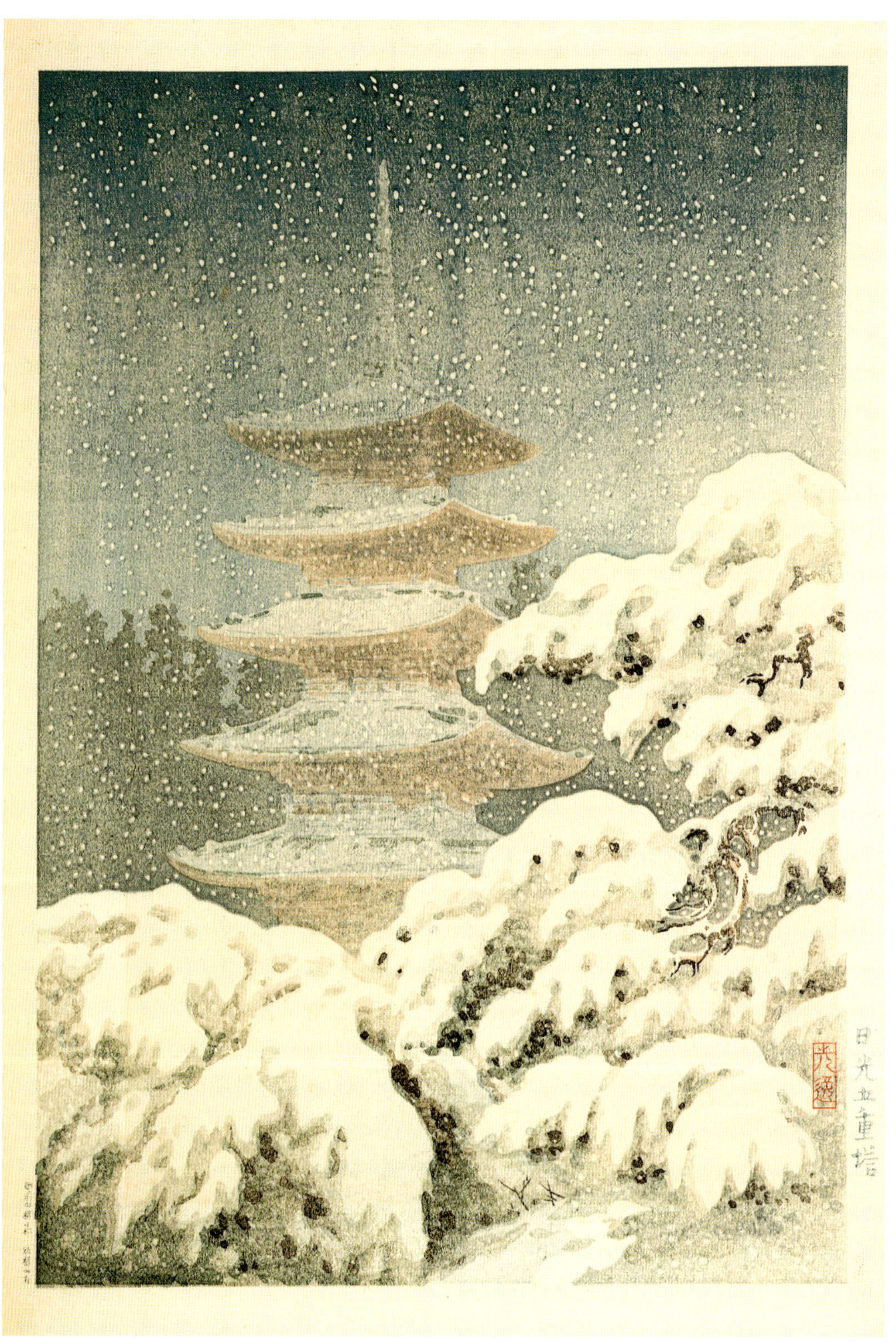

8

"Five-Story Pagoda, Nikkō"

Nikkō gojū tō

DATE Undated, c. 1930

SIGNATURE Unsigned

ARTIST'S SEAL *Kōitsu*

PUBLISHER Sakai/Kawaguchi

SIZE 38.1 x 26.0 cm

PUBLISHER'S STOCK NUMBER 40 (verso)

PROVENANCE Shima Art Co., New York, 1940

ACCESSION NUMBER S2003.8.2773

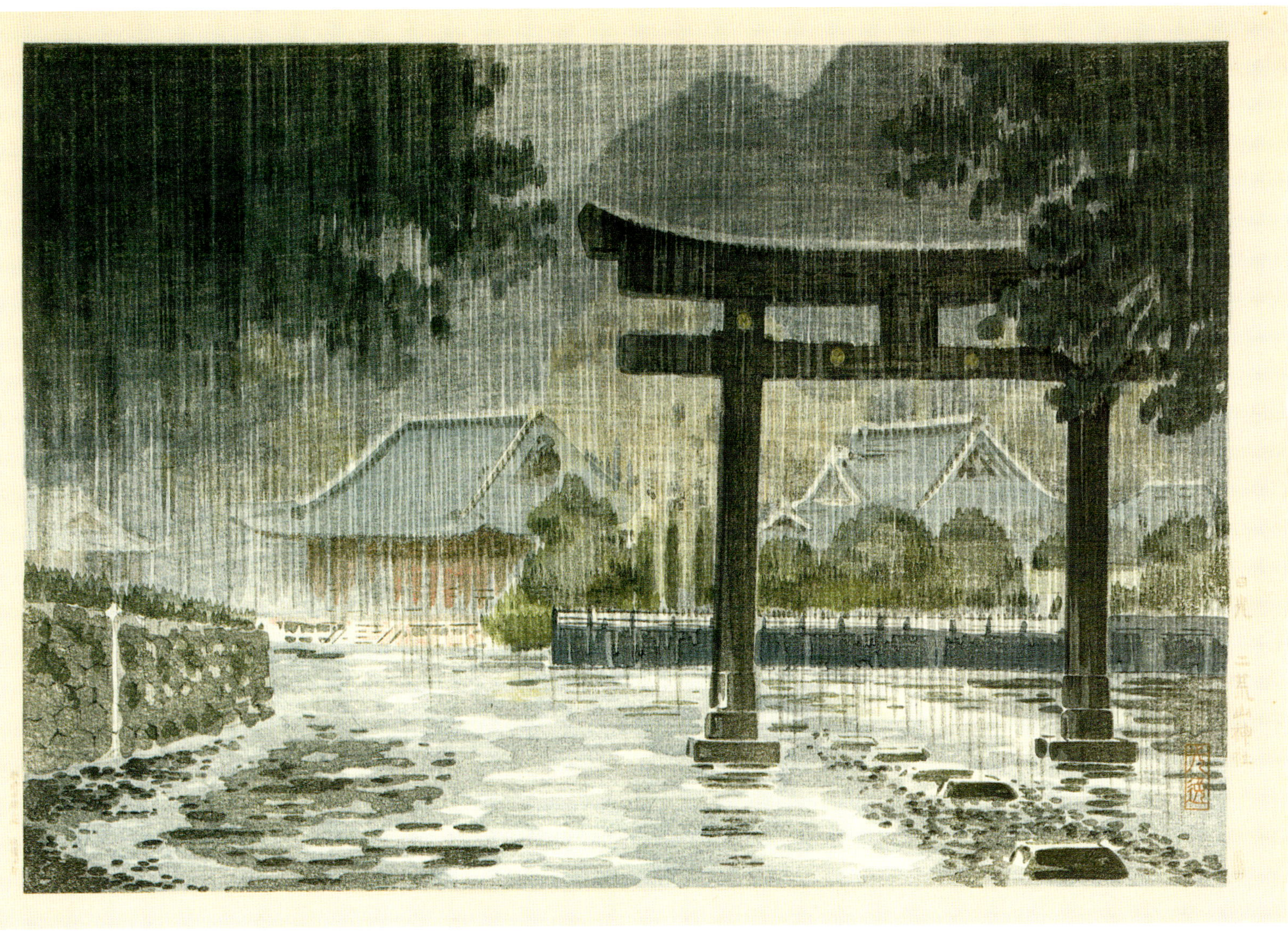

9

"Futarasan Shrine, Nikkō"

Nikkō Futarasan jinja

DATE Undated, c. 1932
SIGNATURE Unsigned
ARTIST'S SEAL *Kōitsu*
PUBLISHER Kawaguchi
SIZE 25.9 x 37.9 cm
PUBLISHER'S STOCK NUMBER 42 (verso)
PROVENANCE Shima Art Co., New York, 1940
ACCESSION NUMBER S2003.8.2768

Kōitsu is considered one of the "second generation" *Shin-hanga* landscape artists. He initially designed ten prints for Watanabe. However, the two prints illustrated here date to a period in the early 1930s, when Kōitsu, like a number of his colleagues, shifted his allegiance from Watanabe to other publishers. In Kōitsu's case it was to Sakai/Kawaguchi, and these two designs are characteristic of their publications: they are printed on a thick, absorbent paper, and the printing itself displays a greater degree of texture, which is perhaps best described as "waxy" (as opposed to a flat surface) and "fuzzy" (as opposed to sharply delineated contour lines). Sakai/Kawaguchi releases contrast the rather flat and lifeless impressions made by the Kyoto publisher Baba Nobuhiko from 1935 onward and Tokyo publisher Doi Sadaichi, who issued about 100 Kōitsu prints. Only eight Doi prints were produced during the artist's lifetime.

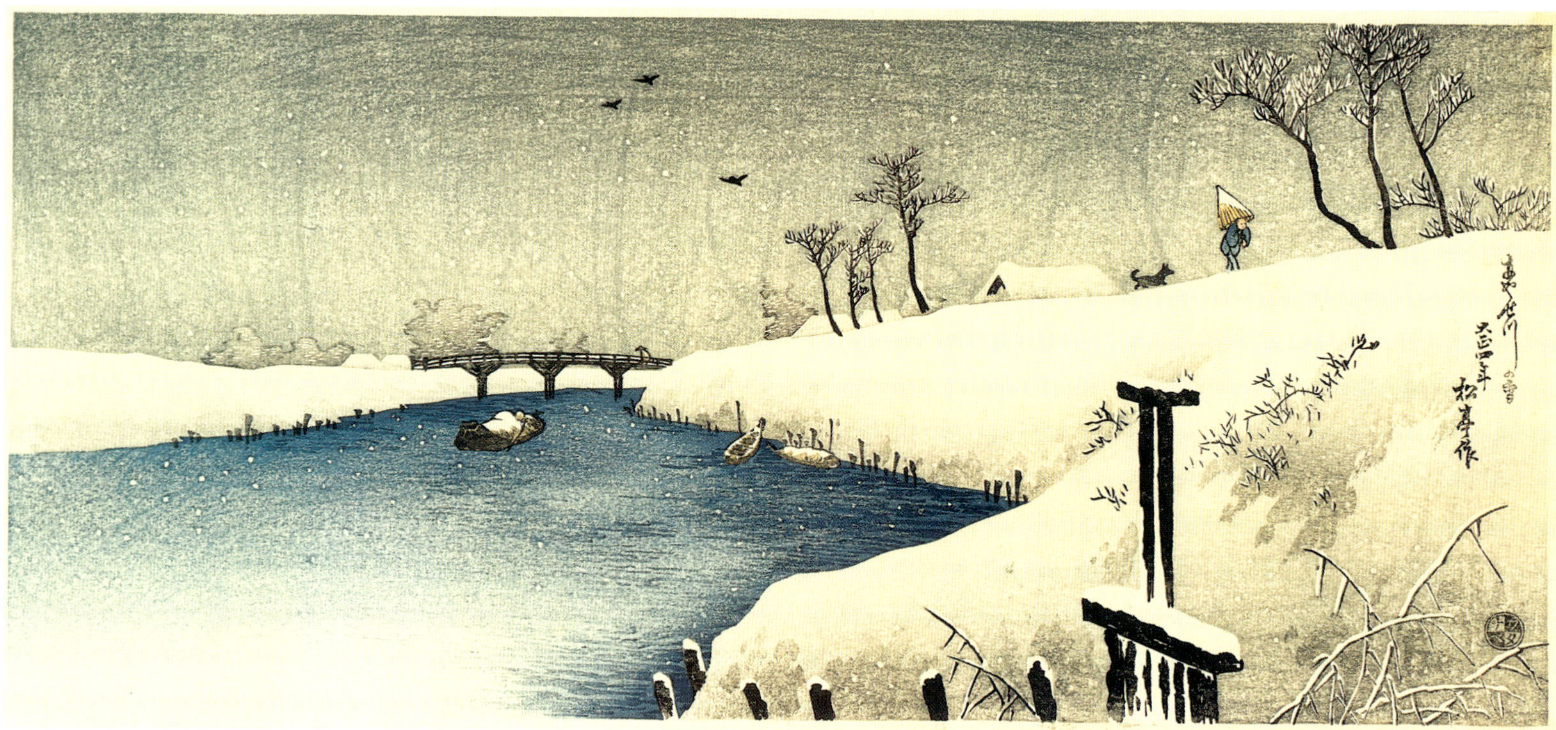

Takahashi Hiroaki (Shōtei) (1871-1945)

Hiroaki was born Matsumoto Katsutarō in the Asakusa district of Tokyo, and as child he was adopted into the Takahashi family. From 1879 he studied *Nihonga* with his uncle, the painter Matsumoto Fūko (1840-1923), from whom he received his artist's name *Shōtei*. At the age of fifteen or sixteen he worked in the design section at the Imperial Household and also illustrated magazines, scientific textbooks and newspapers. Together with the *Nihonga* painter Terazaki Kōgyō (1866-1919), he organized the *Nihon Seinen Kaiga Kyōkai* (Japan Youth Painting Association) in 1891. Sometime around 1906/1907, he began working with the publisher Watanabe Shōzaburō (1885-1962) and signed his prints *Shōtei*. From 1921 he assumed the name *Hiroaki* (also read *Kōmei*), but continued the use of the name *Shōtei* in his artist's seal. According to Watanabe, Hiroaki designed 500 prints, all of which were destroyed by the Great Kantō Earthquake of 1 September 1923. After the earthquake Watanabe states that he produced some 165 prints by Hiroaki in different sizes; however, in actual fact 300 prints issued by Watanabe have been identified (see *www.shotei.com*). In the 1930s Hiroaki also created twenty-seven prints with the publisher Fusui Gabō and collaborated with another publisher, Shōbidō (Tanaka), to make around 180 prints in mostly smaller formats (14.3 x 9.7 cm).

REFERENCES Watanabe Shōzaburō (1936), 105-6; Merritt and Yamada (1992), 142; Stephens (ed.) (1993), 111-14; Hamanaka and Newland (2000), 113-14; *www.shotei.com*

10
"Snow at Ayase River"
Ayasegawa no yuki

DATE 1915 (Taishō 4)
SIGNATURE *Shōtei*
PUBLISHER Watanabe Shōzaburō
SIZE 16.5 x 37.2 cm
ACCESSION NUMBER S2003.8.2327

From around 1906/1907 Hiroaki began to design landscape prints for the Watanabe firm in the narrow *mitsugiriban* ("three-cut format," *c.* 37 x 48 cm), whereby three prints are cut from a sheet of *Minogami* paper. These prints have margins of approximately 3-4 mm on all sides, and the paper tends to be slightly darker than that normally used in traditional *Ukiyo-e*. The title of the print appears within the design and can be followed by a seal reading *Hiroaki* (also read *Kōmei*), *Shōtei* or *Takahashi*. Early examples can have the largest of the circular Watanabe seals, but the majority do not have the publisher's seal.

Hiroaki's work with Watanabe is characteristically atmospheric landscape scenes, with a preference for twilight views and nocturnes. As an artist Hiroaki merits reappraisal, and certainly for his place in the evolution of *Shin-hanga* as the first artist employed by Watanabe in his search for a *Shin-hanga* "ideal." But it appears that Watanabe himself deemed Hiroaki's prints incongruous with this ideal, and perhaps Watanabe's dissatisfaction can be interpreted by the absence of his copyright seals on the majority of Hiroaki's *mitsugiriban*. Hiroaki was, quite undeservedly, not included in the groundbreaking exhibitions at the Toledo Museum of Art in 1930 and 1936. (The website *www.shotei.com* presents an inventory of all Hiroaki prints known to date.)

11

"Evening Glow at Genki Bridge"

Genkibashi no sekishō

DATE Undated, *c.* pre-1923
SIGNATURE Unsigned
ARTIST'S SEAL *Shōtei*
PUBLISHER Watanabe Shōzaburō
SIZE 37.5 × 16.5 cm
PROVENANCE Israel Goldman, London, New York City Print Fair, November 1992
ACCESSION NUMBER S2003.8.2308

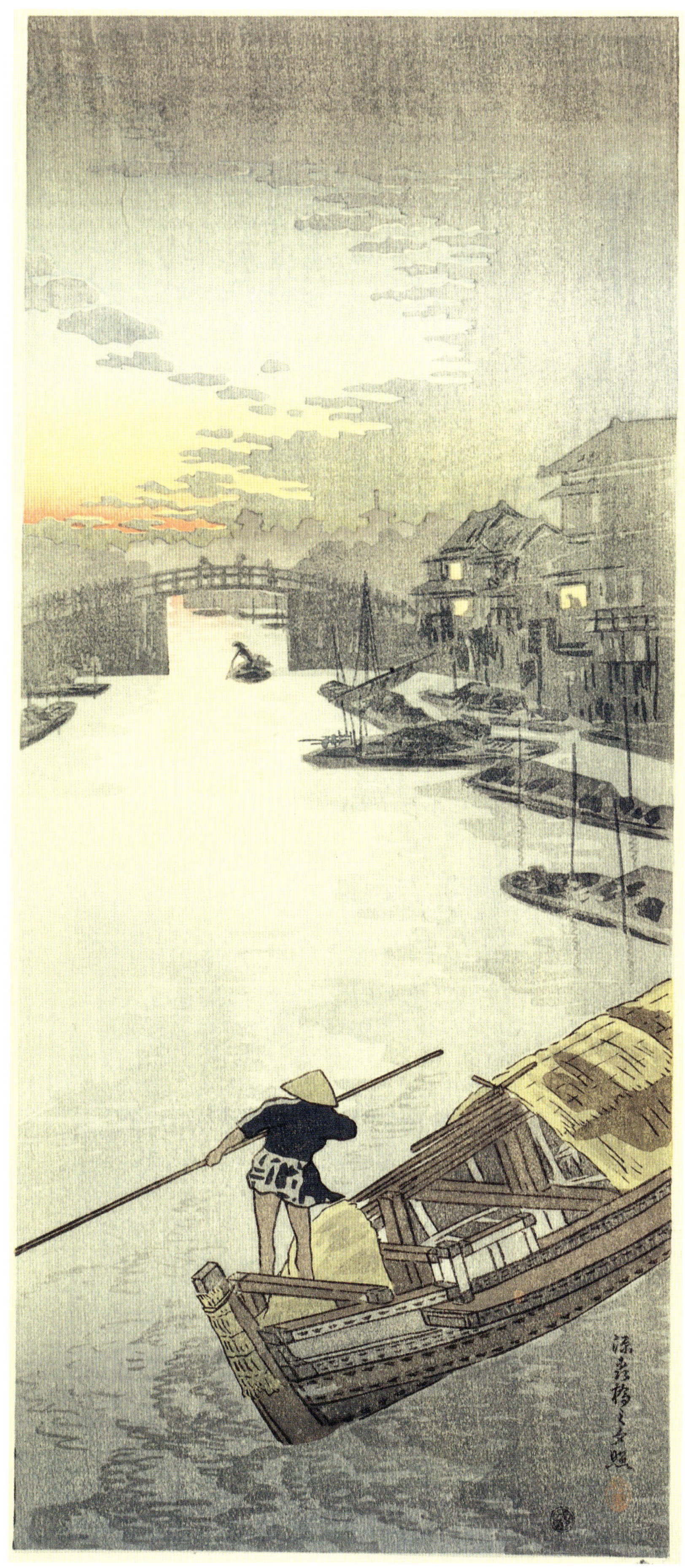

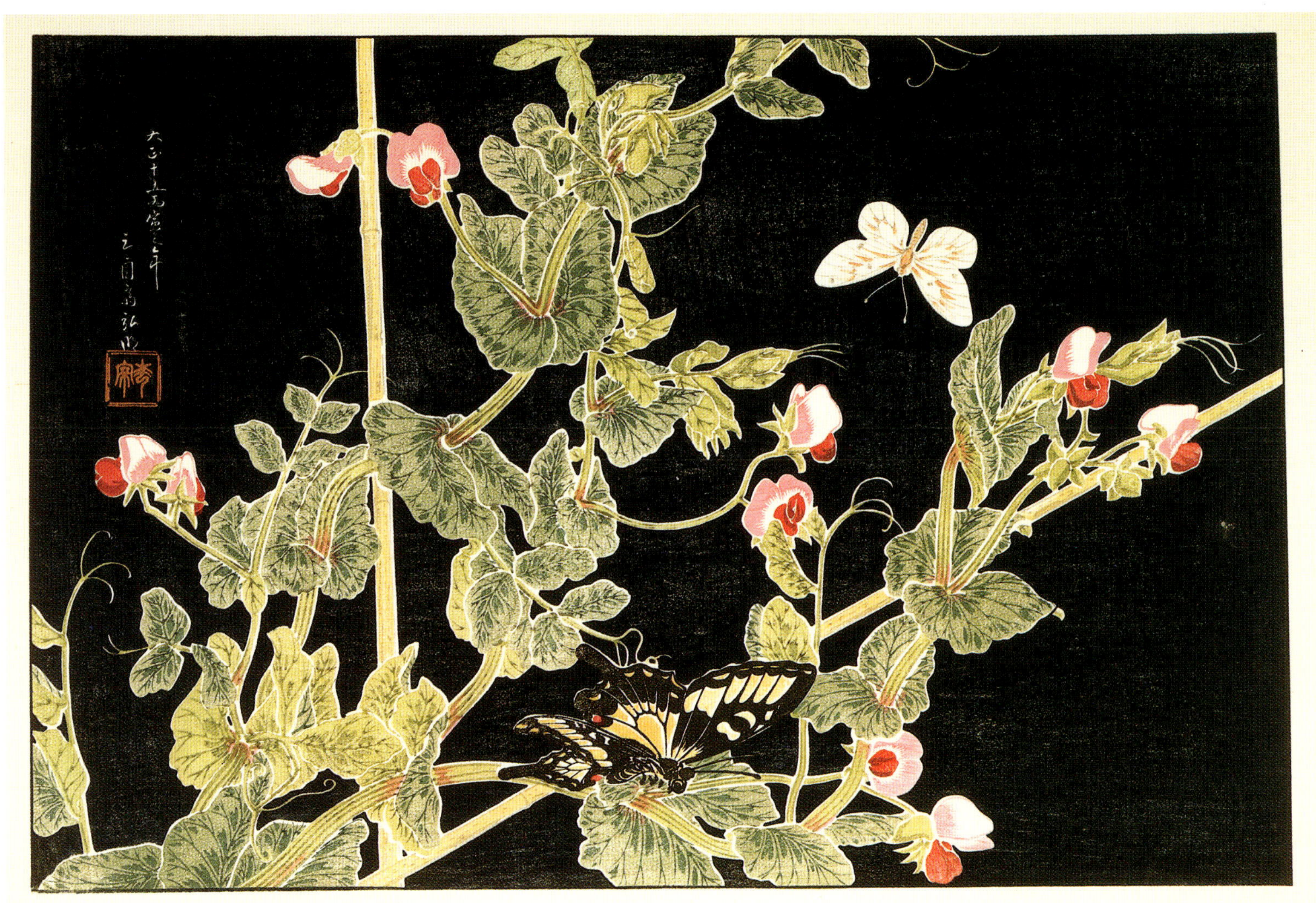

12
"Sweet Pea Flower and Butterfly"

DATE 1926 (Taishō 15)
SIGNATURE *Takahashi Shōtei*
ARTIST'S SEAL *Shōtei*
PUBLISHER Watanabe Shōzaburō
SIZE 24.1 x 36.2 cm
PROVENANCE Joan Mirviss, New York, October 1995
ACCESSION NUMBER S2003.8.2387

This design numbers among the rare *ōban* format prints produced by Hiroaki for the publisher Watanabe Shōzaburō. This highly unusual print of flowers and insects, set against a black ground, was most likely printed in an extremely small run.

13
"Nude Playing with a Cat"

DATE Undated, c. 1930
SIGNATURE AND ARTIST'S SEAL *Hiroaki* (also read *Kōmei*)
PUBLISHER Fusui Gabō
SIZE 41.0 x 25.6 cm
PROVENANCE Kabutoya, Tokyo, May 1980
ACCESSION NUMBER S2003.8.2293
REFERENCE Hamanaka and Newland (2000), no. 147

During the Shōwa period, Hiroaki began to design prints for the publishing firm Fusui Gabō (Fusui Art House), who opened a shop in Hongo, Tokyo in 1924. It is unclear if Hiroaki's shift to Fusui was the result of a quarrel over royalties with Watanabe Shōzaburō. (A number of artists broke with Watanabe due to similar disputes.) From 1929 to 1932, Fusui commissioned new designs from Hiroaki and Yamada Basuke (*d.* 1934). To date, twenty-seven such prints by Hiroaki in *ōban* and *dai-ōban* ("large *ōban*," as here) formats have been identified. The extreme rarity of these often luxuriously printed designs can be explained by the destruction of the Fusui Gabō premises during the Allied bombings of Tokyo during World War II, and along with it all of Hiroaki's blocks.[1] These designs include some of the most daring and sought after twentieth-century Japanese prints. This composition of a nude set against a bright red ground, as she teases a black cat with a length of cloth, imparts a sensuousness not captured in Hiroaki's work with Watanabe.

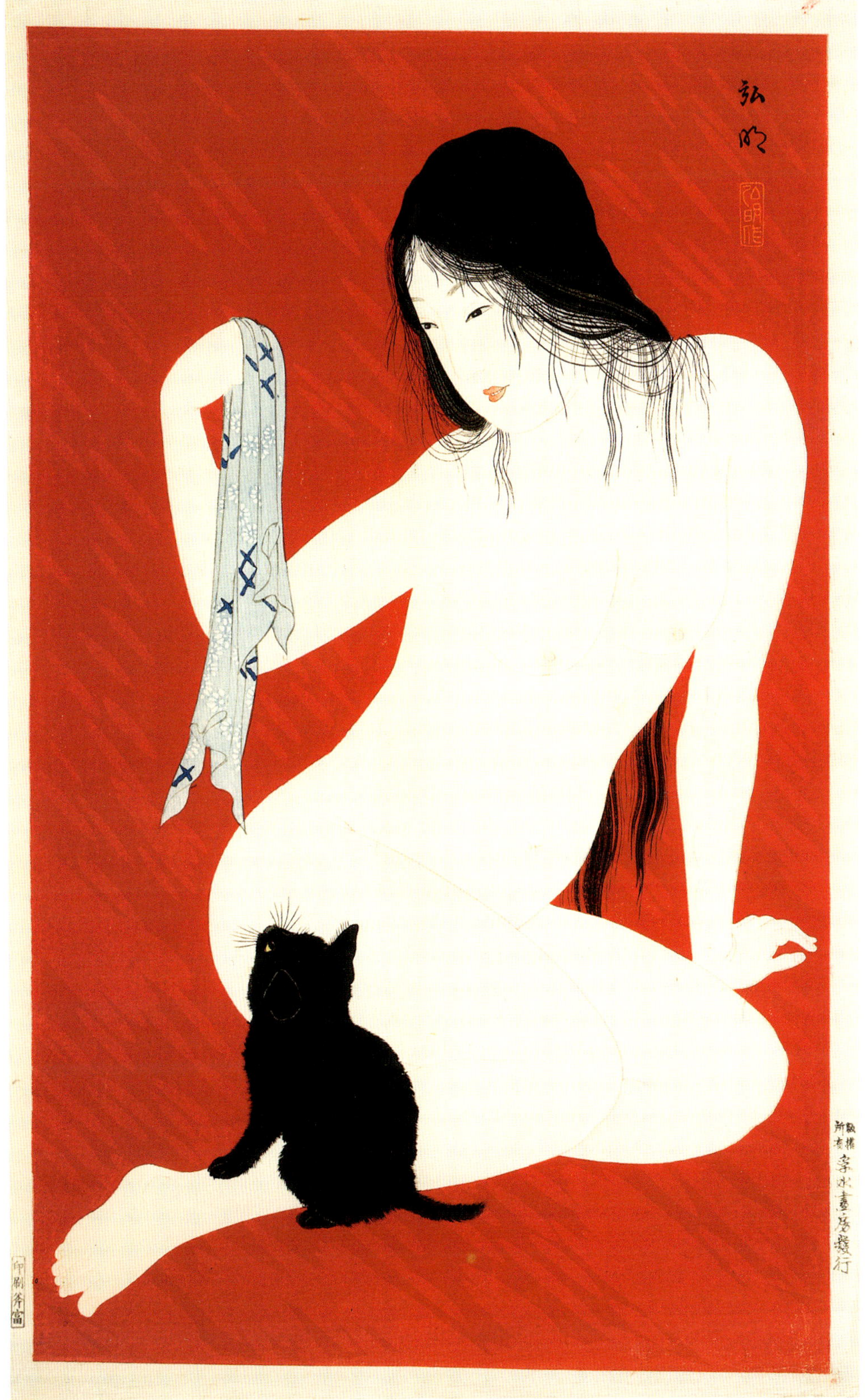

1. Fusui never resumed business after this time; see Shimizu (2002), produced and translated on *www.shotei.com*.

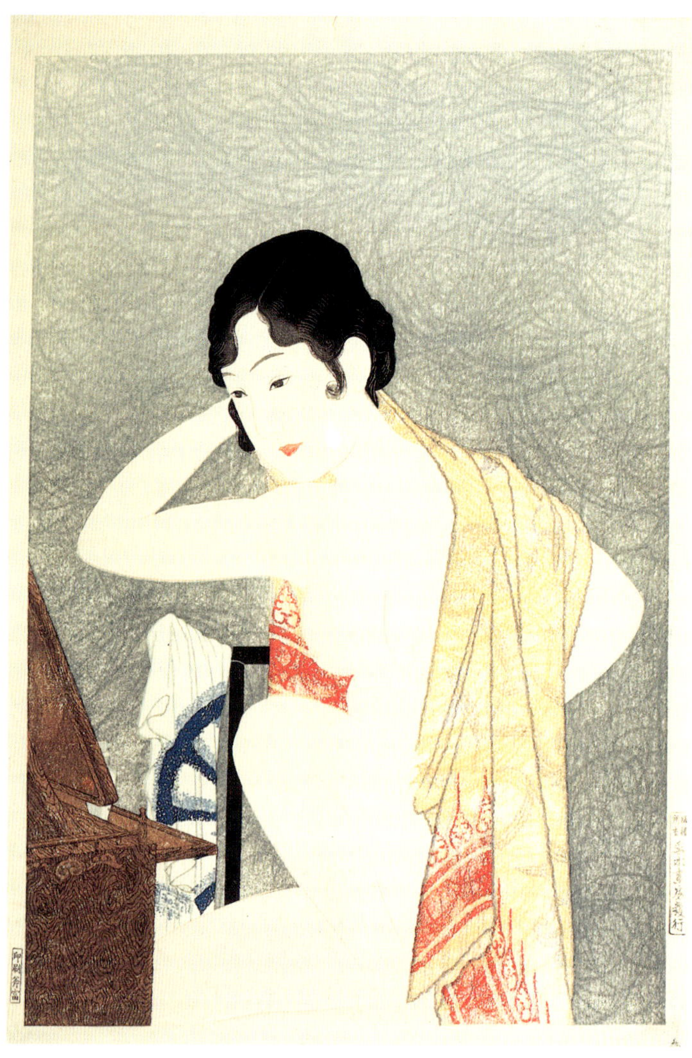

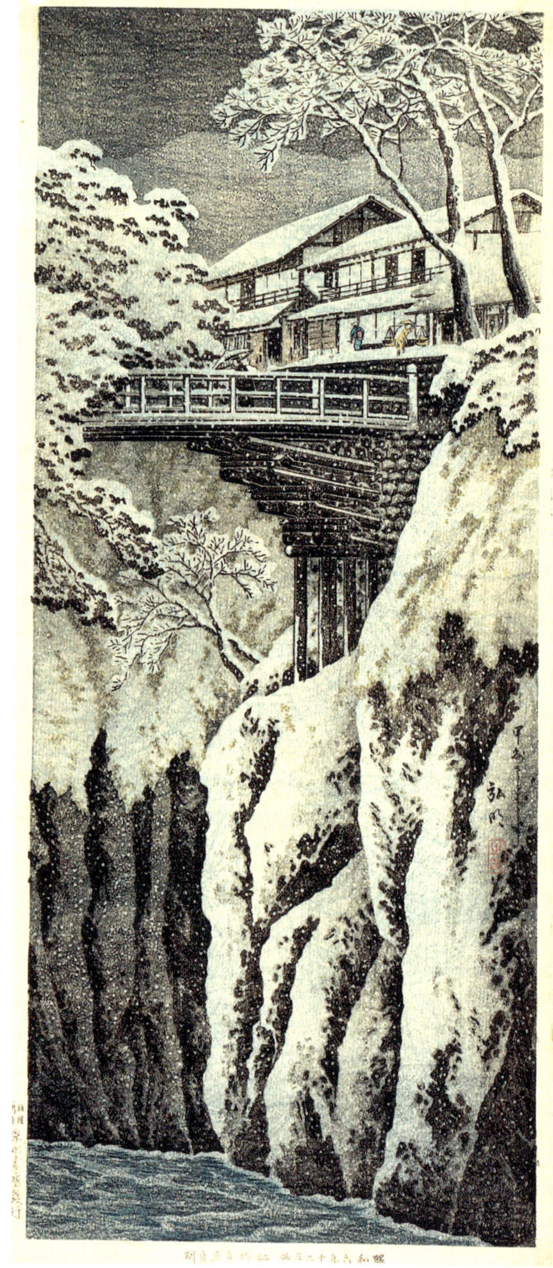

14

"Make-up Before the Mirror"

DATE Undated, *c.* 1927

SIGNATURE AND ARTIST'S SEAL *Hiroaki* (also read *Kōmei*)

PUBLISHER Fusui Gabō

SIZE 39.2 x 26.7 cm

PROVENANCE Kabutoya, Tokyo, May 1981

ACCESSION NUMBER S2003.8.2294

REFERENCE Hamanaka and Newland (2000), no. 149

The contours of the woman's body are accentuated by over-printing in pink and through the use of blind-printing or gauffrage.

15

"The Saru Bridge in Kōshū Province"

Kōshū Saruhashi

DATE 1931 (Shōwa 6), December

SIGNATURE *Hiroaki* (also read *Kōmei*), with unread artist's seal

PUBLISHER Fusui Gabō

Carved by the artist

SIZE 49.8 x 21.0 cm

PROVENANCE Victor Merlo, Santa Barbara, August 1956

ACCESSION NUMBER S2003.8.2381

REFERENCE Stephens (ed.) (1993), cat. no. 93

Hiroaki's supervision of *Ukiyo-e* reproductions for the Fusui Gabō (Fusui Art House), and his earlier experience working with Watanabe Shōzaburō when the publisher was concentrating on the production of deluxe facsimiles of old master *Ukiyo-e* prints, equipped the artist with a sound knowledge of nineteenth-century print masters. The inspiration for this work may have stemmed from the print "Saru Bridge" (*Saruhashi*) in the series *Famous Views in Sixty-odd Provinces* (*Rokujūyoshū meisho zue*, 1853-56) by Utagawa Hiroshige (1797-1858).

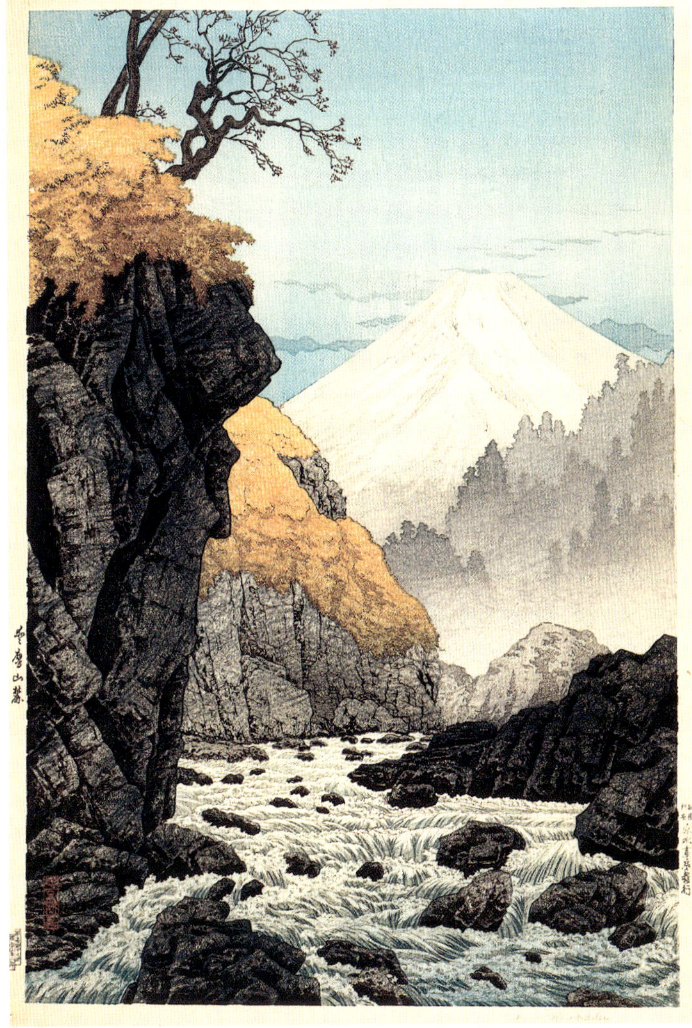

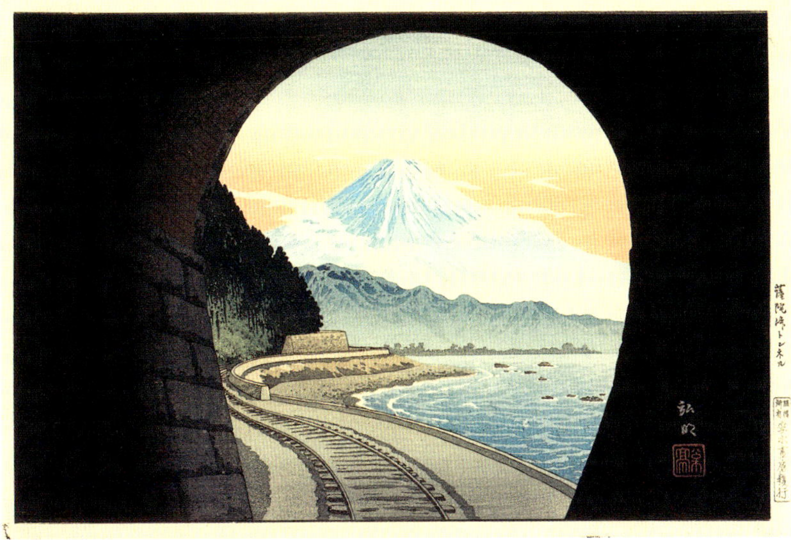

16

"The Foot of Atago Mountain [Autumn]"

Atago Sanroku

DATE 1932 (Shōwa 7), January

SIGNATURE AND ARTIST'S SEAL *Hiroaki* (also read *Kōmei*)

PUBLISHER Fusui Gabō

SIZE 50.8 x 34.3 cm

PROVENANCE W. H. Pinckard, Oakland, May 1982

ACCESSION NUMBER S2003.8.2378

REFERENCE Stephens (ed.) (1993), cat. no. 94a

This strikingly beautiful print demonstrates Hiroaki's ability to compete with better-known artists in the *Shin-hanga* landscape genre such as Kawase Hasui (1883-1957; cat. nos. 52-63) and Yoshida Hiroshi (1876-1950; cat. nos. 18-22) when given the freedom of format and access to first-rate blockcutters and printers. This image exists in two different versions – an autumn and a summer view (*see also* Stephens (ed.) (1993), cat. nos. 94a/94b). The blocks were carved by Takano Shichinosuke and printed by Ono Tomisaburō, two master artisans who had also worked for publisher Watanabe Shōzaburō. The enlisting of master craftsmen like Takano and Ono by the Fusui Gabō is further proof of the firm's confidence in Hiroaki as a viable designer. This print and others shows that Fusui was prepared to invest in larger, more expensive formats.

17

"Satta Mountain Pass Tunnel"

Satta tōge tonneru

DATE Undated, c. 1931

SIGNATURE *Hiroaki* (also read *Kōmei*)

ARTIST'S SEAL *Shōtei*

PUBLISHER Fusui Gabō

SIZE 24.0 x 37.0 cm

PROVENANCE Kabutoya, San Francisco, September 1988

ACCESSION NUMBER S2003.8.2401

Yoshida Hiroshi (1876-1950)

Yoshida Hiroshi was born in Kurume, Fukuoka Prefecture. He received art lessons from Yoshida Kasaburō who, recognizing Hiroshi's talent, adopted him. In 1893 Yoshida left for Kyoto to learn *Yōga* under Tamura Sōritsu (1846-1918), and in the following year he went to Tokyo to study with Koyama Shōtarō (1857-1916). He soon became a member of the *Meiji Bijutsukai* (Meiji Fine Arts Society); in 1898 he exhibited an oil painting with them and also began to study the techniques of Western watercolors. Yoshida traveled widely. His first of three trips to the United States was in 1899 together with the painter Nakagawa Hachirō (1877-1922). In 1902 he participated in the founding of the *Taiheiyō Gakai* (Pacific Western-style Painting Association). From 1903 to 1907 he made a second trip to the United States, traveling back through Europe, and in 1923 he left on his third trip to the United States and his second to Europe. He returned to Japan in 1925 and set up a studio in Tokyo. He was instrumental in the organization of the two very influential exhibitions of Japanese prints at the Toledo Museum of Art in 1930 and 1936; he showed his work in both. In 1930 he made his first trip to India and five years later he joined the *Dainibukai* (The Second Division Society), which opposed a reorganization of the *Teikoku Bijutsuin* (Imperial Fine Arts Academy). He went to China and Korea on a sketching trip in 1936, and between 1938 and 1940 he was dispatched three times to China and Korea as a war artist for the Japanese army. Yoshida was an extremely prolific artist. For example, after his second trip to the United States he submitted 226 paintings with his wife to the sixth *Taiheiyō Gakai* exhibition of 1908. From 1920 to 1941 he designed 259 prints.

REFERENCES Ogura *et al.* (1987); Merritt and Yamada (1992), 176; Stephens (ed.) (1993), 117-21

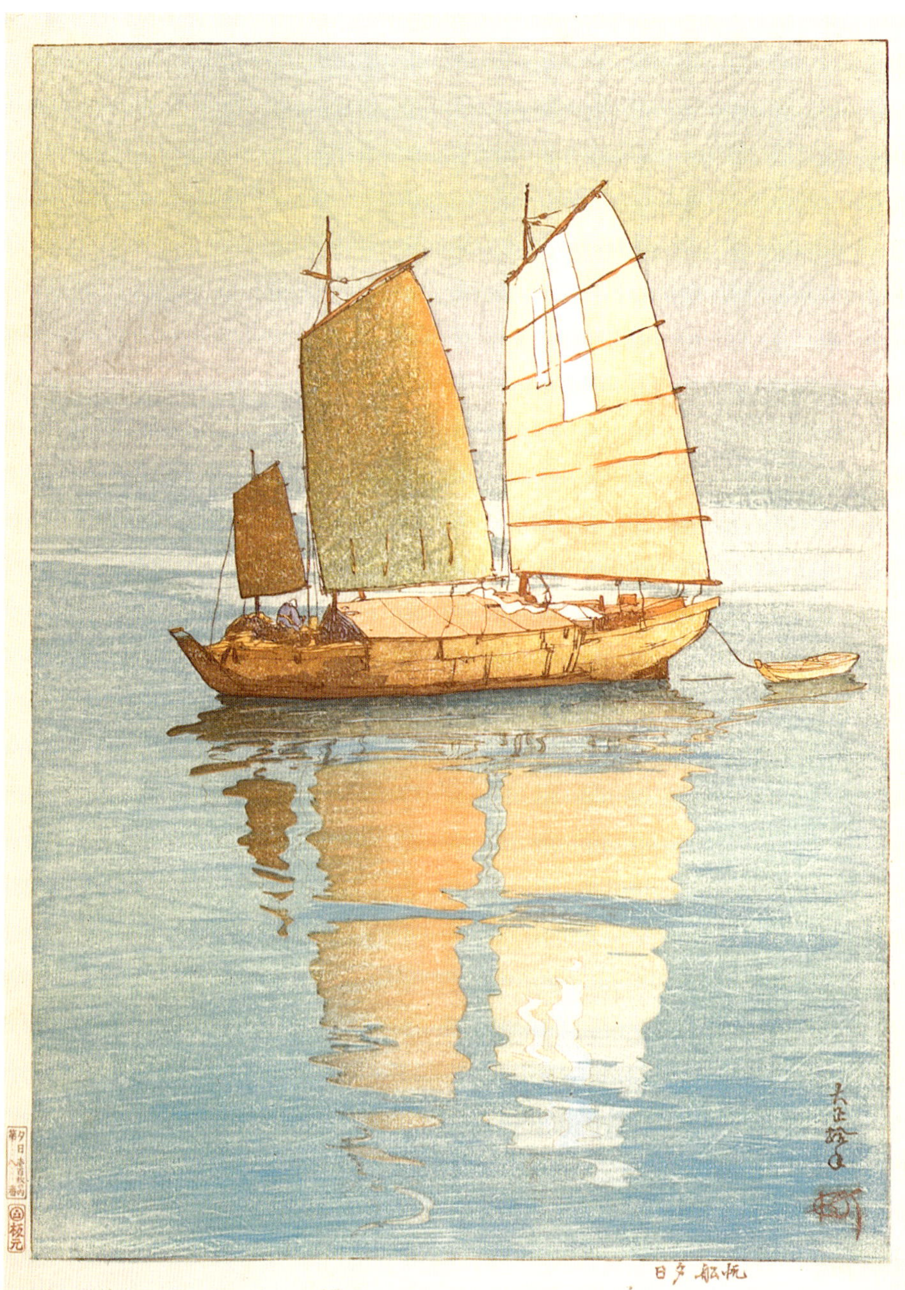

18
"Sailing Boats – The Evening Sun"
Hansen yūhi

DATE 1921 (Taishō 10)
SIGNATURE *Yoshida*
PUBLISHER Watanabe Shōzaburō
EDITION Number 8 from a limited edition of 100 copies
SIZE 45.3 x 33.0 cm
PROVENANCE Yamanaka & Co., Boston, September 1938
ACCESSION NUMBER S2003.8.3450
REFERENCE Ogura *et al.* (1987), no. 6

Yoshida designed eight prints for Watanabe Shōzaburō. The blocks for these and approximately 100 impressions of the eight designs, including the set *Sailing Boats* (one image illustrated here), were destroyed during the Great Kantō Earthquake and ensuing fire that demolished Watanabe's shop in September 1923.

Watanabe rated Yoshida's work highly. During an exhibition in 1921 at the Shirokiya Department Store in Nihonbashi, Tokyo, he priced five of the Yoshida prints at ¥20 each. This was six to seven times the price of a landscape print designed by contemporaries such as Kawase Hasui (1883-1957; cat. nos. 52-63) or Kasamatsu Shirō (1898-1991; cat. nos. 102-4).

19

"Sailing Boats – Night"

Hansen yoru

SERIES *Inland Sea Series (Seto naikai shū)*
DATE 1926 (Taishō 15)
SIGNATURE *Yoshida*
PUBLISHER Self-published
SIZE 50.8 x 36.0 cm
PROVENANCE William Lee Comerford, New York, August 1938
ACCESSION NUMBER S2003.8.3460
REFERENCE Ogura *et al.* (1987), no. 45

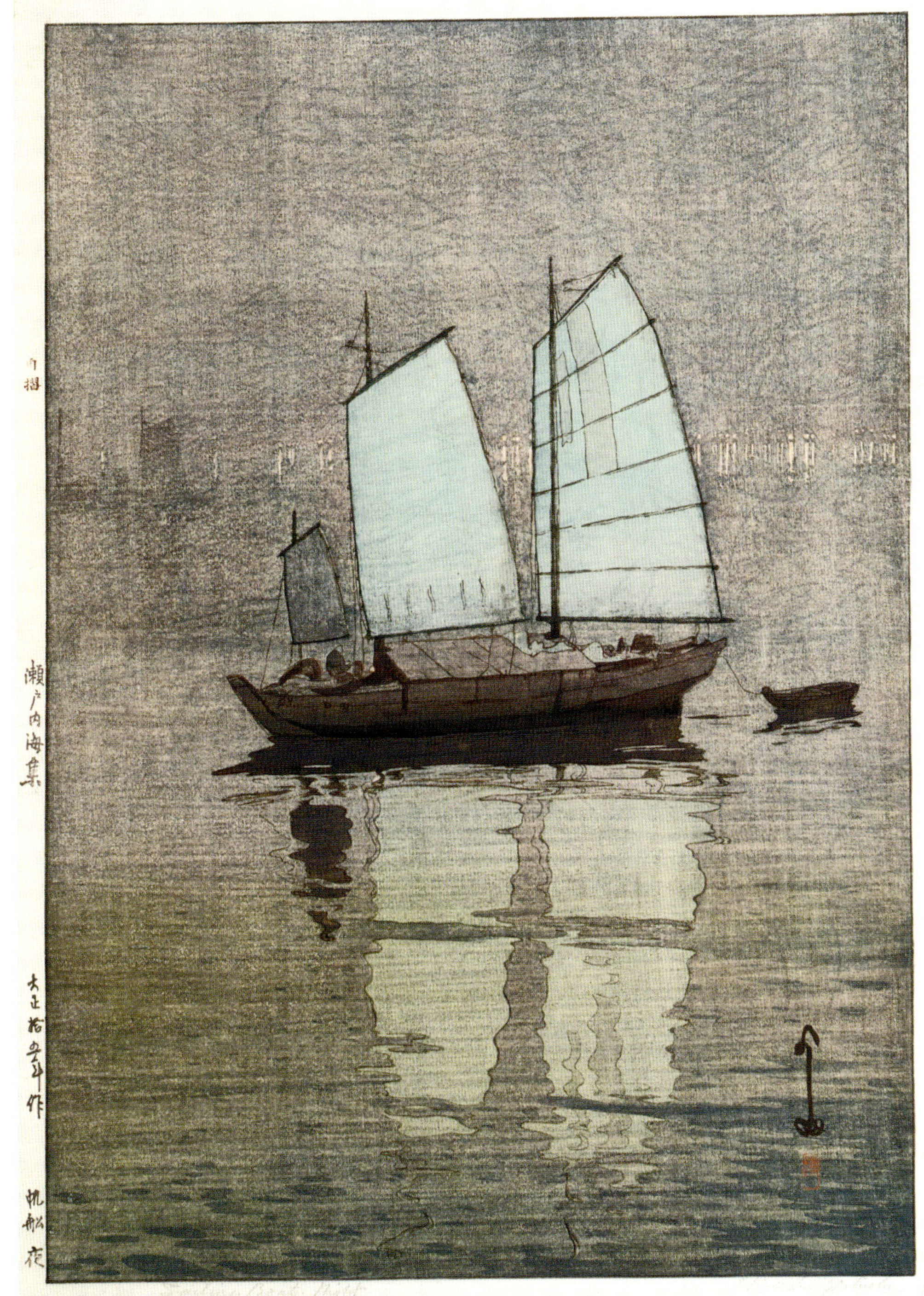

Upon his return to Tokyo in 1925 from his third trip to Europe and the United States, Yoshida sought to capture the sketches of his world tours in the woodblock medium. He took the decision to supervise the entire production process himself, thus breaking his professional relationship with Watanabe Shōzaburō. One of his new projects was a re-issue of the *Sailing Boats* group lost in the Great Kantō Earthquake of September 1923, which he then named *Inland Sea Series* (the earlier set had no titles on the actual images). He increased the size of the prints to 50.9 x 36.1 cm, added two more versions and entered these designs in the eighth *Teiten* of 1927, where they were very well received. The six pieces (four illustrated here: cat. nos. 19-22) were all printed using the same blocks but were inked with different colorants. The result was a sequence of atmospheric depictions of varying times of the day. The catalogue accompanying the 1930 Toledo Museum of Art exhibition rightly emphasizes how skillful the printers were in manipulating the huge blocks needed for the production of these prints, without losing the careful registration needed.

Yoshida Hiroshi has been described as an artist of the "middle ground" between *Shin-hanga* and *Sōsaku-hanga*. In his approach to woodblock printing he retained the traditional division of labor between artist, blockcutter and printer as in *Shin-hanga*. However, he insisted that the overall supervision was in the hands of the artist, which was more in line with *Sōsaku-hanga* practices: the inclusion of the two characters reading *jizuri* ("self-printed") in roughly the center of the left margin is testimony to this. These characters are absent on all posthumous printings of Yoshida's work, and on these later printings his signature *Hiroshi Yoshida*, written in pencil in romanized script, is substituted by a printed version.

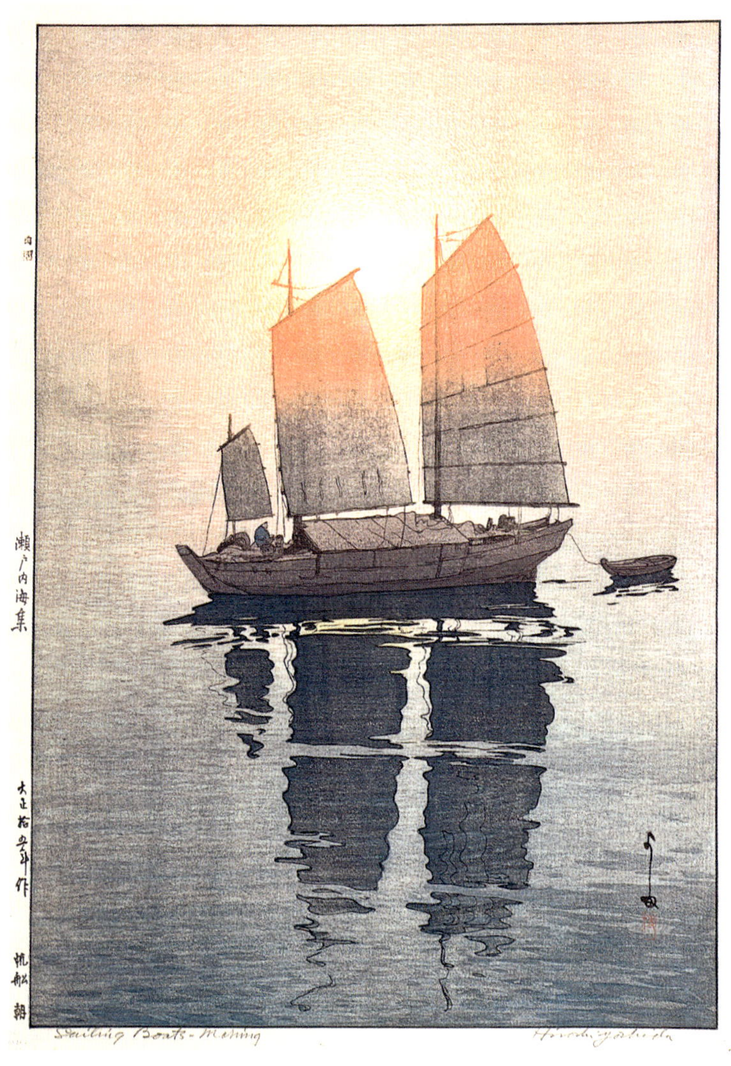

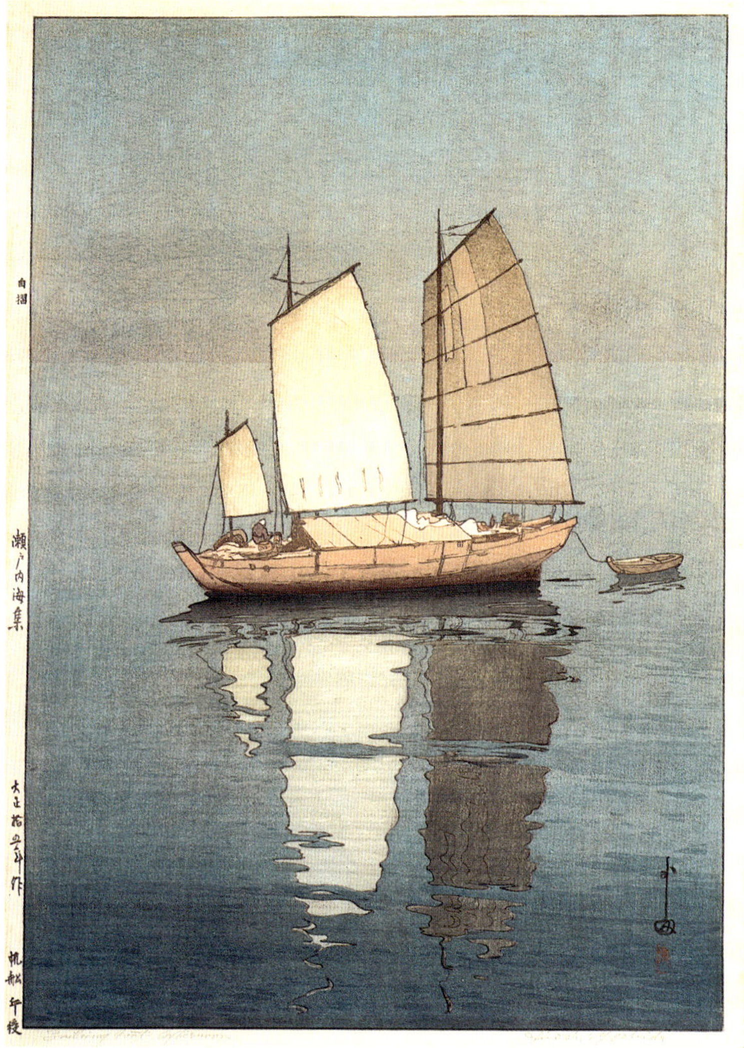

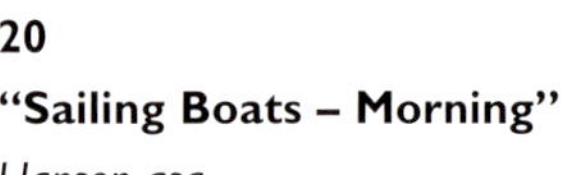

20

"Sailing Boats – Morning"

Hansen asa

SERIES *Inland Sea Series* (*Seto naikai shū*)
DATE 1926 (Taishō 15)
SIGNATURE *Yoshida*
BLOCKCUTTER Maeda Yūjirō (name not listed on print)
PUBLISHER Self-published
SIZE 50.8 x 36.1 cm
PROVENANCE Yamanaka & Co., Chicago, April 1937
ACCESSION NUMBER S2003.8.3461
REFERENCE Ogura *et al.* (1987), no. 40

21

"Sailing Boats – Afternoon"

Hansen gogo

SERIES *Inland Sea Series* (*Seto naikai shū*)
DATE 1926 (Taishō 15)
SIGNATURE *Hiroshi Yoshida*
BLOCKCUTTER Maeda Yūjirō (name not listed on print)
PUBLISHER Self-published
SIZE 50.8 x 36.1 cm
PROVENANCE The Jade Dragon, Ann Arbor, Michigan, New Haven Antique Show, October 1993
ACCESSION NUMBER S2003.8.3458
REFERENCE Ogura *et al.* (1987), no. 42

22
"Sailing Boats – Mist"
Hansen kiri

SERIES *Inland Sea Series (Seto naikai shū)*
DATE 1926 (Taishō 15)
SIGNATURE *Yoshida*
BLOCKCUTTER Maeda Yūjirō (name not listed on print)
PUBLISHER Self-published
SIZE 50.8 x 36.0 cm
PROVENANCE William Lee Comerford, New York, August 1938
ACCESSION NUMBER S2003.8.3459
REFERENCE Ogura *et al.* (1987), no. 43

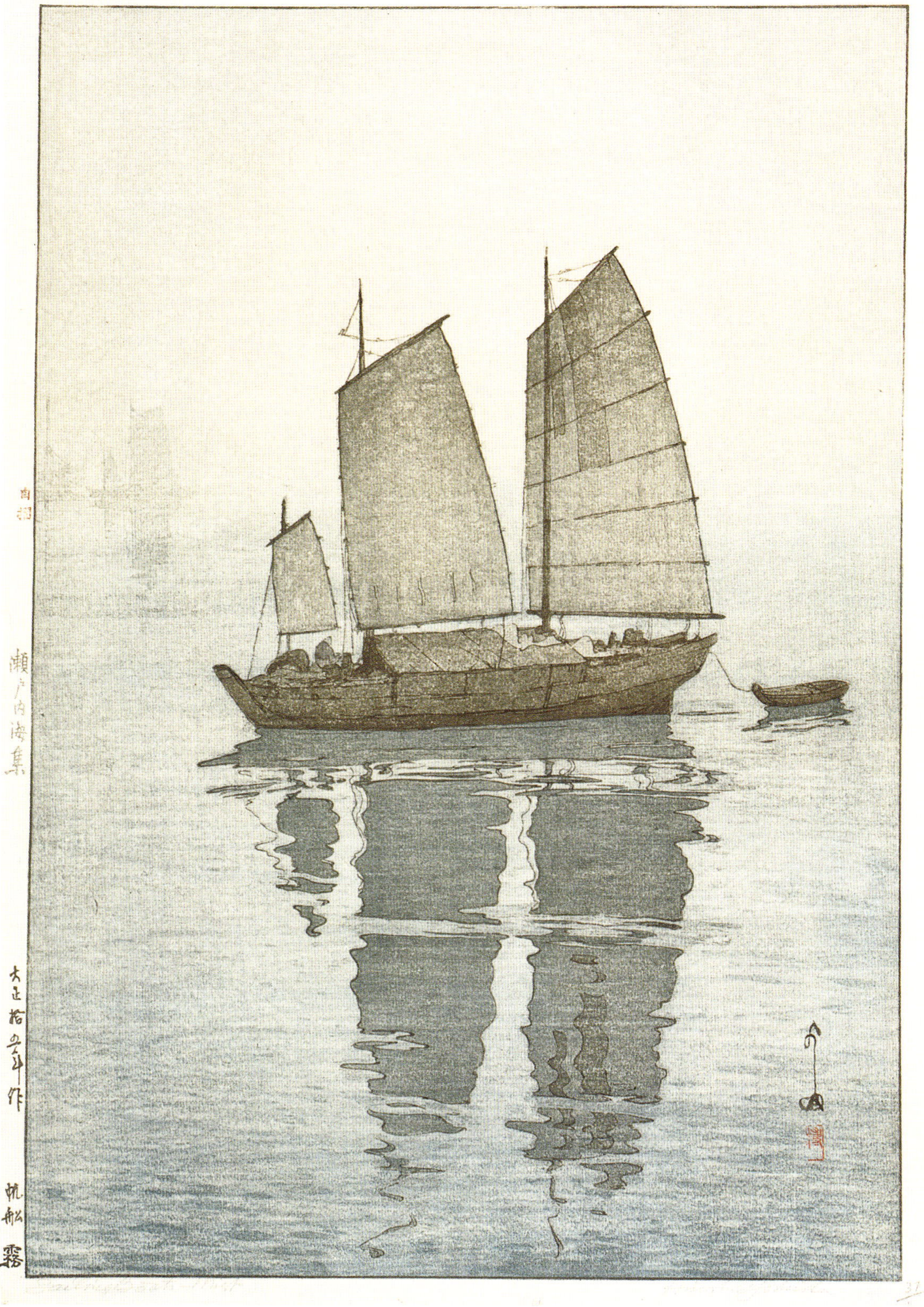

Ohara Koson (1877-1945)

Koson was born Ohara Matao in Kanazawa, Ishikawa Prefecture. He eventually moved to Tokyo to study *Shijō* painting under Suzuki Kason (1860-1919), from whom he received the artist's name *Koson*. Around 1900 he reportedly became a teacher at the *Tōkyō Bijutsu Gakkō* (Tokyo School of Fine Arts), where he is said to have met the American Ernest Fenollosa (1853-1908), then a professor at the *Tōkyō Teikoku Daigaku* (Tokyo Imperial University; present-day University of Tokyo) and an advocate of traditional Japanese arts. Koson may have painted *kachōga* under his guidance. He also designed some prints of the Russo-Japanese War (1904-5), and from around the same time *kachōga* under the name *Koson* with the publishers Daikokuya (Matsuki Heikichi) and Kokkeidō (Akiyama Buemon). In 1926 he began working with the publisher Watanabe Shōzaburō (1885-1962) who, as a result of the devastating Great Kantō Earthquake of 1 September 1923, was looking for new print artists like Koson to rebuild his business. Koson signed his prints issued by Watanabe with the name *Shōson*. In addition to Watanabe, Koson also made prints with the publisher Sakai/Kawaguchi, probably from 1930 onward and signed *Hoson*. Koson is acknowledged as a master of twentieth-century printed *kachōga*, and with some 500 prints to his name, he represents one of the, if not the most, prolific in this field.

REFERENCES Watanabe Shōzaburō (1936), 97; Merritt and Yamada (1992), 116; Stephens (ed.) (1993), 122-25; Hiraki Ukiyo-e Museum (ed.) (1998); Newland *et al.* (2001)

23
"Heron in Moonlight"

DATE Undated, *c.* 1905
SIGNATURE AND ARTIST'S SEAL *Koson*
PUBLISHER Akiyama Buemon
SIZE 49.8 x 21.0 cm
PROVENANCE Shima Art Co., New York, 1940
ACCESSION NUMBER S2003.8.1958
REFERENCE Newland *et al.* (2001), cat. no. 11

Koson's prints can perhaps be best characterized as "printed paintings." Particularly in his early work with the Daikokuya (Matsuki Heikichi), blockcutters and printers convincingly transmitted the painterly feel of his works to the print medium. Matsuki Heikichi was an astute publisher who understood the potential and benefit of marketing works abroad, especially in the United States, and he profited from the demand for Japanese prints in the early decades of the twentieth century. His publications were exhibited at various World Exhibitions, such as the St. Louis World Fair in 1904, where the *One Hundred Views of Mount Fuji* (*Haku Fuji*) by Ogata Gekkō (1859-1920) received a prize. Matsuki printed advertisements in English, underwrote reproductions and the work of many artists who could be considered painters cum printmakers. It is not surprising then that Koson`s prints were clearly designed for a foreign clientele.

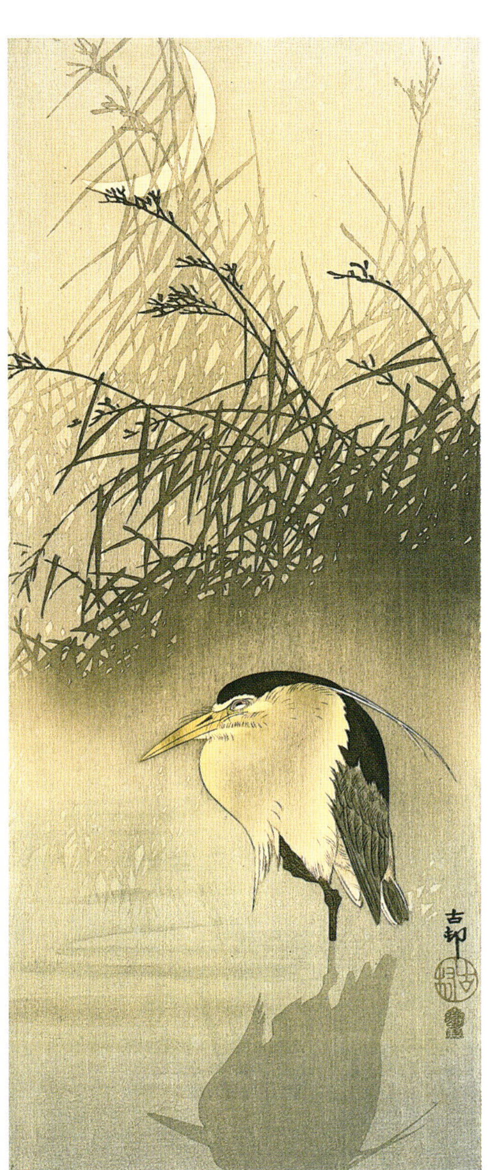

24
"Little Egret with Outstretched Wings on a Willow Branch"

DATE Undated, *c.* 1905
SIGNATURE AND ARTIST'S SEAL *Koson*
PUBLISHER Akiyama Buemon
SIZE 49.8 x 21.0 cm
PROVENANCE Japan Gallery, New York, November 1991
ACCESSION NUMBER S2003.8.1959
REFERENCE Newland *et al.* (2001), K14.16

25
"Bats Against a Full Moon"

DATE Undated, *c.* 1910
SIGNATURE AND ARTIST'S SEAL *Koson*
PUBLISHER Matsuki Heikichi
SIZE 34.6 x 18.7 cm
PROVENANCE Shima Art Co., New York, 1940
ACCESSION NUMBER S2003.8.1838
REFERENCE Newland *et al.* (2001), no. 135

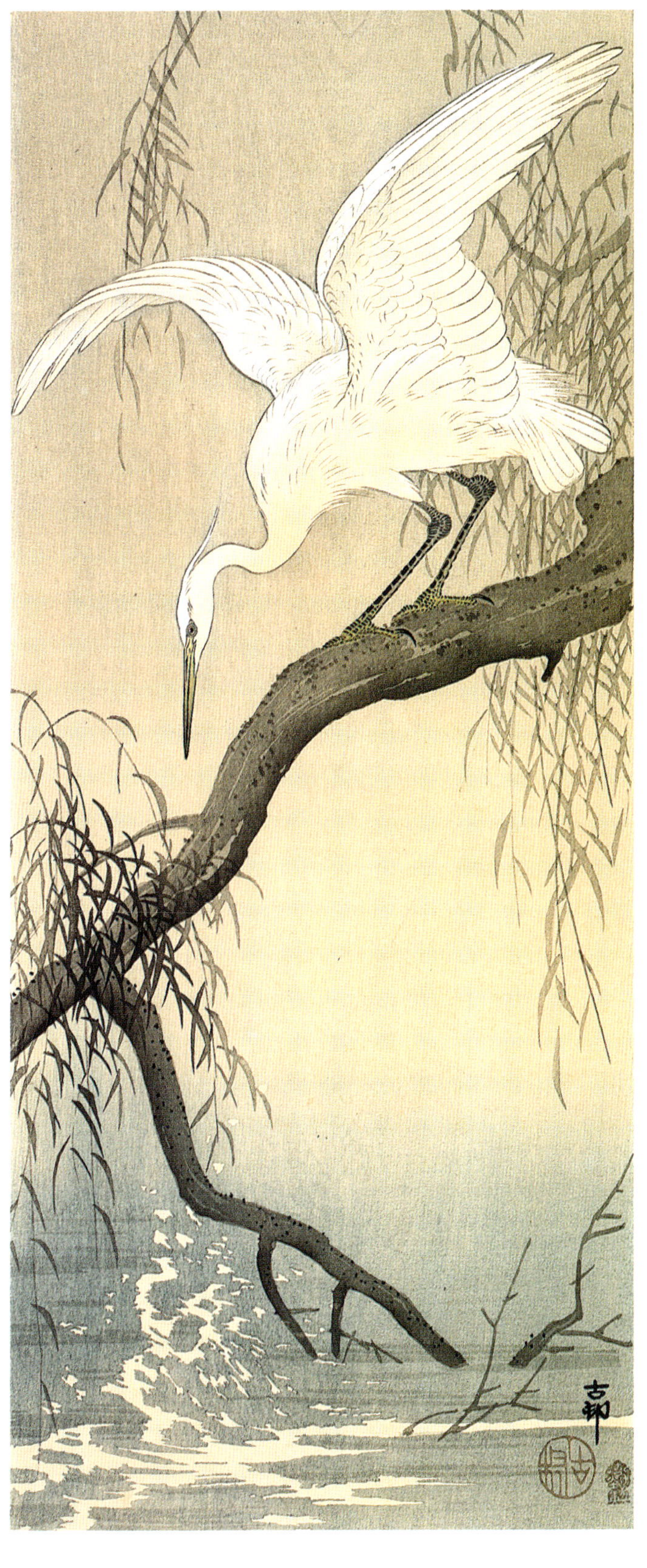

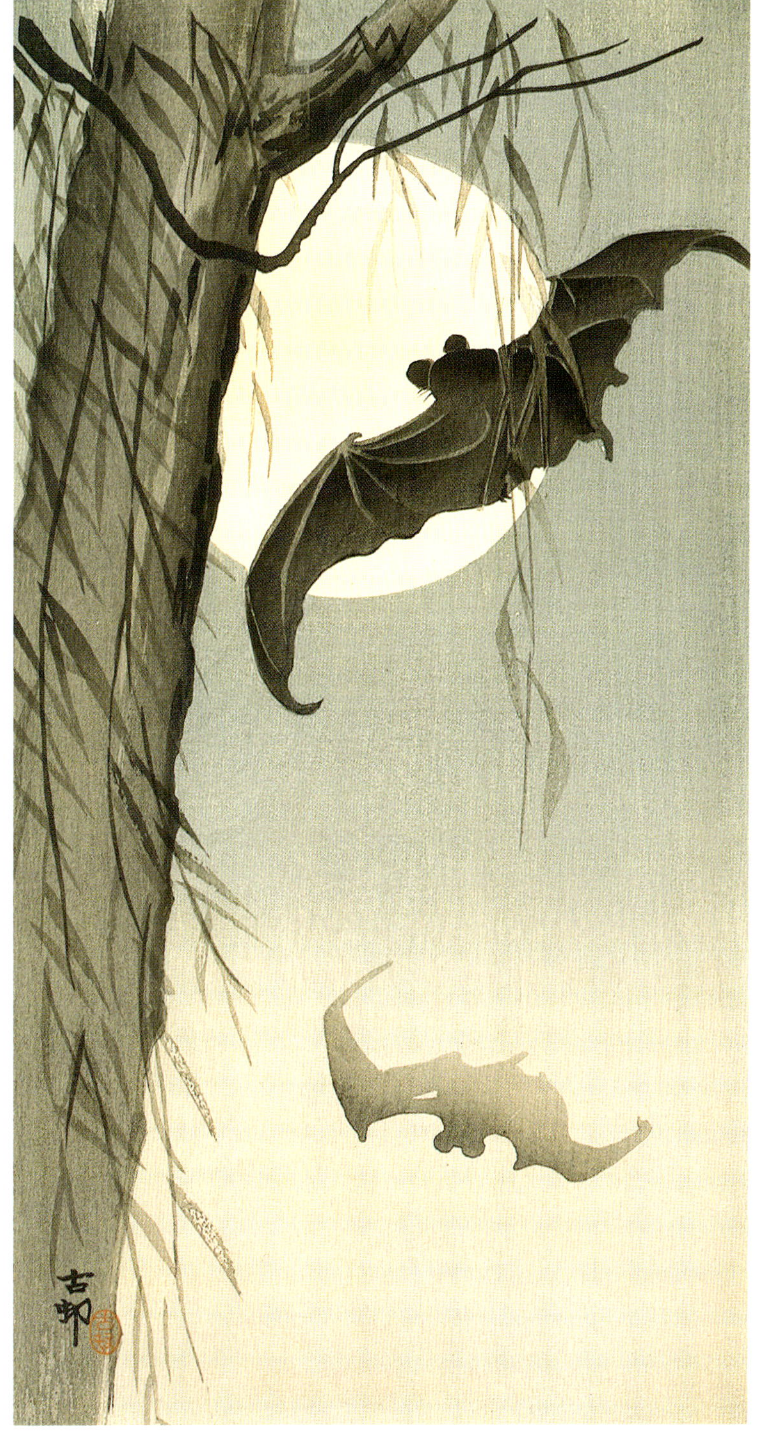

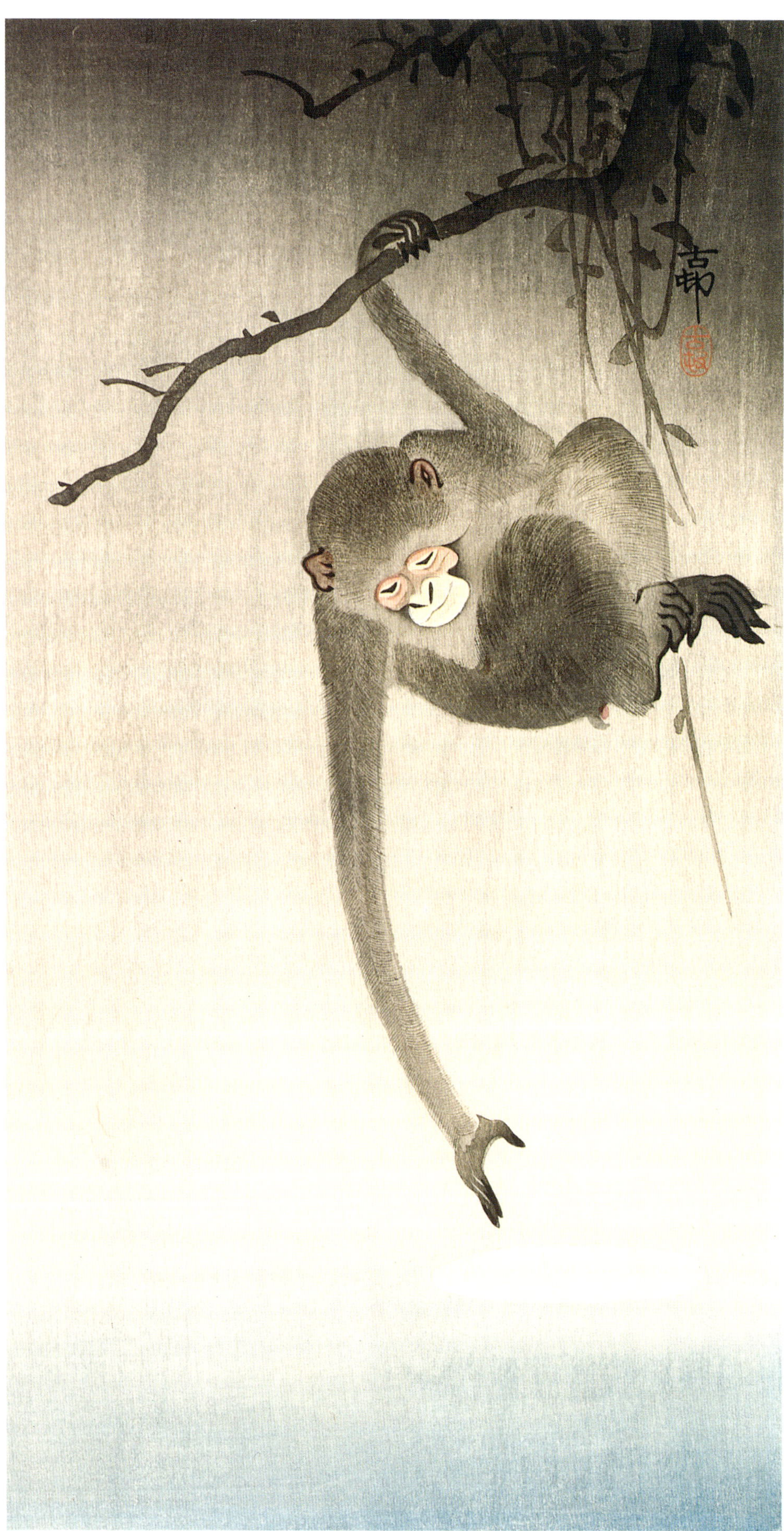

26

"Gibbon Reaching for the Reflection of the Moon"

DATE Undated, *c.* 1910
SIGNATURE AND ARTIST'S SEAL *Koson*
PUBLISHER Matsuki Heikichi
SIZE 34.6 x 18.7 cm
PROVENANCE Shima Art Co., New York, 1940
ACCESSION NUMBER S2003.8.1836
REFERENCE Newland *et al.* (2001), no. 136

The image of a gibbon trying to grab the reflection of the moon is not an uncommon subject in *Kano* and *Maruyama-Shijō* schools of painting, and is one based on Chinese antecedents. This print exemplifies the skill of Matsuki's printers in rendering a beautifully gradated background: the gray sky merges almost imperceptibly with the gray-blue tones of the water below. This technique of gradation, or *bokashi*, was achieved by carefully wiping the color blocks. Also, the grain of the woodblock, which is visible in the background, contributes further to the sense of texture created for the sky.

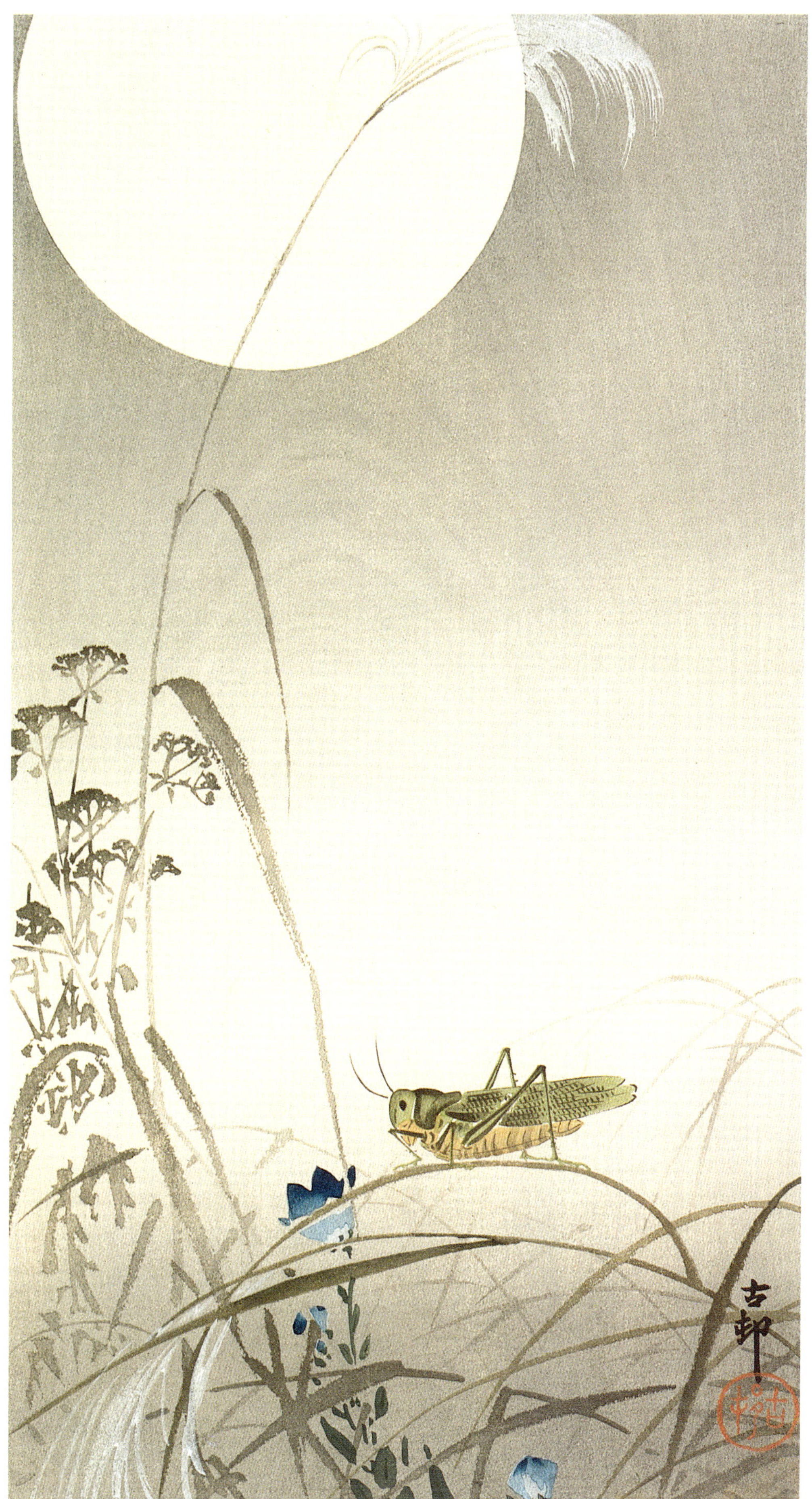

27

"Grasshopper on Autumn Grasses, A Full Moon Above"

DATE Undated, *c.* 1910
SIGNATURE AND ARTIST'S SEAL *Koson*
PUBLISHER Matsuki Heikichi
Number 186 in the Daikokuya sample book
SIZE 33.3 x 18.4 cm
PROVENANCE Daikokuya sample book, received from the Shima Art Co., New York, *c.* 1955
ACCESSION NUMBER S2003.8.1824
REFERENCE Newland *et al.* (2001), K40.8

This design was taken from one of the Daikokuya sample books, which came into the Robert O. Muller collection when he acquired the Shima Art Company in 1940. The sample books contained prints that were pasted in and numbered, and these were used to solicit orders from customers. That they facilitated the ordering process explains their existence in the holdings of the Shima Art Company, who was a regular customer of the Daikokuya during the first three decades of the twentieth century.

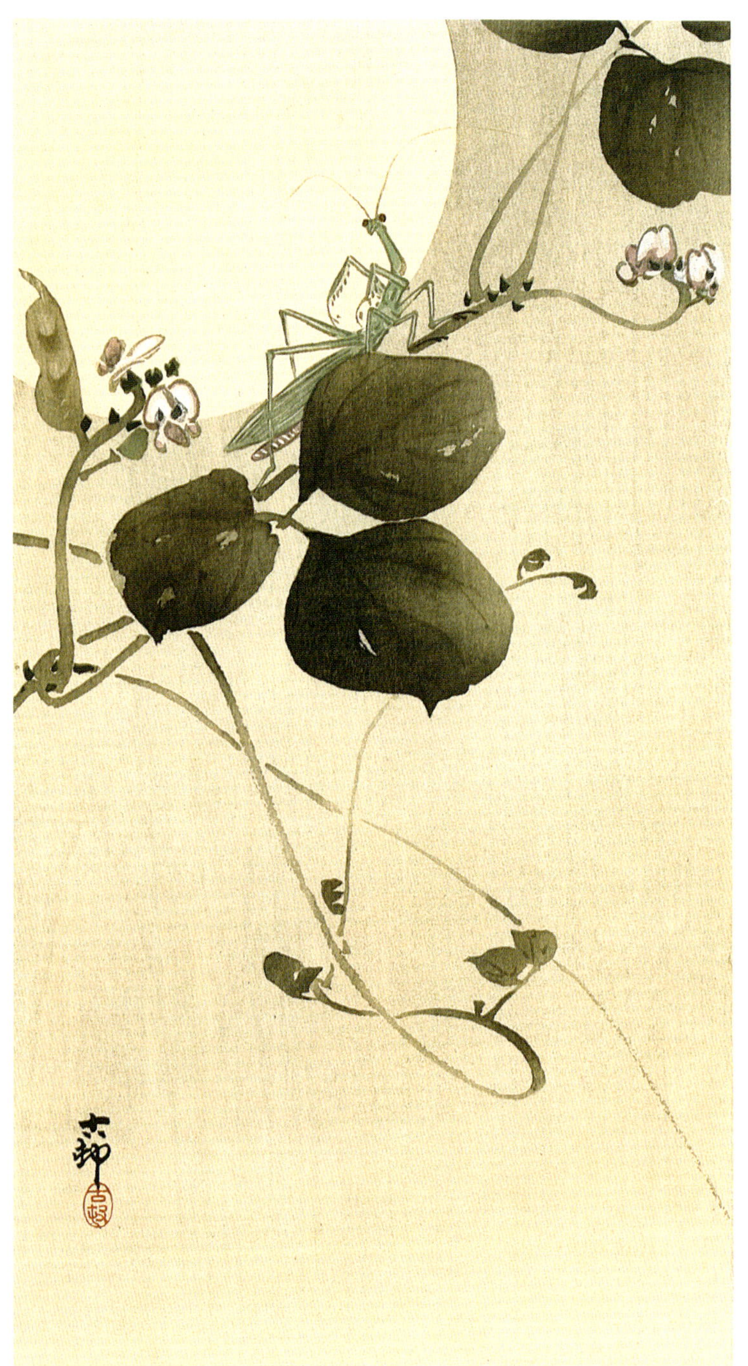

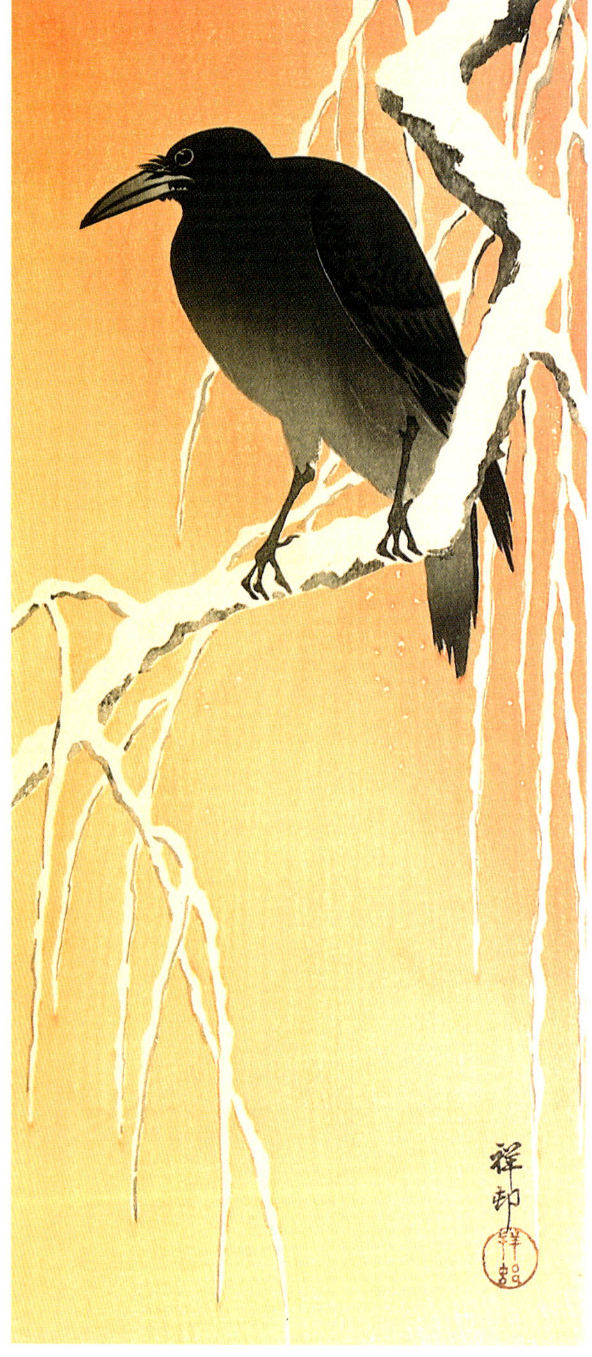

28

"Praying Mantis and Moon"

DATE Undated, c. 1910

SIGNATURE AND ARTIST'S SEAL *Koson*

PUBLISHER Matsuki Heikichi

Number 166 in the Daikokuya sample book

SIZE 33.2 x 18.4 cm

PROVENANCE Daikokuya sample book, received from Hango Sumii, 1956

ACCESSION NUMBER S2003.8.1819

REFERENCE Newland *et al.* (2001), no. 92

29

"Carrion Crow on a Snow-covered Willow Branch at Dawn"

DATE Undated, c. 1926

SIGNATURE AND ARTIST'S SEAL *Shōson*

PUBLISHER Watanabe Shōzaburō

SIZE 37.2 x 16.7 cm.

PROVENANCE Shima Art Co., New York, 1940

ACCESSION NUMBER S2003.8.2058

REFERENCE Watanabe Shōzaburō (1936), no. 257

30
"Egrets"

DATE Undated, *c.* 1926
SIGNATURE AND ARTIST'S SEAL *Shōson*
PUBLISHER Watanabe Shōzaburō
SIZE 36.2 x 23.8 cm
PROVENANCE Kawaguchi, New York, 31 January 1936
ACCESSION NUMBER S2003.8.2046
REFERENCE Newland *et al.* (2001), no. 155

It is believed that Koson's collaboration with Watanabe Shōzaburō in 1926 occasioned the change of his artist's name to *Shōson*. Thereafter his work appears more regularly in the *ōban* format, the most common print size employed by Watanabe. Moreover, Shōson prints assume a more graphic and less painterly feel, the latter quality of which was emphasized by his earlier publishers, namely Akiyama Buemon.

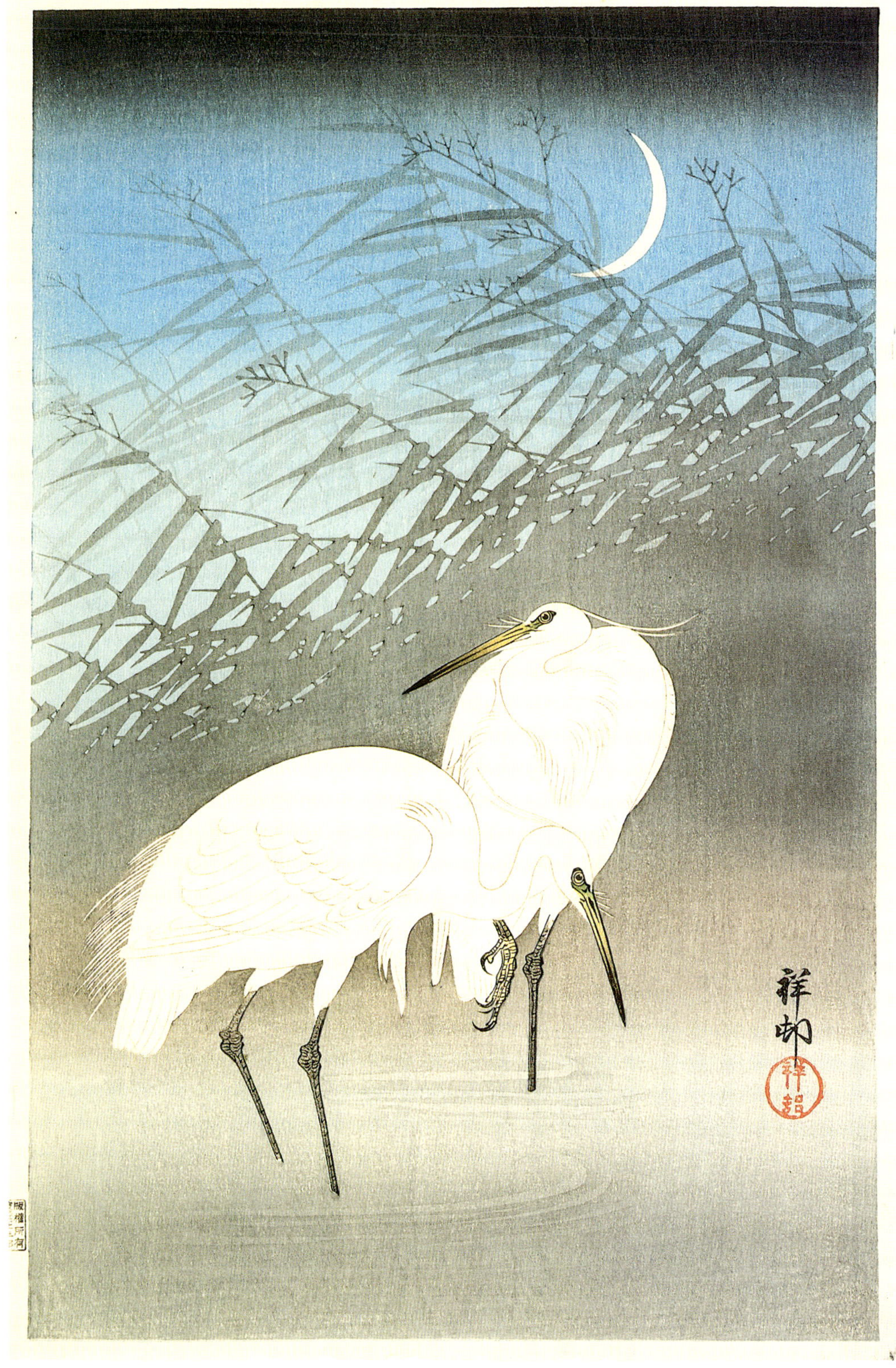

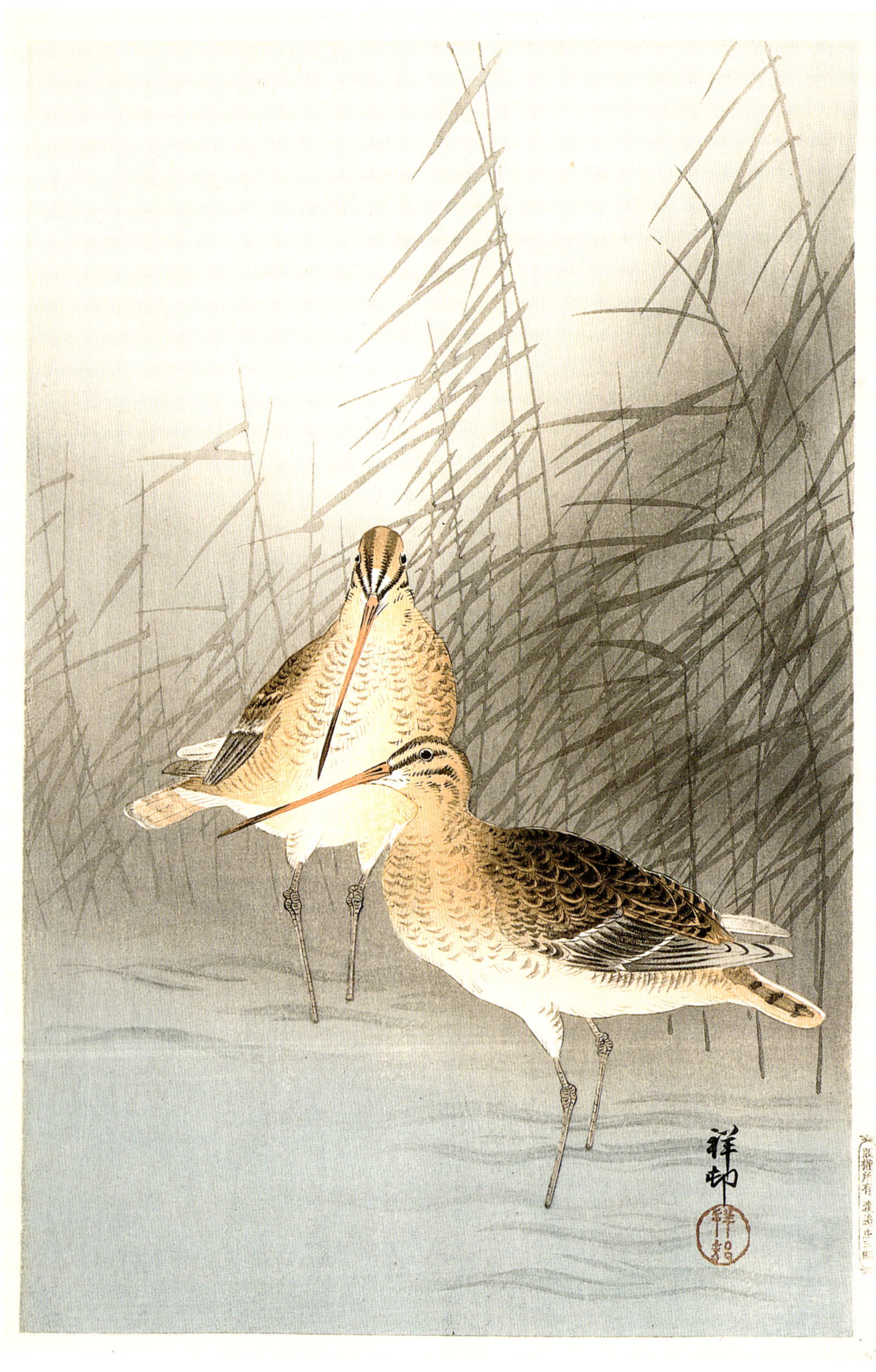

31

"Two Bar-tailed Godwits in Shallow Waters next to Reeds"

DATE Undated, *c.* 1926
SIGNATURE AND ARTIST'S SEAL *Shōson*
PUBLISHER Watanabe Shōzaburō
SIZE 36.2 x 24.0 cm
PROVENANCE Shima Art Co., New York, 1940
ACCESSION NUMBER S2003.8.2041
REFERENCE Newland *et al.* (2001), S24.1

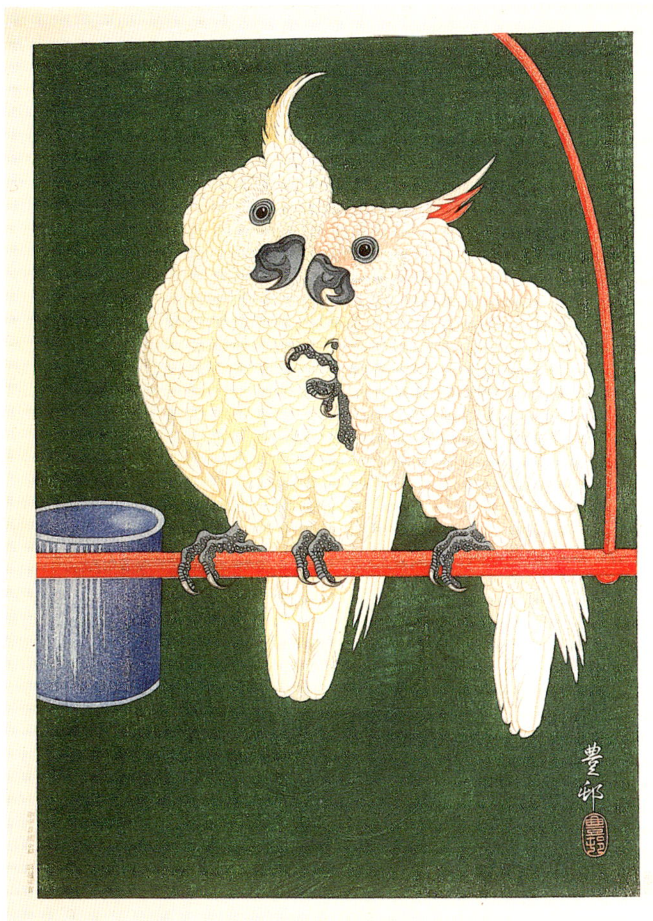

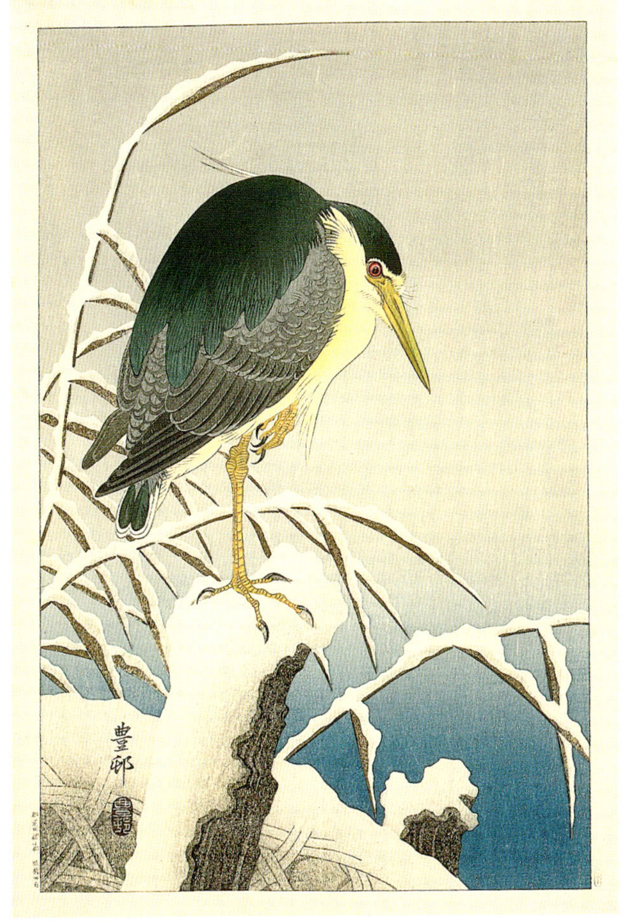

32

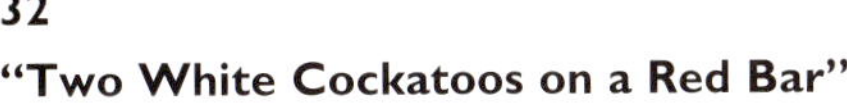

"Two White Cockatoos on a Red Bar"

DATE Undated, *c.* after 1930
SIGNATURE AND ARTIST'S SEAL *Hoson*
PUBLISHER Kawaguchi
PUBLISHER STOCK NUMBER 37 (verso)
SIZE 33.3 x 24.1 cm
PROVENANCE Shima Art Co., New York, 1940
ACCESSION NUMBER S2003.8.2077
REFERENCE Newland *et al.* (2001), H36.1

It seems that after 1930 Koson shifted his allegiance from publisher Watanabe Shōzaburō to Kawaguchi, who was also based in Tokyo. The Kawaguchi releases are identifiable by the wide margins and the artist's signature *Hoson*.

33

"Heron on a Snow-covered Trunk"

DATE Undated, *c.* after 1930
SIGNATURE AND ARTIST'S SEAL *Hoson*
PUBLISHER Kawaguchi
SIZE 36.2 x 24.1 cm
PROVENANCE Japan Gallery (Ayako Abe), New York, December 1992
ACCESSION NUMBER S2003.8.2072
REFERENCE Newland *et al.* (2001), H14.1

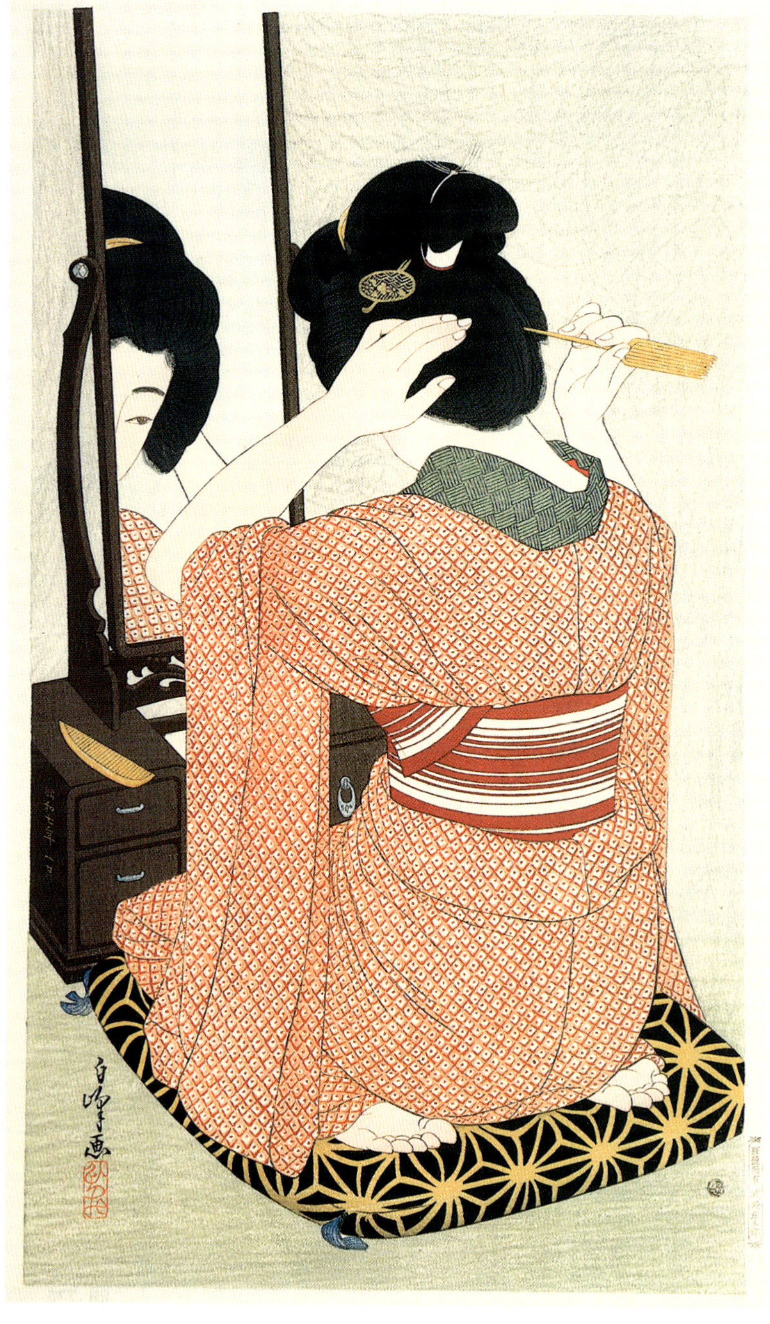

Hirano Hakuhō (1879-1957)

Little is known about Hakuhō, who was born in Kyoto and studied *Ukiyo-e* painting in his youth. He was interested in classical *Kano* painting, *Nihonga* and *Ukiyo-e* printmaking. It seems that he was largely self-taught. From the early 1930s onward he produced six prints with the publisher Watanabe Shōzaburō (1885-1962). Two of these were shown at the Toledo Museum of Art exhibition in 1936. Hakuhō specialized in elegant *bijinga*, with his subjects often depicted in profile or from behind.

REFERENCES The Toledo Museum of Art (ed.) (1936), cat. nos. 1-2; Watanabe Shōzaburō (1936), 115; Merritt and Yamada (1992), 34; Stephens (ed.) (1993), 126; Hamanaka and Newland (2000), 152, 208

34
"Before the Mirror"

DATE 1932 (Shōwa 7), January
SIGNATURE *Hakuhō ga*
ARTIST'S SEAL *Hirano*
PUBLISHER Watanabe Shōzaburō
EDITION Number 13 from a limited edition of 90 copies
SIZE 45.3 x 26.4 cm
PROVENANCE Yamanaka & Co., Boston, February 1937
ACCESSION NUMBER S2003.8.137
REFERENCES The Toledo Museum of Art (ed.) (1936), cat. no. 2; Hamanaka and Newland (2000), no. 208

A young woman sits before a mirror, adding the final touches to her coiffure. "Before the Mirror" was included in the 1936 exhibition of Japanese prints held at the Toledo Museum of Art. The explanation for this print in the accompanying exhibition catalogue (*see* reference above) states that twenty blocks were used for the twenty-five superimposed printings. Moreover, it tells us that each work has a limitation stamp that indicates ninety examples of the image were printed. Such fictitious information is repeatedly encountered in the descriptions of the prints in the Toledo catalogues. This clearly demonstrates the shrewd business acumen of the Japanese organizers of the Toledo shows – principally publisher Watanabe Shōzaburō and print artist Yoshida Hiroshi (1876-1950; cat. nos. 18-22) – and their ability to cater to American audiences who preferred small print runs as this implied a more "exclusive" work.

35

"Summer Kimono, Beppu"

DATE 1936 (Shōwa 11), January
SIGNATURE *Hakuhō*, with unread artist's seal
PUBLISHER Watanabe Shōzaburō
SIZE 48.6 x 23.2 cm
PROVENANCE Watanabe Shōzaburō Color Print Co., Tokyo, April 1940
ACCESSION NUMBER S2003.8.138
REFERENCE Hamanaka and Newland (2000), 212

A still summer's day at a hot-spring resort in Beppu – from a veranda a young woman gazes out on the trees and water below. A light breeze lifts the screen to the right. Her *ikat*-style kimono is intricately printed, lending it an almost translucent quality. This and her jet-black hair contrast the muted tones of her surroundings. Such elements work together to make this print one of the most accomplished *Shin-hanga* designs from the 1930s. This example and "Before the Mirror" (cat. no. 34) reveal Hakuhō's preference for a somewhat narrower format, one that is rarely encountered in the work of his contemporaries.

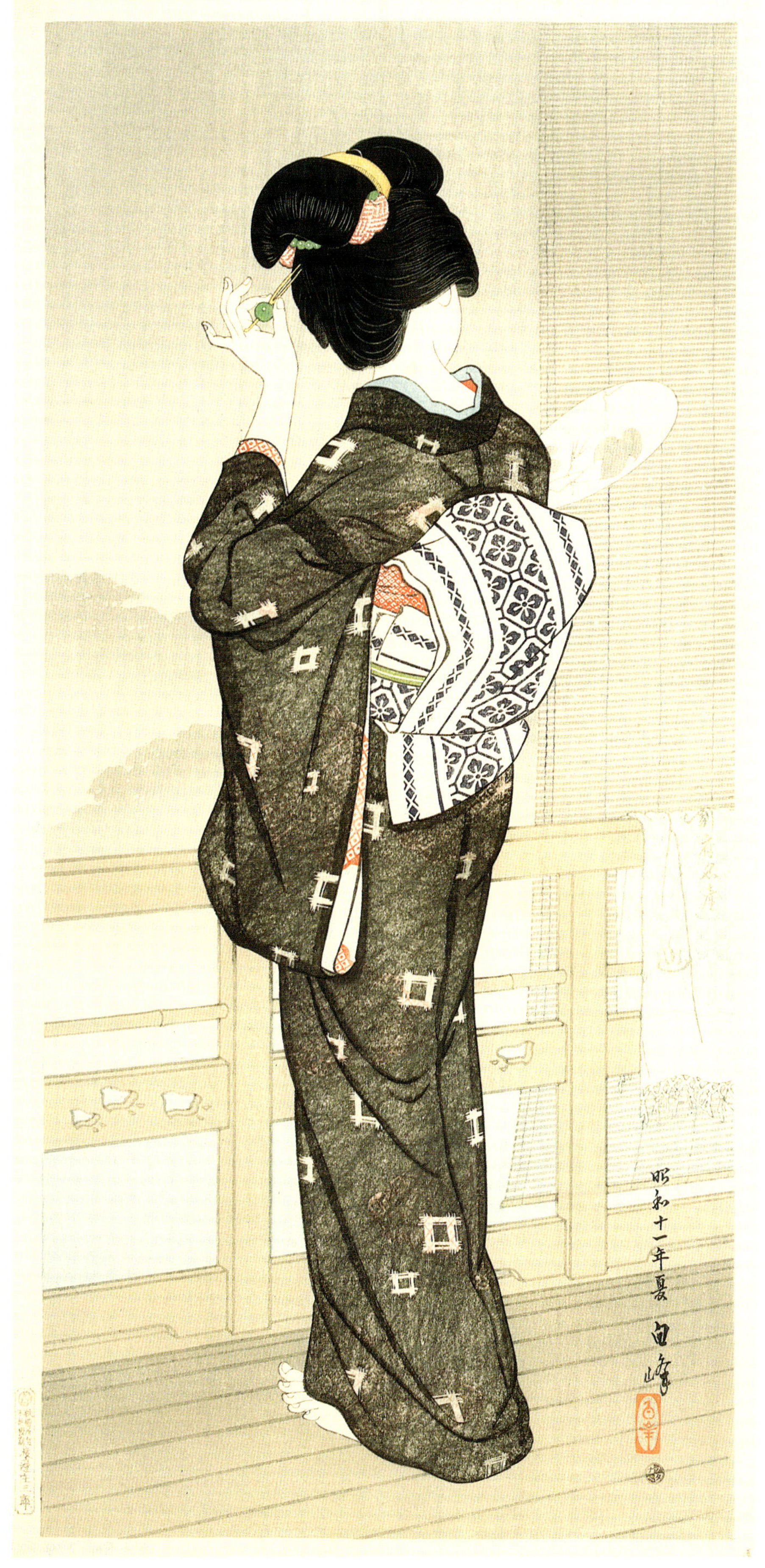

Hashiguchi Goyō (1880-1921)

Hashiguchi Goyō was born Hachiguchi Kiyoshi in Kagoshima, Kyūshū, the son of the *Maruyama-Shijō* painter Hashiguchi Kanemizu. As a child he was trained in the painting style of the *Kano* school. In 1899 he became a pupil of the *Nihonga* painter Hashimoto Gahō (1835-1908) in Tokyo, and from 1901 he studied *Yōga* under Kuroda Seiki (1866-1924). In 1905 Goyō graduated from the *Tōkyō Bijutsu Gakkō* (Tokyo School of Fine Arts) as one of the top students in the Western painting department. At the same time, he was also active as a designer of illustrations for magazines like *Hototogisu* (*Little Cuckoo*) and for covers and illustrations of novels, most notably *Wagahai wa neko de aru* (*I am a Cat*) by Natsume Sōseki (1867-1916). In 1907 he exhibited oil paintings at the *Tōkyō Kangyō Tenrankai* (Tokyo Industrial Exhibition) and at the first *Bunten*, but with limited success. In 1911 he won a poster design contest sponsored by the Mitsukoshi Department Store for his work of a seated young woman leafing through an album of *Ukiyo-e* prints. It was clear that Goyō was to become an important artist in the *bijinga* genre. He was an avid student of *Ukiyo-e* and subsequently published articles on *Ukiyo-e* artists from the Edo period such as Kitagawa Utamaro (1753-1806) and Suzuki Harunobu (1725?-70). From 1916 to 1917 (some sources say 1917-19) he supervised the production of the *Ukiyo fūzoku ya Yamato nishiki e* (*Japanese Manners and Customs and Japanese Color Prints*), a twelve volume series containing around 240 reproductions of famous *Ukiyo-e* prints; his work on this project increased his knowledge about the printmaking process. Goyō designed one print with publisher Watanabe Shōzaburō (1885-1962), after which he decided to publish his prints privately. He died on February 24, 1921 following complications due to meningitis and a severe middle ear infection. Although he made only fourteen prints during his lifetime, they are considered masterpieces of *Shin-hanga*. The several designs that were in progress at the time of his death were completed and issued posthumously by his family.

REFERENCES Riccar Art Museum (ed.) (1976); Merritt and Yamada (1992), 28; Stephens (ed.) (1993), 127-31; Satō *et al.* (1995); Hamanaka and Newland (2000), 39-47, 208

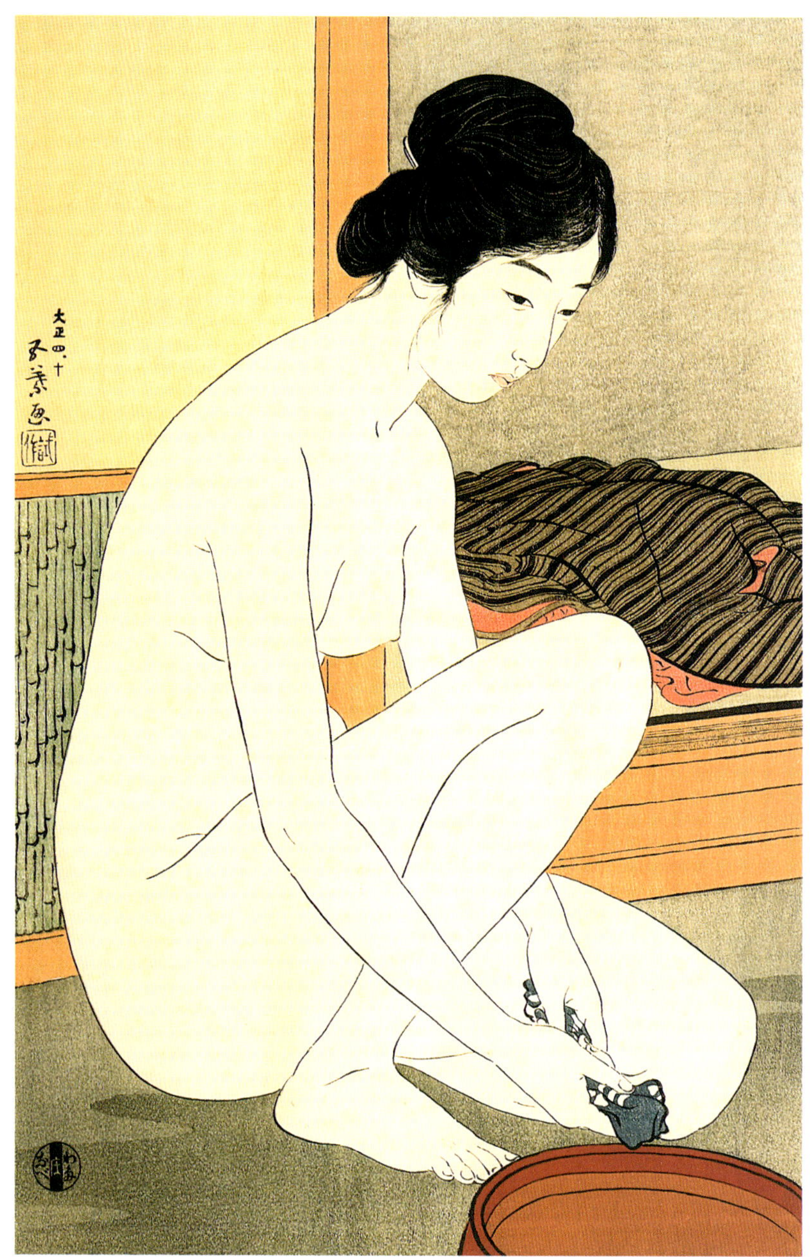

36
"Woman at the Bath"

DATE 1915 (Taishō 4), October
SIGNATURE *Goyō ga*
PUBLISHER Watanabe Shōzaburō
SIZE 40.2 x 26.4 cm
PROVENANCE Yamanaka & Co., New York, August 1936
ACCESSION NUMBER S2003.8.106
REFERENCE Hamanaka and Newland (2000), no. 12

This is Goyō's first print, and the only design to be published by Watanabe Shōzaburō. It is somewhat atypical in style and presentation: the features of the young woman are less idealized and more angular, and the technical perfection so characteristic of his subsequent prints is absent. Perhaps these aspects contribute to the seemingly tranquil simplicity of this work. The scarcity of this design suggests that relatively few copies were sold by Watanabe before the Great Kantō Earthquake of September 1923 destroyed his premises and stock. The model for this print was named Tomi. It appears that Goyō used her frequently, as attested by her appearance in his many surviving sketches and in his famous print designs "Woman Combing Her Hair" (cat. no. 38) and "Woman in a Long Undergarment" (cat. no. 39). The seal that follows the artist's signature reads *shisaku* ("trial work").

37

"Woman Applying Powder"

DATE 1918 (Taishō 7)
SIGNATURE *Goyō ga*
ARTIST'S SEAL *Goyō*
SIZE 50.8 × 36.2 cm
PROVENANCE Yamanaka & Co., New York, February 1936
ACCESSION NUMBER S2003.8.120
REFERENCES Stephens (ed.) (1993), cat. no. 128; Hamanaka and Newland (2000), no. 13

This is one of Goyō's most celebrated designs. It has been conjectured that it owes a great artistic debt to *bijinga* master Kitagawa Utamaro (1753-1806), but the underlying success of this work actually lies in its combination of Western realism with the classical theme of a woman at her toilette. The large size of the print, the solid mica background and the simple color scheme – note the extremely delicate skin tones in the woman's face – augment its expressive power.

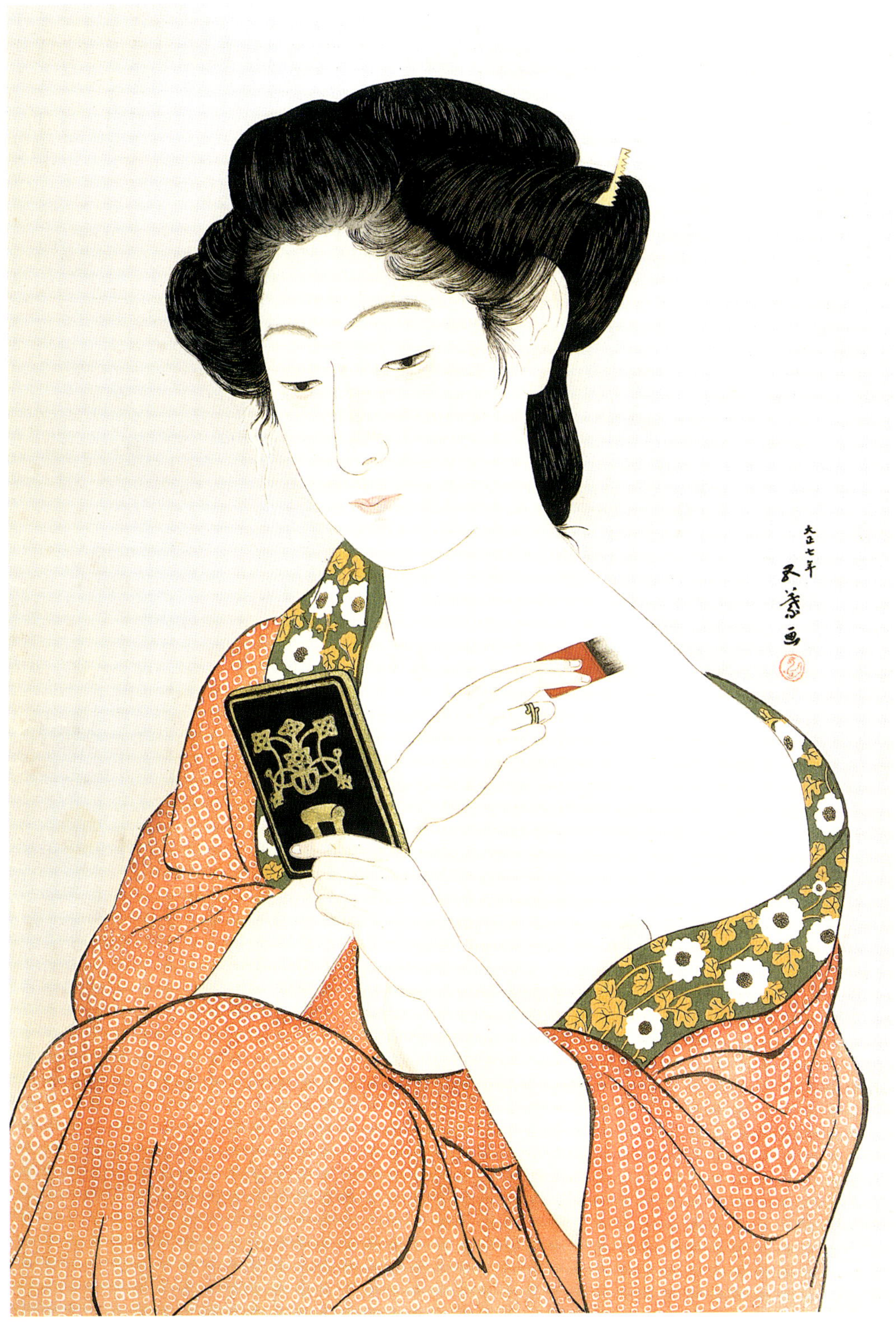

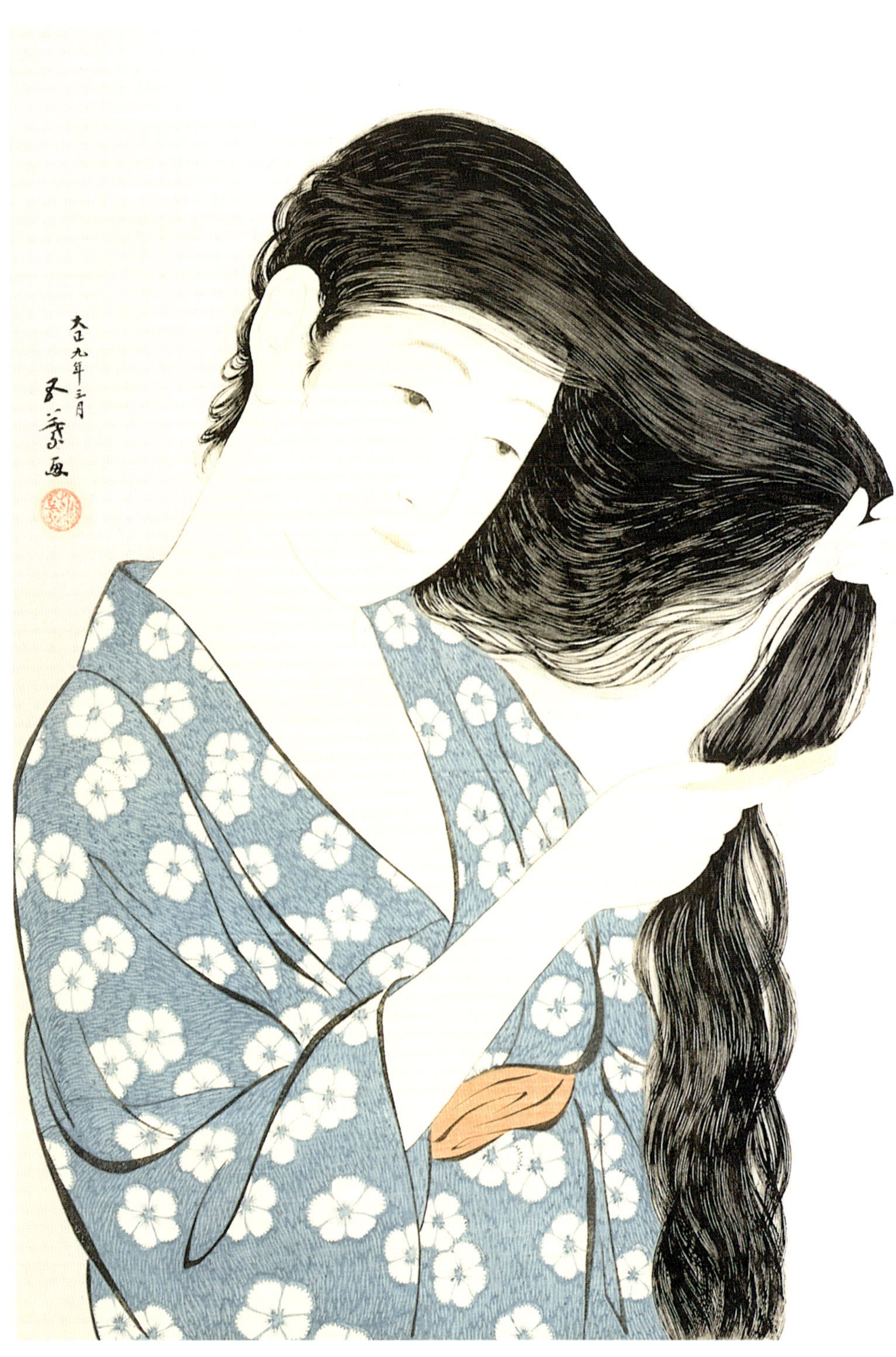

38

"Woman Combing Her Hair"

DATE 1920 (Taishō 9), March
SIGNATURE *Goyō ga*
ARTIST'S SEAL *Hashiguchi Goyō*
PUBLISHER Privately published
SIZE 44.0 x 32.6 cm
PROVENANCE Yamanaka & Co., New York, August 1935
ACCESSION NUMBER S2003.8.121
REFERENCES Stephens (ed.) (1993), fig .8; Hamanaka and Newland (2000), no. 17

Goyō's prints fetched high prices in his native Japan, but soon at auction in New York too. Within five years after its release the sales of this work exceeded most prints by Utagawa Hiroshige (1797-1858) and Katsushika Hokusai (1760-1849).

39

"Woman in a Long Undergarment"

DATE 1920 (Taishō 9), May
SIGNATURE *Goyō ga*
ARTIST'S SEAL *Goyō*
PUBLISHER Privately published
SIZE 47.0 x 13.5 cm
PROVENANCE Watanabe Shōzaburō, Tokyo, March 1937
ACCESSION NUMBER S2003.8.104
REFERENCES Stephens (ed.) (1993), cat. no. 132; Hamanaka and Newland (2000), no. 20

This design exists in at least three versions, each exhibiting differences in the color of the mica background. The extensive use of gauffrage, or blind-printing, in the undergarment is noteworthy. According to Watanabe Shōzaburō's son, Watanabe Tadasu, this print was extremely popular at the time of its publication. It was initially marketed at ¥15, approximately 5 or 6 times the price of a landscape print by Kawase Hasui (1883-1957; cat. nos. 52-63) from the same period. Then, as the work proved increasingly successful, the price was raised to ¥35.

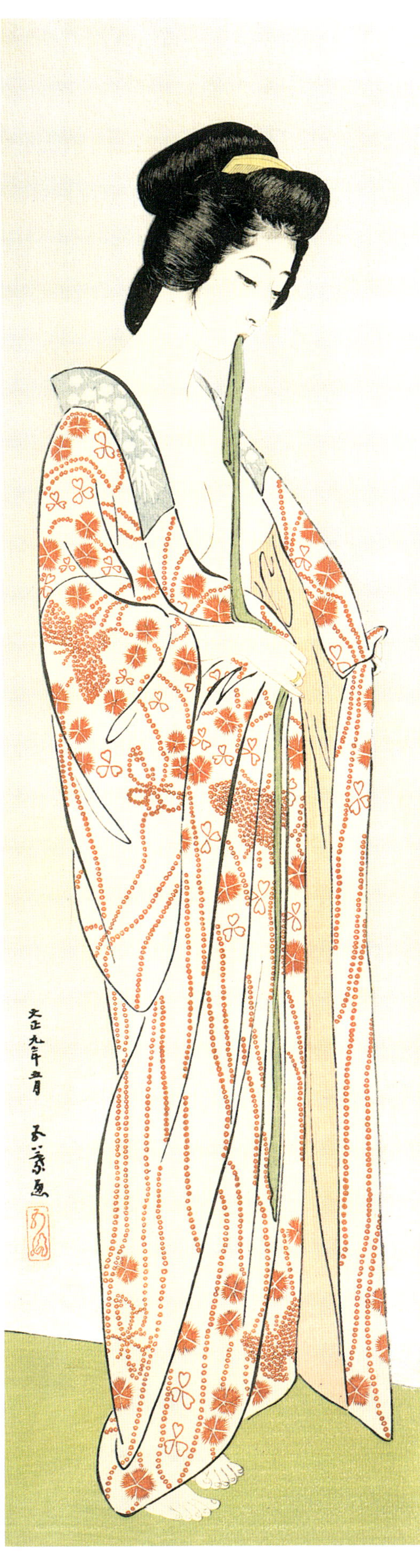

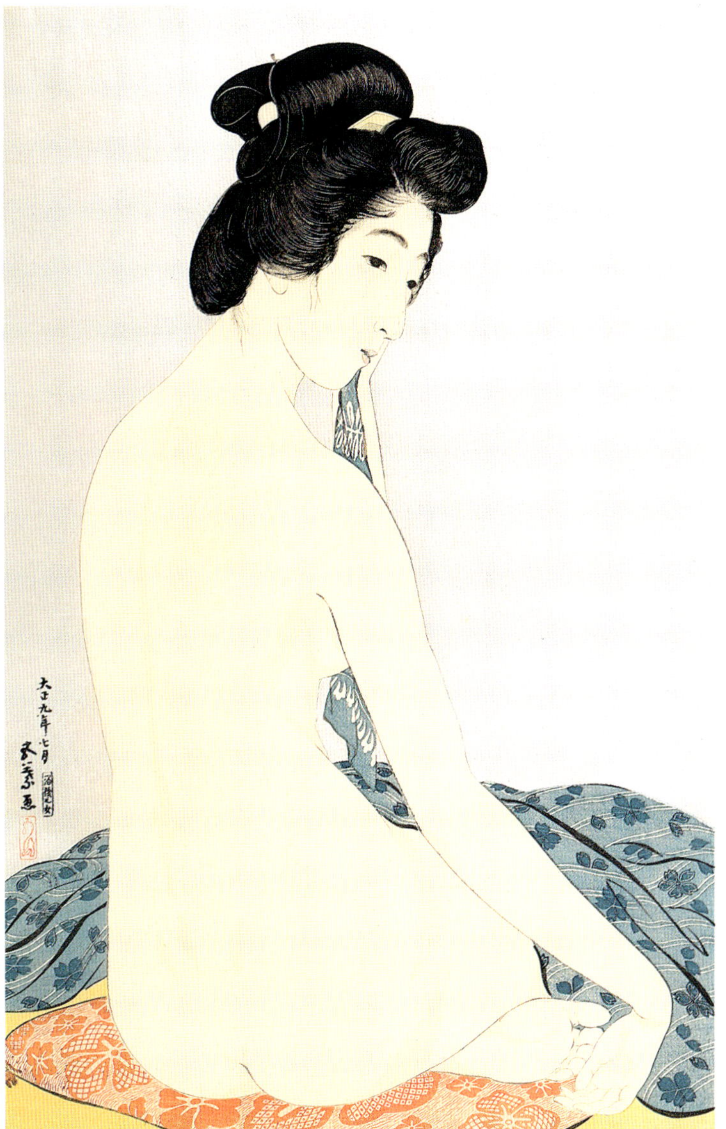

40

"Woman after a Bath"

Yokugo no onna

DATE 1920 (Taishō 9), July

SIGNATURE *Goyō ga*

ARTIST'S SEAL *Goyō*

PUBLISHER Privately published

SIZE 43.8 × 29.0 cm

PROVENANCE Yamanaka & Co., New York, February 1936

ACCESSION NUMBER S2003.8.107

REFERENCES Stephens (ed.) (1993), cat. no. 133; Hamanaka and Newland (2000), no. 16

Goyō did not number his prints, and therefore edition sizes for his works are unknown. However, numerous impressions of this design have surfaced in recent times. The provenance of this design suggests that it dates to before World War II and, as Robert O. Muller believed, provenance was one way to distinguish postwar impressions from originals.

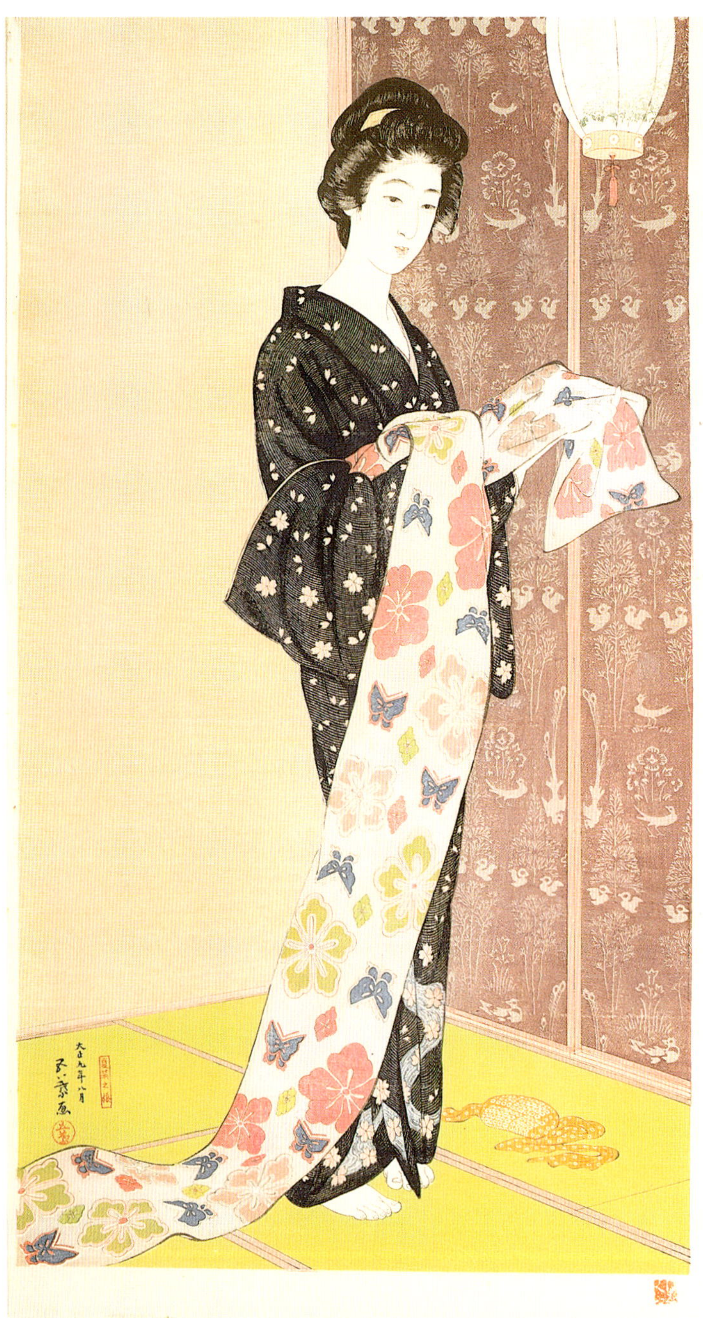

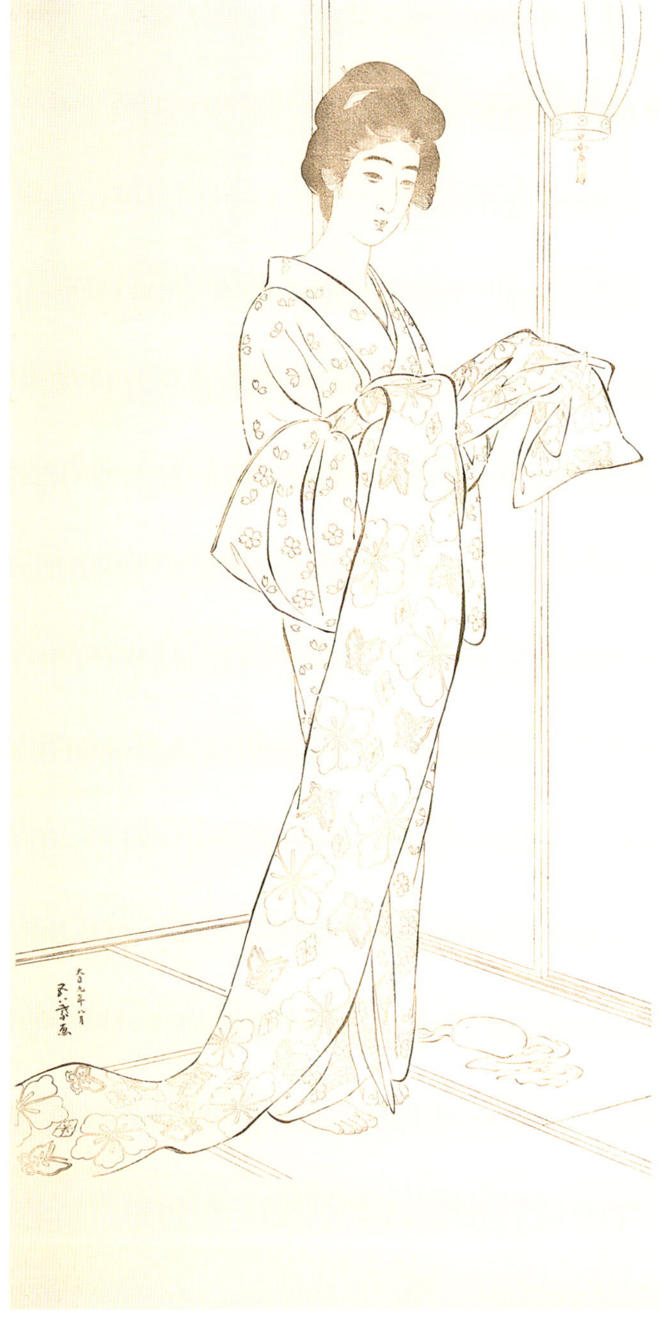

41

"Young Woman in Summer Kimono"

Natsu yosooi no musume

DATE 1920 (Taishō 9), August
SIGNATURE *Goyō ga*
ARTIST'S SEAL *Goyō*
PUBLISHER Privately published
SIZE 52.1 × 29.0 cm
ACCESSION NUMBER S2003.8.105
REFERENCES Stephens (ed.) (1993), cat. no. 135; Hamanaka and Newland (2000), no. 21

42

Keyblock impression for "Young Woman in Summer Kimono"

DATE 1920 (Taishō 9), August
SIGNATURE *Goyō ga*
SIZE 58.8 × 30.5 cm
PROVENANCE Shōbisha (Matsuki Kihachirō), Tokyo, 1940
ACCESSION NUMBER S2003.8.115

Goyō was probably one of the most gifted *Shin-hanga* artists in the depiction of the female form. The quality of his work derives from a deep understanding of his artistic roots, a knowledge that stemmed from his own *Ukiyo-e* studies as well as his involvement in Watanabe Shōzaburō's twelve-volume facsimile set *A Collection of Ukiyo-e Print Masterpieces* (*Ukiyo-e hanga kessaku shū*, 1916-20).

A great many drawings by Goyō still exist and are of great interest as they enable us to see the women that the artist used as his models. In this regard, Goyō stands alone in the history of Japanese printmaking.

43
"Rain at Yabakei Valley, Kyūshū"
Yabakei

DATE 1918 (Taishō 7)
SIGNATURE *Goyō ga*
ARTIST' SEAL *Goyō*
PUBLISHED Privately published
SIZE 37.5 x 49.9 cm
PROVENANCE Yamanaka & Co., New York, April 1936
ACCESSION NUMBER S2003.8.117

Four of Goyō's landscapes – this and the following print included – were part of the 1930 Toledo Museum of Art exhibition of Japanese prints. In the brief biography of Goyō in the accompanying catalogue, it suggests that "his greatest ability is shown in his figure prints rather than in his landscapes or his miscellaneous subjects." But this extremely striking rainscape can compete with any of the best examples in the *Shin-hanga* landscape genre. The rain printed in silver is an indication that this is a first edition.

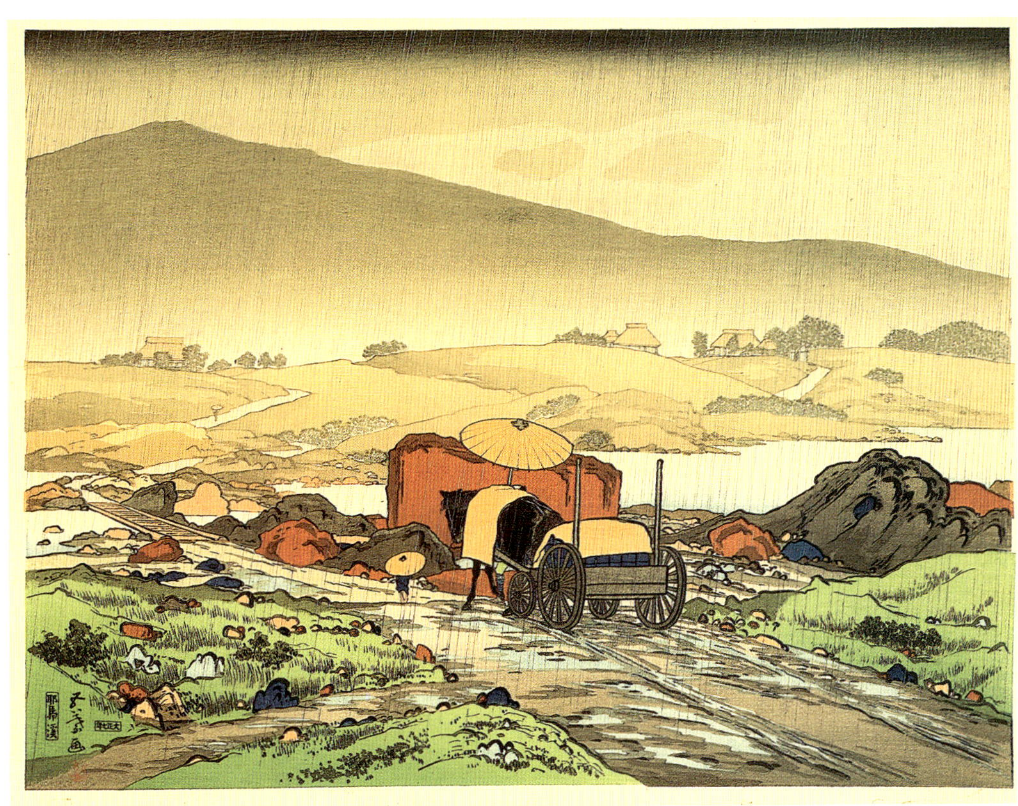

44
"Evening Moon at Kobe"
Kōbe no yoizuki

DATE 1920 (Taishō 9), January
SIGNATURE *Goyō ga*
ARTIST'S SEAL *Goyō*
SIZE 28.1 x 44.7 cm
PROVENANCE Morgenthau Galleries (Auction), New York, February 1938
ACCESSION NUMBER S2003.8.116

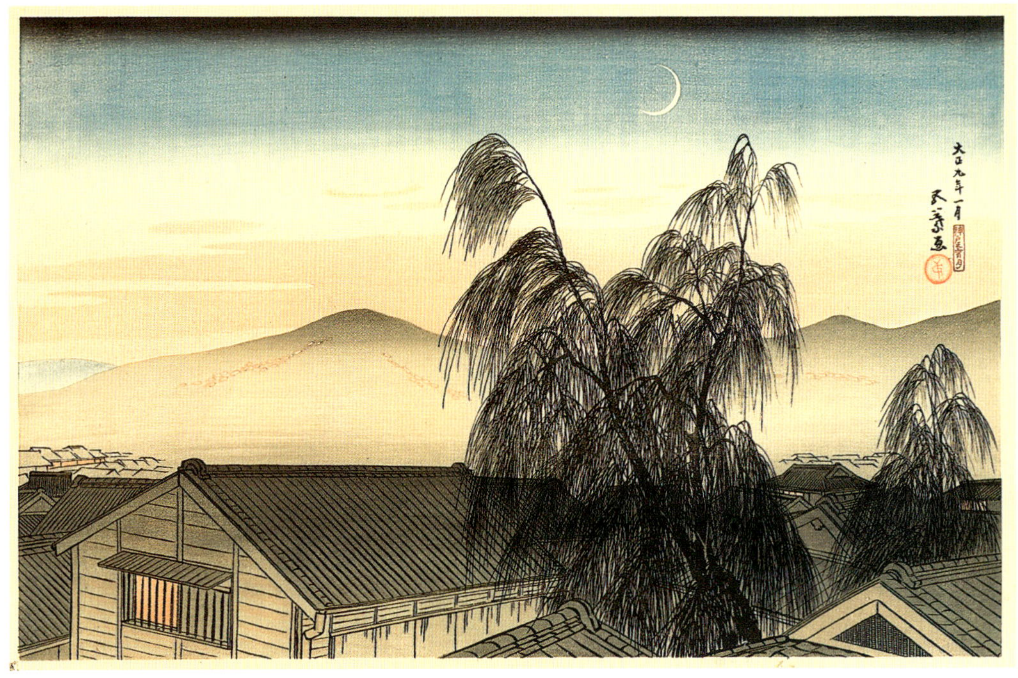

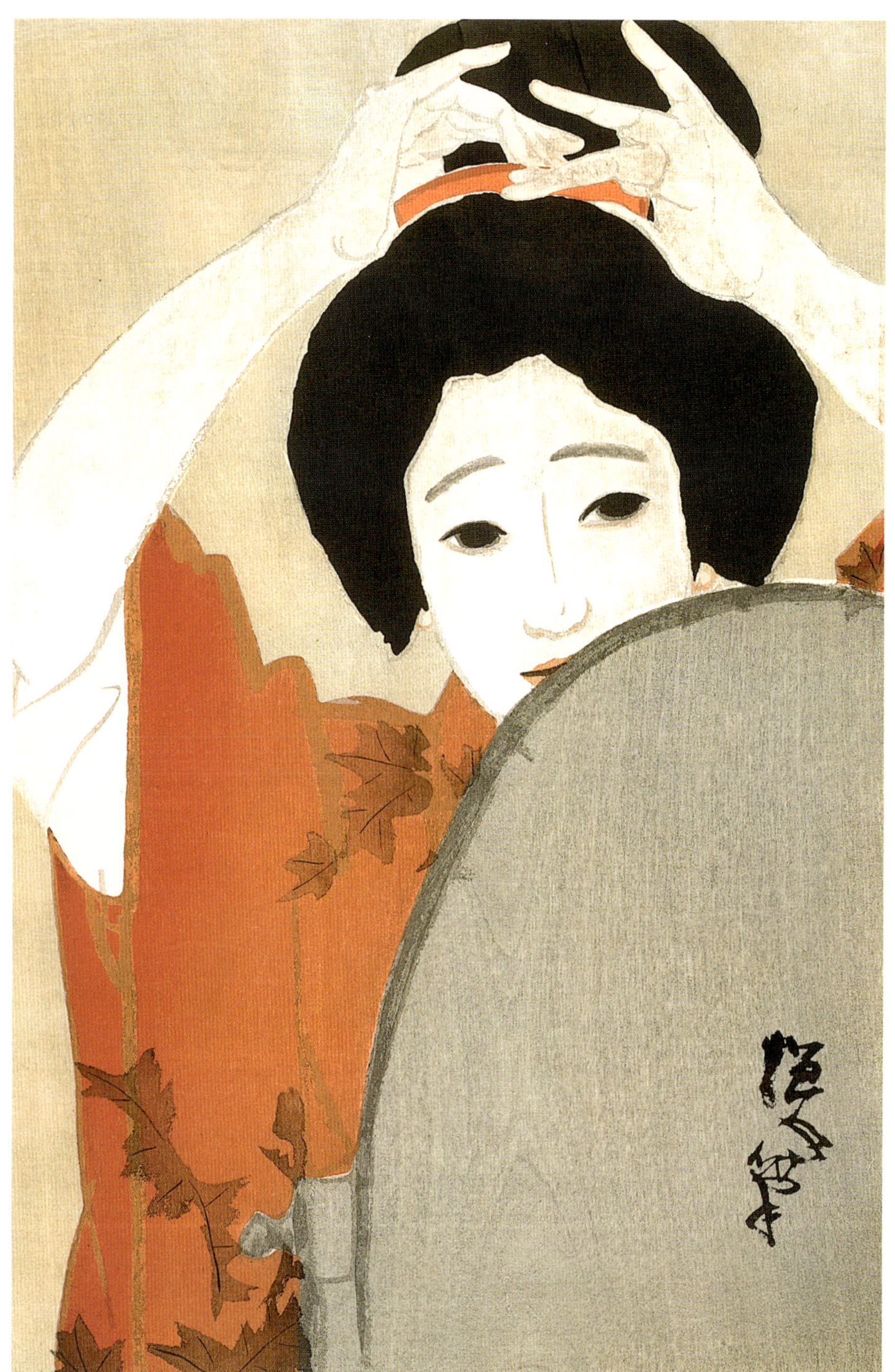

Kitano Tsunetomi (1880-1947)

Tsunetomi was born Kitano Tomitarō in Kanazawa, Ishikawa Prefecture. He became a student of Nishida Suketarō, a minor artist who taught Tomitarō the techniques of *hanshita-e* and of *Nanga* painting. In 1897 he worked as a carver for the newspaper *Hokkoku Shinpō*. The next year he traveled to Osaka to study *Nihonga* with the painter Inano Toshitsune (1858-1907), from whom he received the artist's name *Tsunetomi*. Tsunetomi began producing *kuchi-e* in 1899 and from 1901 he worked as illustrator for the newspaper *Ōsaka Shinbun*, while also pursuing his career as a painter. He became a central figure in Osaka/Kyoto *Nihonga* circles and was active in initiating various organizations, such as the *Ōsaka Bijutsukai* (Osaka Art Association) in 1915, the *Saikō Bijutsuin* (Reorganized Japan Fine Arts Academy) in 1917 and the *Chawakai* ("Tea Table Talk" Association) in 1918. Tsunetomi exhibited frequently at the *Bunten*, *Inten* and numerous other official and private shows. He was the recipient of many prizes, for instance at the fifth *Bunten* in 1911. In 1917 Tsunetomi became a member of the *Teiten* and in 1924 he established the school and publishing house Hakuyōsha. Included among his students were the women artists Shima Seien (1893-1970) and Kitani Chigusa (1890-1947), both of whom would also contribute designs for prints.

REFERENCES Merritt and Yamada (1992), 68; Stephens (ed.) (1993), 132-33; Hamanaka and Newland (2000), 84-8, 210; Tokyo Station Gallery (ed.) (2003)

45
"Winter: In Front of a Mirror"

SERIES *Seasons of the Pleasure Quarters* (*Kuruwa no shunjū*)
DATE 1918 (Taishō 7)
SIGNATURE *Tsunetomi hitsu*
PUBLISHER Nakajima Jūtarō (Nakajima Seikadō, Tokyo)
SIZE 39.1 x 26.0 cm
PROVENANCE Nishinomiya Yosaku, Tokyo, July 1955
ACCESSION NUMBER S2003.8.1087
REFERENCES Stephens (ed.) (1993), cat. no. 13; Hamanaka and Newland (2000), no. 105

This design is from a set of four prints issued together in a folder bearing the title *Kuruwa no shunjū* (*Seasons of the Pleasure Quarters*), the names of publisher and artist, as well as edition size.[1] The set is based on a group of four successful earlier paintings of the same subject by Tsunetomi, in which each composition is linked to one of the four seasons and to one of the pleasure quarters in Osaka. This illustration of a woman adjusting her hair before a mirror stands out as the only half-length portrait in the set. It is associated with "Winter" and the Shinchi district, and is number four in the set. The pigment used to delineate the woman's arms is a metal-based colorant prone to oxidization. The remaining three images are full-length portraits: "After a Bath" (*Yuagari*) for the Nanchi district (Autumn, no. 1), "In Training" (*Keiko no ma*) for Shinmachi (Spring, no. 2) and "Twilight" (*Yūgure*) for Horie (Summer, no. 3).

1. Freis (1994), 138-39.

46
"The Heron Maiden"

DATE Undated, *c.* 1925
SIGNATURE *Tsunetomi hitsu*
BLOCKCUTTER Yamagishi Kazue
PRINTER Nishimura Kumakichi
PUBLISHER Nezu Seitarō
EDITION Number 98 from a limited edition
SIZE 45.1 x 29.9 cm
PROVENANCE Nishinomiya Yosaku, Tokyo, July 1955
ACCESSION NUMBER S2003.8.1085
REFERENCES Stephens (ed.) (1993), cat. no. 139; Hamanaka and Newland (2000), no. 108

Tsunetomi is primarily known as a *Nihonga* painter. Only eleven prints by him are documented, and all are based on paintings. "The Heron Maiden" is undoubtedly the most famous of his prints, in no small measure due to the public acclaim of the original painting. A smaller print with a similar composition was also included in the earlier 1923 set given the title *The Complete Works of Chikamatsu* (*Dai Chikamatsu zenshū*). Although this print is unusual as one of the few examples from the Robert O. Muller collection that is not in pristine condition – the gray mica background is worn and the splashed-on *gofun* for the snowflakes has flaked away in places – it still remains an extremely striking design. This impression is numbered in the bottom margin, and it seems that Tsunetomi numbered every print sold during his lifetime by hand. Following the artist's death, his prints remained in the Kitano family, who has gradually sold them off during the last two decades; these works appear without impression numbers.

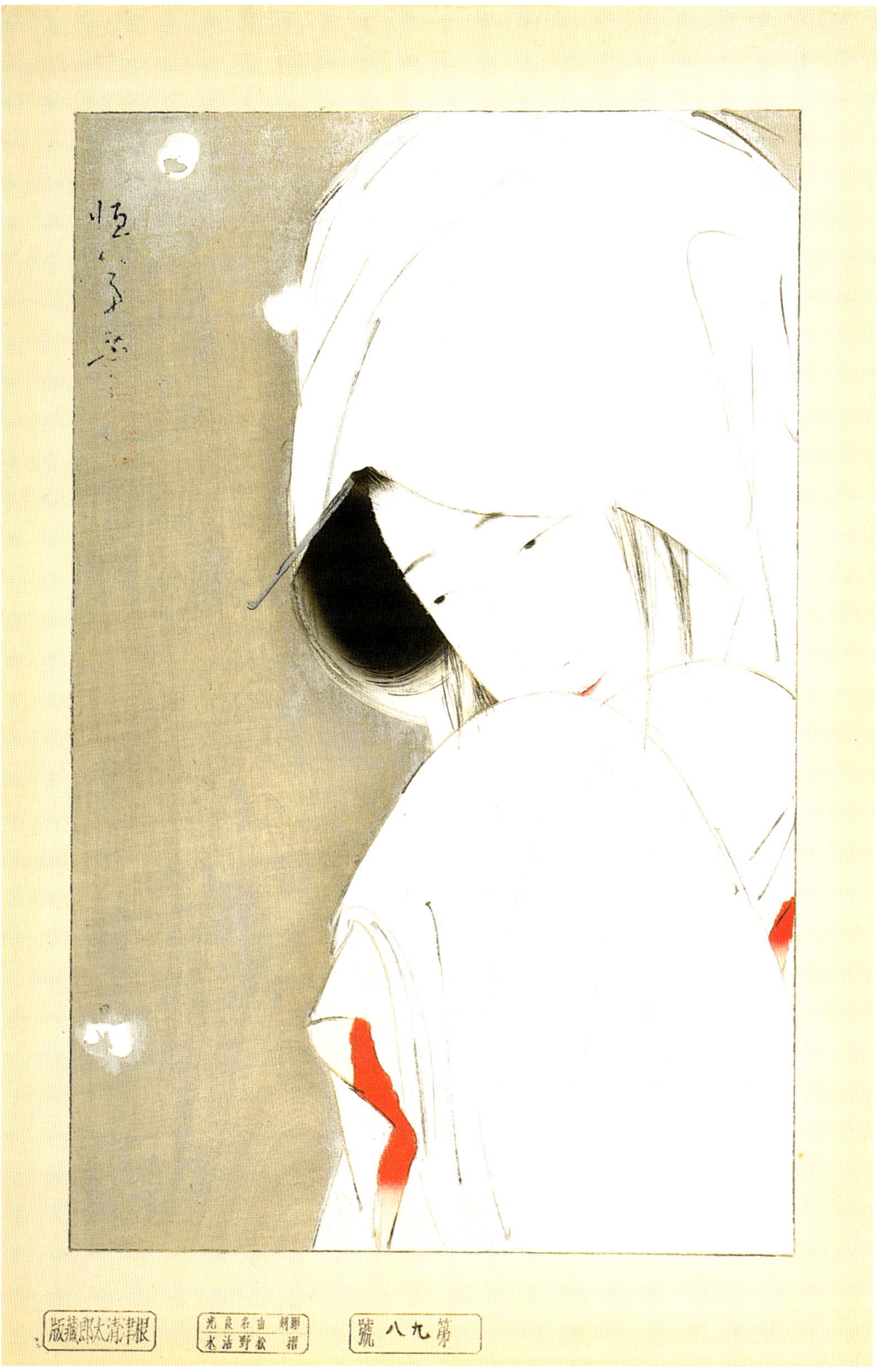

Oda Kazuma (1882-1956)

Oda Kazuma was born in the Shiba district of Tokyo, where he supposedly studied *Yōga* with Kawamura Kiyōo (1852-1934). He went to Osaka to study lithography with Kaneko Masajirō and returned to Tokyo in 1903 to work as a designer at the Koshiba lithography studio. Kazuma became associated with the *Sōsaku-hanga* movement and contributed to their arts and literary magazine *Hōsun* (*Square Inch*) from 1909 to 1911. From 1911 to 1914 he returned to Osaka to work for the newspaper *Teikoku Shinbun* (*Imperial Newspaper*) and to study *Ukiyo-e*. In 1918 he was enlisted by Yamamoto Kanae (1882-1946) to aid in the establishment of the *Nihon Sōsaku-hanga Kyōkai* (Society of Japanese Creative Prints), and he was the only lithographer in the group. Kazuma participated in several official exhibitions, including the *Bunten*, *Teiten* and *Nitten*. He was especially known for his lithographic works, but he also produced six woodblock prints with Watanabe Shōzaburō (1885-1962) in 1924 that were later shown in the Toledo Museum of Art exhibition of 1930. In the same year (1930) he formed the *Yōfū Hangakai* (Western-style Print Association), which was absorbed into the *Nihon Hanga Kyōkai* (Japan Print Association) in 1931. He published several studies on *Ukiyo-e* such as *Ukiyo-e jūhachikō* (*Eighteen Studies on Ukiyo-e*, 1926) and *Ukiyo-e to sashi-e geijutsu* (*Ukiyo-e and The Art of Illustration*, 1931). Kazuma produced at least eight *Shin-hanga* prints, numerous *Sōsaku-hanga* and over 200 lithographs.

REFERENCES Watanabe Shōzaburō (1936), 108; Merritt and Yamada (1992), 114; Stephens (ed.) (1993), 135-36; Fukumitsu Art Museum (ed.) (1996); Machida City Museum of International Graphic Art (ed.) (2000); Chiba City Museum of Art (ed.) (2001)

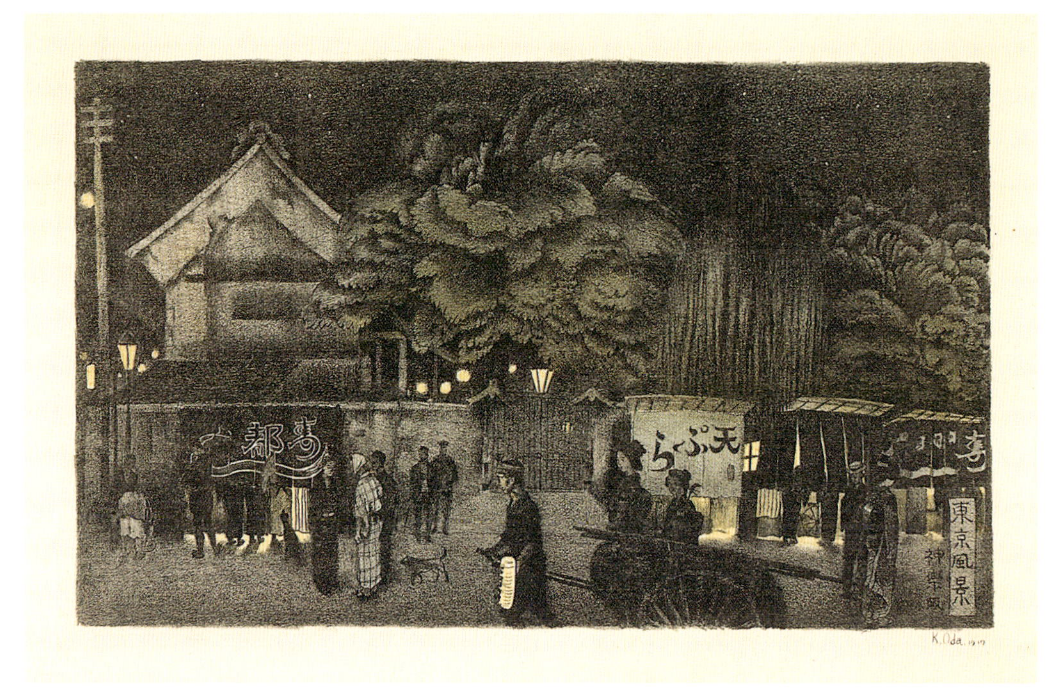

47
"Kagurazaka"
Kagurazaka

SERIES *Views of Tokyo* (*Tōkyō fūkei*)
DATE 1917
SIGNATURE *K. Oda*
PUBLISHER Self-published lithograph
SIZE 26.0 x 43.5 cm
PROVENANCE Merwin's Art Shop, New Haven, Conn., 1963
ACCESSION NUMBER S2003.8.1632
REFERENCE Chiba City Museum of Art (ed.) (1999), no. 151.20

Various reprographic techniques, such as woodblock printing, lithography and photography, were already vying with one other in the publishing industry during the late nineteenth century. At this time, too, hand-colored lithographs (*sekibanga*) of beauties, famous places and historical events became extremely popular. By the early twentieth century a combination of different reprographic techniques characterizes, for example, developments in book illustration: lithographs would be colored by hand or by over-printing with woodblocks. Oda produced many black-and-white lithographs, but also on occasion included (printed, not hand-colored) subdued blues, greens, yellows or reds as striking accents, as seen here.

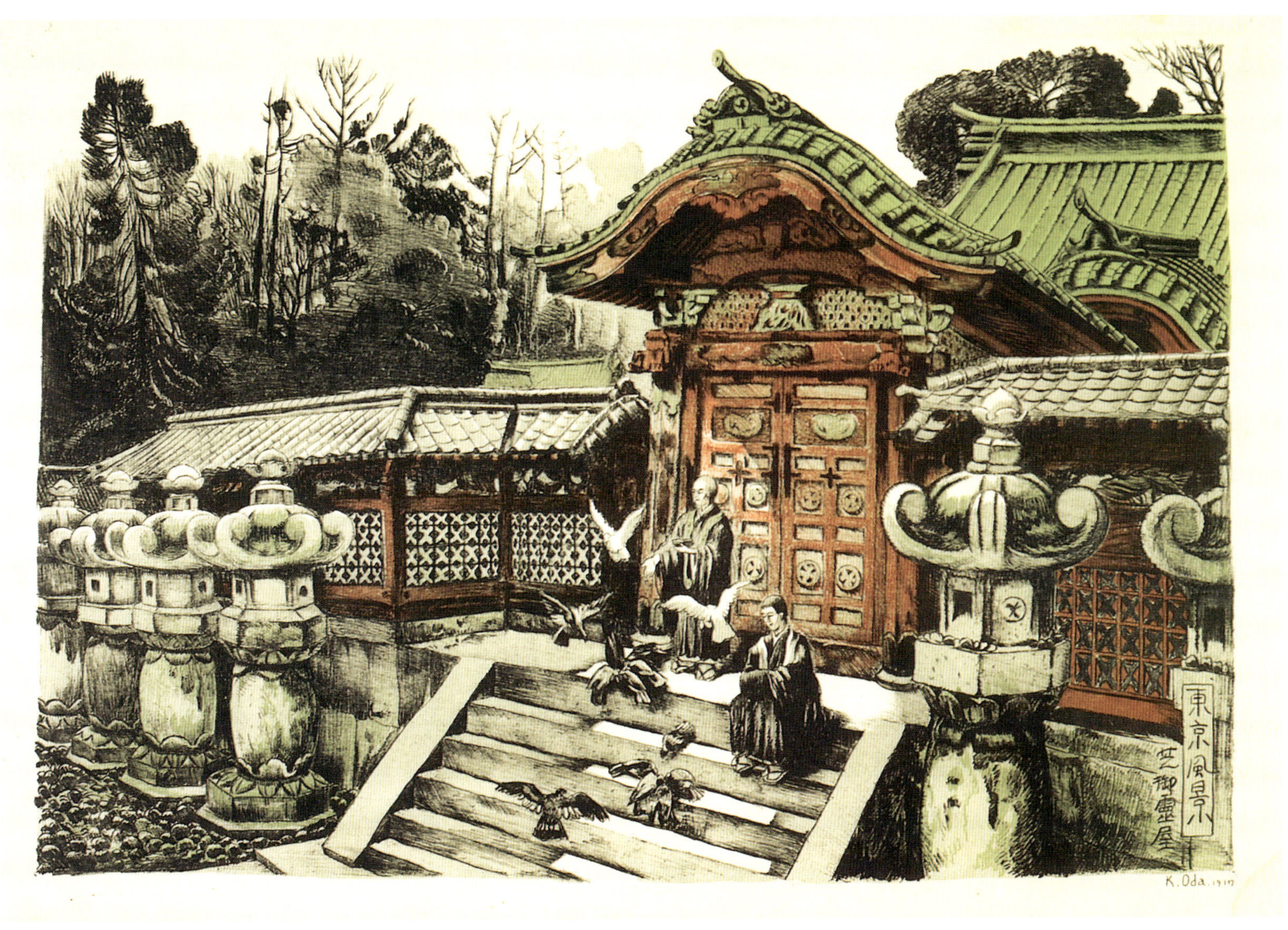

48

"Shiba Shrine"

Shiba Otamaya

SERIES *Views of Tokyo* (*Tōkyō fūkei*)

DATE 1917

SIGNATURE *K. Oda*

PUBLISHER Self-published lithograph

SIZE 30.8 x 45.1 cm

PROVENANCE Merwin's Art Shop, New Haven, Conn., 1963

ACCESSION NUMBER S2003.8.1631

REFERENCE Chiba City Museum of Art (ed.)(1999), no. 151.17

Oda's series *Views of Tokyo* consists of twenty lithographs released from January 1916 to July 1917 and represents the debut of his self-carved work. Compared to his later woodblock prints with Watanabe Shōzaburō from 1924 (*cf.* cat. no. 50), the paper used for these lithographs is generally thinner and the contour line of the lithography stone is visible. The inclusion of Oda's lithographs here emphasizes the notion held by Robert O. Muller and others that the boundaries between *Shin-hanga* and *Sōsaku-hanga* are not always clear. Stylistically these lithographs are closer to *Shin-hanga*, but the control of the production process by the artist is more in keeping with *Sōsaku-hanga*.

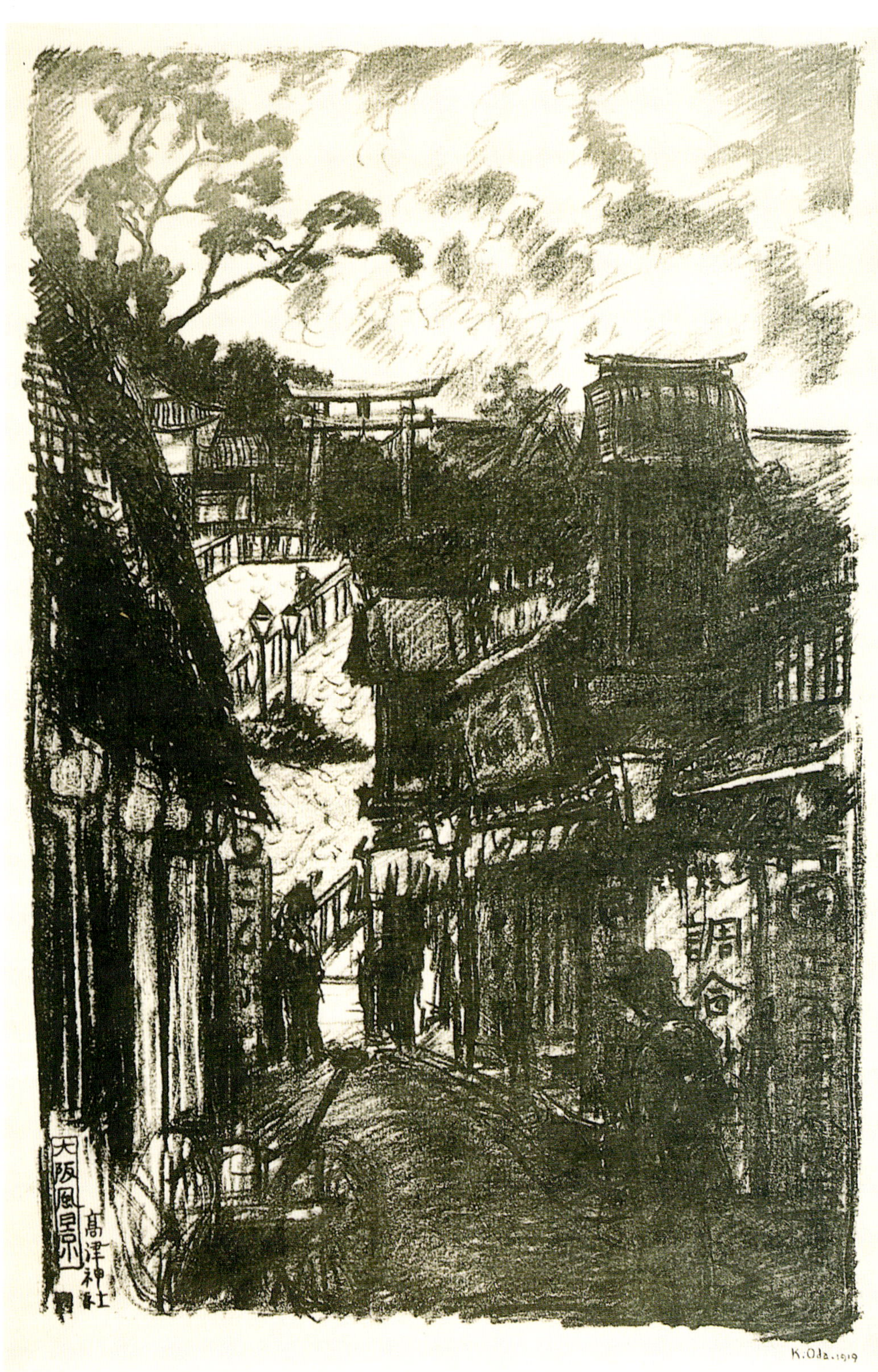

49

"Kozu Shrine"

Kozu jinja

SERIES *Views of Osaka* (*Ōsaka fūkei*)

DATE 1919

SIGNATURE *K. Oda*

PUBLISHER Self-published lithograph

SIZE 44.5 x 29.9 cm

PROVENANCE Merwin's Art Shop, New Haven, Conn., 1963

ACCESSION NUMBER S2003.8.1636

50

"Matsue Great Bridge"

Matsue Ōhashi

DATE 1924 (Taishō 13)
SIGNATURE *Kazuma hitsu*
ARTIST'S SEAL *Oda*
PUBLISHER Watanabe Shōzaburō
SIZE 23.3 x 36.1 cm
ACCESSION NUMBER S2003.8.1626
REFERENCE Stephens (ed.) (1993), cat. no. 141

Oda's prints for Watanabe deal principally with Matsue, the capital of Shimane Prefecture, and its surroundings. It is not clear why Oda – a recognized lithographer – choose to work with the *Shin-hanga* publisher. But in later life he describes this body of work in a less than favorable light, referring to it disparagingly as "reproduction work."

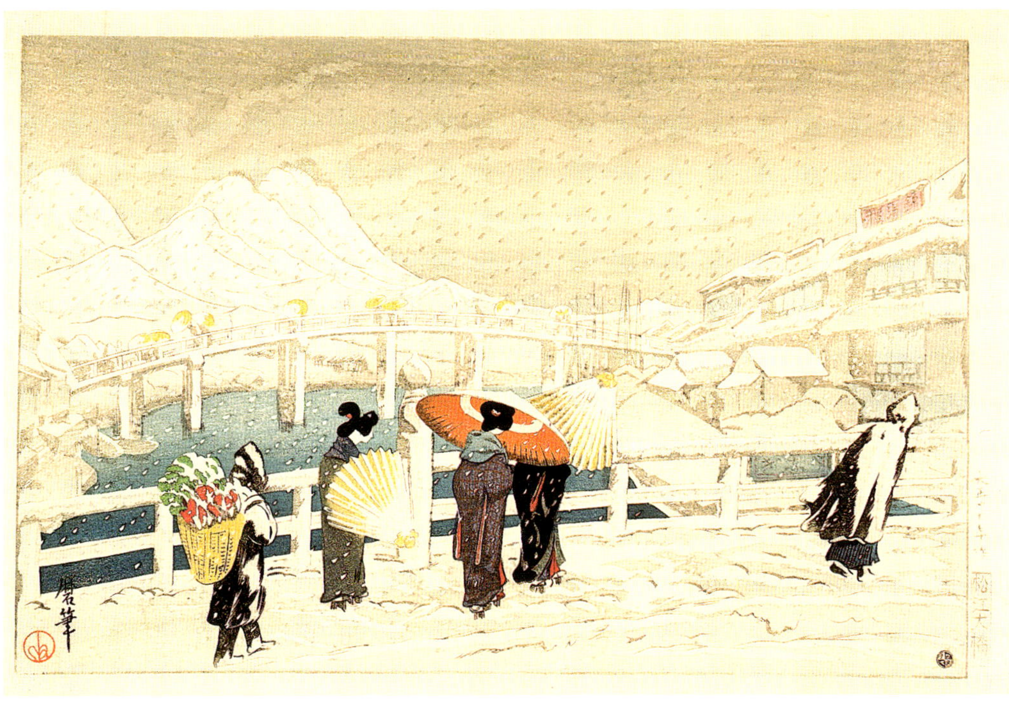

51

"Bridge in Front of Factories"

DATE Undated, *c.* late 1920s
SIGNATURE *Kazuma hitsu*
ARTIST'S SEAL *Oda*
PUBLISHER No publisher's seal
SIZE 22.4 x 34.0 cm
PROVENANCE Yamada Shoten Ltd., Tokyo, March 1983
ACCESSION NUMBER S2003.8.1627

This cityscape utilizes contourless printing (i.e., using just color blocks and no black keyblock). The subject matter is typical of many of Oda's *Sōsaku-hanga* contemporaries, who chose to concentrate on the rapidly changing urban environment of Japan when creating "landscape" prints.

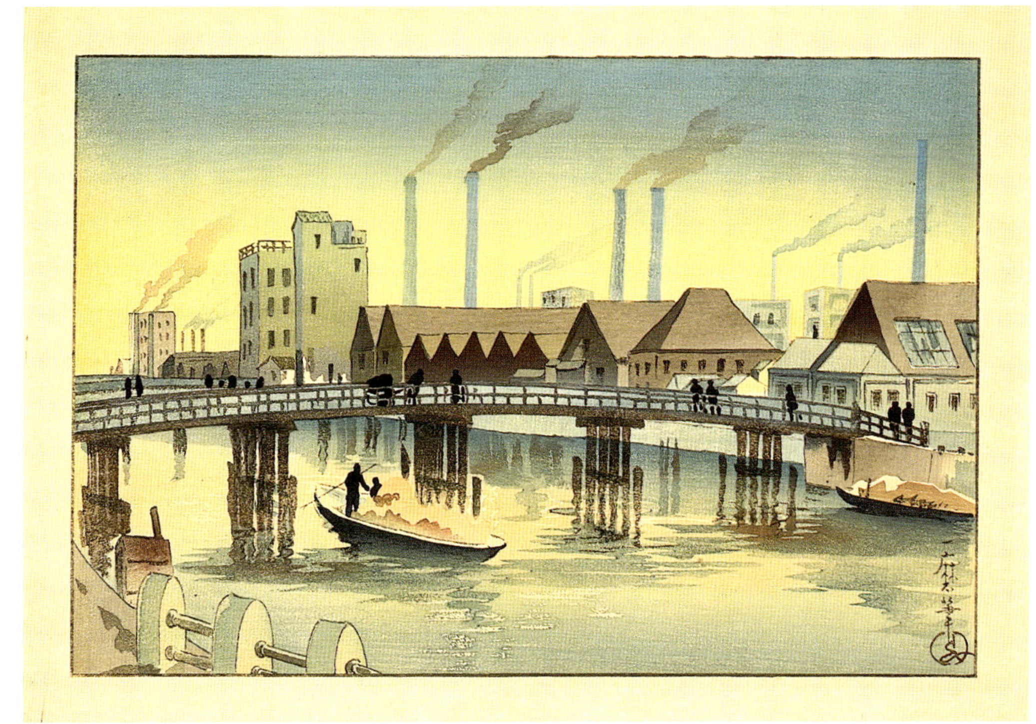

Kawase Hasui (1883-1957)

Kawase Hasui was born Kawase Bunjirō in the Shiba district of Tokyo. He left school at the age of twelve and entered the atelier of the little-known *Nihonga* painter Aoyagi Bokusen two years later. He studied *Yōga* at the *Hakubakai* (White Horse Society) under Okada Saburōsuke (1869-1939) and became a pupil of Kaburagi Kiyokata (1878-1973; cat. nos. 5-7) in 1910. He exhibited *Nihonga* paintings with the *Ugōkai* (Cormorant Society) and *Kyōdokai* (Homeland Society). In 1917 Hasui, impressed by Itō Shinsui's landscape series *Ōmi hakkei* (*Eight Views of Ōmi*; cat. nos. 93-100) that he saw at the seventh *Kyōdokai* exhibition, approached the publisher Watanabe Shōzaburō (1885-1962) and showed him some of his sketches. This marked the beginning of Hasui's career as a printmaker with the Watanabe firm. Hasui traveled extensively in Japan, sketching different landscapes and urban views, intrigued by seasonal and climatic changes and the play of the light. He participated in numerous exhibitions, such as the Watanabe sponsored *Shinsaku-hanga Tenrankai* (New Creative Print Exhibition) in 1921. In September 1923 the Great Kantō Earthquake destroyed Hasui's residence and his sketchbooks as well as most of his prints and blocks stored at Watanabe's publishing house. Hasui's long professional relationship with Watanabe was briefly interrupted from 1930 to 1931, when he worked with several other publishers, including Doi Sadakichi (also read Teiichi) and Sakai/Kawaguchi. Although his house was again destroyed in the Allied bombings of Tokyo in 1944, Hasui continued designing prints during World War II, and in the postwar period quickly picked up his pace of production. While his work never regained the strength of his prewar years, his life-long contribution to printmaking was nonetheless recognized with his designation as a *Ningen Kokuhō* (Living National Treasure) by the Japanese government in 1956. He died on November 27, 1957 from gastric cancer, having produced over 600 full-size prints and numerous smaller, often derivative designs.

REFERENCES Watanabe Shōzaburō (1936), 77-8; Narazaki (ed.) (1979); Merritt and Yamada (1992), 62; Stephens (ed.) (1993), 139-52; Brown *et al.* (2003)

52
"Okane Road, Shiobara"
Shiobara Okane-michi

DATE 1918 (Taishō 7), Autumn
SIGNATURE AND ARTIST'S SEAL *Hasui*
PUBLISHER Watanabe Shōzaburō
SIZE 45.3 x 16.7 cm
PROVENANCE Yamanaka & Co., New York, July 1936
ACCESSION NUMBER S2003.8.560
REFERENCE Brown *et al.* (2003), no. 1

Hasui's first print is one of a group of three featuring his favorite area of Japan: Shiobara. Nine years before the completion of this print, Hasui had visited his aunt in Shiobara for four months to sketch. Hasui's love of Shiobara led to his decision to select scenes from there for his debut prints with publisher Watanabe Shōzaburō. The tall, narrow format is unusual and his first eight designs were all in this format; oddly, he would return to this size only twice in his career. It is interesting to note that the first prints of several other artists who collaborated with Watanabe were in formats other than the standard *ōban* (*c.* 36 x 24 cm; *cf.* Yoshida Hiroshi, cat. no. 18; Yamamura Kōka, cat. nos. 64-5; Natori Shunsen, cat. no. 72; and Itō Shinsui, cat. nos. 85-9) and ones in which they were not to work in again. It was as if Watanabe spared no expense in their early works and was willing to cater to the artists' wishes regardless of cost.

53
"Hataori, Shiobara"
Shiobara Hataori

DATE 1918 (Taishō 7), Autumn
SIGNATURE AND ARTIST'S SEAL *Hasui*
PUBLISHER Watanabe Shōzaburō
SIZE 45.4 x 16.5 cm
PROVENANCE Oshima Kano, New York, January 1936
ACCESSION NUMBER S2003.8.561
REFERENCE Brown *et al.* (2003), no. 2

Sloping fields drenched by a torrential rain, the Hōki River flowing through the cultivated landscape while mist rises between the mountain ridges. This second design from Hasui's Shiobara trilogy is probably one of his most convincing rain scenes.

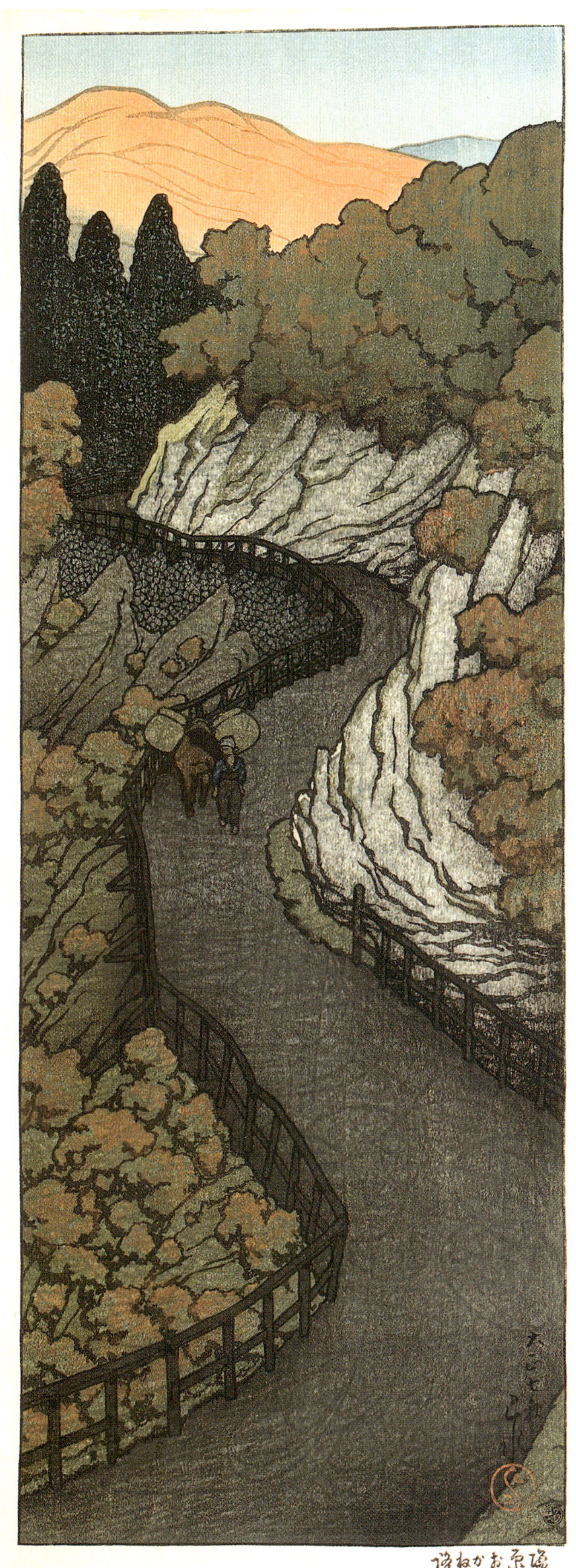
塩原おかね路

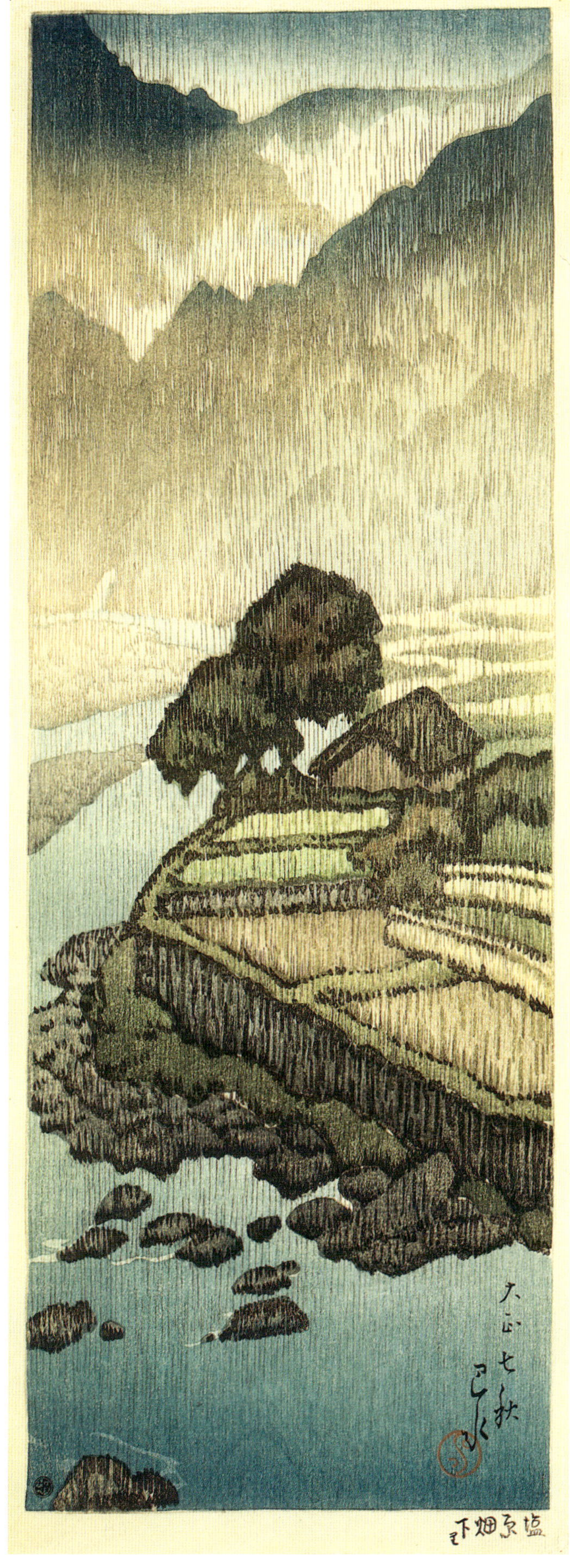
塩原畑下

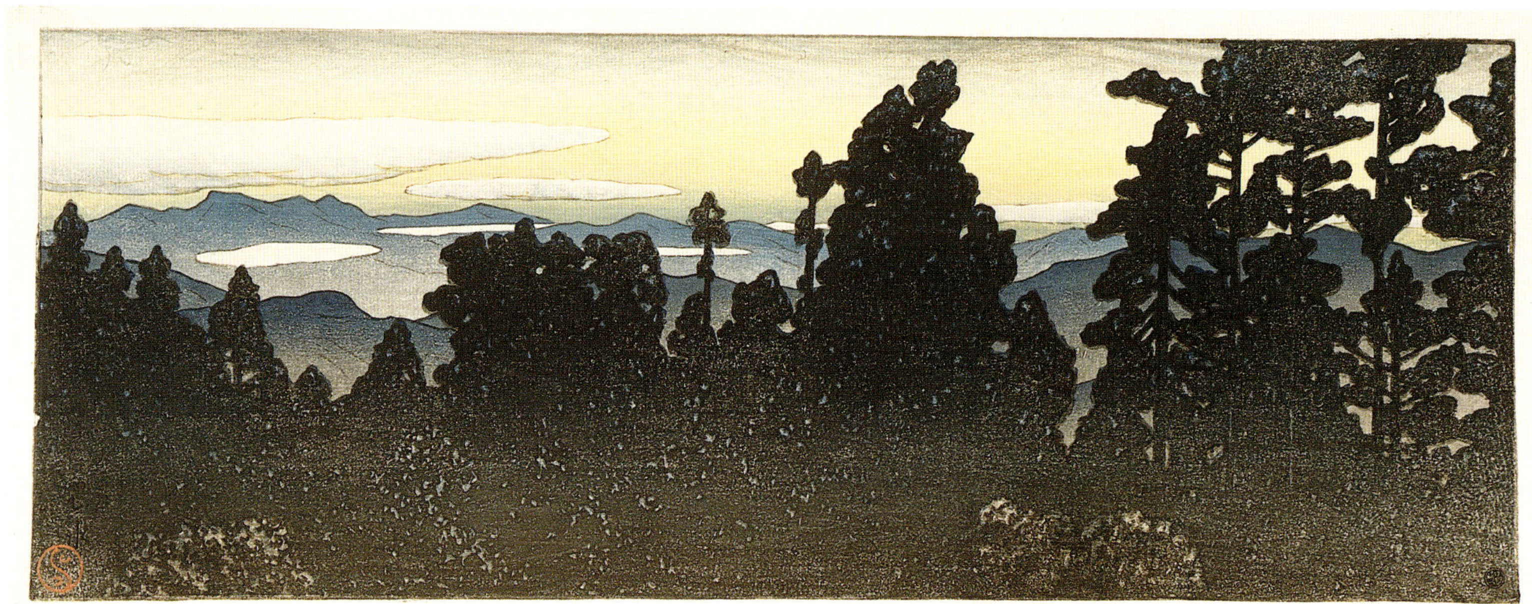

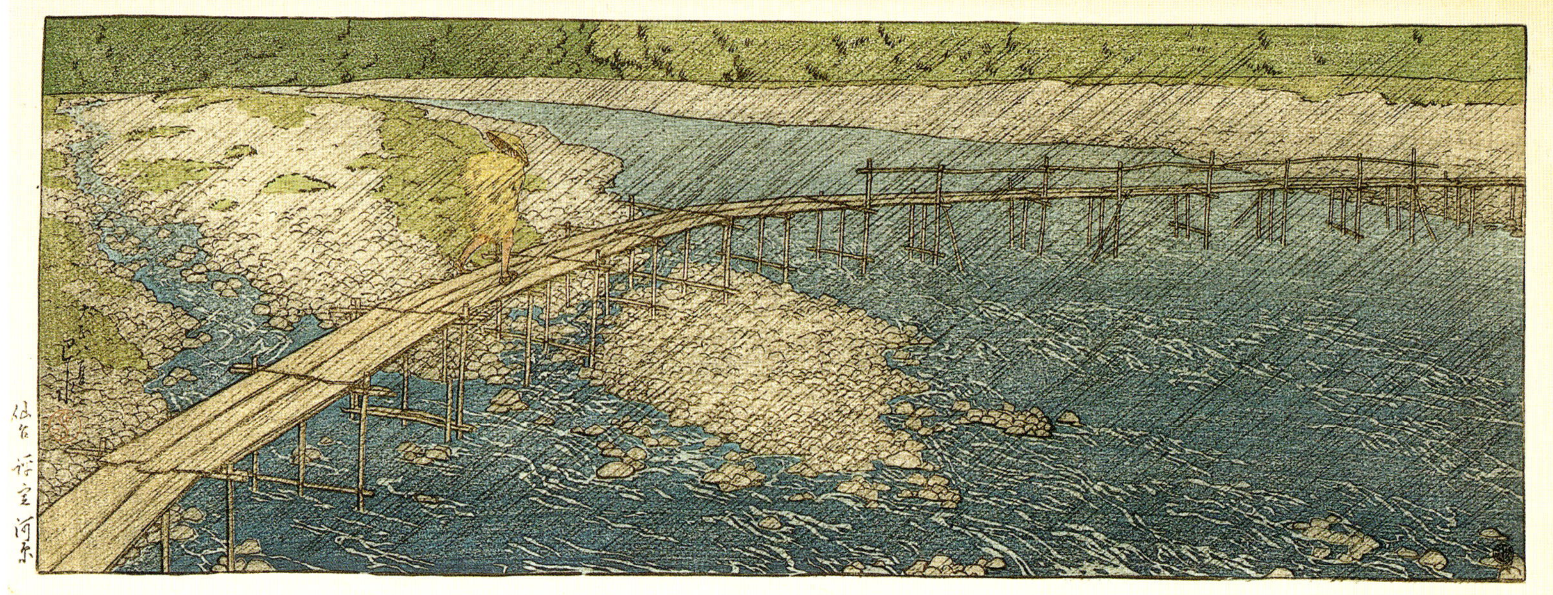

54
"Summer at Ikaho"
Ikaho no natsu

DATE 1919 (Taishō 8), Summer
SIGNATURE AND ARTIST'S SEAL *Hasui*
PUBLISHER Watanabe Shōzaburō
SIZE 16.7 x 45.3 cm
PROVENANCE Watanabe Shōzaburō Co., Tokyo, May 1937
ACCESSION NUMBER S2003.8.564
REFERENCE Brown *et al.* (2003), no. 5

An extremely effective design: trees are silhouetted against a summer's sky above the mountain ranges of Ikaho in Gumma Prefecture.

55
"Hyōjōgawara, Sendai"
Sendai Hyōjōgawara

DATE 1919 (Taishō 8), Summer
SIGNATURE AND ARTIST'S SEAL *Hasui*
PUBLISHER Watanabe Shōzaburō
SIZE 16.5 x 45.6 cm
PROVENANCE Yamanaka & Co., Boston, August 1937
ACCESSION NUMBER S2003.8.567
REFERENCE Brown *et al.* (2003), no. 8

A driving wind and summer rain surprise a traveler crossing a wooden bridge over the Hirose River in Sendai in the northern prefecture of Miyagi.

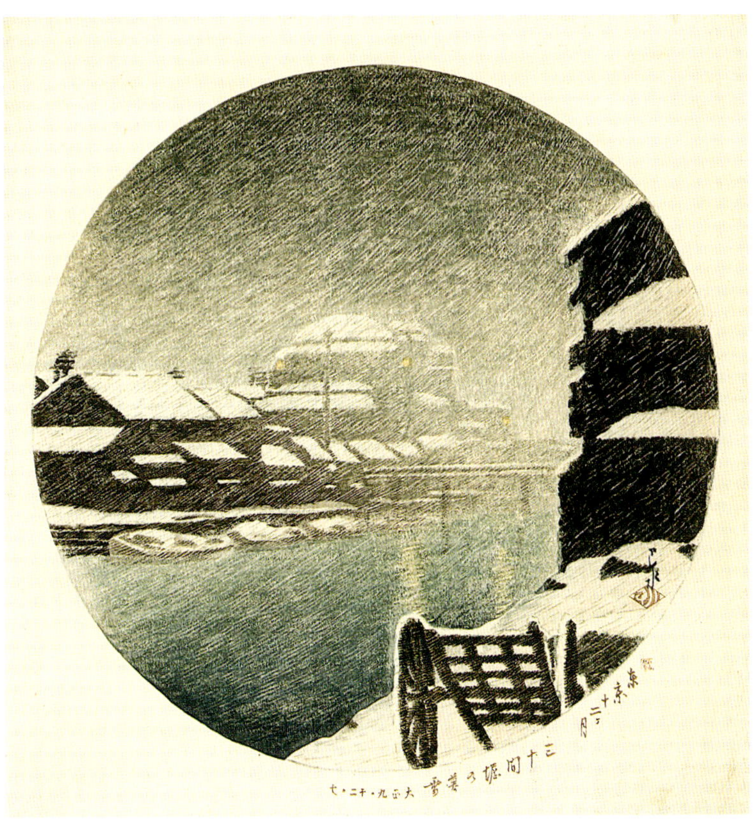

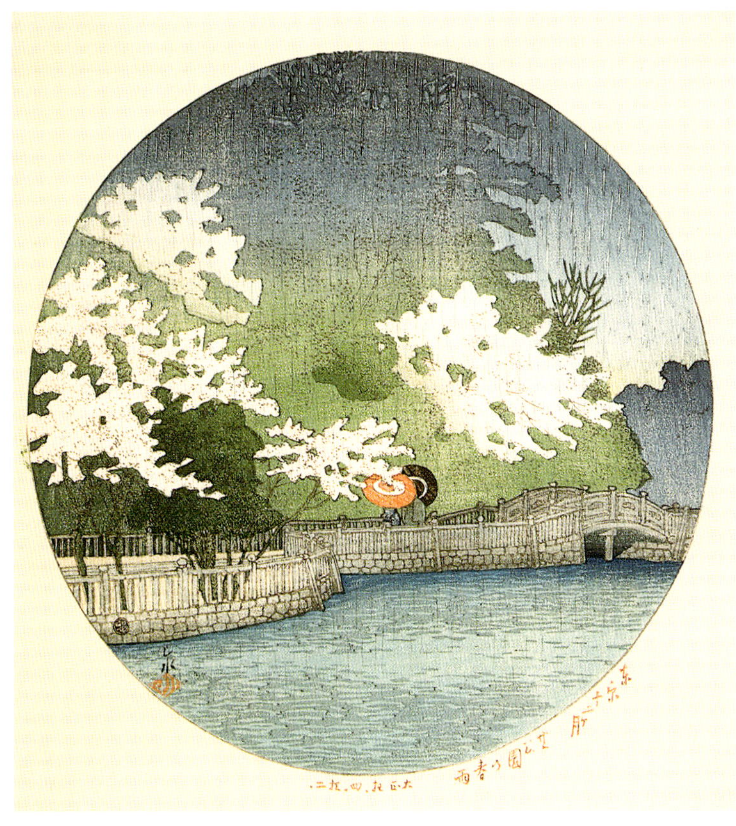

56

"Evening Snow at Sanjūgen Canal"

Sanjūgenbori no bosetsu

SERIES *Twelve Months of Tokyo* (*Tōkyō jūnikagetsu*)
DATE 1920 (Taishō 9), December 7th
SIGNATURE *Hasui*
ARTIST'S SEAL *Kawase*
PUBLISHER Watanabe Shōzaburō
SIZE Diameter: 26.0 cm; paper size: 30 x 28.3 cm
PROVENANCE Yamanaka & Co., New York, April 1936
ACCESSION NUMBER S2003.8.607
REFERENCE Brown et *al.* (2003), no. 38

At the end of Hasui's first year working with publisher Watanabe Shōzaburō, the idea of releasing the artist's prints in serial form is realized. Generally speaking, it is not clear whether *Shin-hanga* series were conceived as such from the beginning or whether the serial aspect was introduced later as a marketing ploy by the publisher to entice customers into subscribing to the entire series. It is highly likely that both strategies existed in tandem. In this series the title is cut into the keyblock, suggesting that the prints were intended as a series from the outset. Only five designs for this series were ever completed. Four were circular designs, and they constitute some of the most intimate landscape designs within Hasui's corpus of work.

57

"Spring Shower at Shiba Park"

Shiba kōen no harusame

SERIES *Twelve Months of Tokyo* (*Tōkyō jūnikagetsu*)
DATE 1921 (Taishō 10), April 12th
SIGNATURE *Hasui*
ARTIST'S SEAL *Kawase*
PUBLISHER Watanabe Shōzaburō
SIZE Diameter: 26.0 cm; paper size: 30 x 28.3 cm
PROVENANCE The Meiji Store, San Francisco, July 1937
ACCESSION NUMBER S2003.8.610
REFERENCE Brown et *al.* (2003), no. 41

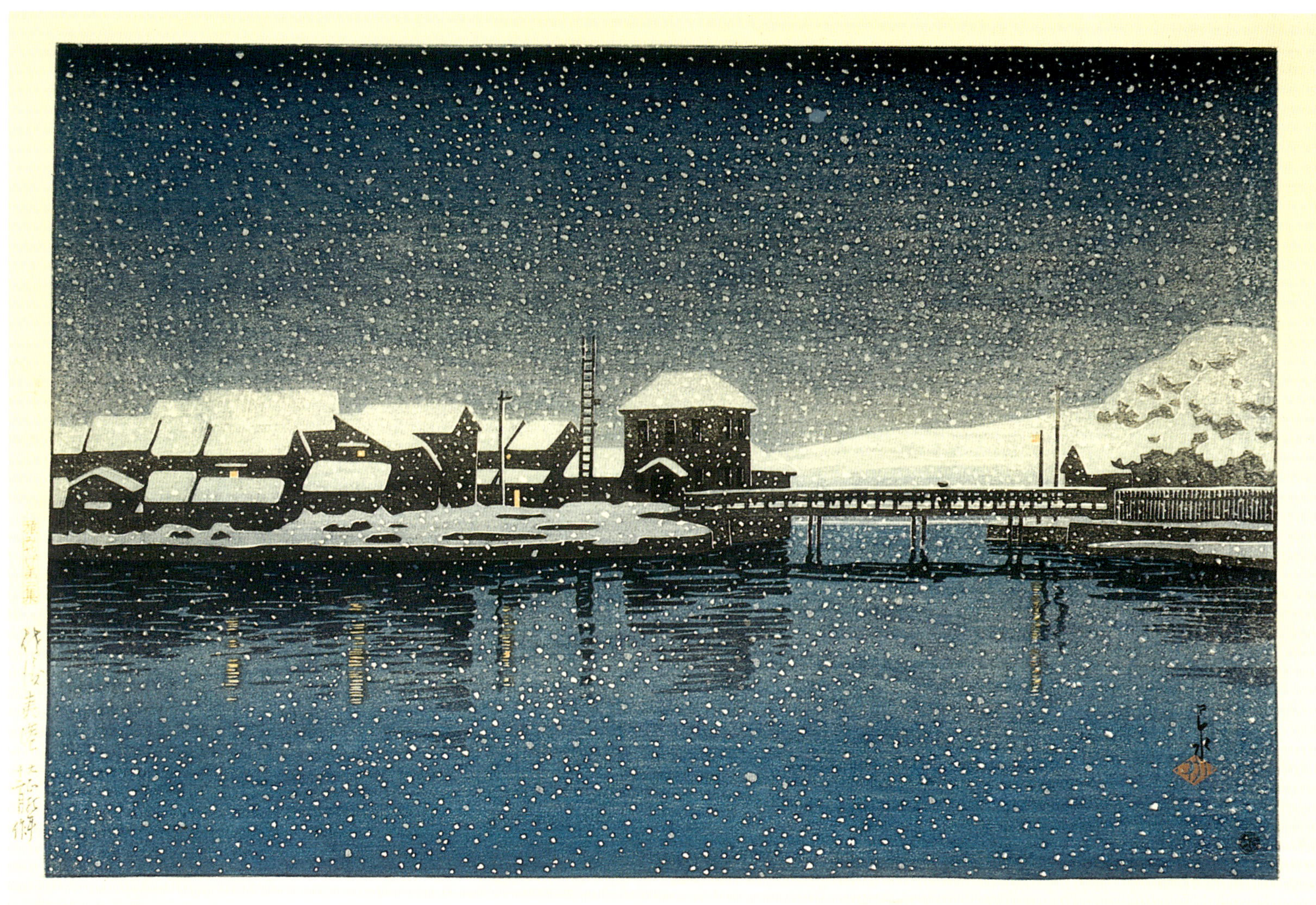

58
"The Port of Ebisu, Sado"
Sado Ebisu wan

SERIES *Souvenirs of Travel, Second Series (Tabi miyage dainishū)*
DATE 1921 (Taishō 10), December
SIGNATURE *Hasui*
ARTIST'S SEAL *Kawase*
PUBLISHER Watanabe Shōzaburō
SIZE 24.0 x 37.2 cm
PROVENANCE Yamanaka & Co., New York, November 1936
ACCESSION NUMBER S2003.8.621
REFERENCE Brown *et al.* (2003), no. 78

Sado is the largest of the islands in the Sea of Japan and is part of Niigata Prefecture. Despite its fame as a beauty spot, historically it was also known as a place of exile. Its most famous guest was undoubtedly the Buddhist priest Nichiren (1222-82). Hasui liked Sado and honored it with eight other prints in this series.

59

"Sunset at Gōmoto, Echigo Province"

Rakuyō (*Gōmoto Echigo*)

DATE 1921 (Taishō 10), August 28th
SIGNED Unsigned
ARTIST'S SEAL *Hasui*
PUBLISHER Watanabe Shōzaburō
SIZE 33.3 x 21.3 cm
PROVENANCE Louis W. Black, Boston, February 1958
ACCESSION NUMBER S2003.8.641
REFERENCE Brown *et al.* (2003), no. 80

The interplay between the traces of the *baren* (a circular implement used to rub the paper on the inked woodblocks) and the wood grain produce an extremely painterly effect. The unusual, slightly smaller print size is noteworthy, as is the obvious misregistration of the blocks for the sky.

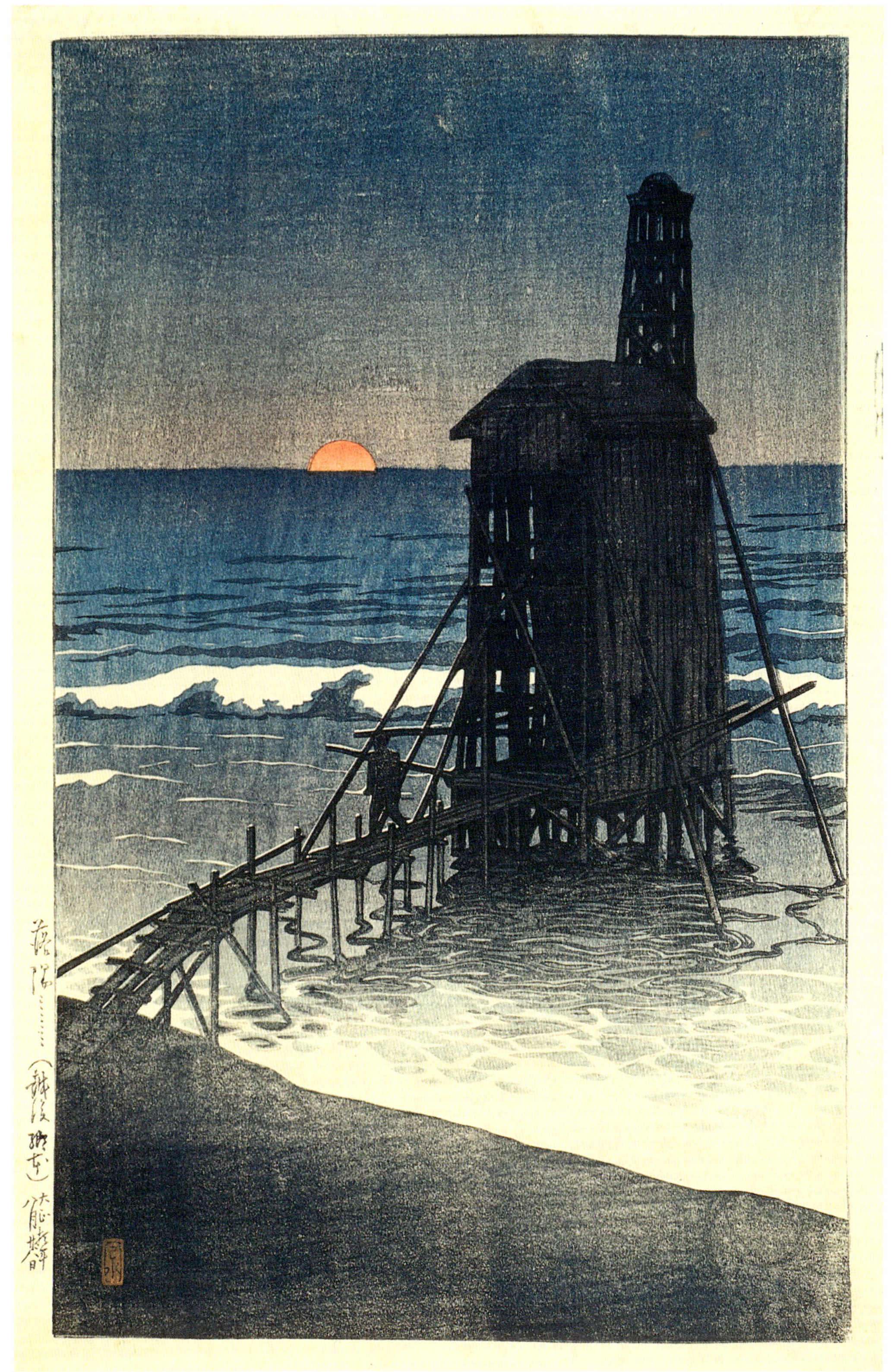

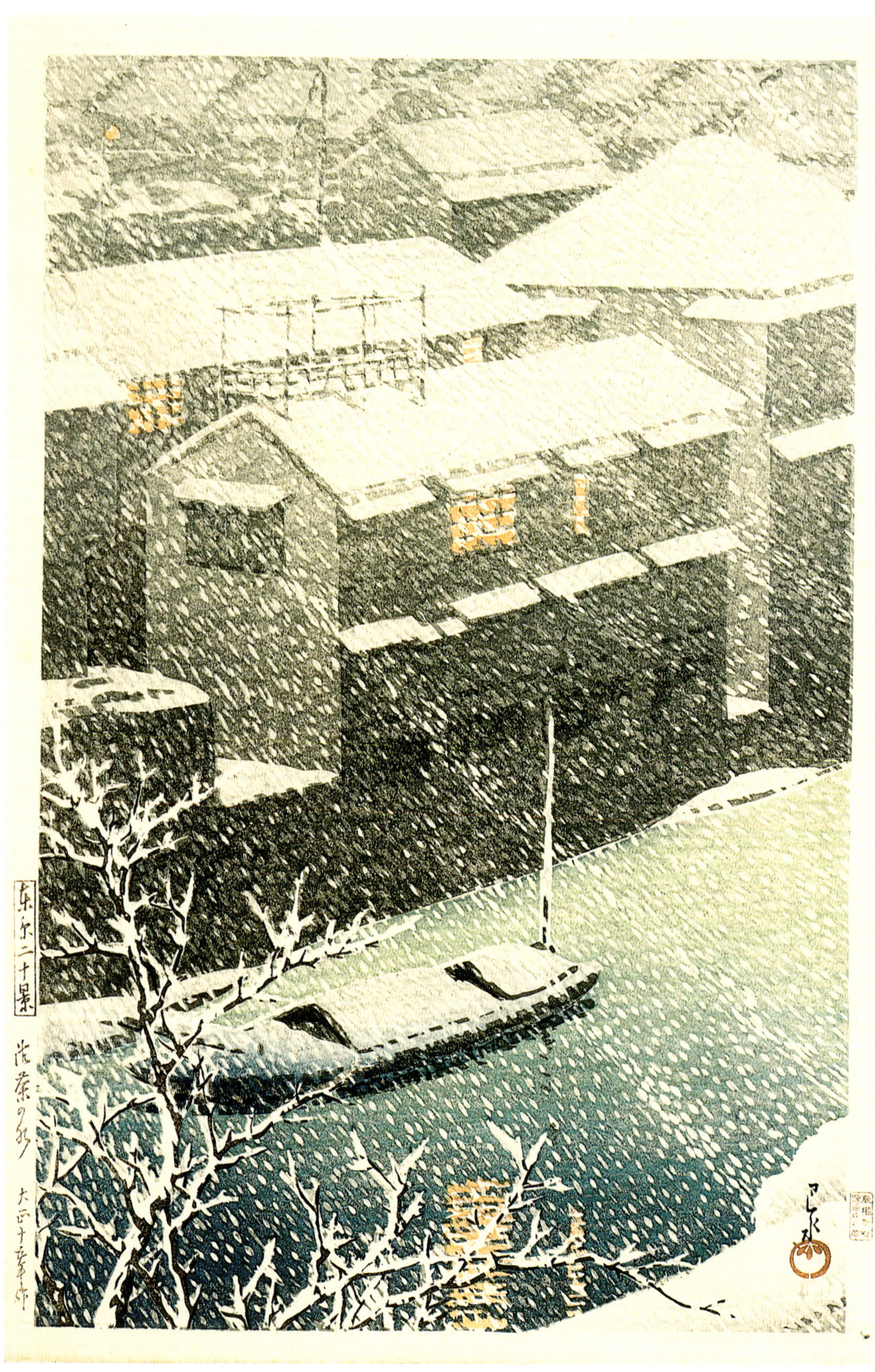

60

"Ochanomizu"

Ochanomizu

SERIES *Twenty Views of Tokyo (Tōkyō nijūkei)*
DATE 1926 (Taishō 15)
SIGNATURE *Hasui*
ARTIST'S SEAL *Kawase*
PUBLISHER Watanabe Shōzaburō
SIZE 36.8 x 24 cm
PROVENANCE Hirota, Boston, April 1935
ACCESSION NUMBER S2003.8.677
REFERENCE Brown *et al.* (2003), no. 150

A winter blizzard blows across a canal from which water was once drawn for tea for the second Tokugawa shogun, Hidetada (1579-1632). Hence the name "Ochanomizu," or "tea water."

61

"Tennō Temple, Osaka"

Ōsaka Tennōji

SERIES *Souvenirs of Travel, Third Series* (*Tabi miyage daisanshū*)
DATE 1927 (Shōwa 2)
SIGNATURE *Hasui*
ARTIST'S SEAL *Kawase*
PUBLISHER Watanabe Shōzaburō
SIZE 36.3 x 23.8 cm
PROVENANCE Hadassah Thrift Shop, New Haven, Conn., April 1977
ACCESSION NUMBER S2003.8.686
REFERENCE Brown *et al.* (2003), no. 135

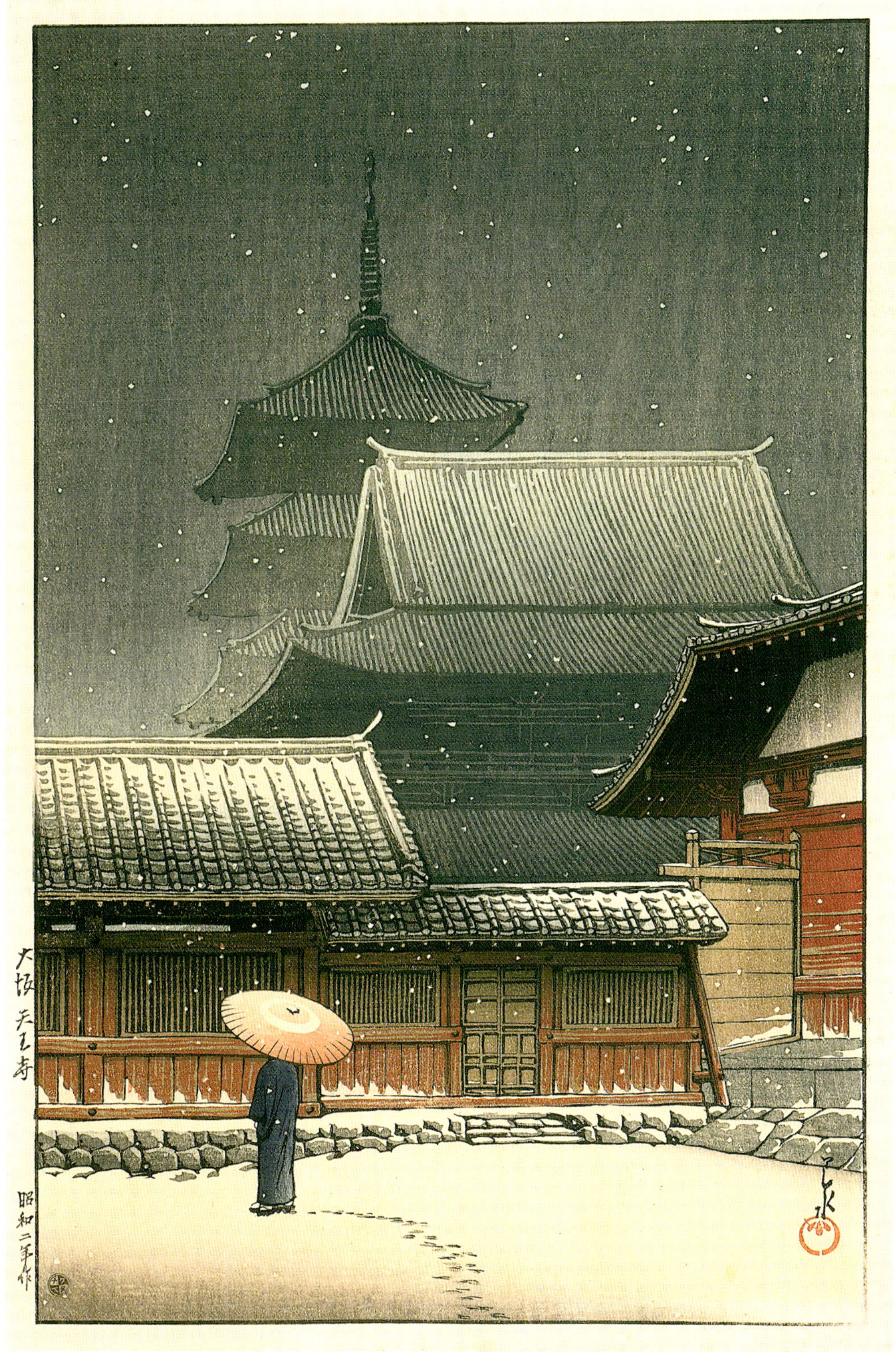

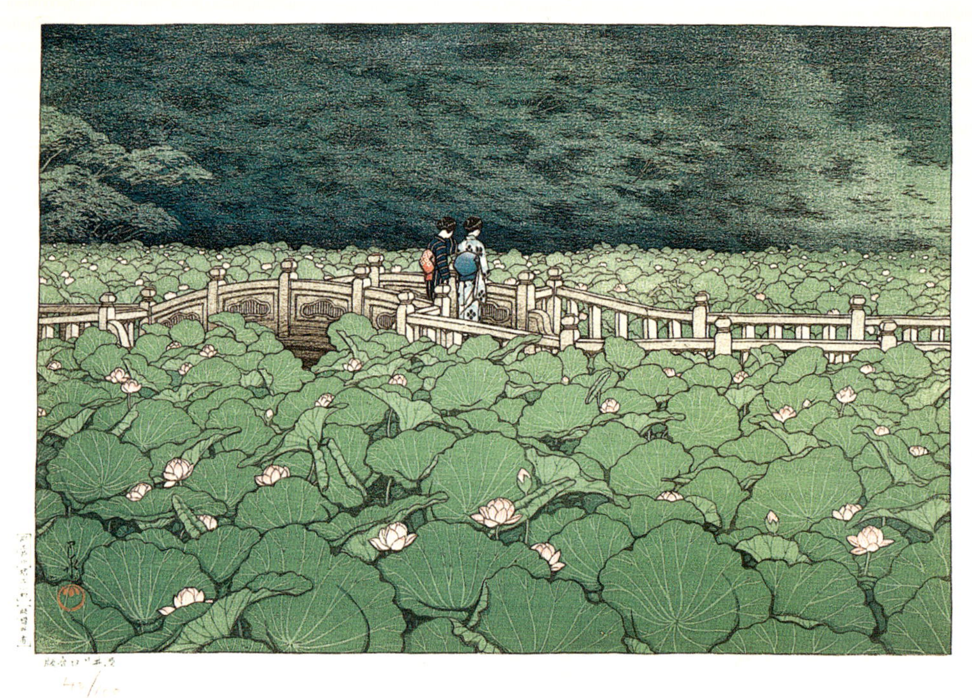

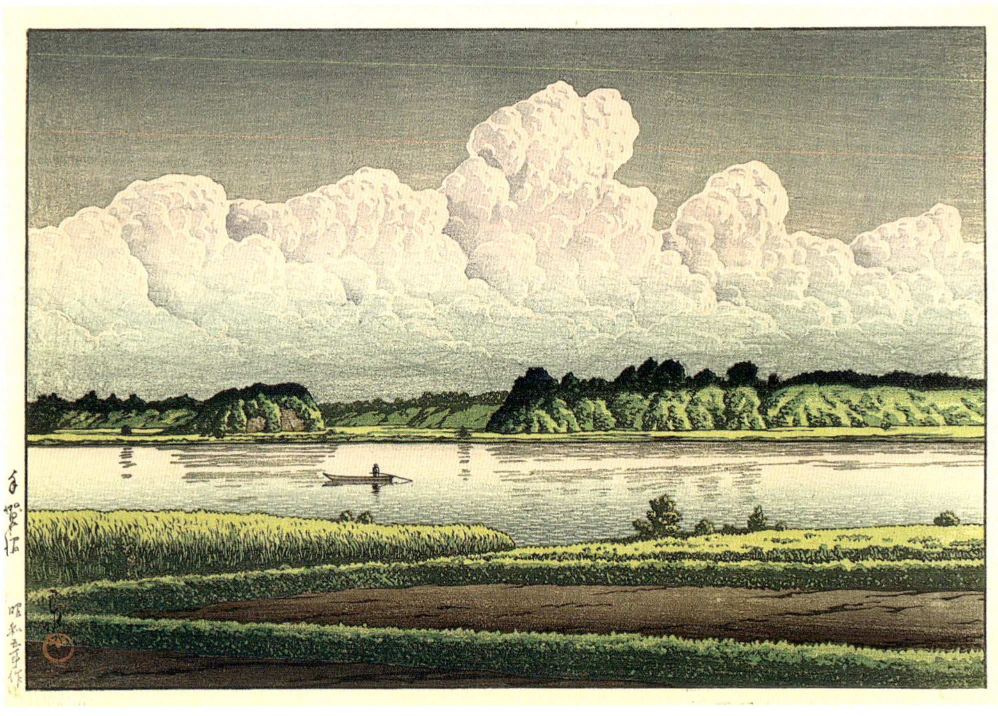

62

"Benten Pond, Shiba"

Shiba Benten ike

DATE 1929 (Shōwa 4), August
SIGNATURE *Hasui*
ARTIST'S SEAL *Kawase*
PUBLISHER Sakai/Kawaguchi
EDITION Number 40 from an edition of 100 copies
SIZE 24.0 x 36.4 cm
PROVENANCE Shima Art Collection, 1940
ACCESSION NUMBER S2003.8.717
REFERENCE Brown *et al.* (2003), no. 186

The join publishers Sakai/Kawaguchi often numbered their prints. It is generally acknowledged that there was a first-edition print run of 100 copies, all numbered on the back in a small rectangular paper seal and signed by the artist. The second edition consists of 350 copies, and a third edition was unnumbered.

Sakai/Kawaguchi prints appear more textured than those issued by the Watanabe firm. The paper can be somewhat thicker and more absorbent, and the design is bordered by much wider margins.

63

"Tega Marsh"

Teganuma

DATE 1930 (Shōwa 5)
SIGNATURE *Hasui*
ARTIST'S SEAL *Kawase*
PUBLISHER Watanabe Shōzaburō
SIZE 23.8 x 36.1 cm
PROVENANCE Ronin Gallery, New York, June 1978
ACCESSION NUMBER S2003.8.724
REFERENCE Brown *et al.* (2003), no. 209

Traces of the circular movement of the *baren* (*see also* cat. no. 59 above) are employed here to add an extra dimension to the lower sections of the clouds.

Yamamura Kōka (Toyonari) (1886-1942)

Yamamura Kōka was born in the Shinagawa district of Tokyo. He was a pupil of Ogata Gekkō (1859-1920) from 1896 and studied *Nihonga* at the *Tōkyō Bijutsu Gakkō* (Tokyo School of Fine Arts). He graduated in 1907 and in the same year he exhibited a painting at the first *Bunten*. He received an award at the fourth *Bunten* in 1910 for the work "Courtier" (*Ōmiyabito*). He also showed at the *Inten* and with the *Ugōkai* (Cormorant Society). Kōka was very interested in the theatrical arts, historical and genre painting. He was also a collector and scholar of *Ukiyo-e*, and in 1919 he published *Shibai nishiki-e shūsei* (*Compendium of Theatrical Woodblock Prints*) together with Machida Hakuzō. His involvement in theatrical subjects led to his collaboration in 1915 with Natori Shunsen (1886-1960; cat. nos. 72-5) and Torii Kotondo (1900-76; cat. nos. 105-11) on the *Shin Nigao-e* (*New Actor Portraits*), a short-lived journal that promoted and advertised the Kabuki theater. In 1916 Kōka became member of the *Saikō Nihon Bijutsuin* (Reorganized Japan Art Institute). He produced the first of some thirty-two prints with Watanabe Shōzaburō (1885-1962) in 1916, after the publisher had seen one of the artist's paintings. From 1920 to 1922 their cooperation resulted in the twelve actor prints in the series *Flowers of the Theatrical World* (*Rien no hana*). After the Great Kantō Earthquake of 1 September 1923 and the destruction of his work at the Watanabe shop, Kōka began to focus on other subjects, such as *bijinga* and landscapes, and his working relationship with Watanabe seems to have ended. Like so many *Shin-hanga* artists, his paintings far outnumbered his printed works. Kōka is also known by the artist's name *Toyonari*, a name that frequently appears on his paintings.

REFERENCES Merritt and Yamada (1992), 172; Stephens (ed.) (1993), 153-58; Yui (1998), 409; Hamanaka and Newland (2000), 89-92, 212

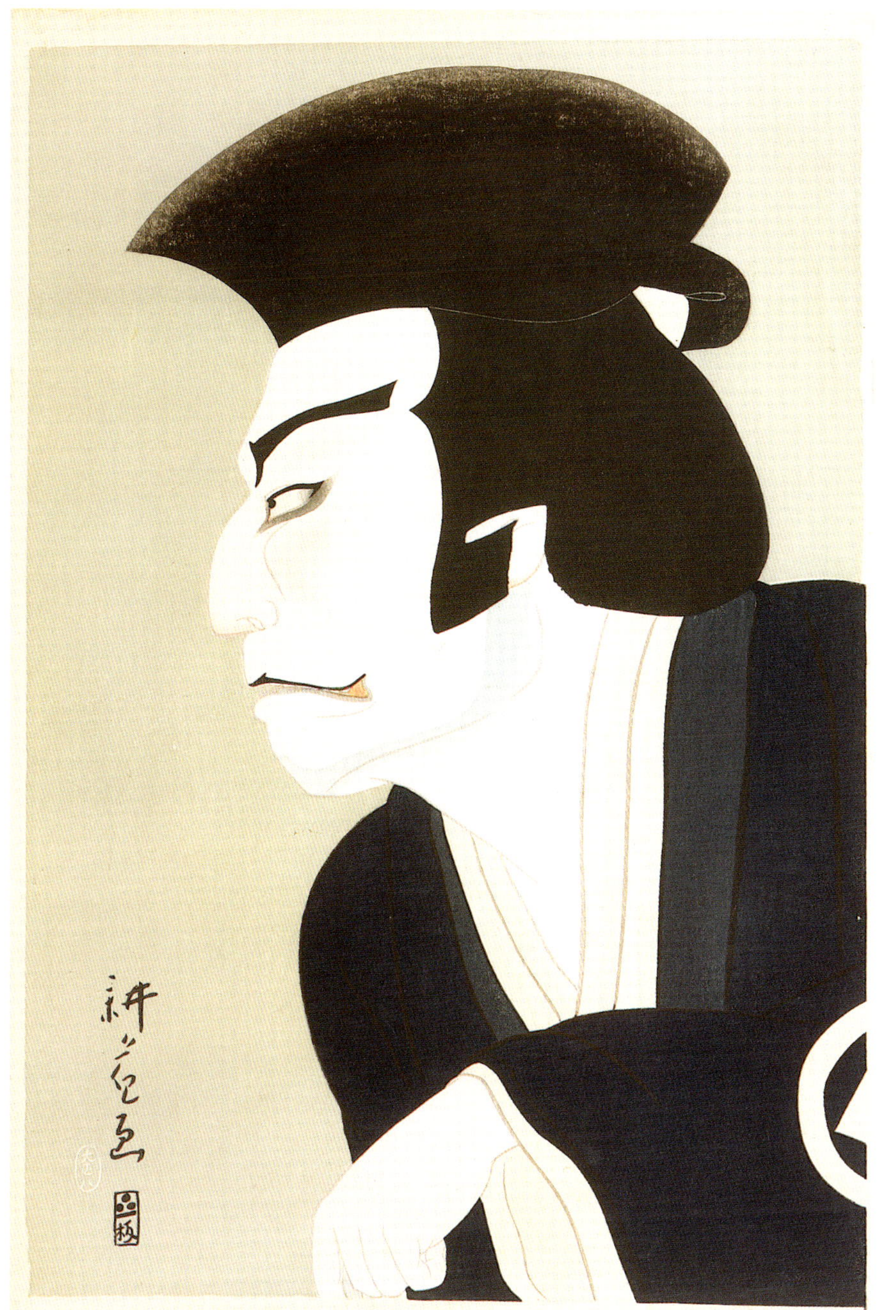

64
"The Actor Ichikawa Danshirō II as Tesshinsai in the Play *Kyōkaku harusame-gasa* (*The Chivalrous Commoner's Spring Raincoat*)"

DATE Undated, c. 1919
SIGNATURE *Yamamura ga*
PUBLISHER Watanabe Shōzaburō
SIZE 27.6 x 40.0 cm
PROVENANCE Shōbisha (Matsuki Kihachirō), Tokyo, June 1940
ACCESSION NUMBER S2003.8.3410
REFERENCES Stephens (ed.) (1993), cat. no. 179; for a synopsis of the play and the role, see page 119

While most would agree that the Kabuki actor print is perhaps not the most easily accessible genre for a Western audience, it can be argued that the marriage between the genre and the medium of printmaking reached new heights in Kōka's work in the combination of graphic abstraction with powerful compositional elements. This "sculpted" profile view of the actor Ichikawa Danshirō II (1855-1922) has an almost Art Deco feel to it. The concise lines, large areas of flat color – can a print be any more "graphic"?

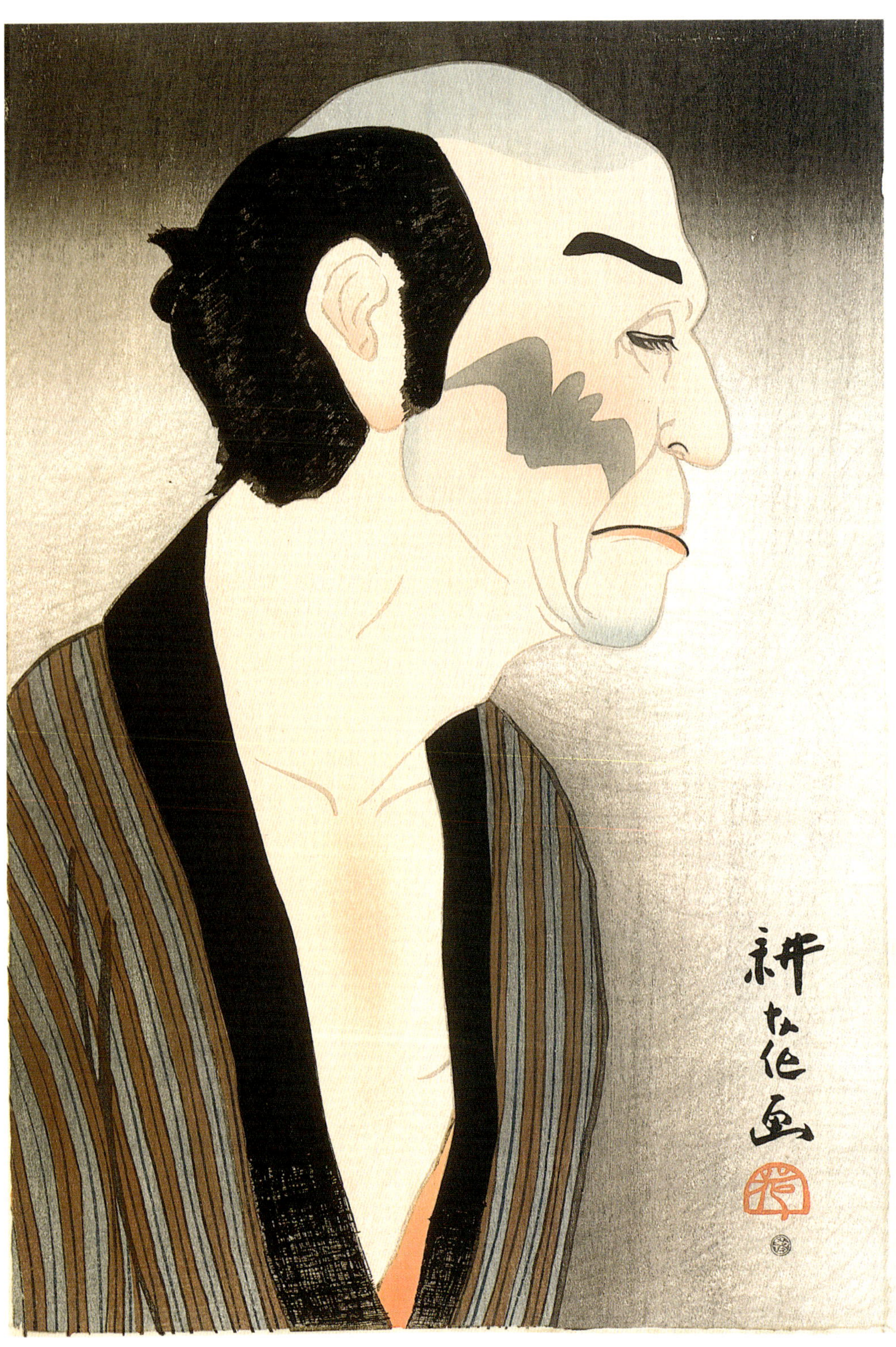

65

"The Actor Onoe Matsusuke IV as Kōmori Yasu in the Play *Yowa nasake ukina yokogushi (The Love Affair of Otomi and Scarface Yosaburō)*"

DATE Undated, *c.* 1919

SIGNATURE *Kōka ga*

ARTIST'S SEAL *Kōka*

PUBLISHER Watanabe Shōzaburō

SIZE 27.7 x 40.0 cm

PROVENANCE Shōbisha (Matsuki Kihachirō), Tokyo, April 1940

ACCESSION NUMBER S2003.8.3434

REFERENCES Stephens (ed.) (1993), cat. no. 177; for a synopsis of the play and the role, see page 119

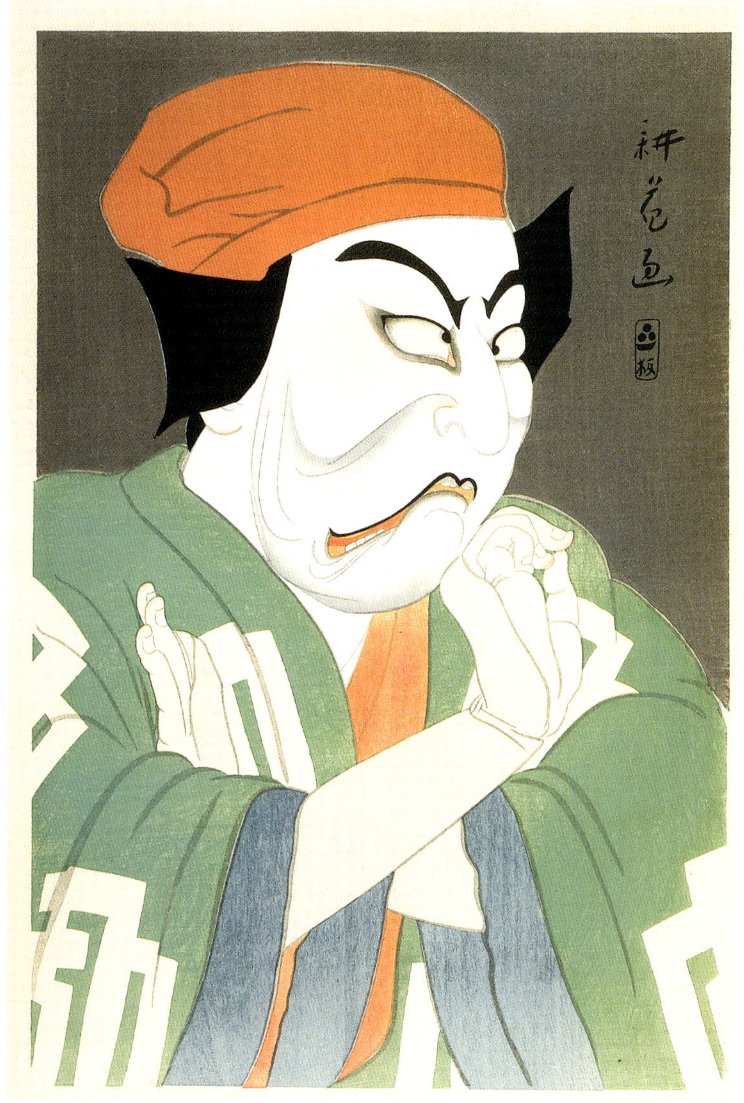

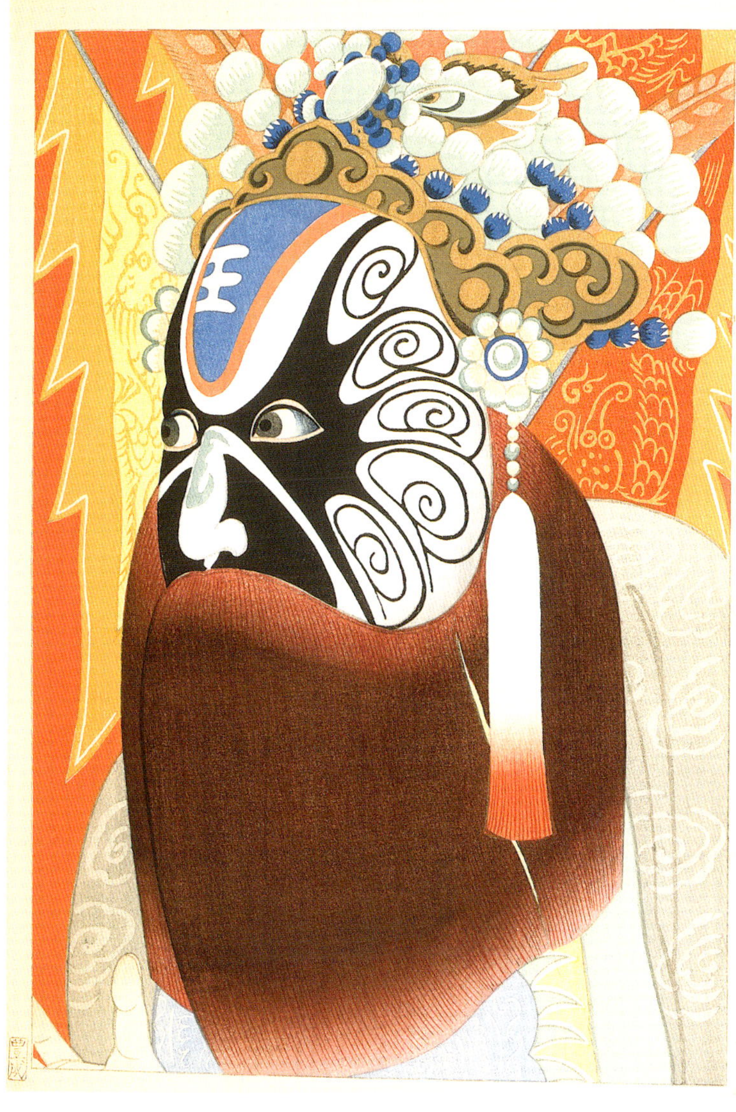

66

"The Actor Matsumoto Kōshirō VII as Sekibei in the Play *Seki no to* (*Love at the Snow-covered Barrier Gate*)"

DATE Undated, c. 1919
SIGNATURE *Toyonari ga*
PUBLISHER Watanabe Shōzaburō
SIZE 27.2 × 39.9 cm
PROVENANCE Shōbisha (Matsuki Kihachirō), Tokyo, June 1940
ACCESSION NUMBER S2003.8.3433
REFERENCES Stephens (ed.) (1993), cat. no. 178; for a synopsis of the play and the role, see page 119

67

"An Actor in an Unidentified Chinese Play"

DATE Undated, c. 1926
SIGNATURE Unsigned
ARTIST'S SEAL *Toyonari*
PUBLISHER Watanabe Shōzaburō
SIZE 26.0 × 37.8 cm
PROVENANCE Shōbisha (Matsuki Kihachirō), June 1940
ACCESSION NUMBER S2003.8.3411

Robert O. Muller kept meticulous records, and he once noted that Watanabe Shōzaburō's son, Watanabe Tadasu, dated this print to 1926. However, Muller felt that it could have been made before the Great Kantō Earthquake of September 1923. The portrayal of a theatrical subject not related to Kabuki is without precedence in *Shin-hanga*. The rarity of this piece suggests, however, that it may not have been a commercial success.

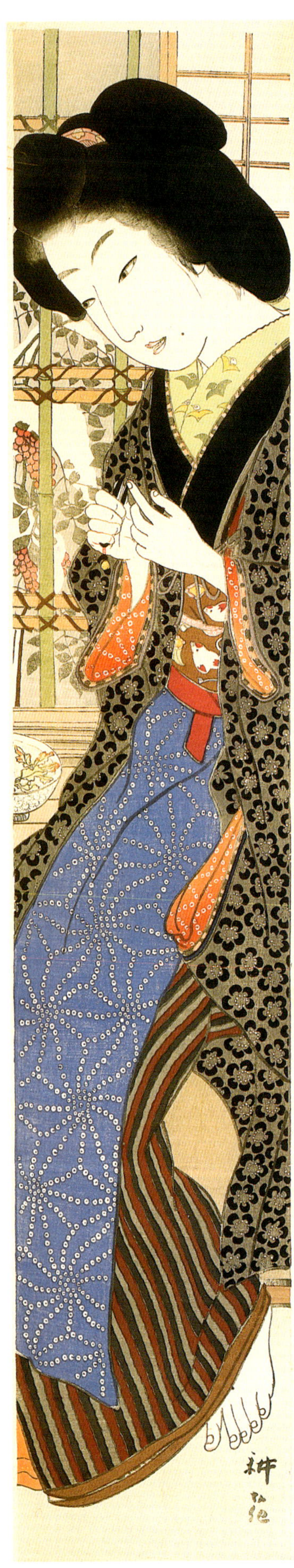

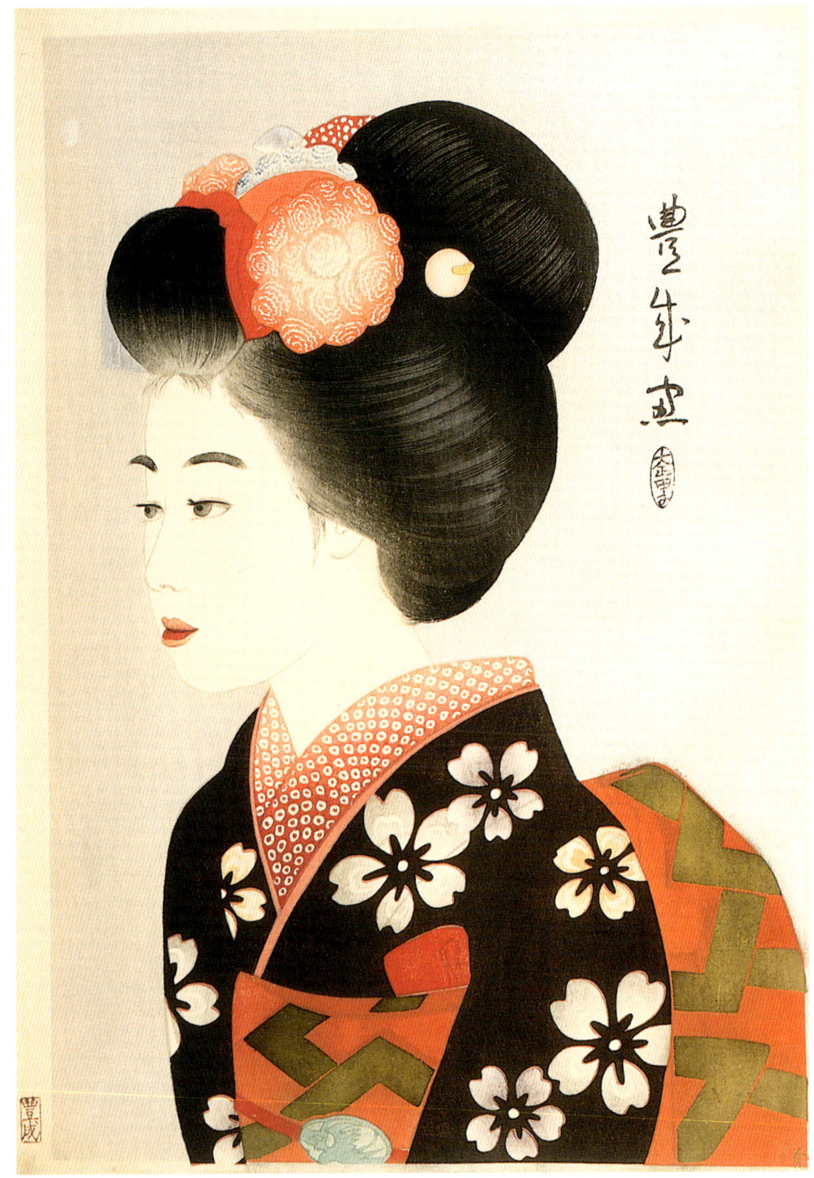

68

"Typical Daughter of Downtown Edo"

DATE Undated, *c.* 1935

SIGNATURE *Kōka*

SIZE 74.3 x 14.0 cm

PROVENANCE Marumiya, Tokyo, 1940, April 1940

ACCESSION NUMBER S2003.8.3408

REFERENCES Stephens (ed.) (1993), cat. no. 187; Hamanaka and Newland (2000), no. 118

This long narrow work, or *hashira-e* (literally, "pillar print"), is the only *Shin-hanga* print in this format. Robert O. Muller purchased this print directly from the artist. In his notes Muller assigns it a date of 1935, which we can assume was given to him by Kōka.

69

"Portrait of a Maiko"

DATE 1924 (Taishō [Year of the] Rat)

SIGNATURE *Toyonari ga*

ARTIST'S SEAL *Toyonari*

PUBLISHER Watanabe Shōzaburō

SIZE 38.3 x 26.4 cm

PROVENANCE Shōbisha (Matsuki Kihachirō), Tokyo, April 1940

ACCESSION NUMBER S2003.8.3407

REFERENCE Hamanaka and Newland (2000), no. 113

70
"Dancing at the New Carlton Hotel in Shanghai"

DATE 1924
SIGNATURE Unsigned
ARTIST'S SEALS (on print) *Kōka* and (left margin) *Toyonari*
PUBLISHER Yamamura Kōka Hanga Kankōkai (Publishing Committee for Yamamura Kōka's Prints)
SIZE 29.7 x 40.0 cm
PROVENANCE Shōbisha (Matsuki Kihachirō), Tokyo, April 1940
ACCESSION NUMBER S2003.8.3419
REFERENCES Hamanaka and Newland (2000), no. 115; Brown and Minichiello (2002), cat. no. 1

In this unique work Kōka depicts "modern" women of the 1920s as they imbibe the nightlife at the New Carlton Hotel in Shanghai, a city which at this time was a bustling cosmopolitan metropolis. These "flappers" are a far cry from the traditional idealized face of Japanese womanhood crystallized in *bijinga* by artists like Itō Shinsui (1898-1972; cat. nos. 85-101) or Hirano Hakuhō (1879-1957; cat. nos. 34-5). Instead, this avant-garde composition is more in league with the work of Kobayakawa Kiyoshi (1899-1948; cat. nos. 81-3).

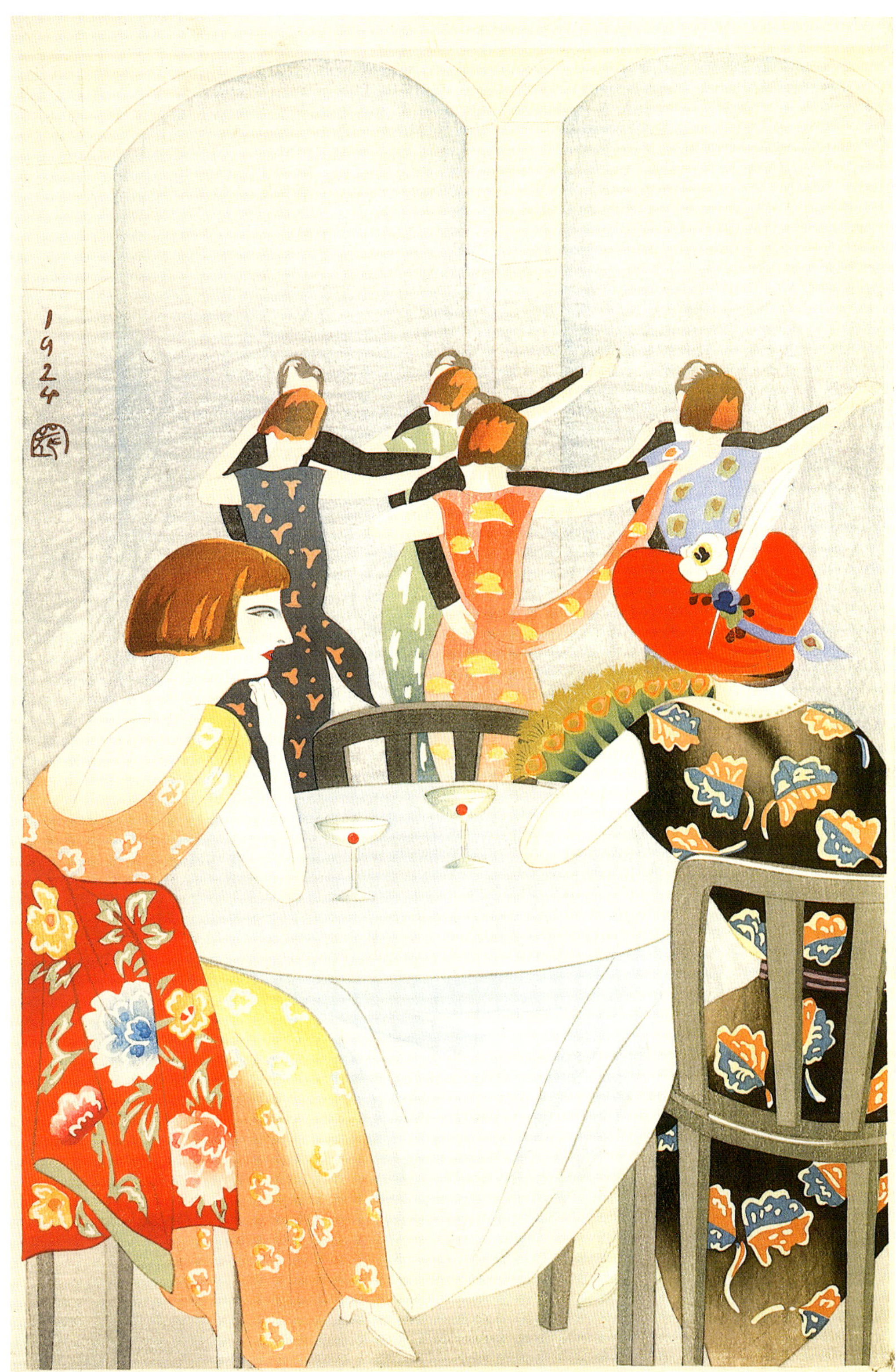

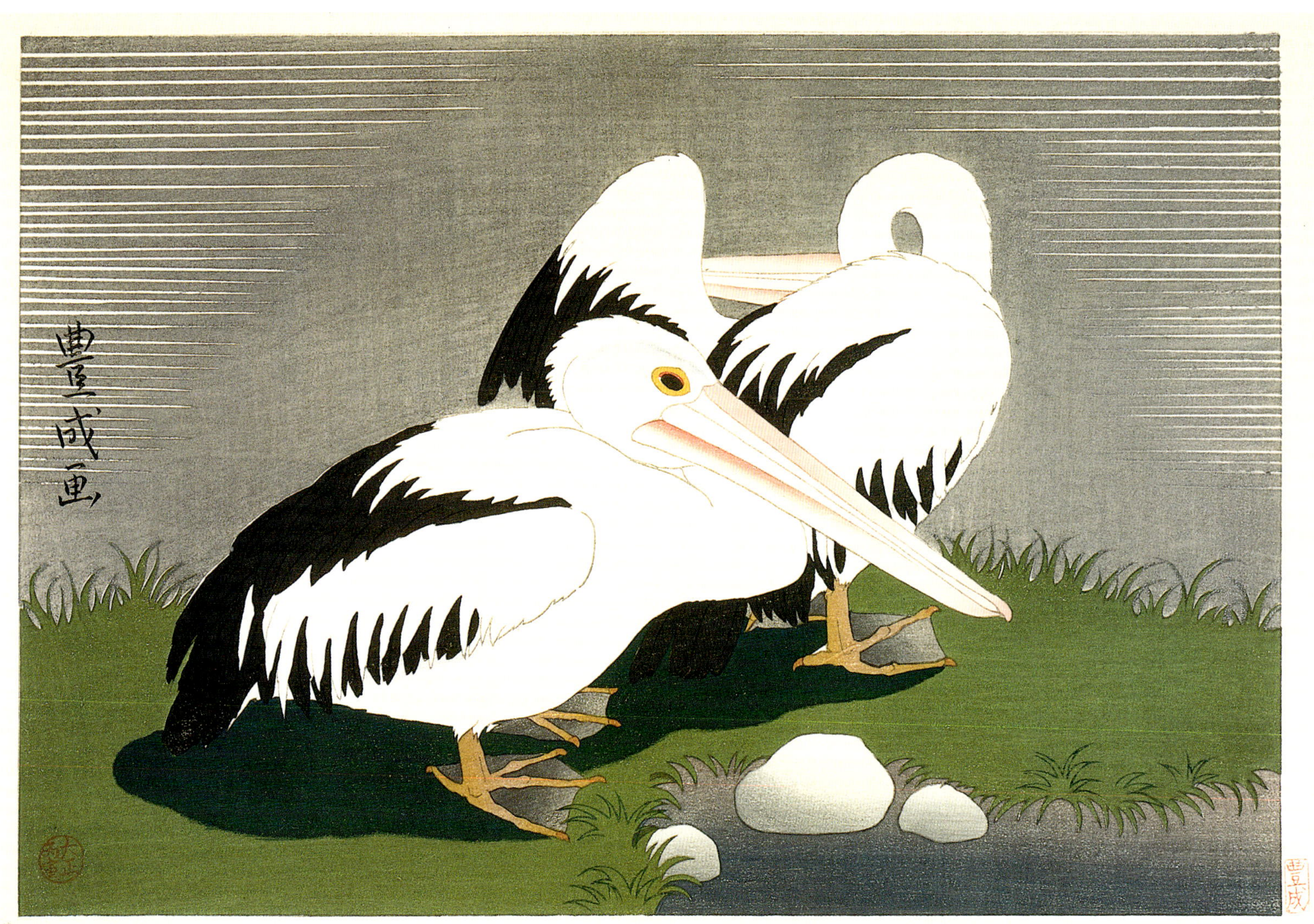

71
"Pelicans"

DATE 1926 (Taishō [Year of the] Tiger)
SIGNATURE *Toyonari ga*
ARTIST'S SEAL *Toyonari*
PUBLISHER Watanabe Shōzaburō
SIZE 25.3 × 37.3 cm
PROVENANCE Yamanaka & Co., New York, September 1937
ACCESSION NUMBER S2003.8.3413

Sumptuously printed with the use of silver colorants and blind-printing or gauffrage, this work is singular within Kōka's oeuvre. It is perhaps more reminiscent of European graphic artists like Fritz Lang (1877-1966) than of Japanese *kachōga* ("bird-and-flower pictures"). Kōka created numerous paintings of subjects drawn from nature, normally in a delicate *Nihonga* style and sometimes imbued with the decorative qualities more closely associated with the *Rinpa* school. By contrast, in his prints Kōka can be considered among the most forward-looking in *Shin-hanga* in terms of assimilating foreign artistic influences.

Natori Shunsen (1886-1960)

Natori Shunsen was born Natori Yoshinosuke in Ogasawara, Yamanashi Prefecture. Following the bankruptcy of his father's business, the Natori family moved to Tokyo in 1887. In 1897 he studied *Nihonga* under Kubota Beisen (1852-1906) and later under Beisen's son Kubota Kinsen (1875-1954). In 1905 he became a pupil of Hirafuku Hyakusui (1877-1933) and worked as an illustrator for the *Tōkyō Asahi Shinbun* (*Tokyo Daily Newspaper*) from 1907. He also illustrated novels, including *Sanshirō* (1908) by Natsume Sōseki (1867-1916), who was a colleague at the *Tōkyō Asahi Shinbun*. Shunsen exhibited at the *Inten*, *Teiten* and at other official shows. From 1915 he began designing actor prints [e.g., *Shin Nigao-e* (*New Actor Portraits*) with Yamamura Kōka (Toyonari) (1886-1942; cat. nos. 64-71) and Torii Kotondo (1900-76; cat. nos. 105-11)], and in the following year issued his first prints with the publisher Watanabe Shōzaburō (1885-1962). He became member of the *Saikō Nihon Bijutsuin* (Reorganized Japan Art Institute) in 1918. Shunsen became an important designer of actor prints and after the 1930 exhibition at the Toledo Museum of Art he received international recognition. In 1933 his prints were shown at the Warsaw International Print Exhibition. Shunsen and his second wife Shigeko committed double suicide on March 30, 1960, after the unexpected death of their daughter Yoshiko from pneumonia in 1958. Shunsen produced eighty-nine *ōban* format prints, many paintings and hundreds of book illustrations.

REFERENCES Watanabe Shōzaburō (1936), 93; Merritt and Yamada (1992), 107-8; Stephens (ed.) (1993), 161-64; Yui (1998), 283; Hamanaka and Newland (2000), 119-22, 211; Ikeda and Balluteau (2001)

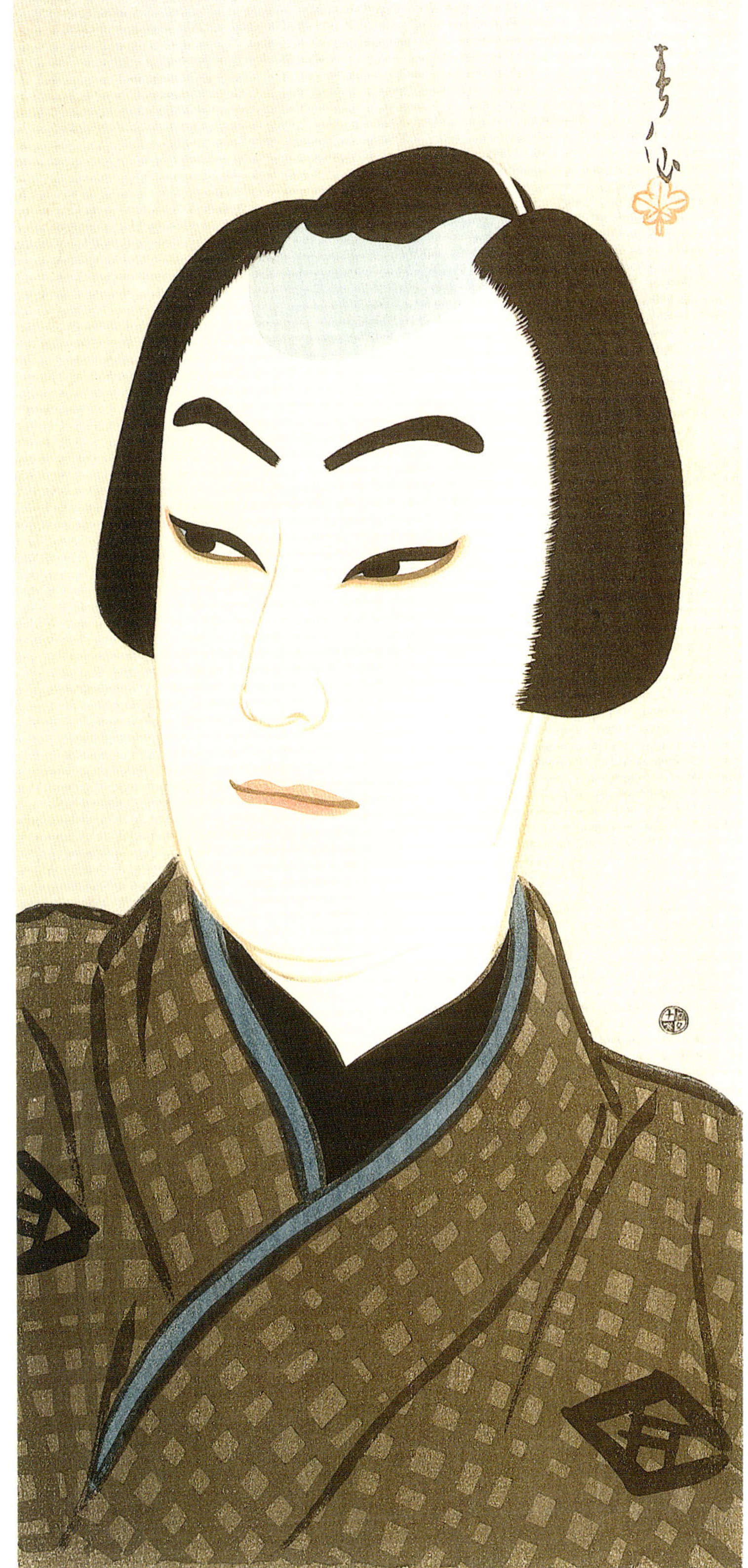

72

"The Actor Nakamura Ganjirō I as Kamiya Jihei in the Play *Shinjū ten no Amijima* (*Love Suicide at Amijima*)"

DATE Undated, c. 1916
SIGNATURE *Shunsen*, with artist's leaf seal
PUBLISHER Watanabe Shōzaburō
SIZE 51.1 x 24.8 cm
PROVENANCE Watanabe Shōzaburō, April 1940
ACCESSION NUMBER S2003.8.1546
REFERENCES Stephens (ed.) (1993), cat. no. 193; Ikeda and Balluteau (2001), 40; for a synopsis of the play and the role, see pages 119-20

This example is Shunsen's first of two prints issued in 1916 with the publisher Watanabe Shōzaburō. Their collaboration was realized after Watanabe saw a painting of the same subject in an exhibition at the Gahakudō Gallery, and they agreed to release a print of it. Both print designs were produced in a long, narrow format. This particular design of Nakamura Ganjirō I (1860-1935) is deservedly a *Shin-hanga* masterpiece: the facial lines have been over-printed in a sepia hue, and the mica background is indicative of the high quality of this piece.

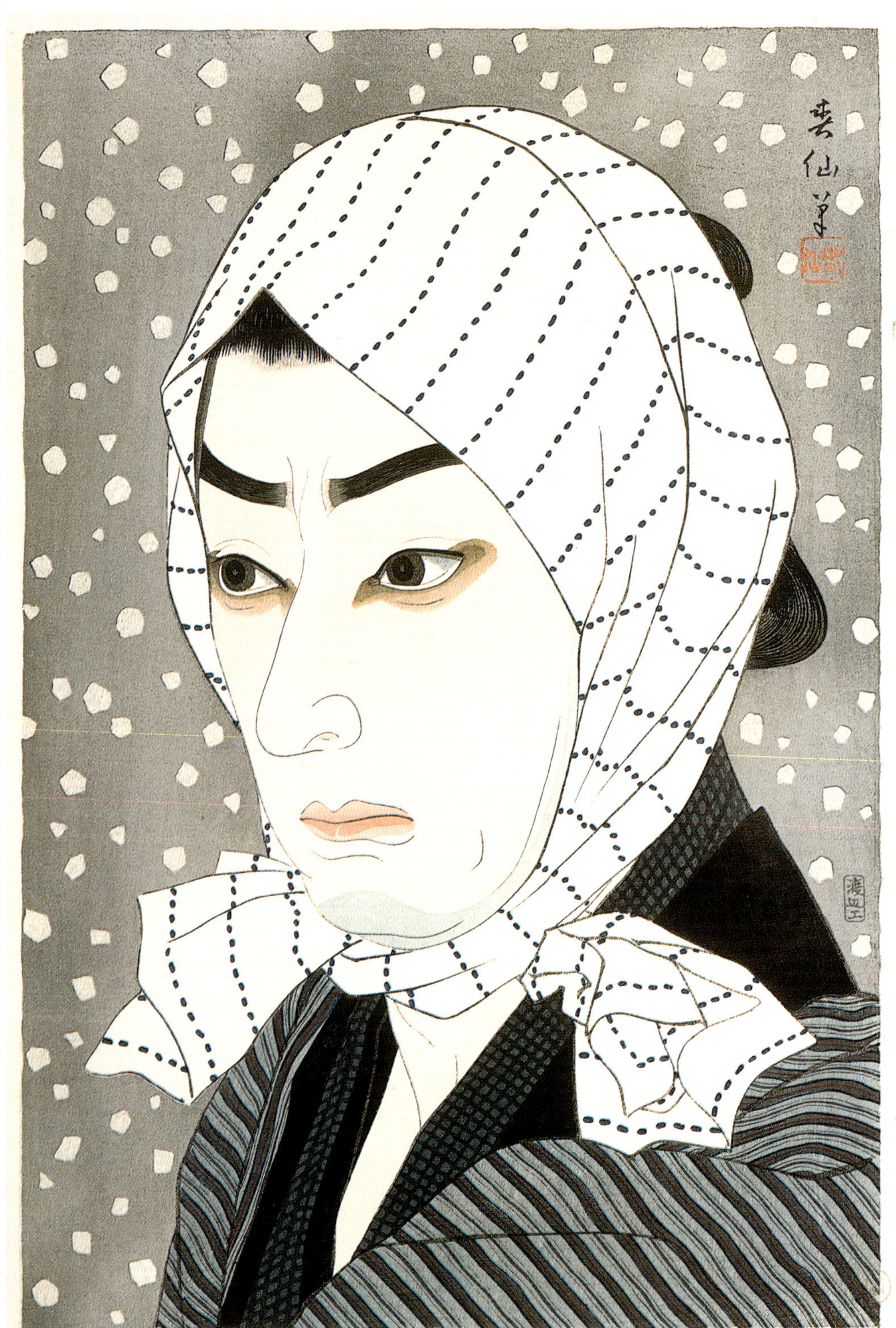

73
"The Actor Ichimura Uzaemon XV as Iriya Naozamurai in the Play *Naozamurai*"

SERIES *Collection of Shunsen Portraits* (*Shunsen nigao-e shū*)
DATE Undated, c. 1925
SIGNATURE *Shunsen hitsu*
ARTIST'S SEAL *Shunsen*
PUBLISHER Watanabe Shōzaburō
SIZE 37.9 x 26.0 cm
PROVENANCE Watanabe Shōzaburō, Tokyo, October 1936
ACCESSION NUMBER S2003.8.1551
REFERENCES The Toledo Museum of Art (ed.) (1930), cat. no. 329; Stephens (ed.) (1993), cat. no. 194; Ikeda and Balluteau (2001) cat. no. 9; Kushigata City Shunsen Museum of Art (ed.) (2002), no. 21; for a synopsis of the play and the role, see page 120

This print belongs to a series of thirty-six actor portraits which Watanabe Shōzaburō released from May 1925 to 1929 (with fifteen more images were added up until 1934). They were issued in a special paper folder, listing the names of the actors and their roles. It is representative of the majority of Shunsen's work: an expressive *ōkubi-e* ("large-head picture") executed with an extreme economy of line. Due to his association with Watanabe, Shunsen must have had access to any number of highly stylized *ōkubi-e* from the late eighteenth and nineteenth centuries designed by *Ukiyo-e* print artists Tōshūsai Sharaku (act. *c.* 1794-95), the Katsukawa-school artists Shunei (1762-1819) and Shunkō (1743-1812), the Utagawa-school artists Kunimasa (1773-1810) and Toyokuni (1769-1825), and others. The last nineteenth-century artist working in the genre was Toyohara Kunichika (1835-1900), whose dedication to the Kabuki subject draws an easy comparison with Shunsen. In 1930 thirty-two of the designs from *Collection of Shunsen Portraits* were exhibited at the Toledo Museum of Art; Shunsen was to contribute only seven prints to the 1936 show.

Many *Shin-hanga* prints – landscapes, beauties and bird-and-flower prints – were reliant on sales to a foreign clientele. But it seems that actor prints by Shunsen, Yamamura Kōka (Toyonari) (1886-1942; cat. nos. 64-71) and Yoshikawa Kanpō (1894-1979; cat. nos. 78-80), his contemporaries in the actor print genre, targeted a domestic audience. Perhaps the disproportionately large number of actor prints in the first 1930 Toledo show can be interpreted as an extra effort to market these prints abroad.

74

"The Actor Ichikawa Kigan V as Otomi in the Play *Yowa nasake ukina yokogushi* (*The Love Affair of Otomi and Scarface Yosaburō*)"

SERIES *Collection of Shunsen Portraits (Shunsen nigao-e shū)*
DATE Undated, *c.* 1927
SIGNATURE AND ARTIST'S SEAL *Shunsen*
PUBLISHER Watanabe Shōzaburō
SIZE 37.9 x 25.4 cm
PROVENANCE Kabutoya, Tokyo, May 1984
ACCESSION NUMBER S2003.8.1556
REFERENCES The Toledo Museum of Art (ed.) (1930), cat. no. 149; Ikeda and Balluteau (2001), cat. no. 22; Kushigata City Shunsen Museum of Art (ed.) (2002), no. 32; for a synopsis of the play and role, see page 120

Any major series of Kabuki actor prints such as this would certainly include designs depicting *onnagata* (literally, "female person"). In the Kabuki theater, all actors were male and the playing of female roles was assumed by *onnagata* – Ichikawa Kigan V (1887-1978) had an established reputation in this difficult dramatic form.

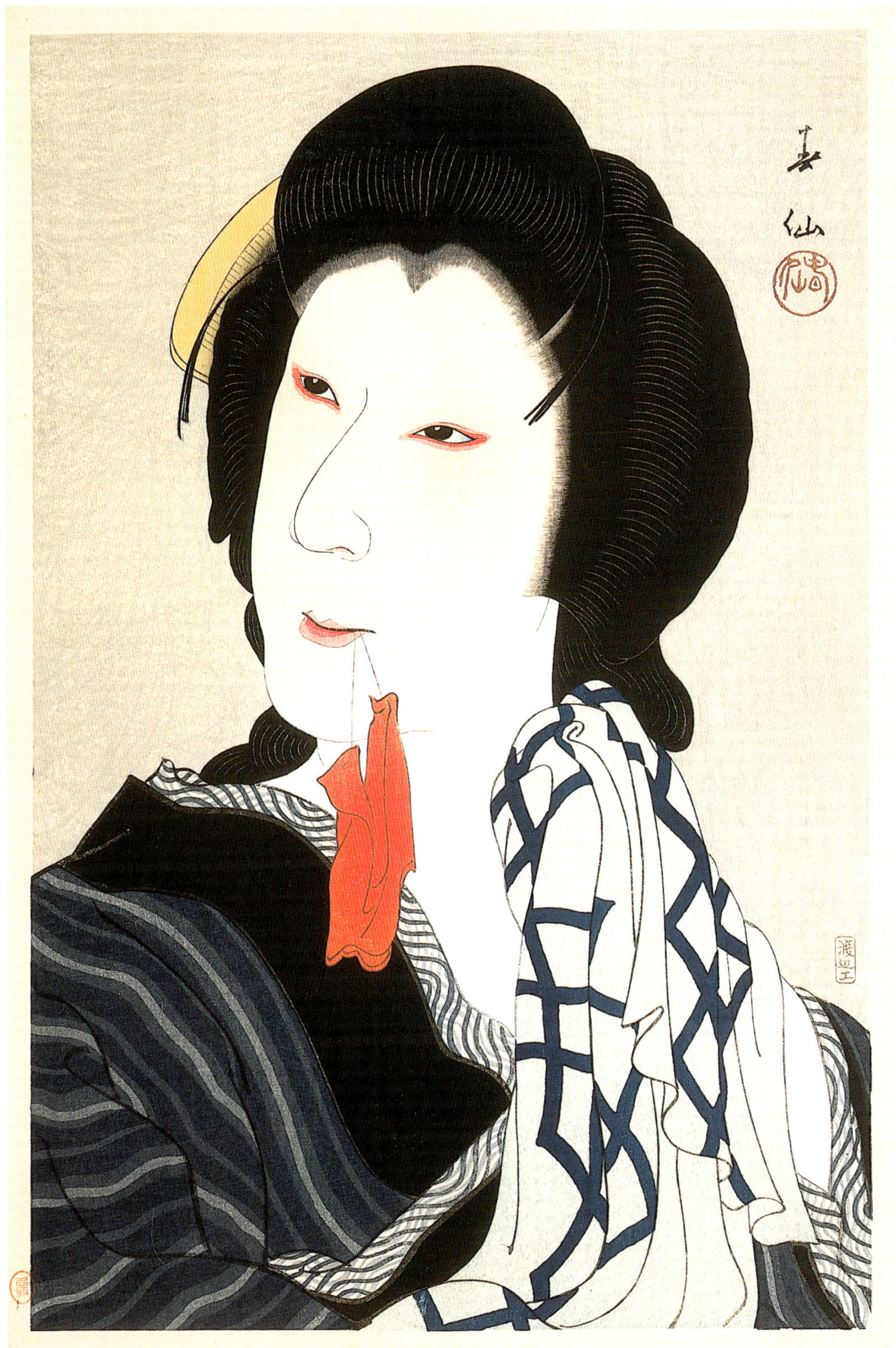

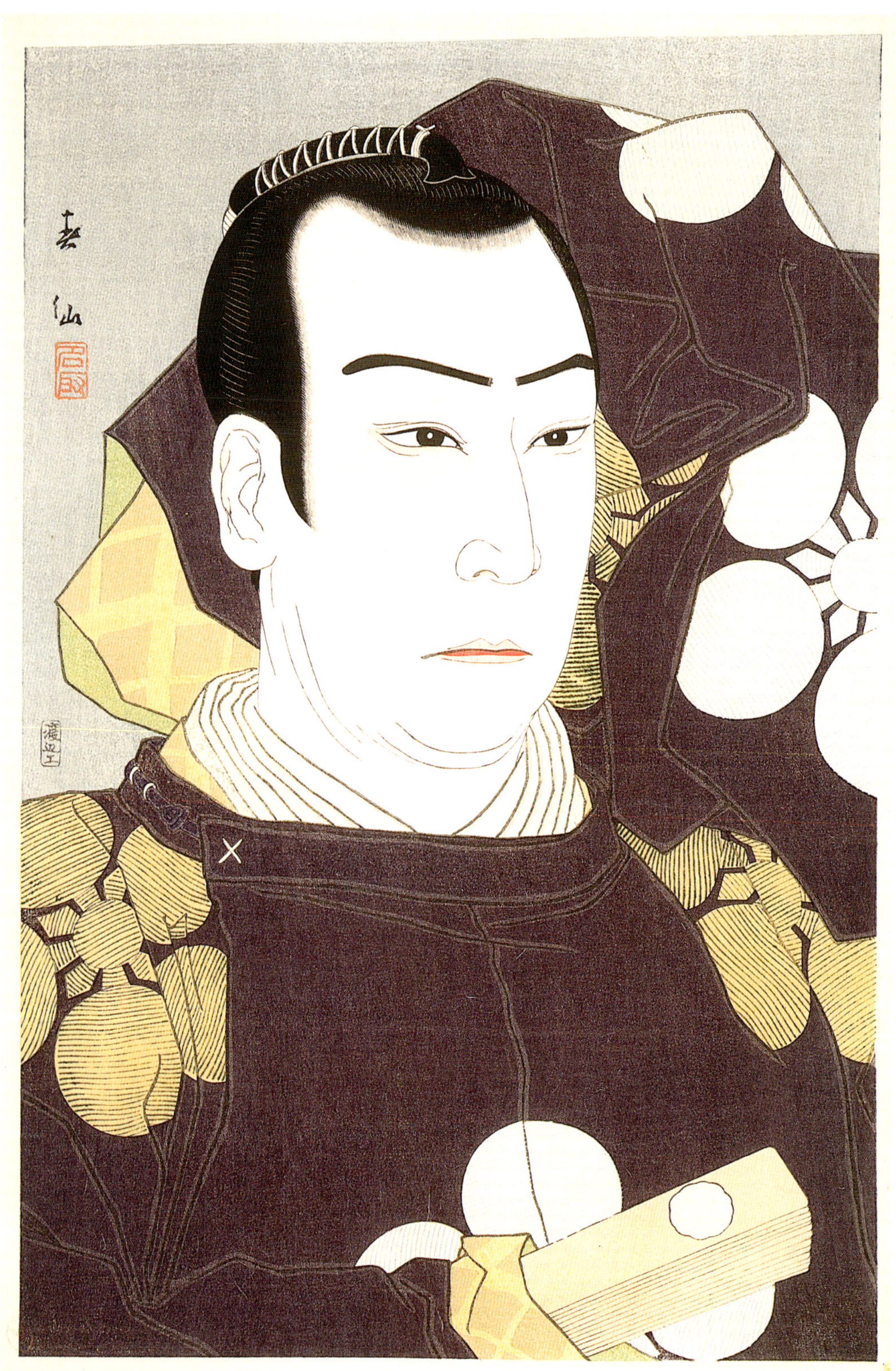

75

"The Actor Ōtani Tomoemon VI as Sugawara no Michizane in the Play *Sugawara denju tenarai kagami (Sugawara's Secrets of Calligraphy)*"

SERIES *Collection of Shunsen Portraits* (*Shunsen nigao-e shū*)
DATE Undated, c. 1927
SIGNATURE *Shunsen*
ARTIST'S SEAL *Natori*
PUBLISHER Watanabe Shōzaburō
SIZE 38.3 x 25.9 cm
PROVENANCE Tokyo, 1963
ACCESSION NUMBER S2003.8.1554
REFERENCES The Toledo Museum of Art (ed.) (1930), cat. no. 147; Ikeda and Balluteau (2001), cat. no. 20; Kushigata City Shunsen Museum of Art (ed.) (2002), no. 29; for a synopsis of the play and role, see page 120

Similar to the print of Ichimura Uzaemon XV (cat. no. 73), this design is typically Shunsen, with a simply delineated subject set against a mica ground. After finishing the fifty-one prints for the *Collection of Shunsen Portraits* in 1929, Shunsen would not return to the genre until the early 1950s. From 1951 to 1954, again in concert with Watanabe Shōzaburō, Shunsen designed the larger series of twenty-four prints entitled *New Prints of Actors on the Stage* (*Shin han butai no sugata-e*). These designs have only recently begun to garner the same praise as his early set, yet no sheets from this second series were in the Robert O. Muller collection. (A complete list of all of Shunsen's prints for Watanabe is included in the Watanabe Shōzaburō (1962), 57-64.)

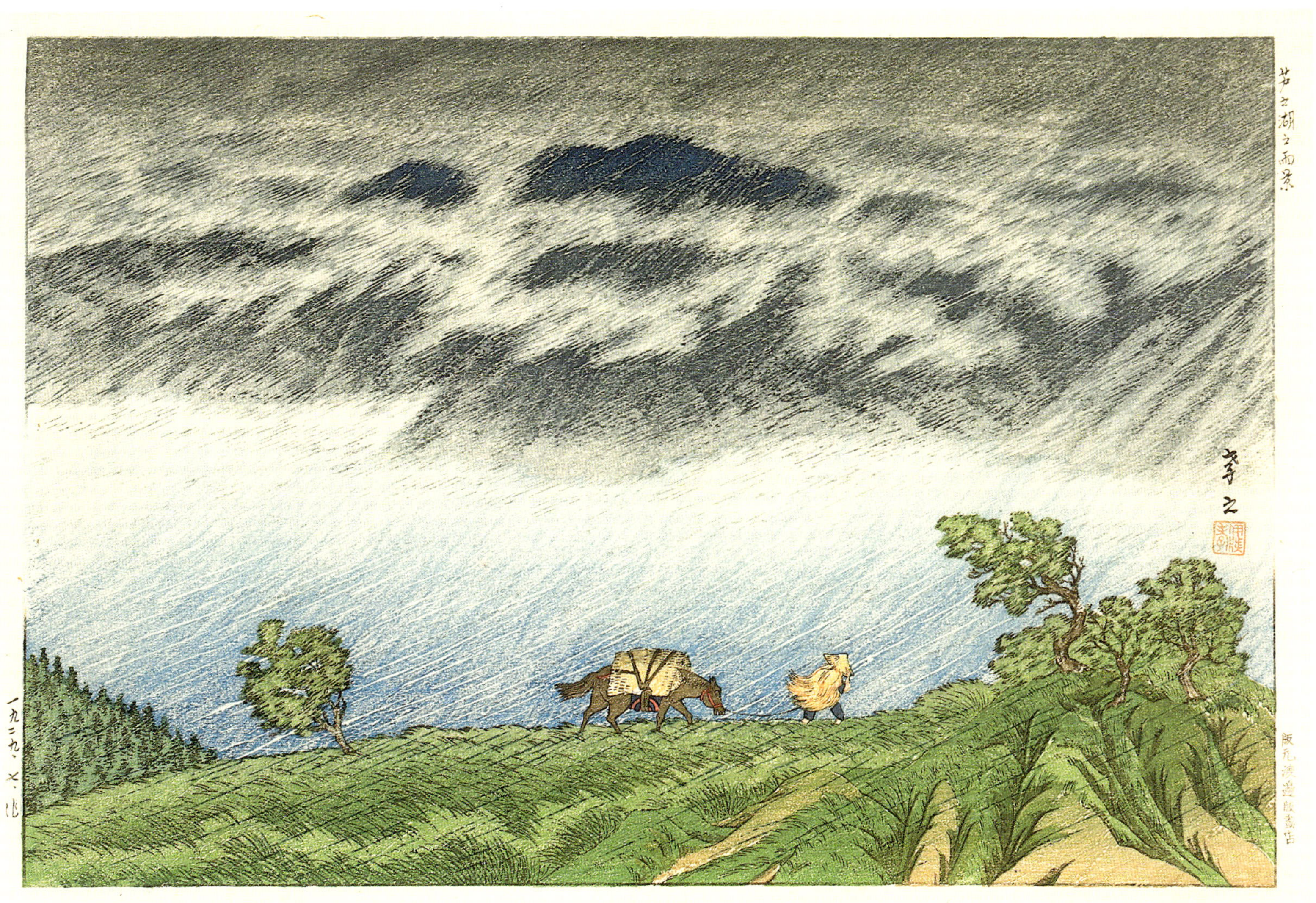

Itō Takashi (1894-1982)

Itō Takashi was born in Kama, Shizuoka Prefecture. He went to Kyoto, where he studied *Yōga* with Totori Eiki (1873-1943) and *Nihonga* with Takeuchi Seihō (1864-1942) at the *Kōtō Kōgei Gakkō* (Kyoto Higher Technical Art School). He later moved to Tokyo where he graduated from the *Tōkyō Bijutsu Gakkō* (Tokyo School of Fine Arts). He also studied *Nihonga* with painter Yūki Somei (1875-1957) and was a pupil of Kaburagi Kiyokata (1878-1973; cat. nos. 5-7). He exhibited paintings at the *Teiten*. Although Takashi worked primarily as a painter, he also produced landscape prints with the publisher Watanabe Shōzaburō (1885-1962) from 1922. His designed around eighty-five prints.

REFERENCES Watanabe Shōzaburō (1936), 109; Merritt and Yamada (1992), 47; Stephens (ed.) (1993), 170-71; Yamanashi Prefectural Art Museum (ed.) (1997)

76

"Lake Ashinoko in Rain (Hakone)"

Ashinoko no ukei

DATE 1929, July

SIGNATURE AND ARTIST'S SEAL *Takashi*

PUBLISHER Watanabe Shōzaburō

SIZE 36.7 x 24.1 cm

PROVENANCE Shima Art Co., New York, 1940

ACCESSION NUMBER S2003.8.378

REFERENCE Stephens (ed.) (1993), cat. no. 209

In this composition the artist transforms Lake Ashinoko in the Hakone area – often depicted as an idyllic beauty spot – into a dramatic scene, an almost hostile environment in which a man, bent against the lashing rain, leads his horse home. Itō seems to have been attracted to mountain scenes in his native Japan for the subject matter of his prints.

The biography of the artist's life included in the 1936 Watanabe sale catalogue is somewhat cryptic. Watanabe describes Itō as an artist who experimented frequently with printing and over-printing, and that he also carved one design himself entitled "Sinking Sun" which illustrated the courtyard of Tokyo Imperial University (present-day University of Tokyo). "Sinking Sun" was apparently not published by Watanabe and was distributed by Itō to members of the Edo-Picture Appreciation Society. Watanabe also states that at the time of the Great Kantō Earthquake in September 1923 a number of trial prints by Itō, done in conjunction with Watanabe's printers, were in progress. They were subsequently abandoned due to the destruction of his shop premises. Perhaps Itō's "experimental approach" explains the interesting treatment of light above the clouds in this moody rainscape.

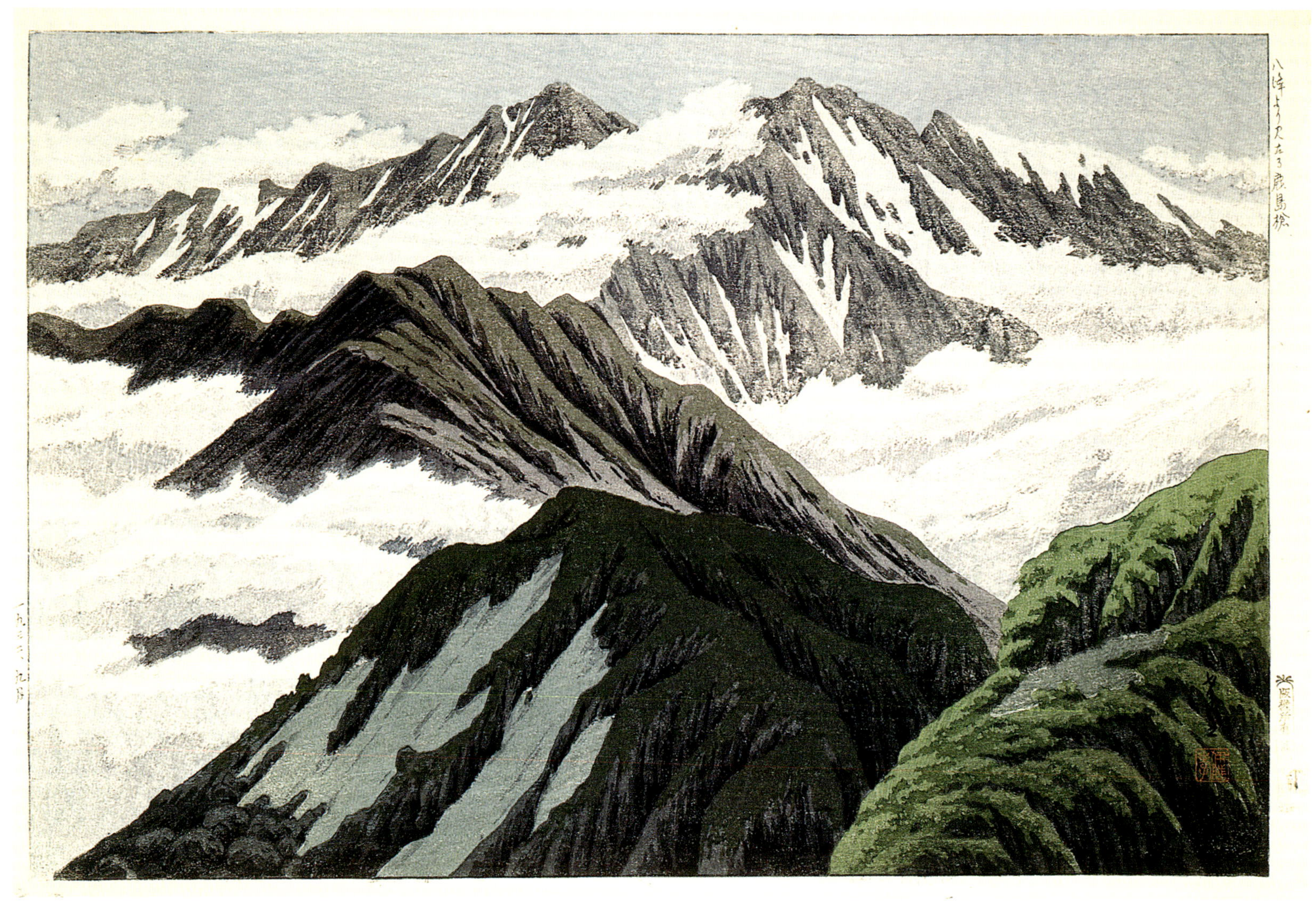

77
"Mount Kashimayari from Mount Happō [Japanese Alps]"
Happō yori mitaru Kashimayari

DATE 1932, September
SIGNATURE AND ARTIST'S SEAL *Takashi*
PUBLISHER Watanabe Shōzaburō
SIZE 24.1 x 36.4 cm
PROVENANCE Arts & Design of Japan (Peter Gilder), San Francisco, October 1991
ACCESSION NUMBER S2003.8.384

Yoshikawa Kanpō (1894-1979)

Yoshikawa Kanpō was born Yoshikawa Kenjirō in Kyoto. From 1901 he studied *Nihonga* painting with Nishibori Tōsui, and from 1909 briefly enlisted as a pupil of Takeuchi Seihō (1864-1942) and started his study of *Ukiyo-e*. In 1914 he entered the *Kyōto-shi Kaiga Senmon Gakkō* (Kyoto Municipal Specialist School of Painting) and graduated in 1918. He subsequently worked as a theatrical designer for the Shōchiku firm, which by the 1920s dominated ownership of the country's Kabuki theaters and had entered into the motion picture industry. In the early 1920s Kanpō produced a few prints with the Kyoto-based publisher Satō Shōtarō, and in 1923 he founded the *Kojitsu Kenkyūkai* (Association of Antiquities Studies). In 1925 Kanpō exhibited prints and paintings with his Kyoto colleague Miki Suizan (1887-1957), a specialist in *bijinga* whose prints were also published by Satō Shōtarō. After 1926 he no longer participated in public exhibitions, and only created prints and paintings on commission. Kanpō had a keen interest in the history of Kabuki theater, its music and costumes, as well as in aspects of traditional everyday life. He authored publications such as *Nihon fūzoku daizushū* (*History of Japanese Manners and Customs*, 1934) and *Obi no hensenshi* (*History of the Transition of the Japanese Sash*, 1963). Kanpō amassed a substantial collection of prints and objects documenting Edo- and Meiji-period life. He designed only ten prints.

REFERENCES Merritt and Yamada (1992), 178; Stephens (ed.) (1993), 172-74; Hamanaka and Newland (2000), 93, 212; The Museum of Kyoto (ed.) (2002)

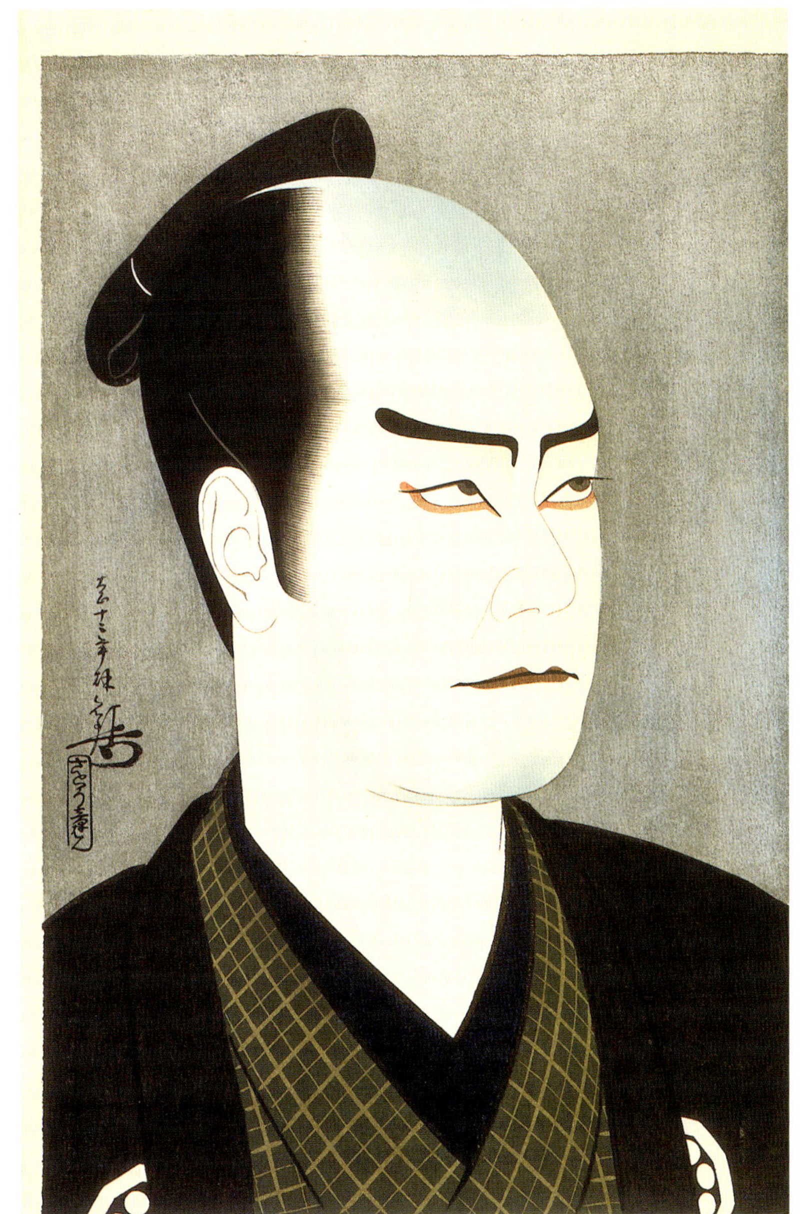

78
"The Actor Ichikawa Sadanji II as Hishikawa Gengobei in the Play *Imayō Satsuma no uta* (*The Song of Satsuma in Modern Style*)"

SERIES *Kanpō's Creative Prints, First Series* (*Kanpō sōsaku-hanga shū daiisshū*)
DATE 1923 (Taishō 12), Autumn
SIGNATURE *Kanpō*
PUBLISHER Satō Shōtarō
EDITION Number 37 from a limited edition of 200 copies
SIZE 40.1 x 26.5 cm
PROVENANCE Yamanaka & Co., New York, May 1938
ACCESSION NUMBER S2003.8.3629
REFERENCES The Toledo Museum of Art (ed.) (1930), cat. no. 330; Stephens (ed.) (1993), cat. no. 214; for a synopsis of the play and role, see pages 120-21

Kanpō holds a special place among *Shin-hanga* artists as he hailed from Kyoto *and* he produced actor prints. All of his prints were published by the established Kyoto publisher, print dealer and collector Satō Shōtarō, and they were shown in the 1930 exhibition at the Toledo Museum of Art. Kanpō's actor prints are characterized by a subdued palette, with beautifully printed mica backgrounds, and a refined deportment in the depiction of his subjects. All first-edition prints (1920s) by the artist have limitation seals on the back of the print. Postwar printings tend to be done on very white paper that is generally thinner than first editions.

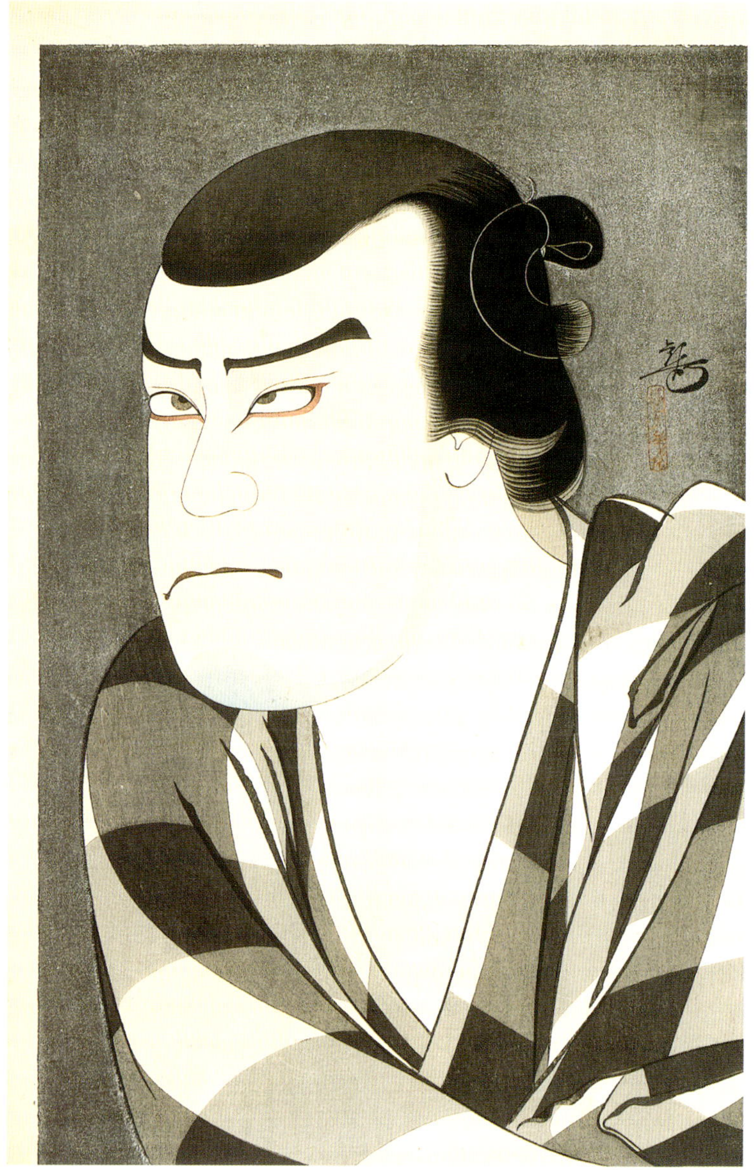

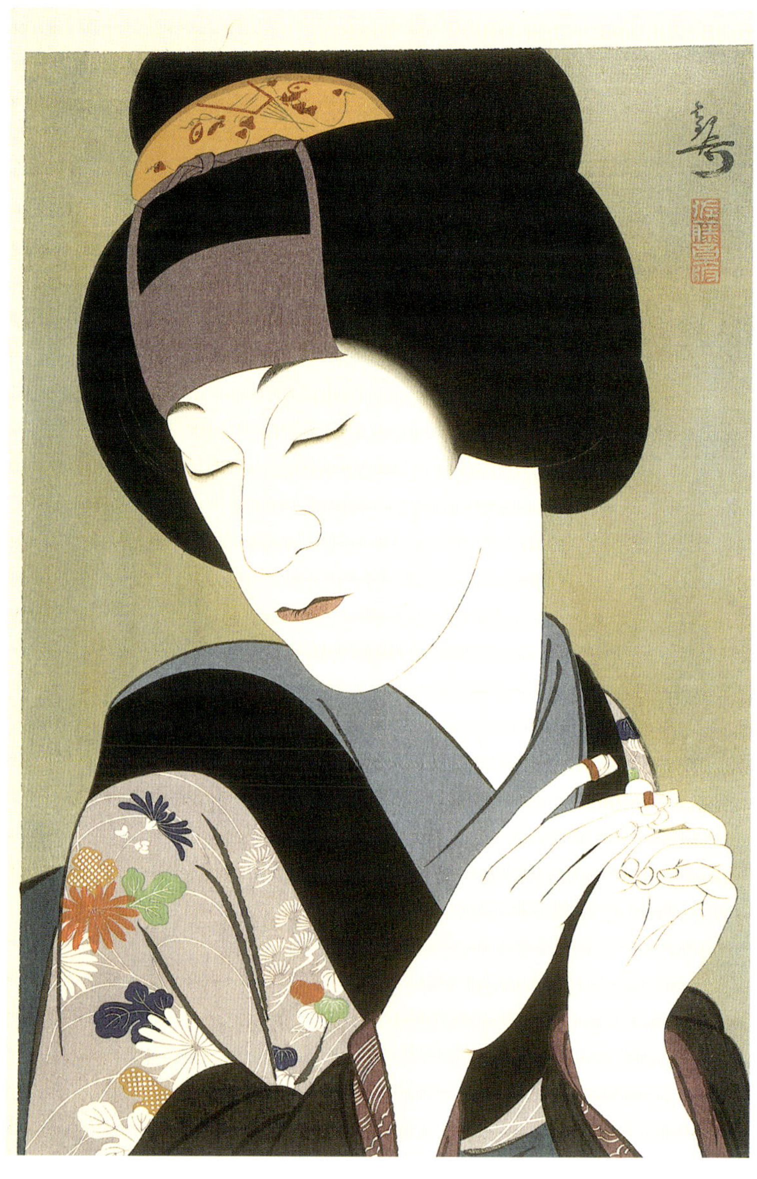

79

"The Actor Jitsukawa Enjaku II as Igami no Gonta in the Play *Yoshitsune senbonzakura* (*Yoshitsune and the Thousand Cherry Trees*)"

SERIES *Kanpō's Creative Prints, First Series* (*Kanpō sōsaku-hanga shū daiisshū*)
DATE 1923 (Taishō 12)
SIGNATURE *Kanpō*
PUBLISHER Satō Shōtarō
EDITION Number 37 from a limited edition of 200 copies
SIZE 39.7 x 26.2 cm
PROVENANCE Yamanaka & Co, New York, January 1939
ACCESSION NUMBER S2003.8.3628
REFERENCES The Toledo Museum of Art (ed.) (1930), cat. no. 328; for a synopsis of the play and role, see page 121

80

"The Actor Kataoka Gadō IV as Asagao in the Play *Shō utsushi Asagao nikki* (*Diary of the Morning Glory*)"

SERIES *Kanpō's Creative Prints, First Series* (*Kanpō sōsaku-hanga shū daiisshū*)
DATE 1924 (Taishō 13)
SIGNATURE *Kanpō*
PUBLISHER Satō Shōtarō
EDITION Number 37 from a limited edition of 200 copies
SIZE 40.0 x 27.0 cm
PROVENANCE Yamanaka & Co., New York, April 1939
ACCESSION NUMBER S2003.8.3631
REFERENCES The Toledo Museum of Art (ed.) (1930), cat. no. 329; Stephens (ed.) (1993), cat. no. 216; for a synopsis of the play and the role, see page 121

All three of the actor prints by Kanpō reproduced here are part of a set of six entitled *Kanpō's Creative Prints, First Series* (*Kanpō sōsaku-hanga shū daiisshū*), which was designed by the artist from 1922 to 1923. The remaining three prints all date to 1922: "The Actor Nakamura Ganjirō I as Kamiya Jihei', "Moon" (*Tsuki*) and "Hinazō."

Kobayakawa Kiyoshi (1899-1948)

Kobayakawa Kiyoshi was born in Hakata, Fukuoka Prefecture, where he took lessons from the *Nanga* painter Ueda Tekkō. When he was in his late teens, he moved to Tokyo and studied *bijinga* under Kaburagi Kiyokata (1878-1973; cat. nos. 5-7). He participated in several prestigious exhibitions starting with the fifth *Teiten* in 1924, when he entered the *Nihonga*-style *bijin* painting entitled "Okiku of Nagasaki" (*Nagasaki no Okikusan*). Kiyoshi would draw on Nagasaki for a number of his works. He subsequently exhibited with the *Kyōdokai* (Homeland Society), *Teiten* and *Bunten*. Sometime in the mid-1920s he designed his first woodblock print; his interest in woodblock prints also extended to collecting *Ukiyo-e* and research into their colorants. He self-published the six-print series *Styles of Contemporary Make-up* (*Kindai jiseshō no uchi*) in 1930-31 and received special mention at the *Teiten* in 1933 for his painting "Ichimaru." Kiyoshi's corpus of paintings is extensive, but he produced only thirteen prints. Twelve of these were included in the Japanese print exhibition at the Toledo Museum of Art in 1936.

REFERENCES Watanabe Shōzaburō (1936), 117; Merritt and Yamada (1992), 70; Stephens (ed.) (1993), 176-77; Yui (1998), 172; Hamanaka and Newland (2000), 141-48, 210

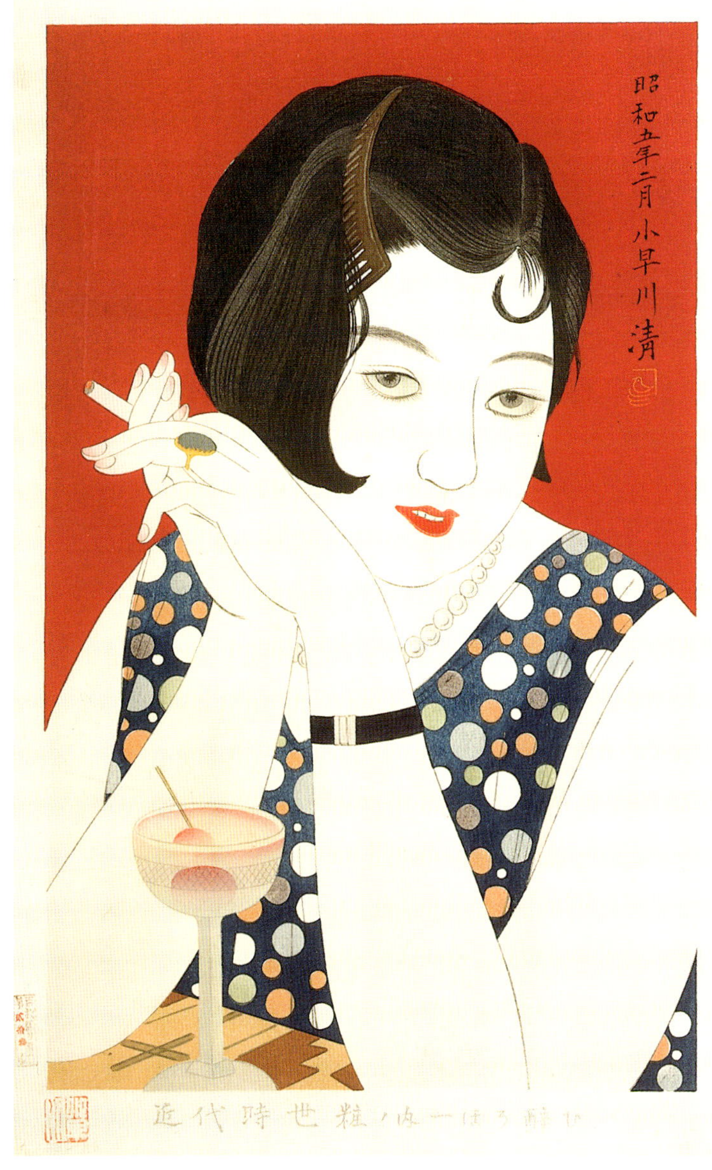

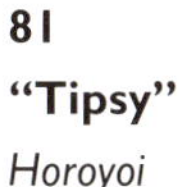

81
"Tipsy"
Horoyoi

SERIES *Styles of Contemporary Make-up, No. 1* (*Kindai jiseshō no uchi ichi*)
DATE 1930 (Shōwa 5), February
SIGNATURE *Kobayakawa Kiyoshi*, with artist's duck seal
PUBLISHER Privately published
EDITION Number 23 from a limited edition of 100 copies
SIZE 43.5 x 27.4 cm
PROVENANCE Kawaguchi, New York, December 1936
ACCESSION NUMBER S2003.8.1092
REFERENCES Stephens (ed.) (1993), cat. no. 220; Hamanaka and Newland (2000), cat. no. 189; Brown and Minichiello (2002), cat. no. 2

Kobayakawa Kiyoshi is unique within *Shin-hanga* for his totally different approach in the illustration of women: they are not the ethereal, romanticized Japanese beauties incarnate in the prints of Itō Shinsui (1898-1991; cat. nos. 85-101), Hashiguchi Goyō (1880-1921; cat. nos. 36-44) or Hirano Hakuhō (1879-1957; cat. nos. 34-5), but an up-to-date *modan gâru* or *moga* ("modern girl"). As Kendall H. Brown describes this "new Taishō woman," one which he suggests was already defined by the mid-1920s, "... she strolled along the urban streets or danced in Jazz cafés, the *moga* exhibited a newly found independence. With her typically short hair and Western clothes, her growing economic freedom and often defiant sexuality, the *moga* appeared to react against traditional woman's roles of obedience and sacrifice as codified in the official ideology of *ryōsai kenbō* (Good Wife and Wise Mother)."[1]

Kiyoshi's celebrated design is the embodiment of the *moga* ideal: a bared-arm, slightly inebriated young coquette with bobbed hair, red lipstick and daring polka-dot dress and pearls holds a cigarette, wears a cabochon ring and modern watchband. A cocktail is set before her. Her countenance is flirtatious, her forward sexuality apparent and her attitude is anything but subservient.[2] Although the number of this work appears as part of the print and series title located in the bottom margin, unnumbered examples do exist. Differences between numbered and unnumbered examples of this particular composition are often restricted to the visibleness of the silver smoke emanating from the woman's cigarette, and the flesh tones on her arms, body and face.

1. Kendall H. Brown, "Moderating Modernity: The *Moga*," 65-76, in Brown *et al.* (1996), 65.

2. For more on the *moga* phenomenon, see Miriam Silverberg, "The Modern Girl as Militant," 239-66, in Bernstein (ed.), 1991.

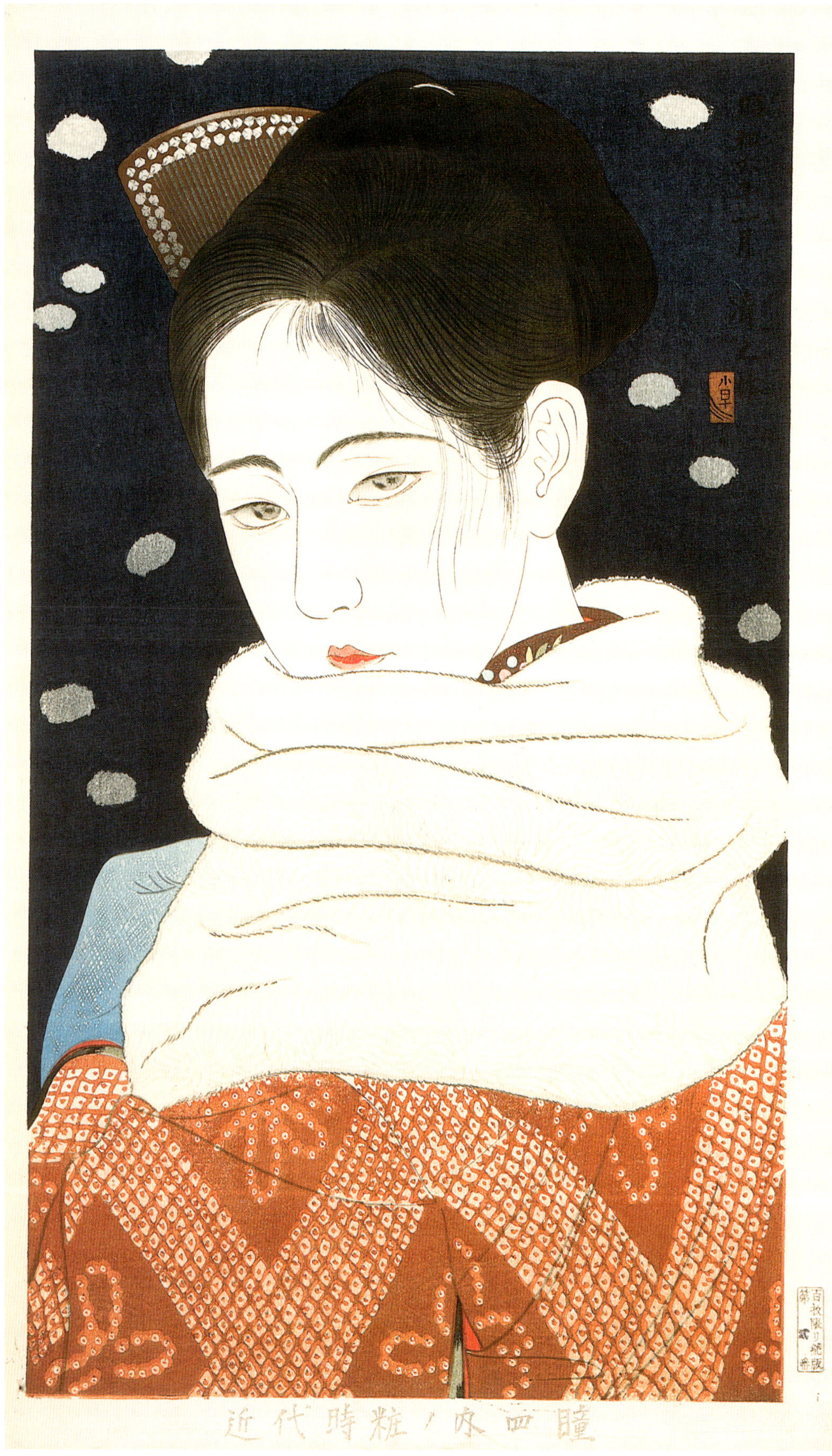

82
"Eyes"
Hitomi

SERIES *Styles of Contemporary Make-up, No. 4*
(*Kindai jiseshō no uchi yon*)
DATE 1931 (Shōwa 6), January
SIGNATURE *Kiyoshi*
ARTIST'S SEAL *Kobayakawa*
PUBLISHER Privately published
EDITION Number 2 from a limited edition of 100 copies
SIZE 46.0 x 27.0 cm
PROVENANCE Kawaguchi, New York, December 1936
ACCESSION NUMBER S2003.8.1094
REFERENCES Stephens (ed.) (1993), cat. no. 221; Hamanaka and Newland (2000), no. 192

Of the six prints in the series *Styles of Contemporary Make-up*, three show women attending to their toilette[1] and a fourth is the alluring "Tipsy" above. The remaining two images, illustrated here and in cat. no. 83, portray women in modern kimono and hairstyles. They demonstrate Kiyoshi's ability to find a compromise between the defiantly in-vogue *moga* and the traditional Japanese beauty. Here a young woman is dressed against the cold of a snowy night, her white shawl displays a distinctive pattern printed in silver, which contrasts handsomely with the *ikat* silk over-kimono. The viewer is immediately drawn toward the seductive, almost cat-like stare of the woman's eyes: the careful gray shading and almost transparent quality of her pupils (*hitomi* literally means "pupils of the eyes") differ enormously from the rather emotionless expressions of women in *bijinga* by artists like Itō Shinsui (1898-1972; cat. nos. 85-101). This is a jewel of Shōwa-period printmaking.

1. These are "Makeup" (*Keshō*, 1930; no. 2), "Nails" (*Tsume*, 1930; no. 3) and "Black Hair" (*Kurokami*; no. 5, 1931).

83

"Lipstick"

Kuchibeni

SERIES *Styles of Contemporary Make-up, No. 6*
(*Kindai jiseshō no uchi roku*)
DATE 1931 (Shōwa 6), March
SIGNATURE *Kiyoshi*
ARTIST'S SEAL *Kobayakawa*
PUBLISHER Privately published
EDITION Number 25 from a limited edition of 100 copies
SIZE 49.5 x 28.3 cm
PROVENANCE Kawaguchi, New York, December 1936
ACCESSION NUMBER S2003.8.1093
REFERENCE Hamanaka and Newland (2000), no. 194

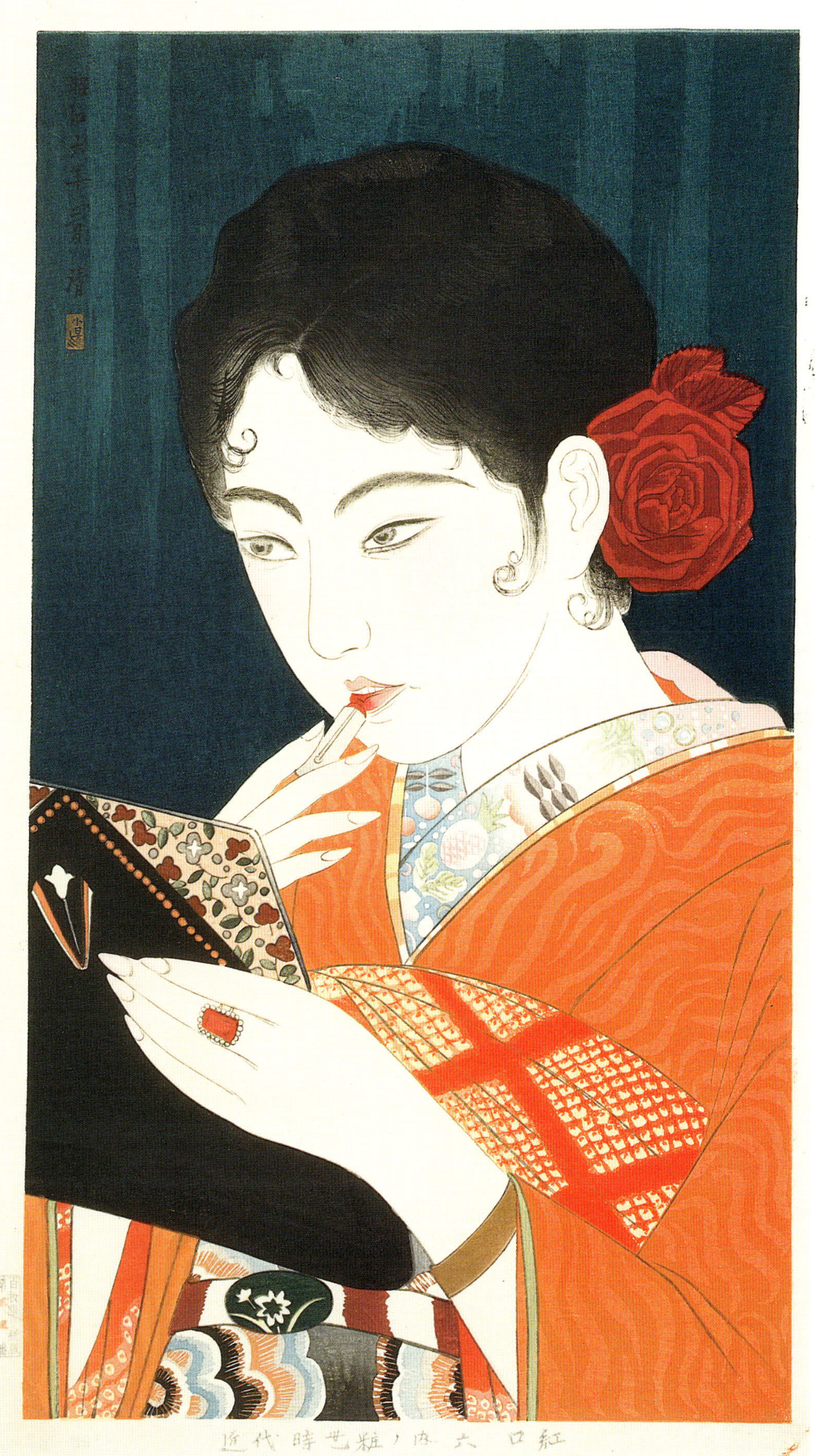

Kiyoshi designed thirteen prints of beauties and his most important work, the six-print series *Styles of Contemporary Make-up*, was privately published. It is not known why the prints in this series were not marketed through an established publisher. It might have been that the subject was too risky for a large-scale, commercial, and relatively conservative publisher like Watanabe Shōzaburō in that *moga* were more than symbols of a passing fashion statement. They were emblems of the era, and their impact was such that the Japanese government banned in 1930 "the stockingless fad for girls in foreign style dress." In the same year employers fired female employees who were "forever staining their lips," while police rounded up women applying make-up in the streets![1] Kiyoshi himself defended his choice to portray a more contemporary vision of Japanese women: "I do not just draw customs and manners but try to capture the essence of the time in which we live."[2] Here a young woman in an up-to-date kimono and coiffed hairdo applies lipstick while looking into an elegantly decorated compact.

Of Kiyoshi's remaining seven prints, three were published by the well-known producer of reproductions (*fukusei*) Takamizawa Enji (Ensendō), three were issued by the export publishing firm Hasegawa and one by Watanabe.[3]

1. Brown and Minichiello (2002), 66.
2. Stephens (ed.) (1993), 177.
3. "Dance" (*Odori*, 1932), "The Mistress Okichi" (*Tōjin Okichi*, 1932), and "Dancer" (*Dansâ*, n.d.) were issued by Hasegawa; "Dressing her Hair" (*Kamiyui*), "The Geisha Ichimaru" (*Geisha Ichimaru*, c. 1933), and "After the Bath" (*Yuagari*, n.d.) by Takamizawa, and "Western-style Dancing" (*Butō*) by Watanabe. They were incorrectly listed in Hamanaka and Newland (2000).

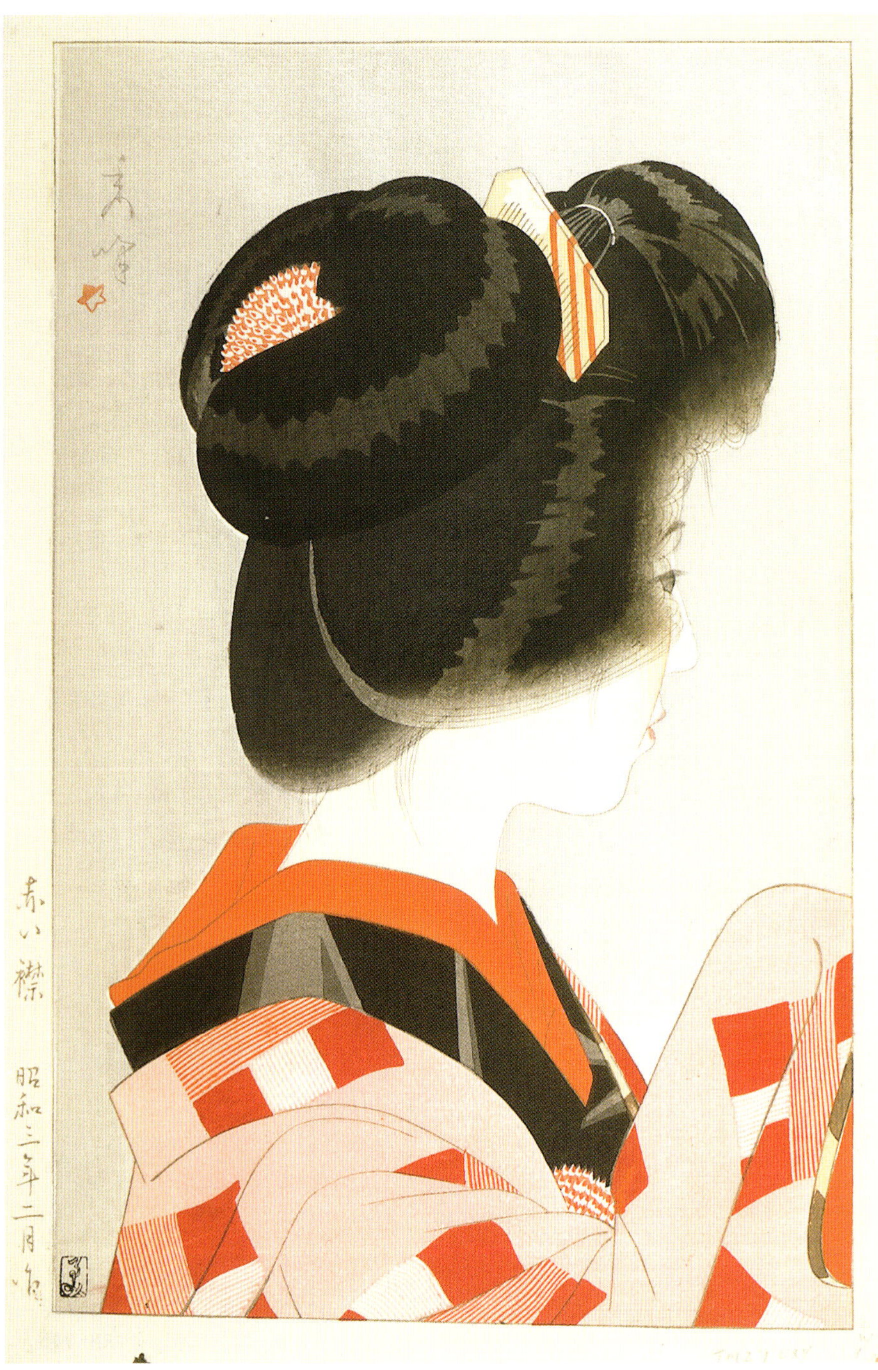

Yamakawa Shūhō (1898-1944)

Yamakawa Shūhō was born Yamakawa Yoshio in Kyoto, the son of a designer of textile patterns. When he was a child the family moved to Tokyo. There he studied *kachōga* under the artist Ikegami Shūhō (1874-1944), from whom he received his artist's name *Shūhō*. He later became a student of *bijinga* master Kaburagi Kiyokata (1878-1973; cat. nos. 5-7), and together with Torii Kotondo (1900-76; cat. nos. 105-11), Itō Shinsui (1898-1972; cat. nos. 85-101) and Kobayakawa Kiyoshi (1899-1948; cat. nos. 81-3) he numbers among Kiyokata's stellar students. Shūhō worked as an illustrator and painter, and exhibited at the *Teiten* for the first time in 1919 with his *Nihonga* paintings. In the late 1920s he produced his first *bijin* prints, showed at several exhibitions and received awards for his paintings at the ninth and eleventh *Teiten*. In 1939 he and Shinsui established the *Seikinkai* (Blue Collar Society). Shūhō's career was cut short in 1944 with his death from a cerebral hemorrhage; he produced some twenty prints with Watanabe Shōzaburō (1885-1962) and the Tokyo-based Bijutsusha.

REFERENCES Merritt and Yamada (1992), 170; Stephens (ed.) (1993), 179; Yui (1999), 399; Hamanaka and Newland (2000), 116-18, 212

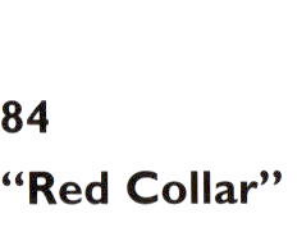

84
"Red Collar"
Akaieri

SERIES *Four Subjects of Women* (*Fujo yondai*)
DATE 1928 (Shōwa 3), February
SIGNATURE *Shūhō*, with artist's maple leaf-pattern seal
PUBLISHER Bijutsusha
SIZE 36.5 x 23.7 cm
PROVENANCE Shima Art Co., New York, September 1938
ACCESSION NUMBER S2003.8.3332
REFERENCES Stephens (ed.) (1993), cat. no. 226; Hamanaka and Newland (2000), no. 154

This composition of a young woman, probably a geisha, in profile and set against a light mica ground, is the most successful of a group of four designs issued as a set with wrapper by the Bijutsusha in 1927-28. Each image portrays a kimono-clad beauty with associations to one of the four seasons: this "Red Collar" is linked to spring.[1] Like Kobayakawa Kiyoshi, Shūhō was interested in the portrayal of contemporary woman as evinced in his superb paintings on silk and screens, although in style his work is colored more by tradition and his training with Kaburagi Kiyokata.

The first edition of this print carries the publisher's seal and is identified by the pink flush on the woman's cheek.

1. The remaining three images are: "Autumn" (*Aki*), "Looks like Snow" (*Yukimoyoi*) for Winter and "Dusk" (*Tasogare*) for Summer. All four appear in Hamanaka and Newland (2000), nos. 152-55.

Itō Shinsui (1898-1972)

Itō Shinsui was born Itō Hajime in the Fukagawa district of Tokyo. At age nine he was forced to leave school due to his family's straitened circumstances, and he found employment at a lithography studio. He also found time to study *Nihonga* with Nakayama Shuko (1872-?). In 1911 he began work at the *Tōkyō Insatsu* (Tokyo Printing Company) where he became an assistant typographer and lithographer in their drawing department. In the same year he became a pupil of Kaburagi Kiyokata (1878-1973; cat. nos. 5-7), from whom he received his artist's name *Shinsui*. In 1912 one of his paintings was shown at the *Tatsumi Gakai* (Southeast Painting Society) and he won the second prize at the *Heiwa Kinen Tōkyō Hakurankai* (Peace Memorial Tokyo Exhibition). In 1916, after having seen one of his paintings, Watanabe Shōzaburō (1885-1962) published Shinsui's first print "Before the Mirror" (cat. no. 85); this began a long and fruitful working relationship. Shinsui often exhibited with the *Kyōdokai* (Homeland Society), as well as the *Nihon Bijutsuin* (Japan Fine Art Institute) and *Bunten*. In 1933 he became a judge for the *Teiten*, *Shin-Bunten* and *Nitten*. Together with Yamakawa Shūhō (1898-1944; cat. no. 84), he founded the *Seikinkai* (Blue Collar Society) in 1939. Shinsui was considered the most important *Shin-hanga* artist in the *bijin* genre. As early as 1931 he had over 100 students working for him in the *Rōhōgajuku* (Clear Peak Painting Academy), a school he established in Ikegami, Tokyo in 1930. In 1958 he was honoured by membership to the *Nihon Geijutsuin* (Japan Art Academy) and in 1970 was awarded the *Kyokujitsushō* (Order of the Rising Sun). Although primarily a painter, Shinsui produced some 135 prints with Watanabe.

REFERENCES Watanabe Shōzaburō (1936), 74-5; Hamada and Hosono (eds.) (1981-82); Merritt and Yamada (1992), 47; Stephens (ed.) (1993), 180-81; Hamanaka and Newland (2000), 49-83, 209

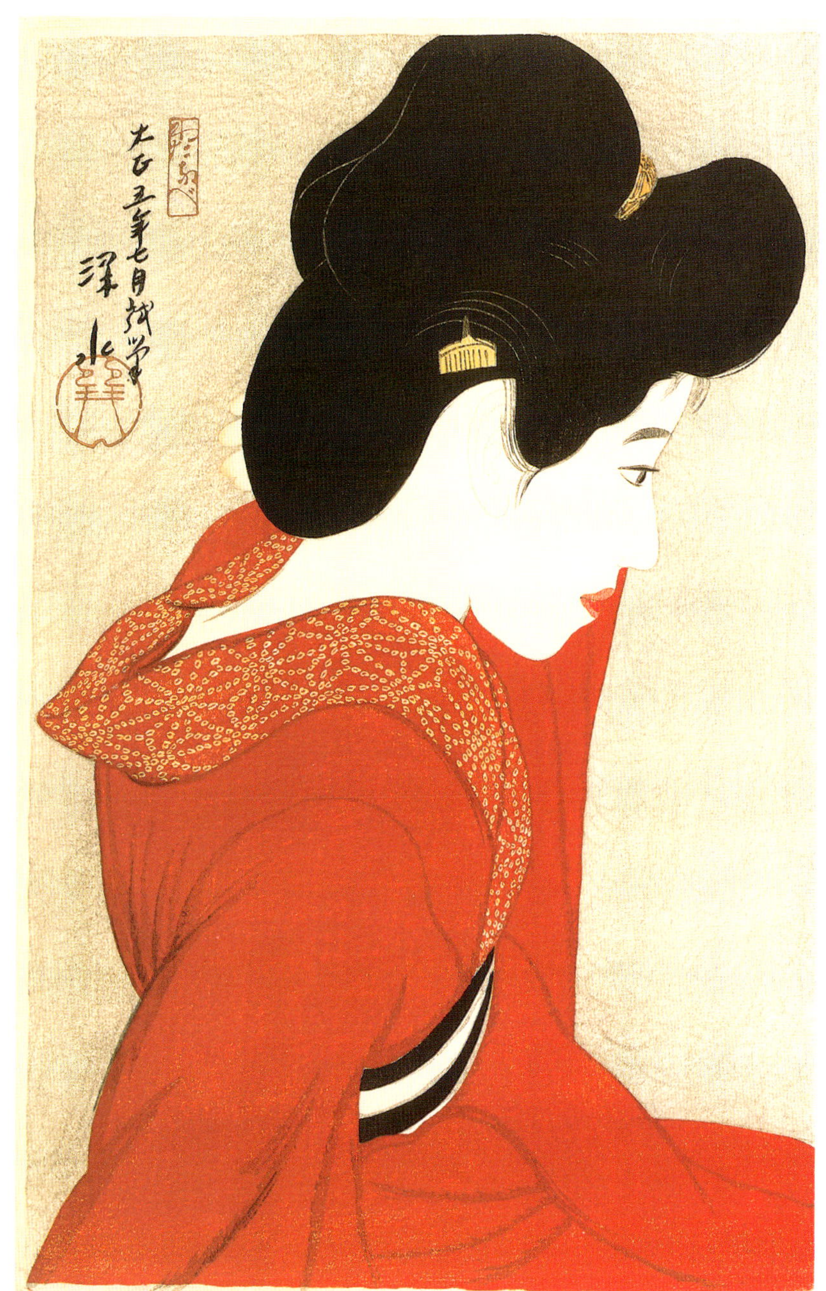

85
"Before the Mirror"

DATE 1916 (Taishō 5), July
SIGNATURE *Shinsui*
ARTIST'S SEAL *Tatsumi*
PUBLISHER Watanabe Shōzaburō
EDITION Number 113 from a limited edition of 150 copies
SIZE 43.2 x 28.1 cm
PROVENANCE J. C. Morgenthau & Co., March 2 1937
ACCESSION NUMBER S2003.8.250
REFERENCES Iino *et al.* (eds.) (1992), cat. no. 1; Hamanaka and Newland (2000), no. 26

This was Shinsui's first print with publisher Watanabe Shōzaburō. Regarding this work, Shinsui writes: "My main purpose in painting was to show the beauty of the small space between the black hair and the kimono. To get the correct red for the kimono Mr. Watanabe Shōzaburō got the best material from the manufacturer, and gave great attention to printing it correctly." In turn, the publisher Watanabe explains that "I made 100 of these for domestic customers and 50 for foreign customers, and each piece has been numbered. In a short time I sold them out. Then I bought back three to exhibit at the Shirakiya [Shirokiya] Dept. Store" (as noted by Robert O. Muller).

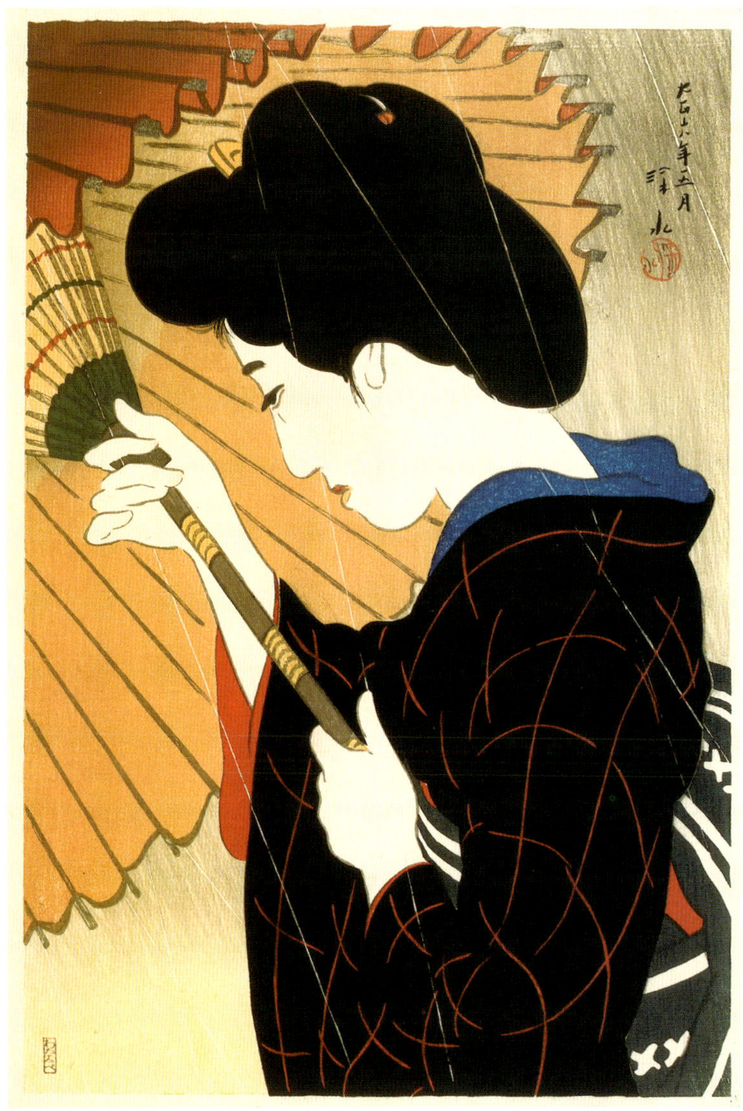

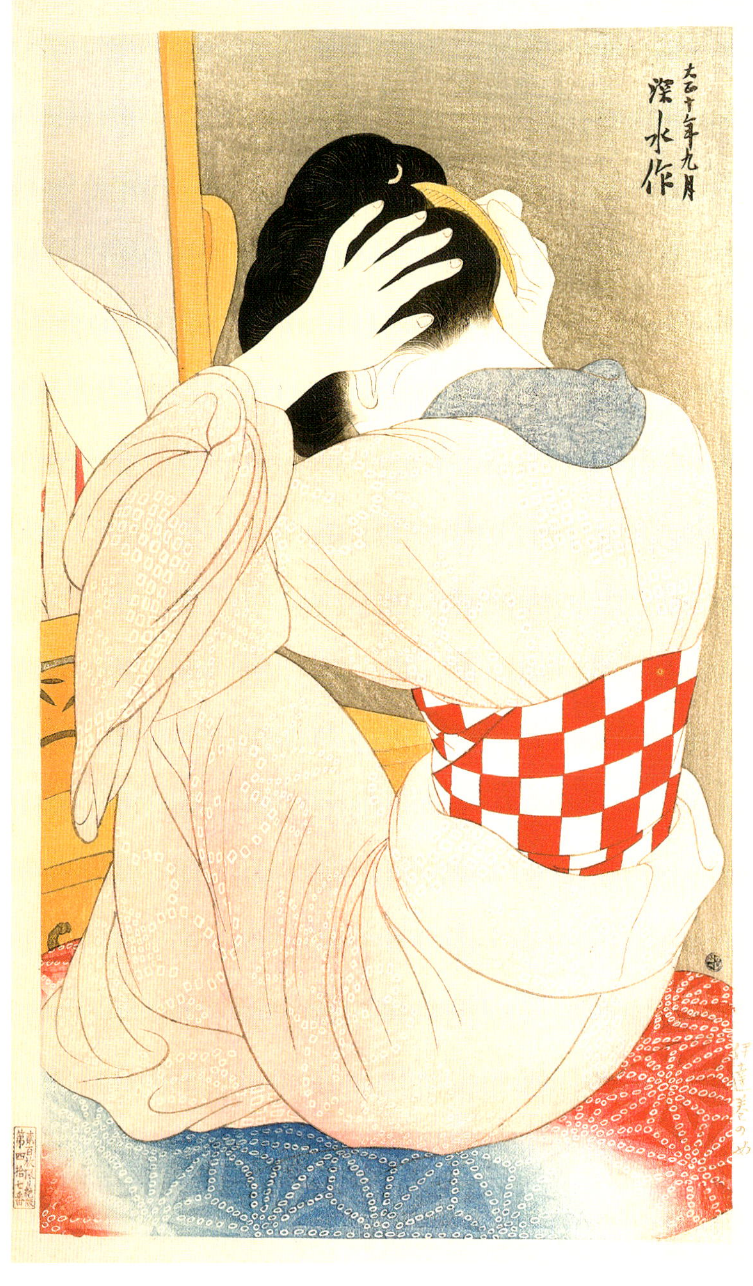

86
"Passing Rain"

DATE 1917 (Taishō 6), May
SIGNATURE AND ARTIST'S SEAL *Shinsui*
PUBLISHER Watanabe Shōzaburō
EDITION Number 16 from a limited edition of 100 copies
SIZE 42.2 × 28.6 cm
PROVENANCE Morgenthau Galleries, New York, March 1937
ACCESSION NUMBER S2003.8.255
REFERENCES Iino *et al.* (eds.) (1992), cat. no. 9a; Stephens (ed.) (1993), cat. no. 233; Hamanaka and Newland (2000), no. 30.1

In his description of this print, Shinsui states how he attempted to adapt the "painterly" color scheme to the printmaking medium by keeping the palette simple.[1] It is certainly true that the graphic qualities are enhanced by the strong contrast of color and compositional elements.

1. Stephens (ed.) (1993), 183.

87
"A Woman in Undersash"
Datemaki no onna

DATE 1921 (Taishō 10), September
SIGNATURE *Shinsui saku*
PUBLISHER Watanabe Shōzaburō
EDITION Number 47 from a limited edition of 200 copies
SIZE 40.8 × 24.2 cm
PROVENANCE Yamanaka & Co., New York, December 1938
ACCESSION NUMBER S2003.8.256
REFERENCES Iino *et al.* (eds.) (1992), cat. no. 1; Hamanaka and Newland (2000), no. 24

This composition of a young woman seated before a mirror, here printed with mica, numbers among Shinsui's most successful designs.

88

"Evening Cool"

Suzumi

SERIES *Twelve Forms of New Beauties* (*Shin bijin jūnisugata*)
DATE 1922 (Taishō 11), Summer
SIGNATURE *Shinsui*
ARTIST'S SEAL *Itō*
PUBLISHER Watanabe Shōzaburō
EDITION Number 115 from a limited edition of 200 copies
SIZE 24.1 x 41.3 cm
PROVENANCE S. H. Mori (Shintarō Mori), Chicago, March 1937
ACCESSION NUMBER S2003.8.262
REFERENCES Iino *et al.* (eds.) (1992), cat. no. 35; Hamanaka and Newland (2000), no. 36

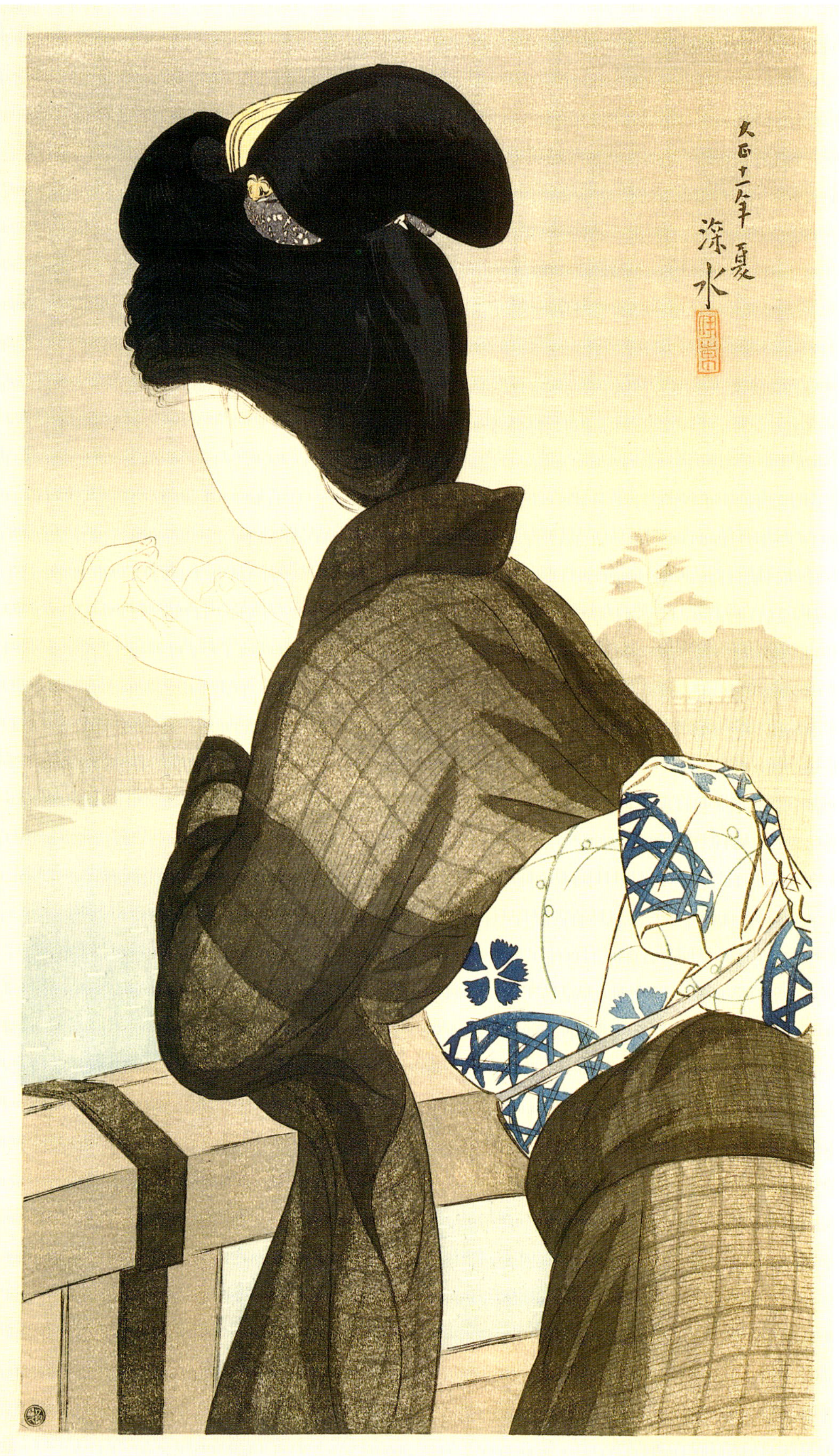

Similar to the previous selection (cat. no. 87), in this work Shinsui chooses to portray his subject from behind. Here a young woman, dressed in a plain *ikat*-style kimono, leans against the railing of a bridge – presumably the Ryōgoku Bridge – and gazes dreamingly toward the Sumida River as she enjoys the cool of a summer's evening. Eleven prints from this series, *Twelve Forms of New Beauties*, the first monumental set of *Shin-hanga* in the *bijinga* genre, were published from June 1922 onward. A new design was issued each month and distributed by the *Ukiyo-e Kenkyūkai* (Association of Ukiyo-e Research). The Great Kantō Earthquake of September 1923 disrupted the regular monthly publication cycle, and the last design "Contemplating the Coming Spring" (*Haru chikaki omoi*) appeared in May 1924.

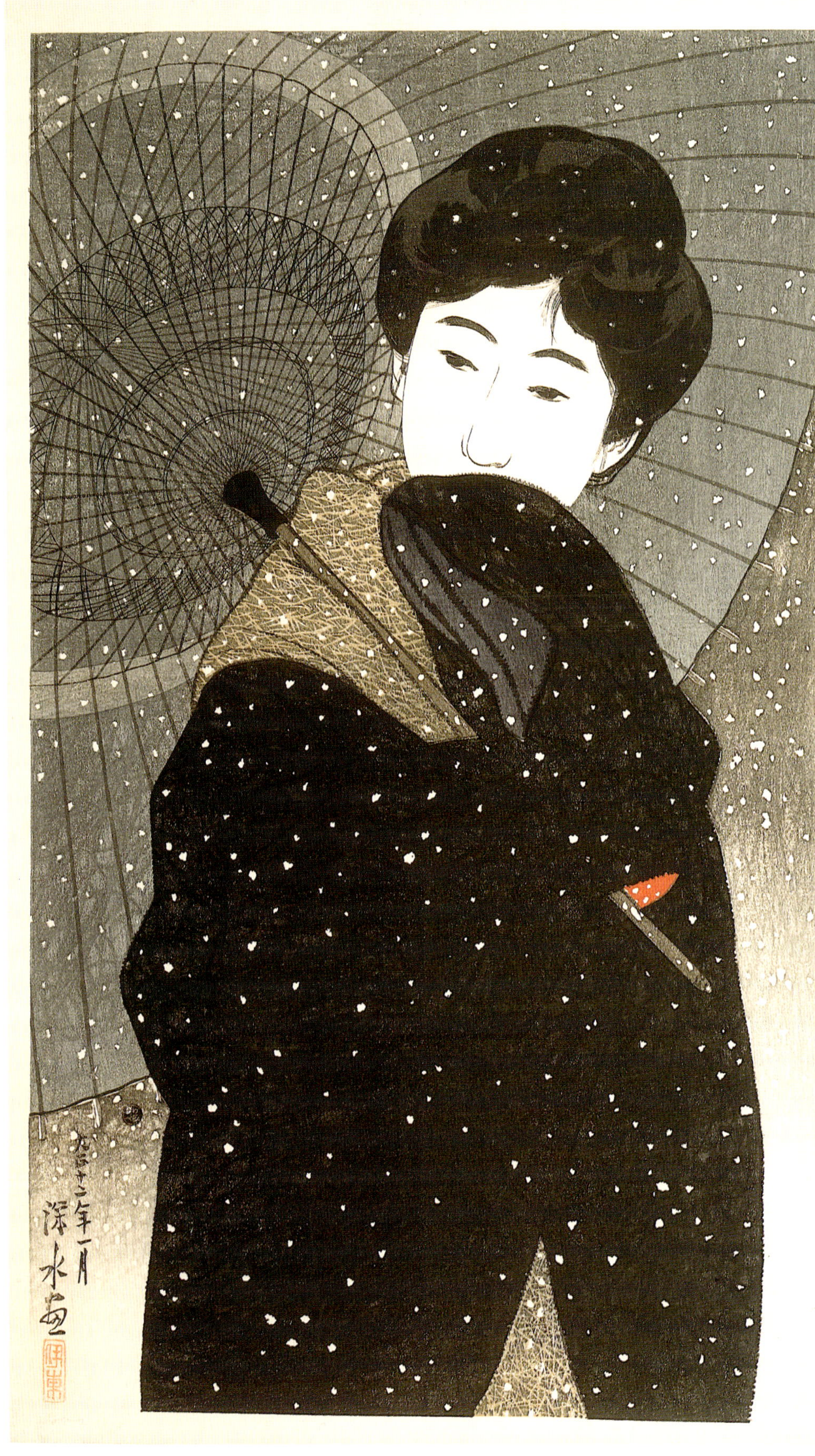

89

"Snowy Night"

Yuki no yoru

SERIES *Twelve Forms of New Beauties* (*Shin bijin jūnisugata*)

DATE 1923 (Taishō 12), January

SIGNATURE *Shinsui*

ARTIST'S SEAL *Itō*

PUBLISHER Watanabe Shōzaburō

EDITION Number 102 from a limited edition of 200 copies

SIZE 40.6 x 24.1 cm

PROVENANCE Yamanaka & Co., London, September 1936

ACCESSION NUMBER S2003.8.265

REFERENCES Iino *et al.* (eds.) (1992), cat. no. 39; Stephens (ed.) (1993), cat. no. 245; Hamanaka and Newland (2000), no. 39

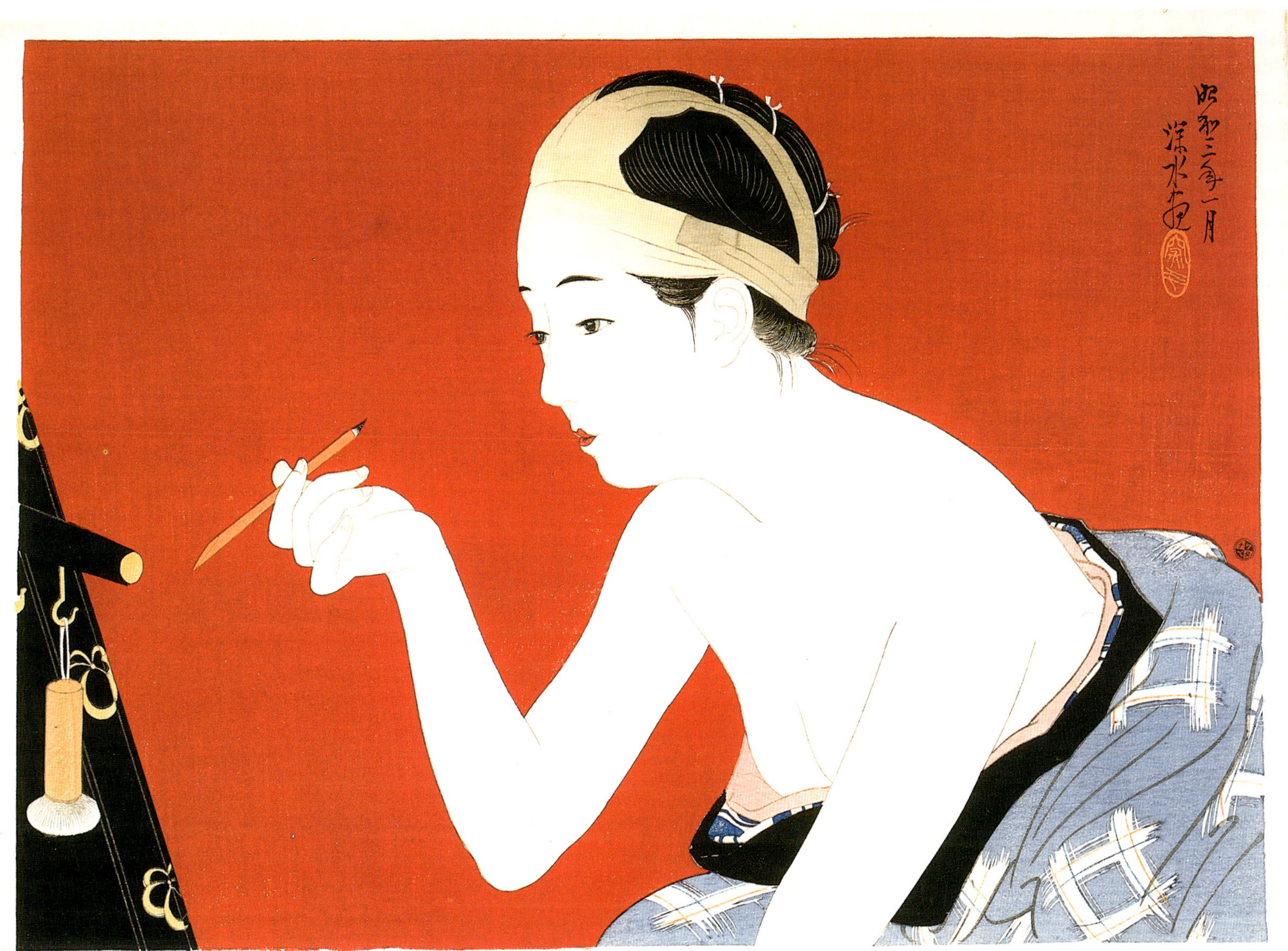

90

"Painting the Eyebrows"

Mayuzumi

DATE 1928 (Shōwa 3), January

SIGNATURE *Shinsui ga*

ARTIST'S SEAL *Shinsui*

PUBLISHER Watanabe Shōzaburō

EDITION Number 142 from a limited edition of 200 copies

SIZE 37.9 × 27.0 cm

PROVENANCE The Tokaido Inc. (J. D. McLaughlin), Boston, March 1939

ACCESSION NUMBER S2003.8.289

REFERENCES Iino *et al.* (eds.) (1992), cat. no. 46; Stephens (ed.) (1993), cat. no. 249; Hamanaka and Newland (2000), no. 52

Immediately striking is the richly printed red background, but subtleties in printing are visible in the facial tones around the eyes. The horizontally oriented format is extremely unusual for prints in the *bijin* genre. The subject here is an actress backstage applying her make-up.

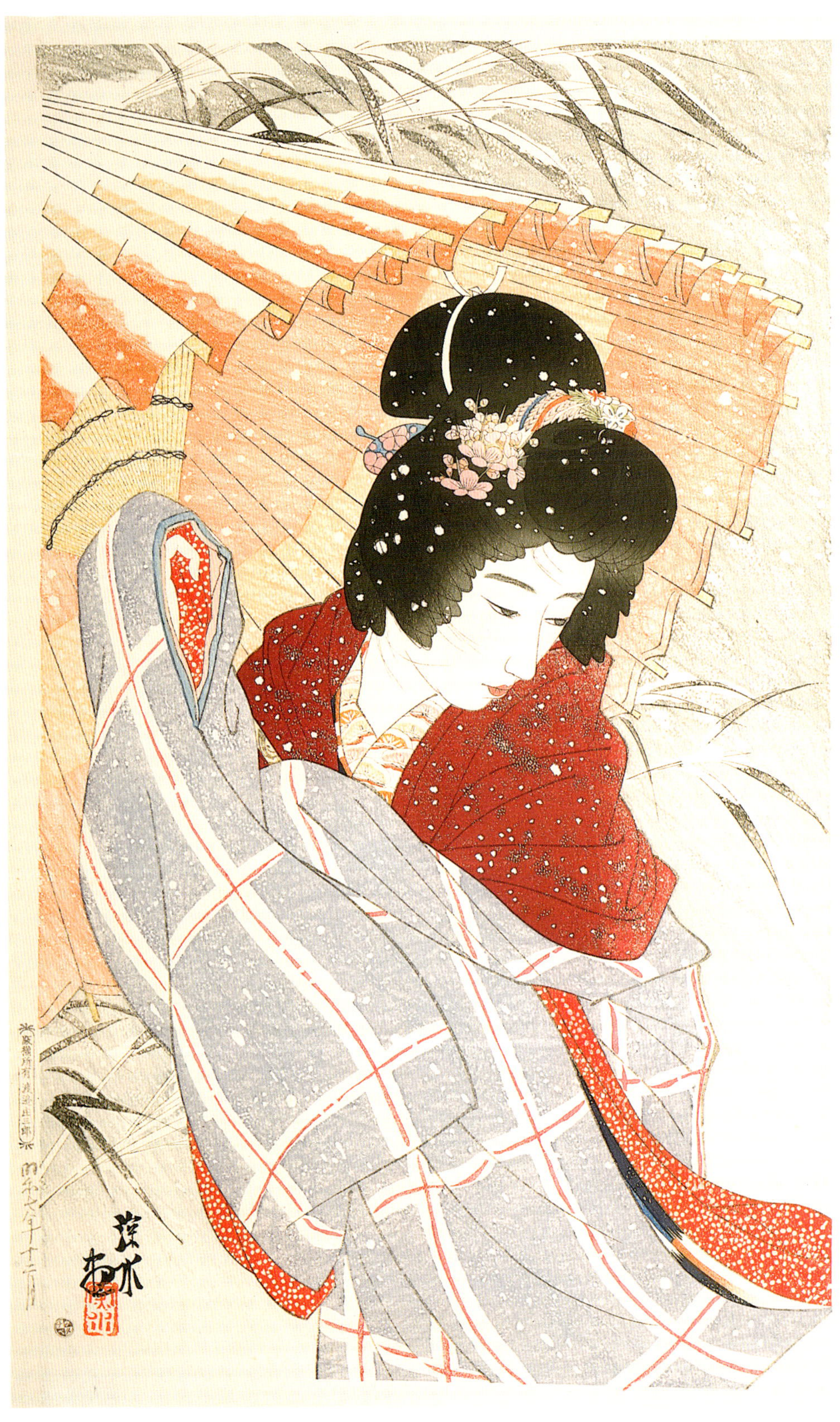

91
"Snowstorm"
Fubuki

SERIES *Collection of Modern Beauties, Second Series (Gendai bijinshū dainishū)*
DATE 1932 (Shōwa 7), December
SIGNATURE *Shinsui ga*
ARTIST'S SEAL *Shinsui*
PUBLISHER Watanabe Shōzaburō
EDITION Number 101 from a limited edition of 250 copies
SIZE 41.6 x 25.6 cm
PROVENANCE Yamanaka & Co., New York, December 1936
ACCESSION NUMBER S2003.8.312
REFERENCES Iino *et al.* (eds.) (1992), cat. no. 67; Stephens (ed.) (1993), cat. no. 252; Hamanaka and Newland (2000), no. 73

Shinsui has created a truly dynamic design: the down-turned head of the woman as she braces herself against a blizzard accentuates the diagonal line of the blowing wind and snow from top left to lower right. This sense of movement is missing from many Shinsui *bijinga*. However, the composition is typically Shinsui in the adherence to a traditional and romanized portrayal of Japanese female beauty. He incorporates neither the Western stylistic sensibilities seen in the work of Hashiguchi Goyō (1880-1921; cat. nos. 36-44) nor the image of the "modern girl" of the 1920s and 1930s limned by Kobayakawa Kiyoshi (1899-1948; cat. nos. 81-3). One wonders whether this conservatism was tied to his strict allegiance to publisher Watanabe Shōzaburō.

92
"Hand Mirror"
Tekagami

DATE Undated, 1954
SIGNATURE AND ARTIST'S SEAL *Shinsui*
PUBLISHER Watanabe Shōzaburō
SIZE 46.8 × 32.7 cm
PROVENANCE Watanabe Shōzaburō, Tokyo, *c.* 1956
ACCESSION NUMBER S2003.8.314
REFERENCES Iino *et al.* (eds.) (1992), cat. no. 129; Hamanaka and Newland (2000), no. 91

This is probably Shinsui's most accomplished print from his later career: print size, palette and the contrasting elements of the kimono design are effectively combined. It might lead to the conclusion that Shinsui is perhaps at his best when his female subject is depicted in profile view or from the back.

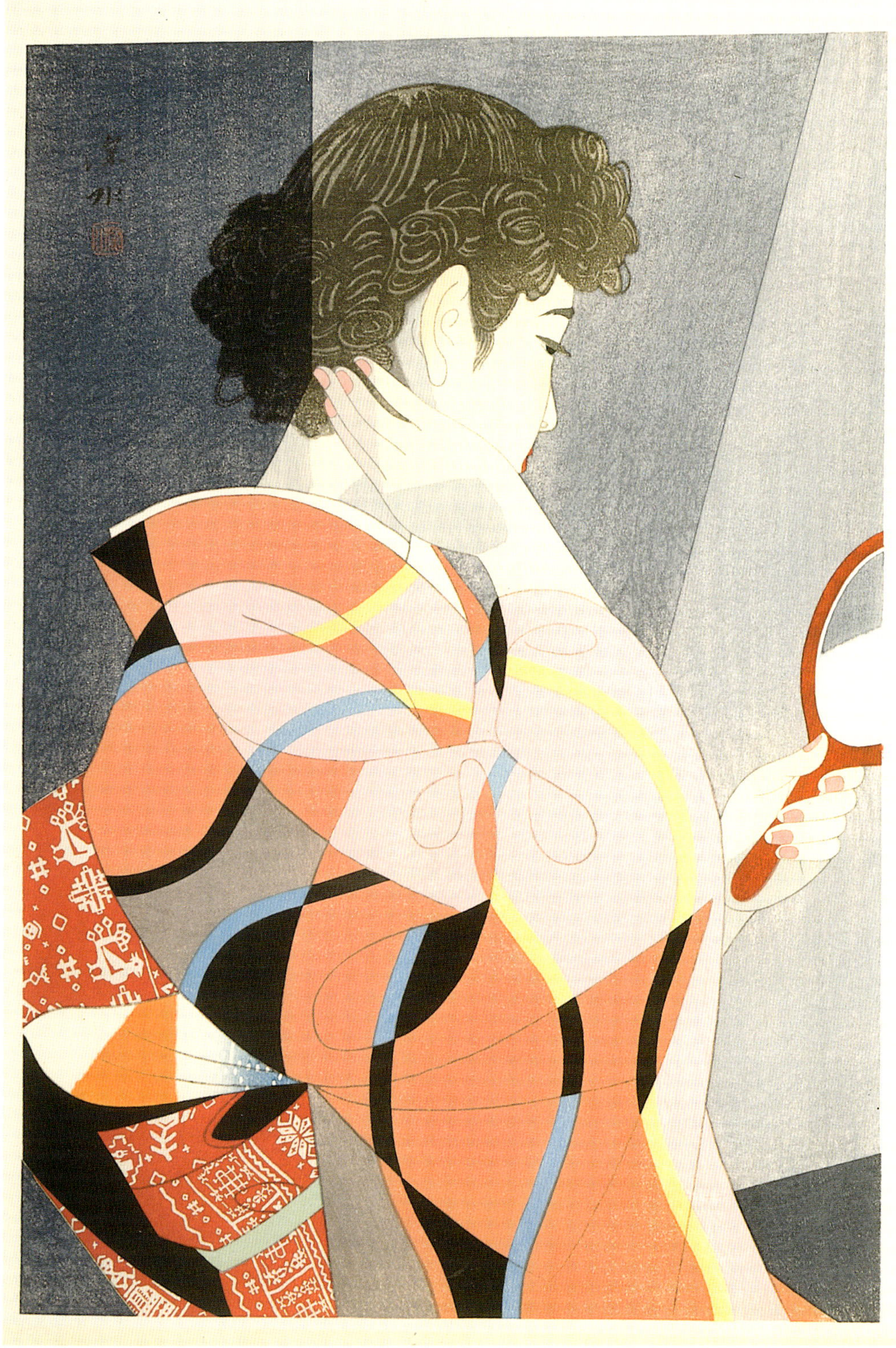

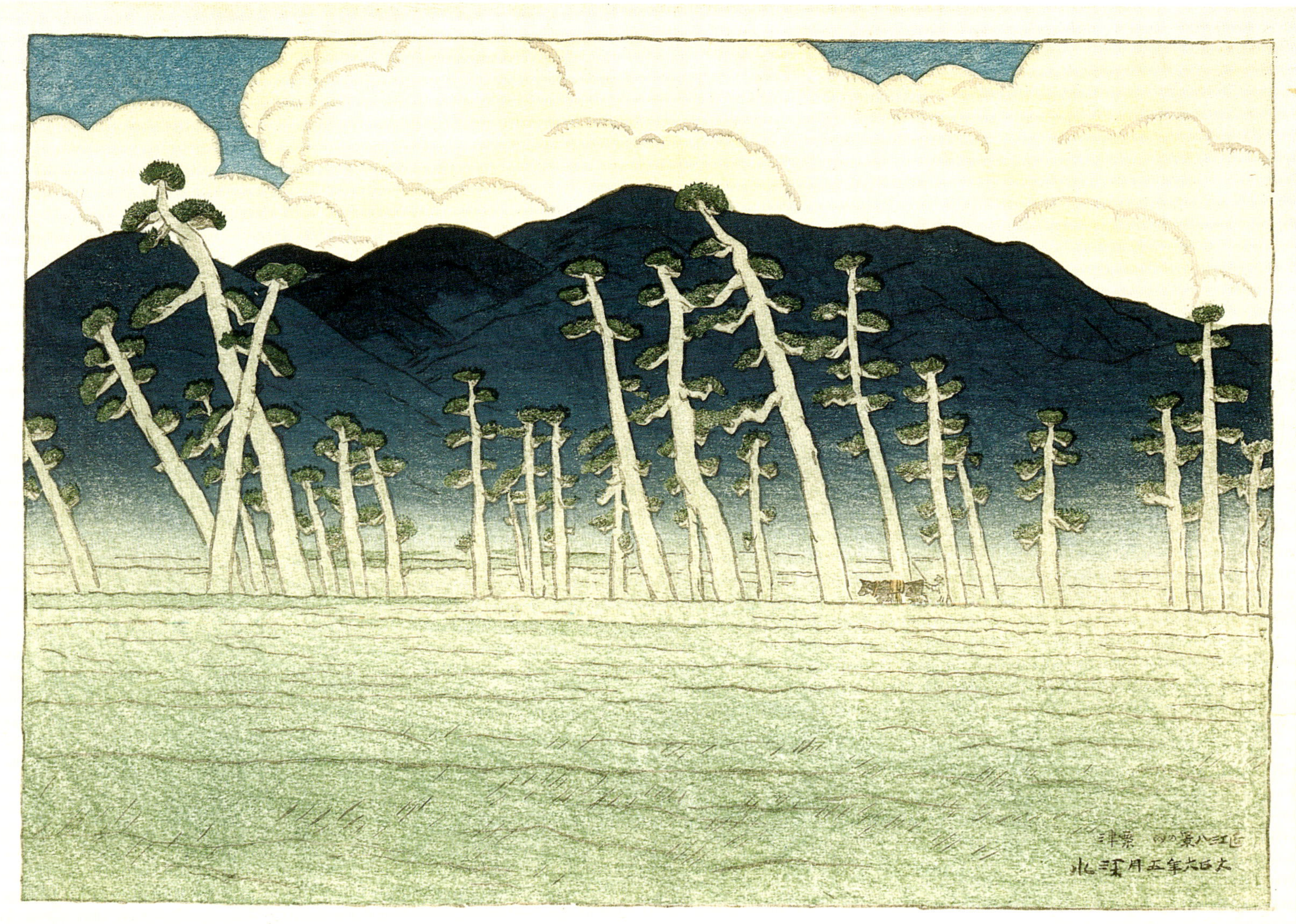

93
"Awazu"
Awazu

SERIES *Eight Views of Ōmi [Lake Biwa] (Ōmi hakkei no uchi)*
DATE 1917 (Taishō 6), May
SIGNATURE *Shinsui*
PUBLISHER Watanabe Shōzaburō
EDITION Number 2 from a limited edition of 200 copies
SIZE 20.0 x 29.7 cm
PROVENANCE S. H. Mori (Shintarō Mori), Chicago, June 1936
ACCESSION NUMBER S2003.8.271
REFERENCES Iino *et al.* (eds.) (1992), cat. no. 11; Stephens (ed.) (1993), cat. no. 235

The following eight prints illustrate in full one of the most intimate yet expressive landscape sets ever produced in the history of Japanese printmaking.

The theme of the "Eight Views of Ōmi" was originally drawn from the Chinese canon for landscape depiction, "Eight Views of the Xiaoxiang Rivers" (*Xiao Xiang bajing*), and appeared in Japanese art from the sixteenth century onward. Shinsui included, numerous Japanese landscape print artists such as Katsushika Hokusai (1760-1849) and Utagawa Hiroshige (1797-1858) were to be inspired by this classical sequel. But in his series Shinsui created a truly personalized view that did not adhere strictly to the classical canon of the eight views.[1]

Shinsui is best remembered as the foremost twentieth-century Japanese artist in the portrayal of the female image. Therefore, it is interesting that Kawase Hasui (1883-1957; cat. nos. 52-63) recounts that after seeing the entire *Eight Views of Ōmi* at an exhibition of the *Kyōdokai* (Homeland Society), he was so overwhelmed by the beauty of Shinsui's landscapes that he decided himself to embark on a career as a landscape print designer.[2] The *Eight Views of Ōmi* was published in a folder in a limited edition of 200 copies (numbered on the back). Unnumbered copies also exist, suggesting that publisher Watanabe extended the print run after the completion of the 200 sets.

1. These traditional Eight Views include: "Lingering Snow at Hira" (*Hira no bosetsu*), "Evening Bell at Mii Temple" (*Miidera no banshō*), "Night Rain at Karasaki" (*Karasaki no yau*), "Evening Glow at Seta" (*Seta no sekishō*), "Glorious Sunset Sky at Awazu" (*Awazu no seiran*), "Returning Ships at Yabase" (*Yabase no kihan*) and "Autumn Moon at Ishiyama" (*Ishiyama no shūgatsu*).
2. Stephens (ed.) (1993), 139.

94
"Hira"
Hira

SERIES *Eight Views of Ōmi [Lake Biwa] (Ōmi hakkei no uchi)*
DATE 1917 (Taishō 6), May
SIGNATURE *Shinsui*
PUBLISHER Watanabe Shōzaburō
EDITION Number 2 from a limited edition of 200 copies
SIZE 20.0 x 29.8 cm
PROVENANCE S. H. Mori (Shintarō Mori), Chicago, June 1936
ACCESSION NUMBER S2003.8.270
REFERENCES Iino *et al.* (eds.) (1992), cat. no. 12; Stephens (ed.) (1993), cat. no. 234

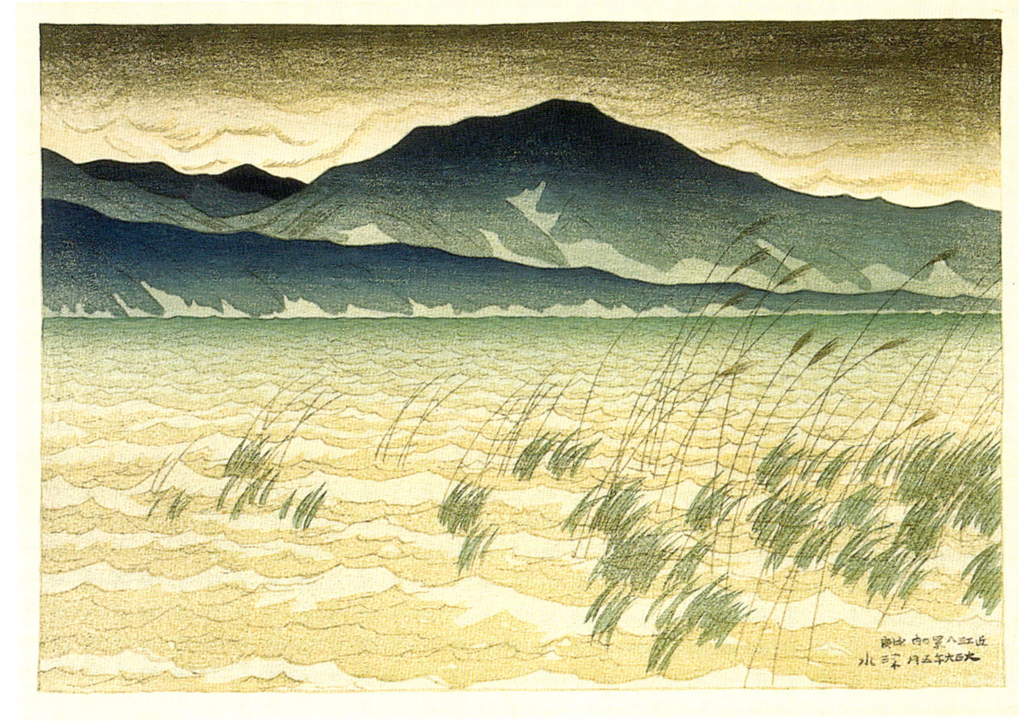

95
"Yabase"
Yabase

SERIES *Eight Views of Ōmi [Lake Biwa] (Ōmi hakkei no uchi)*
DATE 1917 (Taishō 6), July
SIGNATURE *Shinsui*
PUBLISHER Watanabe Shōzaburō
EDITION No edition number
SIZE 19.7 x 29.9 cm
PROVENANCE S. H. Mori (Shintarō Mori), Chicago, June 1936
ACCESSION NUMBER S2003.8.273
REFERENCE Iino *et al.* (eds.) (1992), cat. no. 13

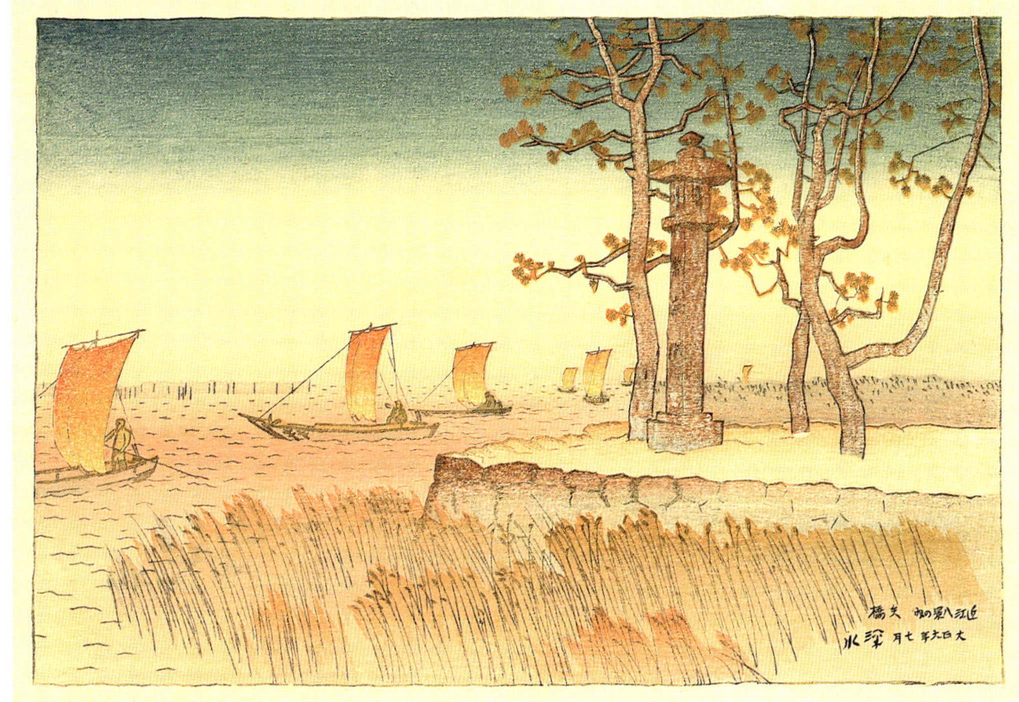

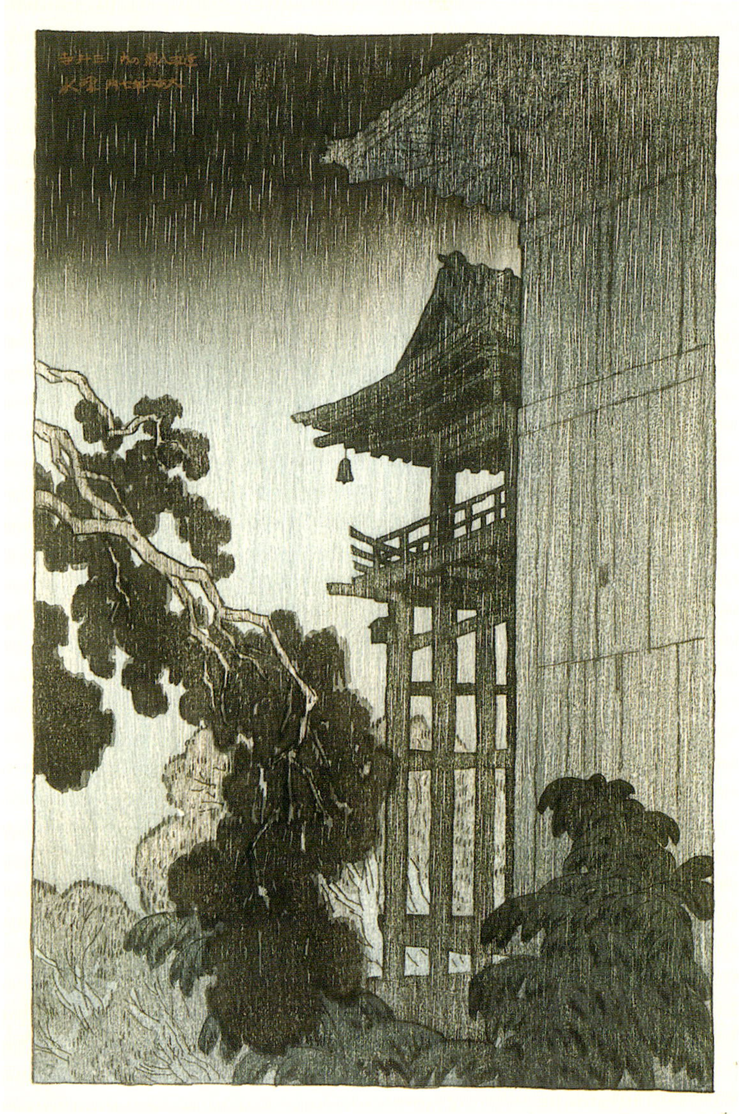

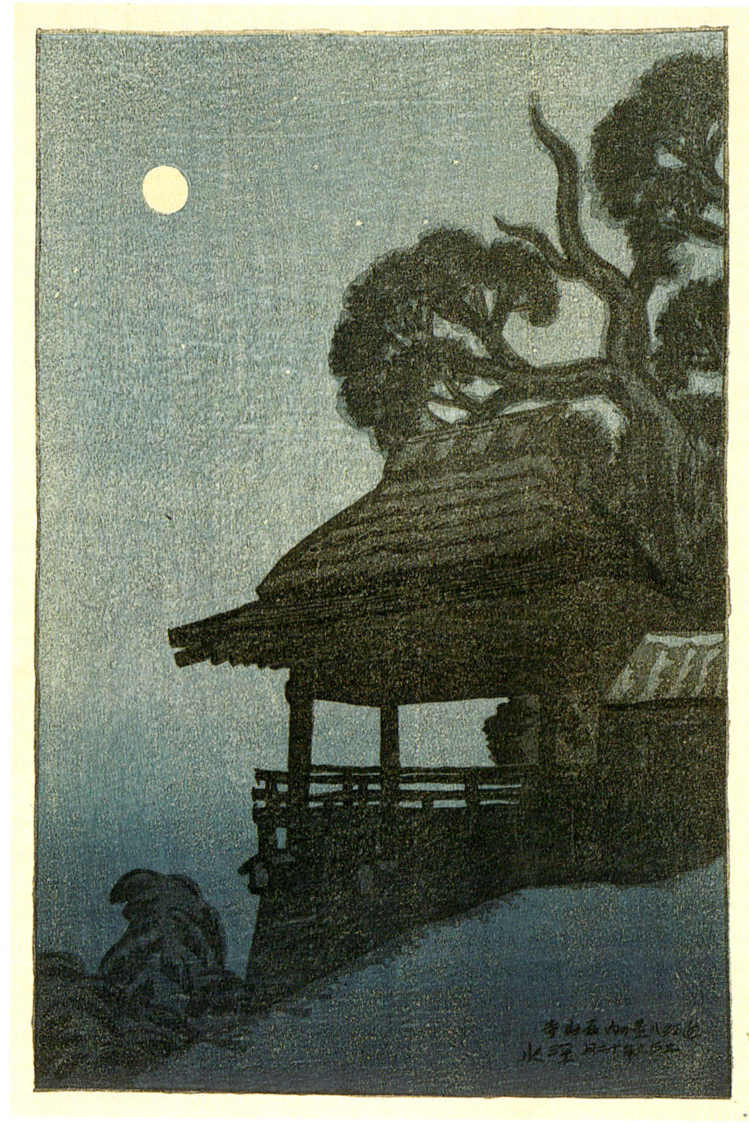

96
"Mii Temple"
Miidera

SERIES *Eight Views of Ōmi [Lake Biwa]* (*Ōmi hakkei no uchi*)
DATE 1917 (Taishō 6), July
SIGNATURE *Shinsui*
PUBLISHER Watanabe Shōzaburō
EDITION Number 52 from a limited edition of 200 copies
SIZE 29.8 x 20.0 cm
PROVENANCE Yamanaka & Co., New York, May 1936
ACCESSION NUMBER S2003.8.272
REFERENCES Iino *et al.* (eds.) (1992), cat. no. 14; Stephens (ed.) (1993), cat. no. 237

97
"Ishiyama Temple"
Ishiyamadera

SERIES *Eight Views of Ōmi [Lake Biwa]* (*Ōmi hakkei no uchi*)
DATE 1917 (Taishō 6), December
SIGNATURE *Shinsui*
PUBLISHER Watanabe Shōzaburō
EDITION Number 2 from a limited edition of 200 copies
SIZE 32.0 x 21.8 cm
PROVENANCE S. H. Mori (Shintarō Mori), Chicago, June 1936
ACCESSION NUMBER S2003.8.274
REFERENCES Iino *et al.* (eds.) (1992), cat. no. 15; Stephens (ed.) (1993), cat. no. 238

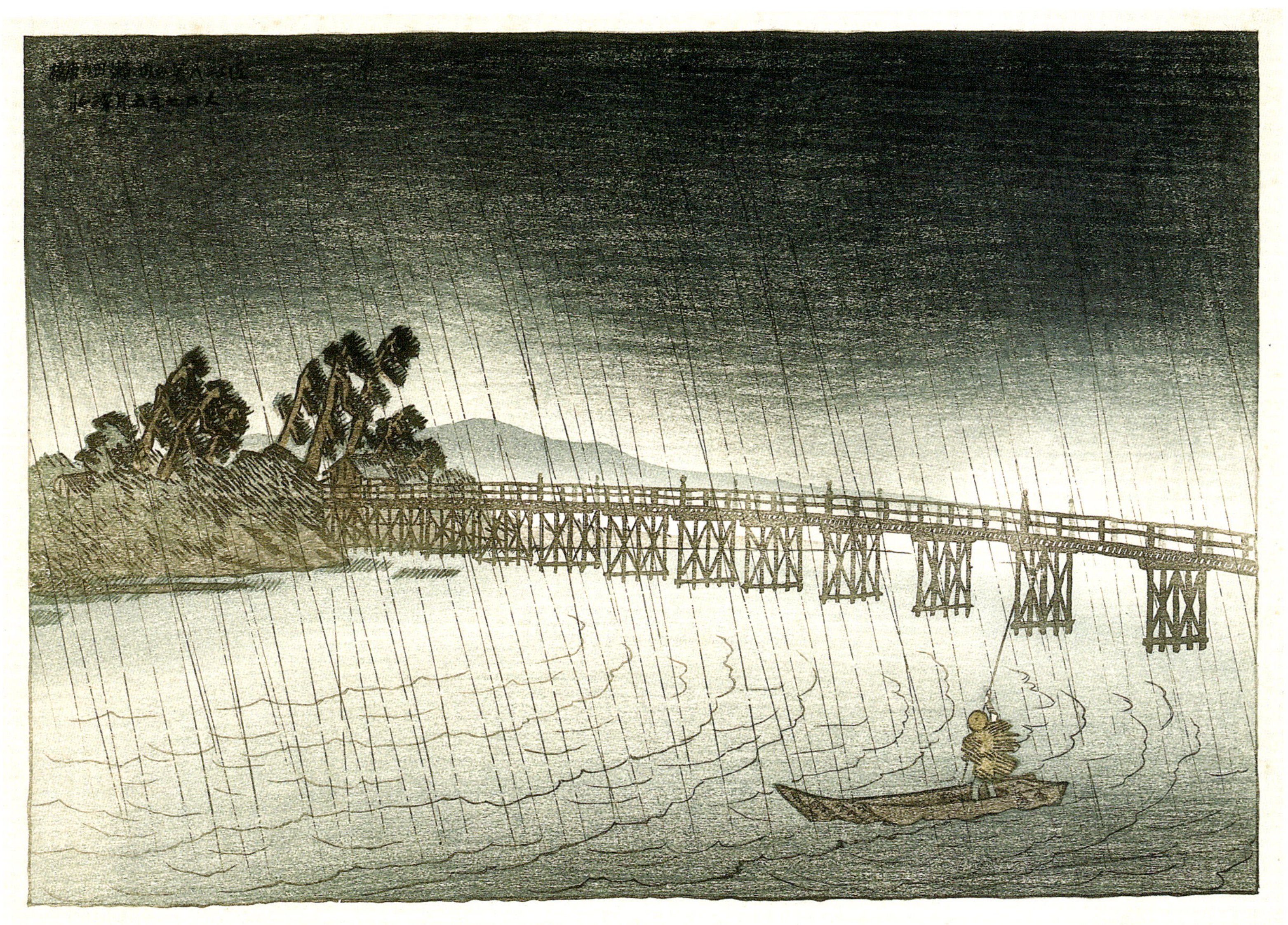

98

"Kara Bridge at Seta"

Seta no Karahashi

SERIES *Eight Views of Ōmi [Lake Biwa] (Ōmi hakkei no uchi)*

DATE 1918 (Taishō 7), May

SIGNATURE *Shinsui*

PUBLISHER Watanabe Shōzaburō

EDITION No edition seal

SIZE 20.0 x 29.8 cm

PROVENANCE S. H. Mori (Shintarō Mori), Chicago, June 1936

ACCESSION NUMBER S2003.8.275

REFERENCES: Iino *et al.* (eds.) (1992), cat. no. 16; Stephens (ed.) (1993), cat. no. 239

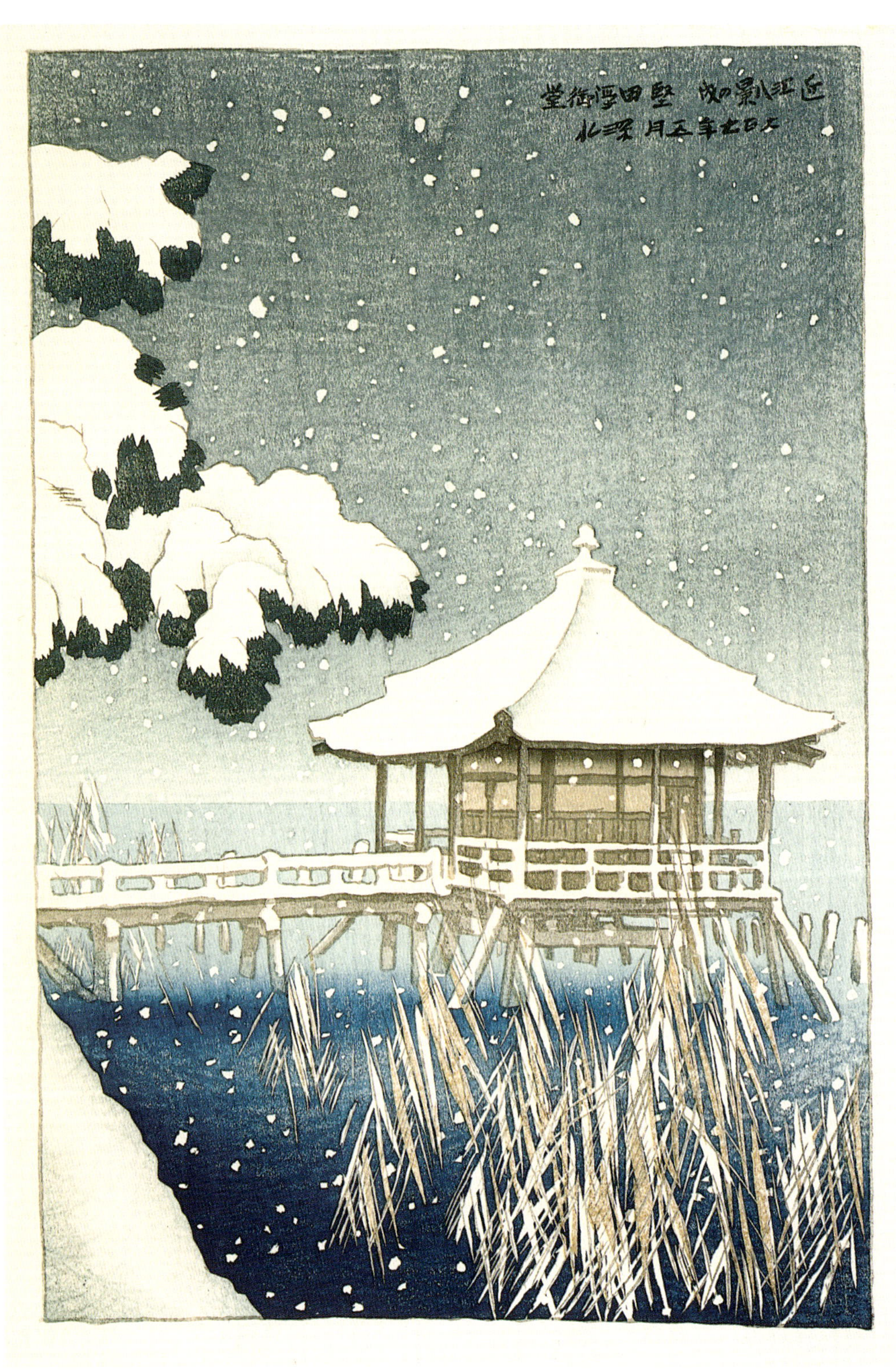

99

"Floating Pavilion at Katada"

Katada Umidō

SERIES *Eight Views of Ōmi [Lake Biwa] (Ōmi hakkei no uchi)*

DATE 1918 (Taishō 7), May

SIGNATURE *Shinsui*

PUBLISHER Watanabe Shōzaburō

EDITION Number 2 from a limited edition of 200 copies

SIZE 20.0 x 29.4 cm

PROVENANCE S. H. Mori (Shintarō Mori), Chicago, June 1936

ACCESSION NUMBER S2003.8.277

REFERENCES Iino *et al.* (eds.) (1992), cat. no. 18; Stephens (ed.) (1993), cat. no. 236

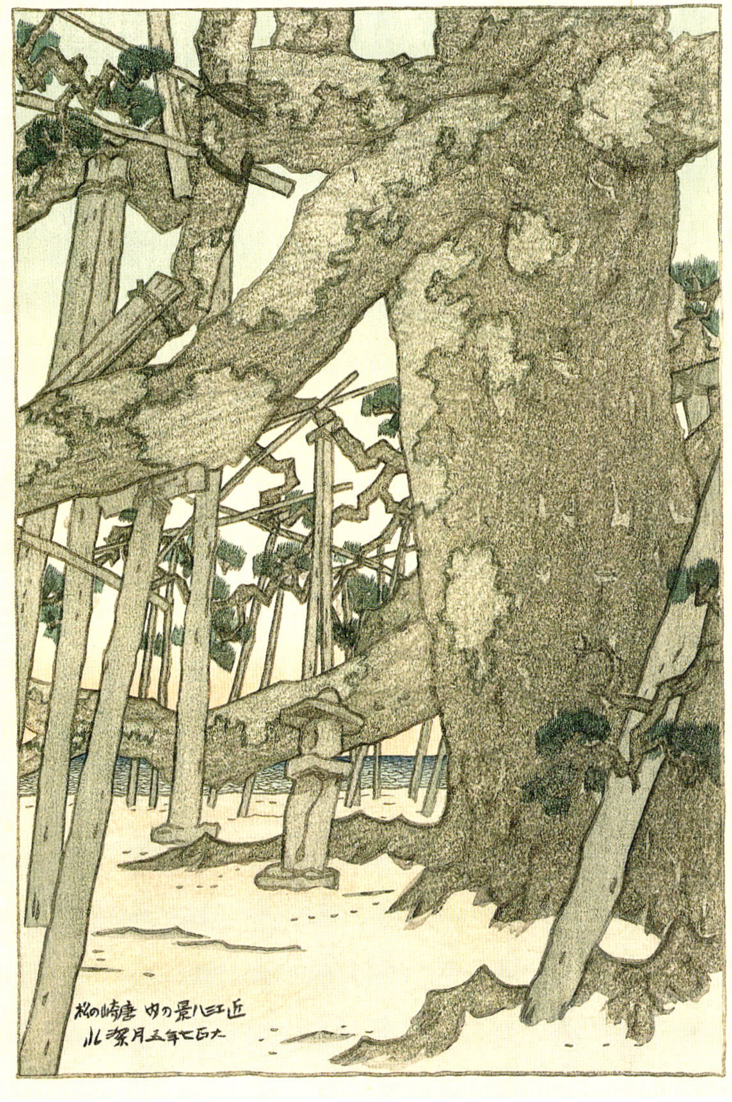

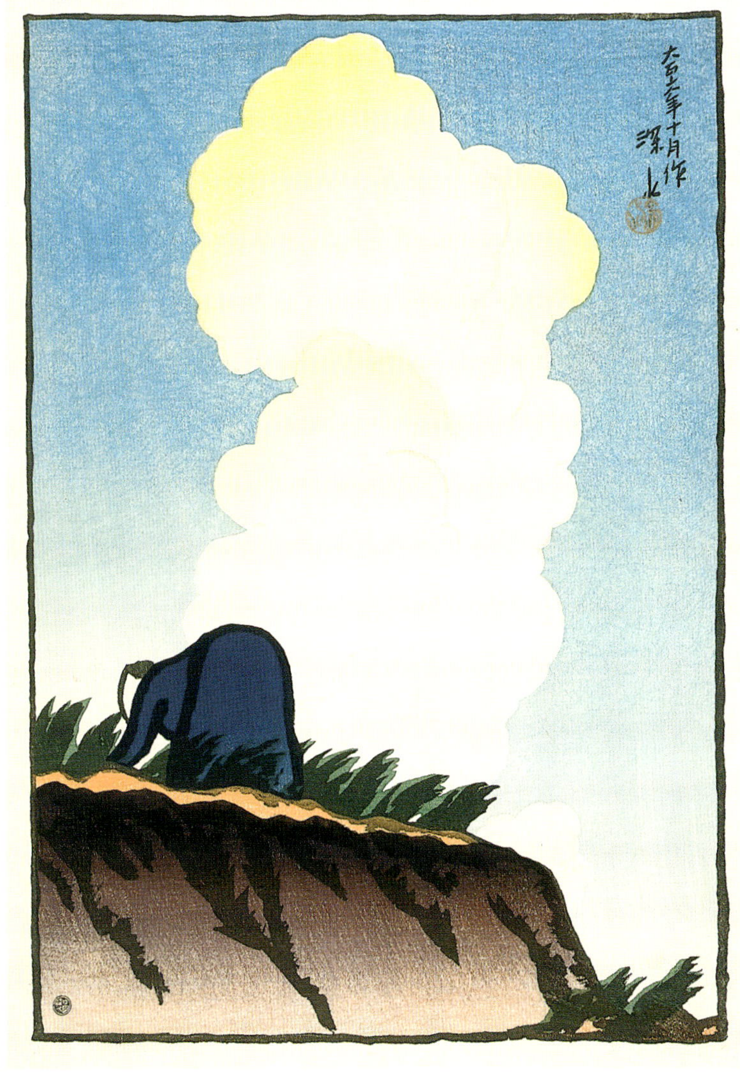

100

"Pine Trees at Karasaki"

Karasaki no matsu

SERIES *Eight Views of Ōmi [Lake Biwa] (Ōmi hakkei no uchi)*
DATE 1918 (Taishō 7), May
SIGNATURE *Shinsui*
PUBLISHER Watanabe Shōzaburō
EDITION Number 2 from a limited edition of 200 copies
SIZE 29.7 × 20.2 cm
PROVENANCE S. H. Mori (Shintarō Mori), Chicago, June 1936
ACCESSION NUMBER S2003.8.276
REFERENCE Iino *et al.* (eds.) (1992), cat. no. 17

101

"A Summer's Midday"

DATE 1919 (Taishō 6), October
SIGNATURE AND ARTIST'S SEAL *Shinsui*
PUBLISHER Watanabe Shōzaburō
SIZE 33.0 × 23.2 cm
PROVENANCE Yamanaka & Co., Boston, April 1937
ACCESSION NUMBER S2003.8.279
REFERENCES Iino *et al.* (eds.) (1992), cat. no. 10; Stephens (ed.) (1993), cat. no. 240

A woman, bent-over, works in a field. A highly abstract landscape in which the woman, the field and the grass are delineated in rough strokes, while a huge billowy cloud is offset against the sky through the use of blind-printing or gauffrage.

Kasamatsu Shirō (1898-1991)

Kasamatsu Shirō was born in the Asakusa district of Tokyo. From about 1911 he studied *Nihonga* with Kaburagi Kiyokata (1878-1973; cat. nos. 5-7) and studied the art of woodblock printing, even though he would not turn to printmaking until around 1916. Shirō showed his paintings at several exhibitions, including the *Bunten*, *Sengakai* (The Select Art Society) exhibition, where he won a prize in 1916, and *Kokumin Bijutsu Kyōkai* (The People's Art Society). He was active in the *Tatsumi Gakai* (Southeast Painting Society), *Seikinkai* (Blue Collar Society) and *Kyōdokai* (Homeland Society). His first print, "Wind Blowing Through Verdure" (*Aoarashi*), was released in 1919 by publisher Watanabe Shōzaburō (1885-1962). In September 1923 many of the blocks for his prints were destroyed in the Great Kantō Earthquake. He was one of the artists included in the 1936 Japanese print exhibition at the Toledo Museum of Art, and in around 1945 he ceased designing prints for Watanabe. Although he started initially as a *Shin-hanga* artist, from the 1950s onward he became increasingly interested in *Sōsaku-hanga*. He carved the blocks and printed works himself from the mid to late 1950s. According to the Wagōkai Foundation, Shirō produced 290 prints during his life, and his body of work is testimony to his specialization in landscapes.

REFERENCES Watanabe Shōzaburō (1936), 118; Merritt and Yamada (1992), 54-5; Stephens (ed.) (1993), 195-97; Wagōkai (ed.) (2002), 69-70

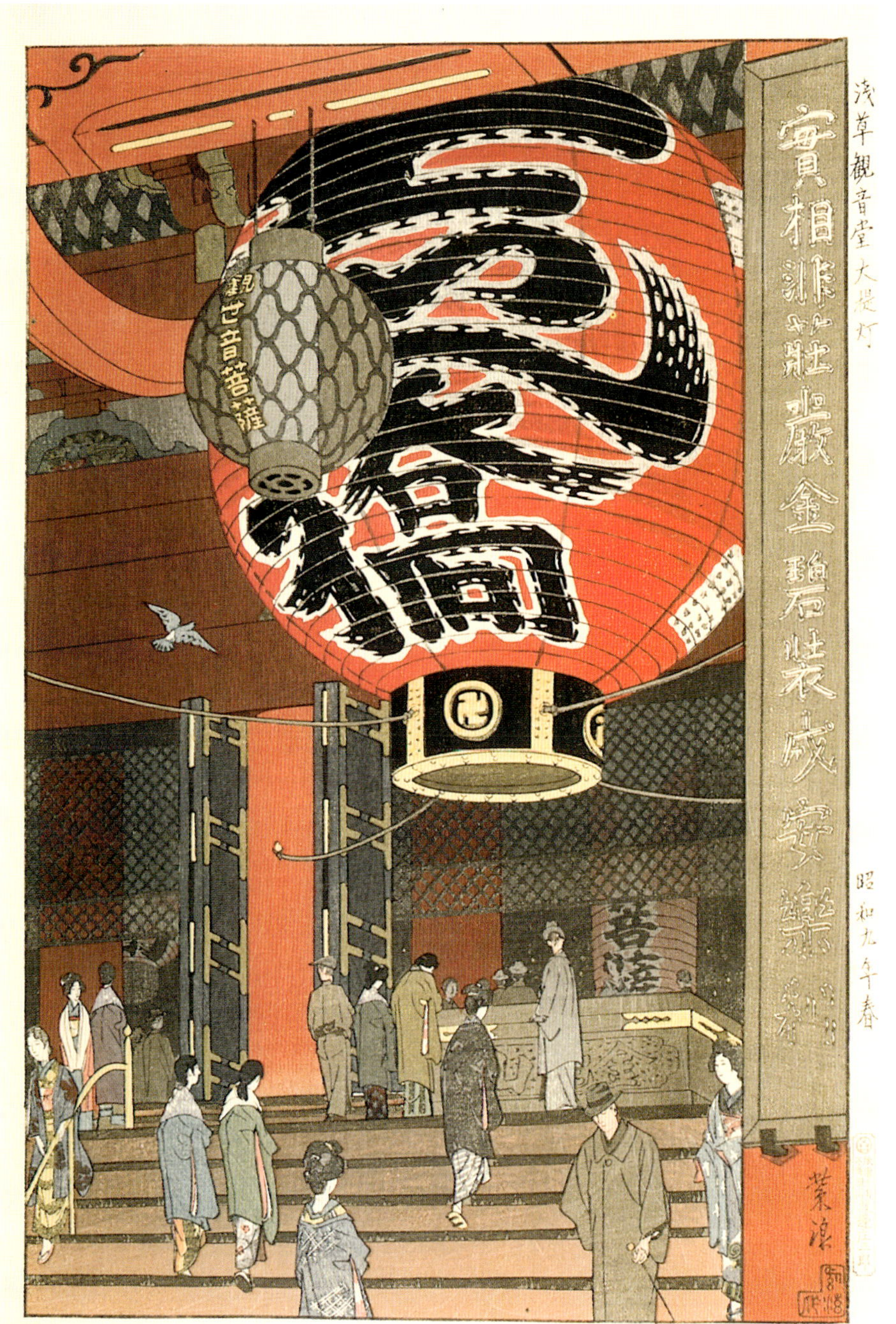

102
"The Great Lantern of the Sensō Temple, Asakusa"
Asakusa Sensōji daichōchin

DATE 1934 (Shōwa 9), Spring
SIGNATURE *Shirō*
PUBLISHER Watanabe Shōzaburō
SIZE 36.2 x 24.1 cm
ACCESSION NUMBER S2003.8.472
REFERENCES Watanabe Shōzaburō (1936), K-11; Wagōkai (ed.) (2002), 14

The enormously popular Asakusa Kannon Temple (also know as Sensō Temple) in Tokyo's Asakusa district figures prominently in the traditional annual calendar of events and festivals, especially during the temple visits at the New Year which attract large crowds. This print is characteristic of Shirō's early period. It is representative of the works released by the Watanabe publishing house, as seen in the similar styles of Shirō's contemporaries, Kawase Hasui (1883-1957; cat. nos. 52-63), Tsuchiya Kōitsu (1870-1949; cat. nos. 8-9) and others.

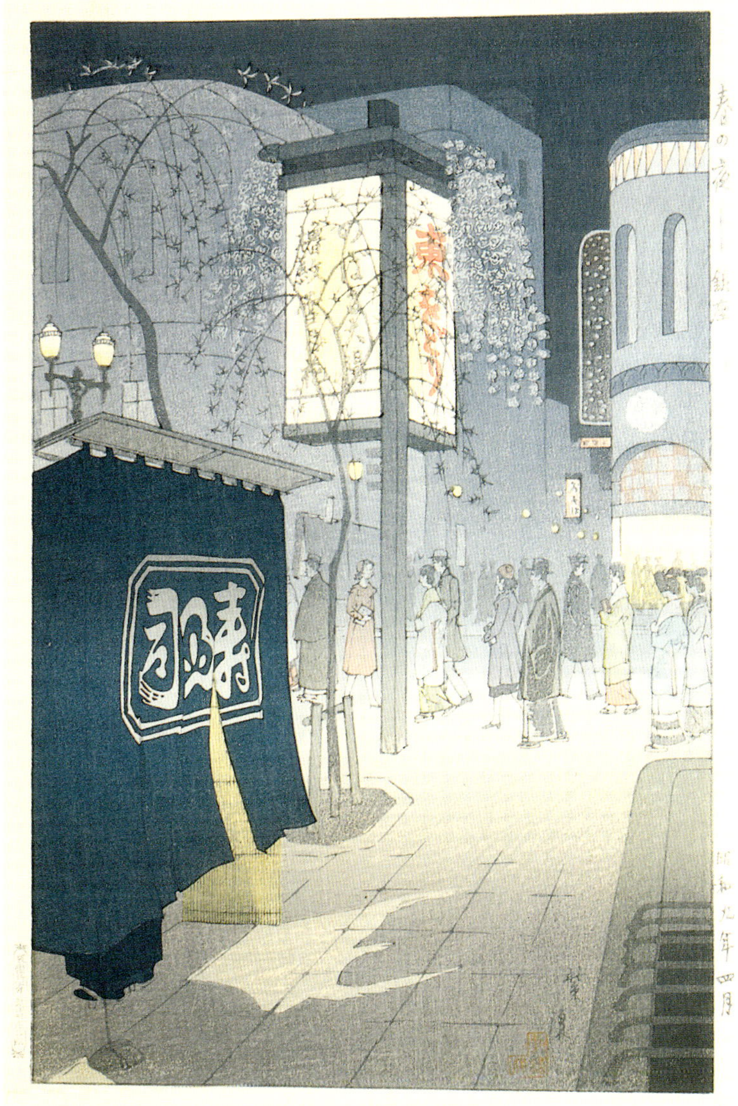

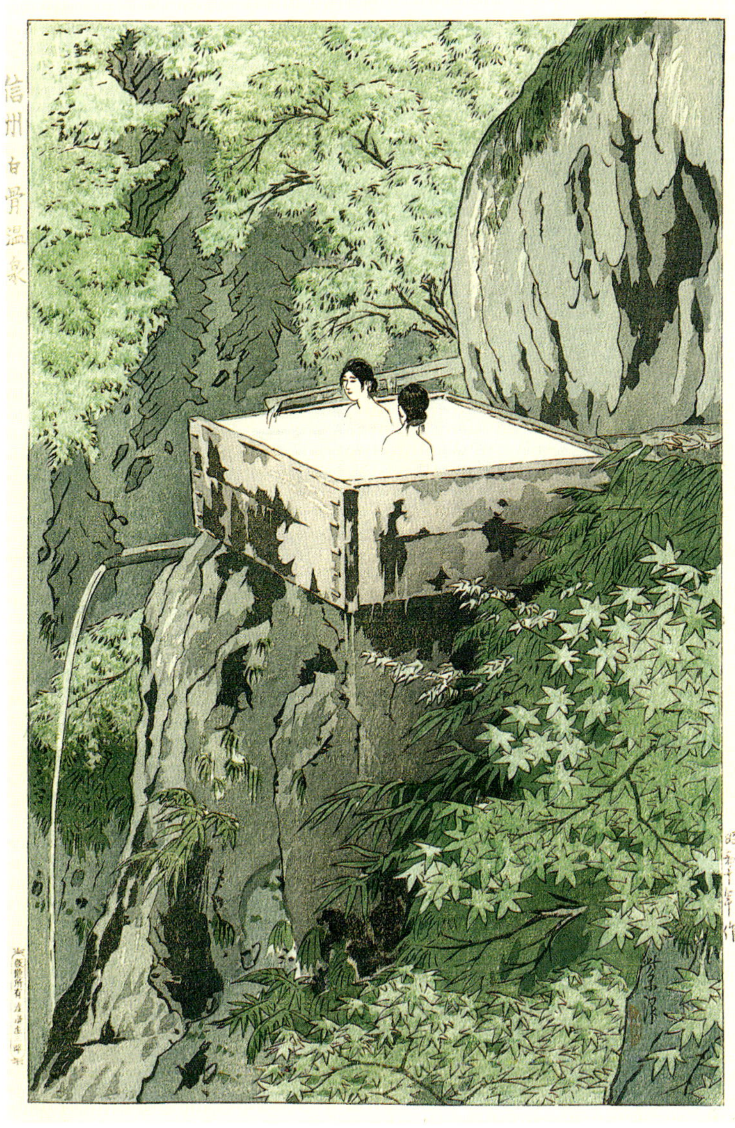

103

"Spring Night at Ginza"

Haru no yoru Ginza

DATE 1934 (Shōwa 9), April
SIGNATURE *Shirō*
ARTIST'S SEAL *Shirō saku*
PUBLISHER Watanabe Shōzaburō
SIZE 36.4 x 23.8 cm
PROVENANCE Shima Art Co., New York, 1940
ACCESSION NUMBER S2003.8.473
REFERENCES The Toledo Museum of Art (1936), cat. no. 171; Watanabe Shōzaburō (1936), K-9; Wagōkai (ed.) (2002), 14

This piece stands as one of Shirō's most delightful designs: a view of the bustling Ginza district in Tokyo during the 1930s, with a streetside food stall to the left, and on the right a large advertisement for the traditional geisha dance, *azuma odori* (literally, "dance of the Eastern Capital [Tokyo]"). Alexandra Marmion suggests that in his prints Shirō attempts to poeticize, or "Edocize," the most aggressively modern district of Tokyo by eliminating any reference to modern culture and defining the subject through elements with romantic, nostalgic connotations – the blossoming cherry tree, the food stall, and the reference to Edo in the advertisement.[1]

1. A. J. Marmion, "The Cultural Landscape: Modernity and Japan's Ideological Reaction," 22-33, in Brown *et al.* (1996), 26.

104

"Shirahone Hot Spring, Shinshū"

Shinshū Shirahone onsen

DATE 1935 (Shōwa 10)
SIGNATURE *Shirō*, with half moon-shaped artist's seal
PUBLISHER Watanabe Shōzaburō
SIZE 36.2 x 24.1 cm
ACCESSION NUMBER S2003.8.458
REFERENCES Watanabe Shōzaburō (1936), K-15; Wagōkai (ed.) (2002), 52 (not illustrated)

Shirō's print production up until World War II resulted in some fifty-six designs, after which time he designed no prints for ten years. His prints dating to the postwar era are more in keeping with the *Sōsaku-hanga* style of artists like Kiyoshi Saitō (1907-97) than with examples of *Shin-hanga*.

Torii Kotondo (1900-76)

Kotondo was born Saitō Akira in the Nihonbashi district of Tokyo. He studied *Yamato-e* painting, ancient court and military arts with the painter Kobori Tomone (1864-1931). At the age of fifteen he was adopted by Torii Kiyotada IV (1875-1941), the seventh-generation head of the Torii School. Kotondo assisted in the production of Kabuki billboards, thus receiving the "classical" training in the time-honored tradition of Torii actor print design. He also illustrated magazines, such as the *Engi gahō* (*Illustrated Entertainment News*), and designed theatrical programs using the name *Kotondo*. In 1917 he entered the studio of Kaburagi Kiyokata (1878-1973; cat. nos. 5-7), where he studied *bijinga* and was exposed to the work of other Kiyokata students like Itō Shinsui (1898-1972; cat. nos. 85-101). His work was admitted to the *Inten* of 1925, and he succeeded his adoptive father Kiyotada in 1929 as the eight-generation head of the Torii line (he assumed the name Kiyotada V in 1941). In 1929 the firms of Sakai/Kawaguchi co-published Kotondo prints of Shōwa-period beauties. The publisher Ikeda produced another twelve exquisite prints of beauties between 1932 and 1934. Kotondo continued to paint beautiful women and actors, but also created some surprising *kachōga*. Kotondo exhibited at the *Nitten* in 1952 and worked as an art director for Kabuki theaters, an art consultant for television, and a teacher of dramatic arts at the *Nihon Daigaku* (Nihon [Japan] University) from 1966 to 1972. Kotondo used four different artist's names throughout his career: Kotondo, Masahiko, Kiyonobu and Kiyotada V.

REFERENCES Merritt and Yamada (1992), 155; Stephens (ed.) (1993), 198; Hamanaka and Newland (2000), 125-40, 212; Ōta Memorial Museum of Art (ed.) (2000)

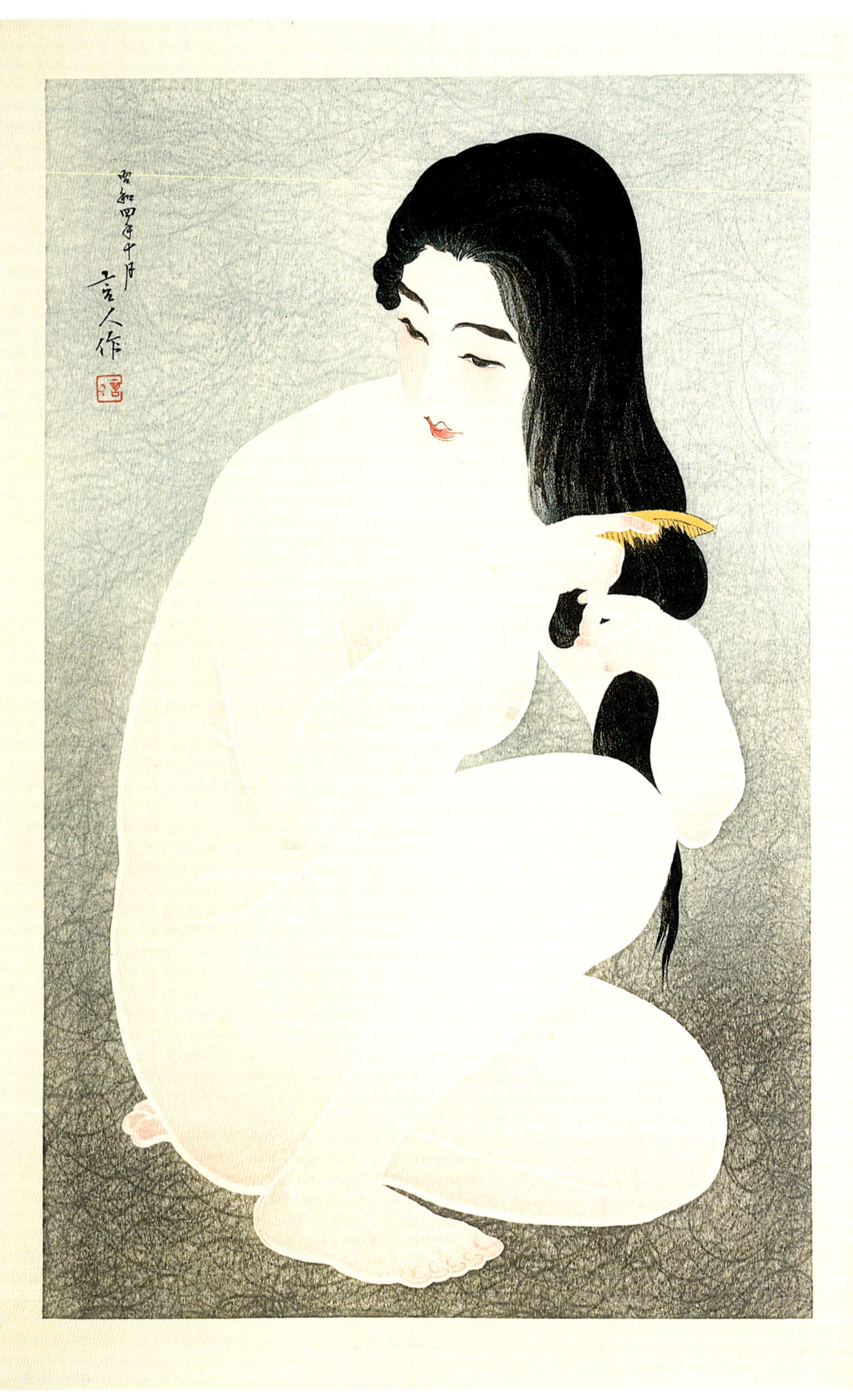

105
"Combing Hair"
Kamisuki

DATE 1929 (Shōwa 4), October
SIGNATURE *Kotondo saku*
ARTIST'S SEAL *Kotondo*

PUBLISHER Sakai/Kawaguchi
EDITION Number 5 from a limited edition of 200 copies
SIZE 41.0 x 26.2 cm
PROVENANCE Shima Art Co., New York, 1940
ACCESSION NUMBER S2003.8.2539
REFERENCES Stephens (ed.) (1993), cat. no. 264; Hamanaka and Newland (2000), no. 170

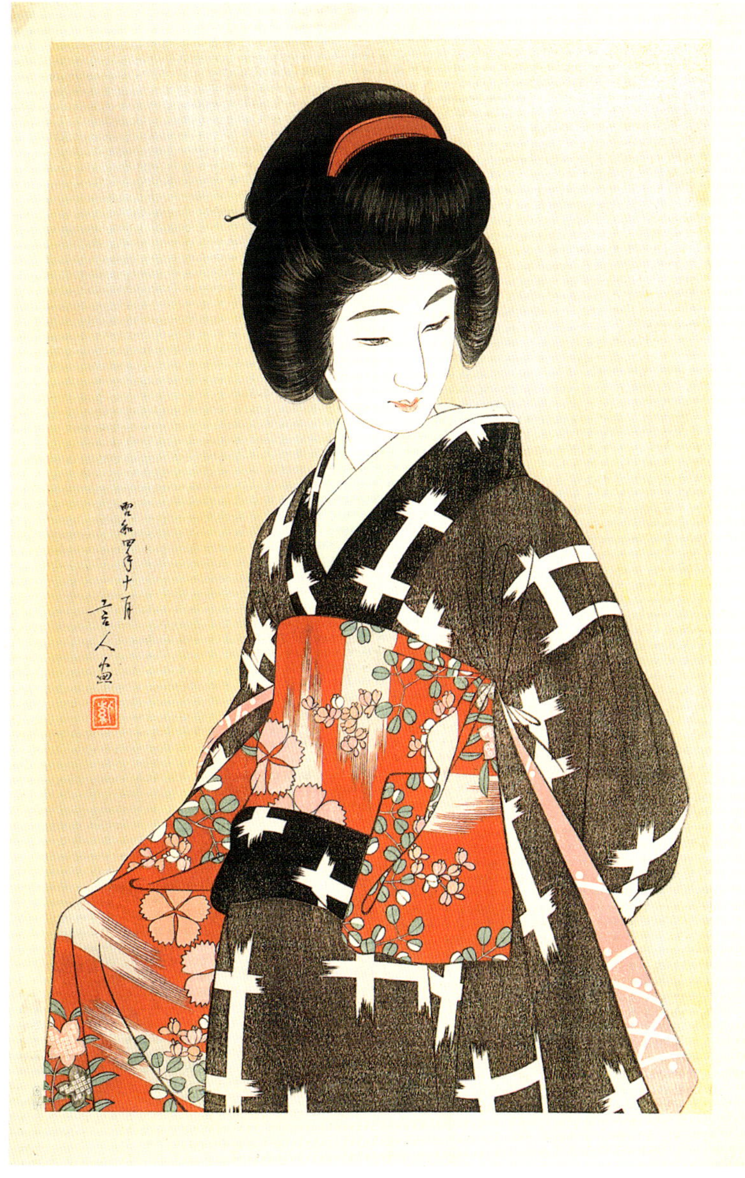

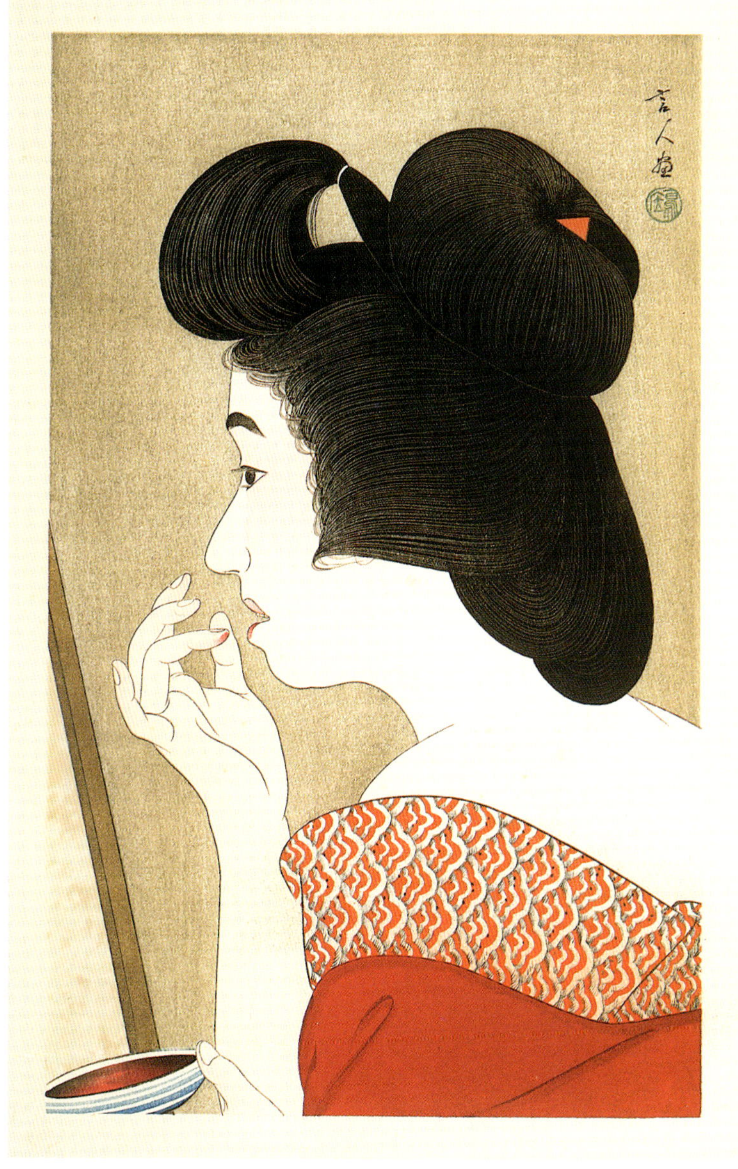

106
"Sash"

DATE 1929 (Shōwa 4), November
SIGNATURE *Kotondo ga*
ARTIST'S SEAL *Shi*
PUBLISHER Kawaguchi
EDITION Number 137 from a limited edition of 350 copies
SIZE 41.0 x 26.2 cm
PROVENANCE Shima Art Co., New York, 1940
ACCESSION NUMBER S2003.8.2555
REFERENCE Hamanaka and Newland (2000), no. 168

Kotondo and the joint publishers Sakai/Kawaguchi experimented with the color for several of the artist's designs. This composition is known in at least three versions, in which the color of the *obi* sash and kimono vary, as does the tint of the mica background. Sakai/Kawaguchi co-produced six prints by Kotondo. Kawaguchi continued on his own after 1930, adding two new designs and reprinting most of the joint productions.

107
"Rouge"

DATE Undated, c. 1930
SIGNATURE *Kotondo ga*
ARTIST'S SEAL *Torii Kotondo*
PUBLISHER Ikeda
SIZE 25.4 x 40.7 cm
PROVENANCE The Tokaido Inc. (J. D. McLaughlin), Boston, August 1937
ACCESSION NUMBER S2003.8.2552
REFERENCE Hamanaka and Newland (2000), no. 179

Some of Kotondo's best designs were issued by Ikeda, a small publishing company in Tokyo. That we know virtually nothing about the Ikeda firm is remarkable in view of the extremely high quality of their Kotondo prints. Their editions were generally limited to 100 impressions.

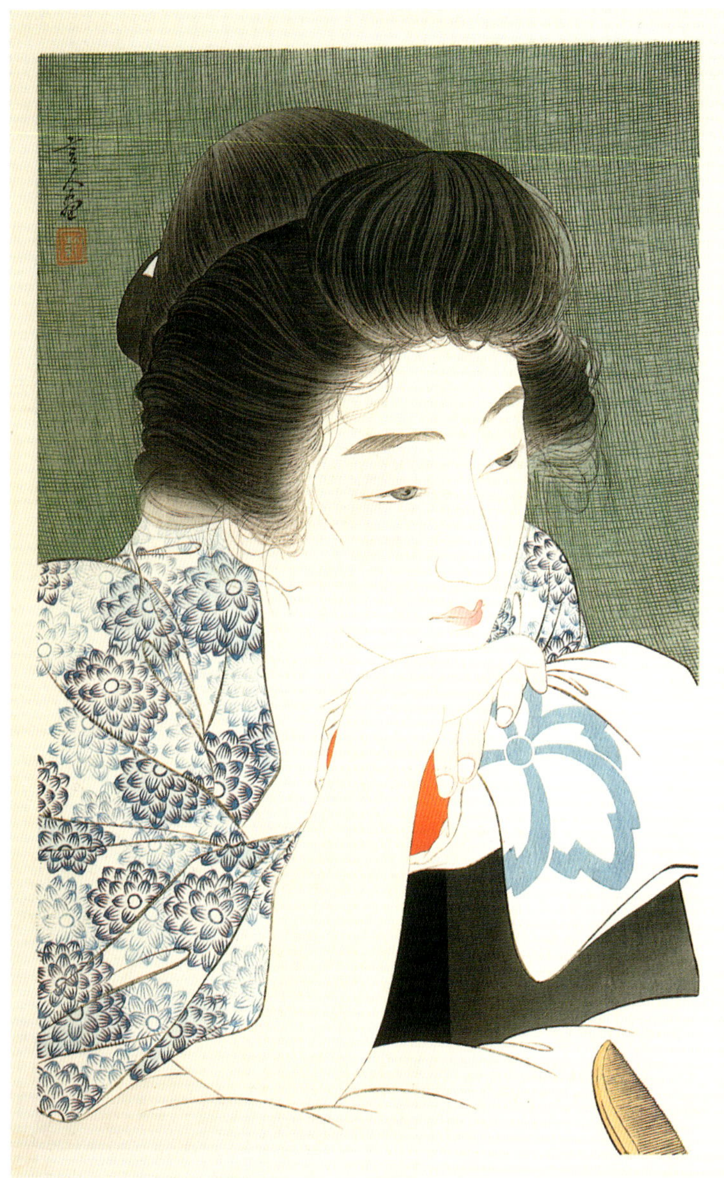

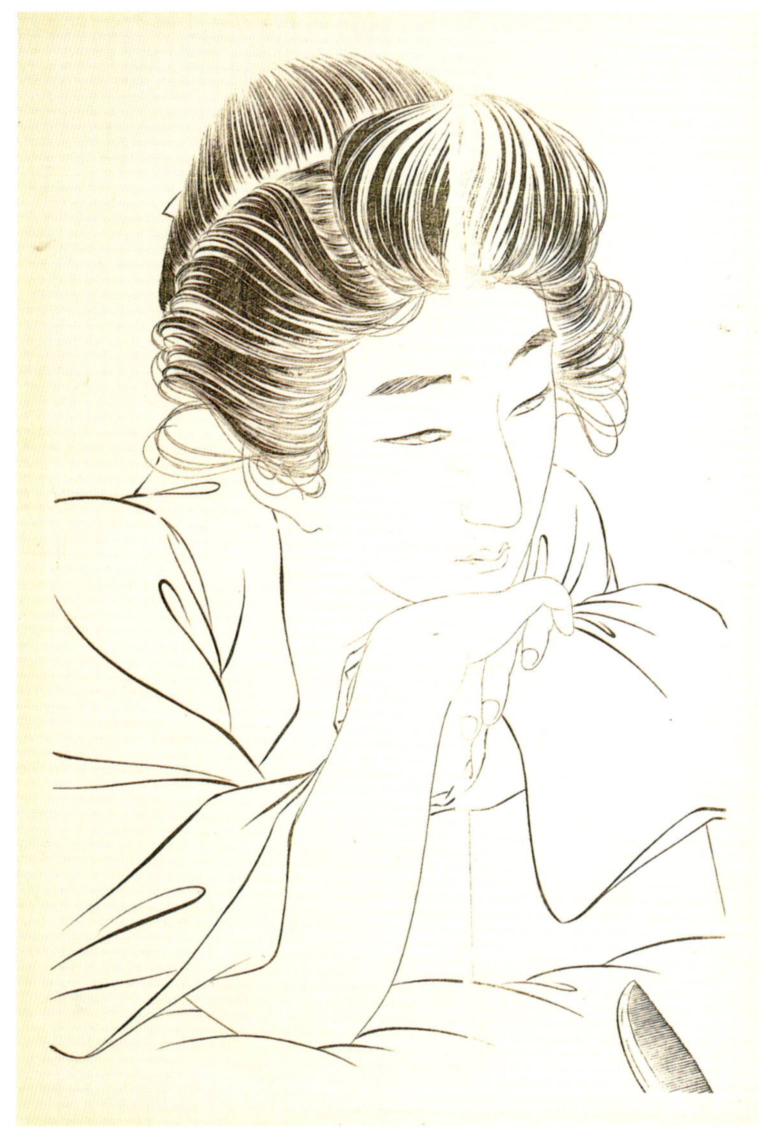

108
"Morning Hair"

DATE 1930 (Shōwa 5)
SIGNATURE *Kotondo ga*
ARTIST'S SEAL *Shi*
PUBLISHER Ikeda
EDITION Number 29 from a limited edition of 200 copies
SIZE 25.6 x 40.8 cm
PROVENANCE The Tokaido Inc. (J. D. McLaughlin), Boston, September 1938
ACCESSION NUMBER S2003.8.2550
REFERENCES Stephens (ed.) (1993), cat. no. 268; Hamanaka and Newland (2000), no. 178

Captured in a moment of dream-like revelry, this beauty is perhaps reliving a meeting with her paramour the night before. An unsubstantiated report states that the underlying message conveyed by this print was considered salacious by the authorities, and therefore only seventy prints were sold before the keyblock was destroyed. Nevertheless, this work represents a high point in *Shin-hanga* history.

109
Keyblock impression for "Morning Hair"

PROVENANCE Shima Art Co., 1940
ACCESSION NUMBER S2003.8.2551
REFERENCE Stephens (ed.) (1993), cat. no. 269

This keyblock print demonstrates how a keyblock is canceled, thereby assuring the limitation of an edition. All thirteen blocks for this print were cut by Maeda Kentarō (*c.* 1891-?), who worked for several publishers including Watanabe Shōzaburō and artists such as Hashiguchi Goyō (1880-1921; cat. nos. 36-44).

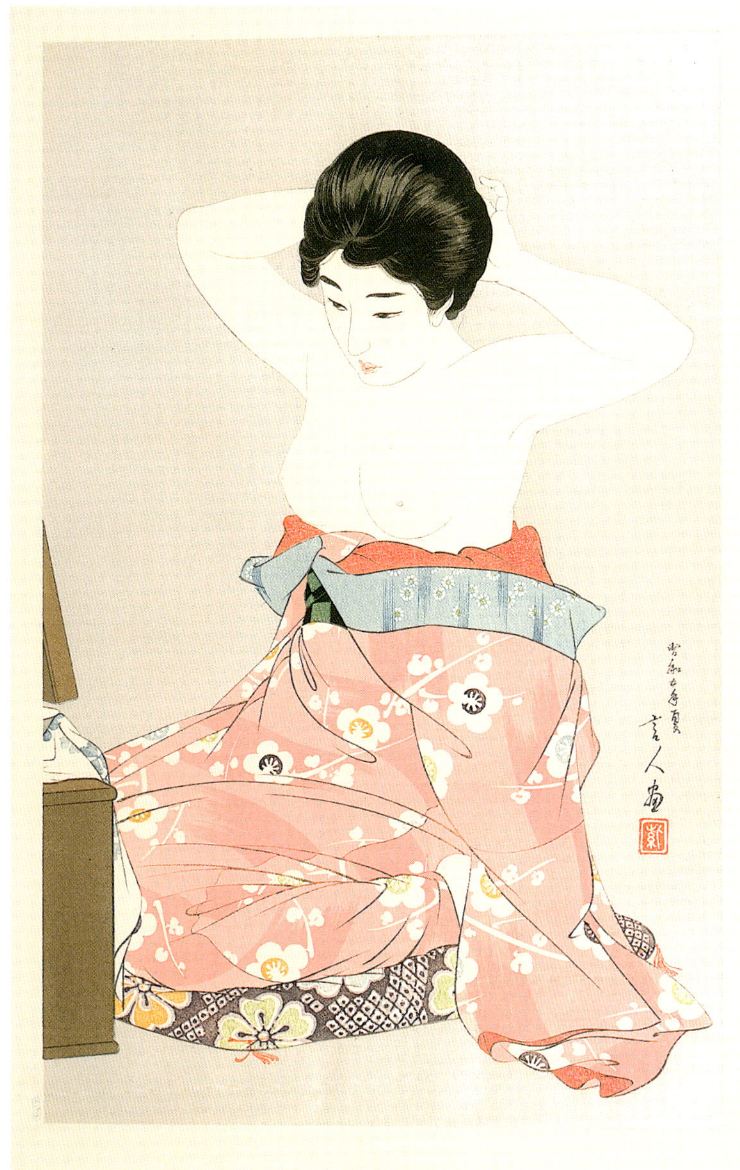

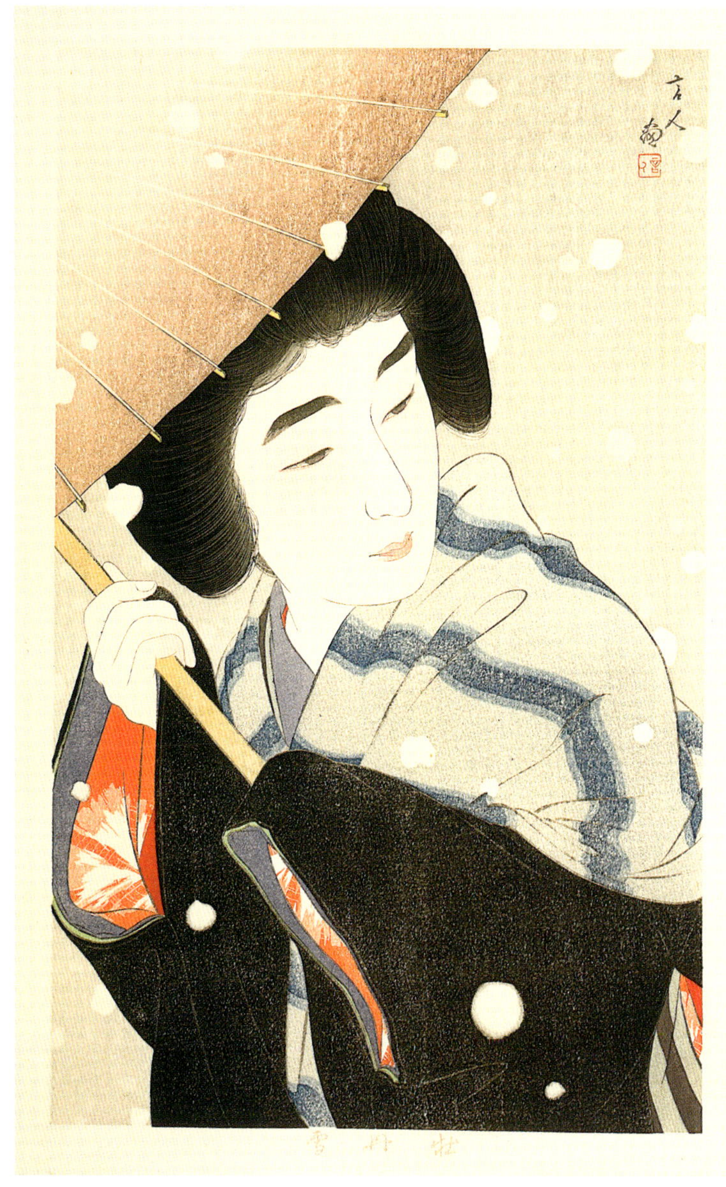

110
"Make-up"

DATE 1930 (Shōwa 5), Summer
SIGNATURE *Kotondo ga*
ARTIST'S SEAL *Shi*
PUBLISHER Kawaguchi
EDITION Number 137 from a limited edition of 350 copies
SIZE 40.8 x 26.2 cm
PROVENANCE The Tokaido Inc. (J. D. McLaughlin), Boston, February 1939
ACCESSION NUMBER S2003.8.2541
REFERENCES Stephens (ed.) (1993), cat. no. 267; Hamanaka and Newland (2000), no. 174

Striking in its forward sensuousness, this design of a woman attending to her toilette is another example of the expensive materials and the high-quality printing that typified Kawaguchi publications. The use of a solid silver mica background and the minimal interior furnishings serve to emphasize the form of the young woman, who immediately draws our attention.

111
"Peony Snow"
Botanyuki

DATE Undated, c. 1931
SIGNATURE *Kotondo ga*
ARTIST'S SEAL *Kotondo*
PUBLISHER Ikeda
EDITION Number 57 from a limited edition of 100 copies
SIZE 40.8 x 25.4 cm
PROVENANCE The Tokaido Inc. (J. D. McLaughlin), Boston, February 1939
ACCESSION NUMBER S2003.8.2558
REFERENCES Stephens (ed.) (1993), cat. no. 271; Hamanaka and Newland (2000), no. 181

The title of this print underlies a clever, layered word play. The large snowflakes are reminiscent of the blossoms of a peony and therefore the title *botanyuki* (literally, "peony snow"). But there is also a special type of "winter peony" (*fuyu botan*) that is often protected against the frost by a small thatched cover, much in the same way as the umbrella shields this beauty from the falling snow. Therefore here we have the comparison of the size of the snowflakes to the peony and of the woman's beauty to the flower's delicate blossoms.

Appendix

Kabuki Actor Prints

Henk Herwig

The following section briefly details the plays and the roles depicted in the ten Kabuki actor prints in this publication.

64

Yamamura Kōka(1886-1942)

"The Actor Ichikawa Danshirō II as Tesshinsai in the Play *Kyōkaku harusame-gasa* (*The Chivalrous Commoner's Spring Raincoat*)," c. 1919

Tesshinsai is a masterless samurai (*rōnin*) and the leader of a gang of hoodlums who terrorize the townspeople (*chōnin*) community. His nemesis is Gyōu, a Robin Hood-like character (*otokodate* or *kyōkaku*) who champions the *chōnin* class in his fight against Tesshinsai and his gang. *The Chivalrous Commoner's Spring Raincoat*, written by Fukuchi Ōchi (1841-1906) in 1897, met with immediate public acclaim as it gave a voice to the hostility felt by many *chōnin* towards the samurai class. Today it might interpreted as an important early protest in Japan against class discrimination. Kōka has cleverly captured the evil character of Tesshinai as performed by the actor Ichikawa Danshirō II (1855-1922). Danshirō's dramatic hairstyle, coupled with striking contrast of tonalities, reinforces the character's fierce countenance.

Fukuchi Ōchi was an influential journalist and politician who became the head of the newspaper *Tōkyō Nichinichi Shinbun* (*Tokyo Daily News*). He was also the co-founder and proprietor of the Kabuki Theater in Tokyo. But he is best remembered for his efforts to raise the social status of the Kabuki theater during the Meiji era from a merely populist form to one receiving official recognition.

65

Yamamura Kōka (1886-1942)

"The Actor Onoe Matsusuke IV as Kōmori Yasugorō in the Play *Yowa nasake ukina yokogushi* (*The Love Affair of Otomi and Scarface Yosaburō*)," c. 1919

The handsome haberdasher, Kirare Yosaburō ("Scarface Yosa") is attacked and severely cut on his face when his clandestine affair with Otomi, a former Fukagawa geisha turned gangster's moll, is found out. He and his crony "Kōmori Yasugorō" ("Yasu the Bat") now earn a living as petty thieves, and one day they conspire to extort money from the owner of a house in the Genyadana district of Edo. Yasugorō or "Yasu" enters first and he spins a yarn to the woman of the house about how his friend who, badly injured in a fight, needs traveling money to visit a hot spring so that he can convalesce. After some pressure, the woman acquiesces and hands over a small amount of money. As Yasu leaves, content with himself, Yosa enters, shouting that the money is not sufficient. He recognizes the woman as his former lover Otomi who he believed had drowned in the sea following his attack. However, Otomi had been saved by the merchant Tazaemon, who subsequently installs Otomi in the modest Genyadana house and acts as her benefactor. Yosa incorrectly assumes that Tazaemon is Otomi's lover and in a long soliloquy he compares her new found luck with his miserable life. Tazaemon arrives, explains the situation, and offers Yosa and Yasu a large sum of money to start a new life. Yosa reluctantly accepts the money, and after leaving the house he and Yasu quarrel about their share of the loot. Kōka's print depicts Onoe Matsusuke IV (1843-1928) as Yasu, identifiable by the prominently tattooed bat on his cheek that gave rise to his nickname "Yasu the Bat." (*See also below* "The Actor Ichikawa Kigan V as Otomi" by Natori Shunsen.)

66

Yamamura Kōka (1886-1942)

"The Actor Matsumoto Kōshirō VII as Sekibei in the Play *Seki no to* (*Love at the Snow-covered Barrier Gate*)," c. 1919

This two-scene dance set begins at the barrier gate on Mount Ōsaka, which is guarded by Sekibei. (Sekibei is actually the evil courtier Ōtomo no Kuronushi in disguise.) Sekibei allows Princess Ono no Komachi to pass through the gate so that she can meet the barrier guardian and her lover Yoshimune Munesada. A dance scene between the three follows and Munesada realizes Sekibei's true identity when he sees the bloody sleeve of his brother Yasusada, who had been killed by Sekibei's followers, carried by a hawk in flight overhead.

One day during a drunken bout Sekibei spies the reflection of stars in his drinking cup, a sign that he will become emperor if he performs a ritual using the burnt wood of a cherry tree. When he is about to fell a nearby cherry, the spirit of the tree appears in the form of Yasusada's mistress, Sumizome, and fights off Sekibei with a flowering branch. In the ensuing dance – imitating the liaison between a courtesan and her client – she forces him to reveal his true nature. In a spectacular quick costume change (*bukkaeri*) on stage, Sekibei changes from his green padded coat and simple brown cap into the magnificent back costume and headdress of the courtier Kuronushi. The scene depicted in Kōka's print captures Sekibei during an emotional pose (*mie*) just before his transformation. The crest (*mon*) on his coat comprises three stylized Chinese characters (connoting "three men") that are associated with the creator of this role, Nakamura Nakazō I (1736-90). Kōka's subject, however, is the actor Matsumoto Kōshirō VII (1870-1949).

72

Natori Shunsen (1886-1960)

"The Actor Nakamura Ganjirō I as Kamiya Jihei in the Play *Shinjū ten no Amijima* (*Love Suicide at Amijima*)," c. 1916

The role of the somewhat naïve character of Kamiya Jihei is performed in the so-called gentle *wagoto* style, typical of plays based on daily life (*sewamono*) in the Edo period. Based on an actual event, the play *Love Suicide at Amijima* was written in 1720 for the puppet theater by Japan's most distinguished historical playwright, Chikamatsu Monzaemon (1653-1724). Successful puppet performances were often followed very soon afterwards by Kabuki adaptations, but in the case of *Love Suicide at Amijima* it was nearly 200 years before a faithful version of the story was staged. Nakamura Ganjirō I (1860-1935) starred in the role of Jihei, a role which has since become a specialty of the Nakamura family.

The plot of the story revolves around a love affair that ends in a double suicide (*shinjū*). Jihei, a paper merchant, is married to Osan and has two children. Even so, he falls in love with Koharu, a courtesan of the Kinokuniya brothel in the Shinmachi pleasure district of Kyoto. Following rumors that some well-to-do person wants to ransom Koharu from her indenture with the brothel, Osan writes Koharu and implores her to give up her husband. Yet at the same time Osan sells her clothes and those of the children to earn enough money for Jihei's ransom of Koharu. The situation becomes even more convoluted when Osan's father comes to take his daughter back home, leaving the children behind. The two lovers Jihei and Koharu see no way out. Torn between obligation (*giri*) and emotion (*ninjō*) they decide to commit double suicide. Plays about love suicides were banned in 1723 because too many young people were following the example set on the stage.

73

Natori Shunsen (1886-1960)

"The Actor Ichimura Uzaemon XV as Iriya Naozamurai in the Play *Naozamurai*," c. 1925

During the Meiji era, Japan experienced a period of "modernization" as it opened its borders to foreign trade. The feudal class system that had prevailed during the previous Edo period was replaced by imperial rule, and sweeping social changes occurred in its wake. One consequence was the abolition of the samurai's once privileged position. The leading Meiji playwright Kawatake Mokuami (1816-93), conscious of the shifting social milieu, produced several bandit plays (*shiranami mono*) recounting tales of samurai who have fallen on hard times. The role of the romantic bandit as illustrated here was created by Mokuami in 1881 for the piece entitled *Naozamurai*. Although part of the longer play *Kumo ni magō Ueno no hatsuhana*, *Naozamurai* was performed as an independent piece in 1910 at the Kabuki Theater in Tokyo. Ichimura Uzaemon XV (1874-1945) starred as Naozamurai (literally, "faithful samurai").

Kataoka Naojirō, better known as Naozamurai, has become a member of a gang of criminals. They are sought after by the authorities and Naozamurai is trying to escape from Edo. On a cold, snowy night he arrives at a noodle shop in Iriya near the Yoshiwara, where he overhears that his mistress, the courtesan Michitose, is suffering from his neglect. Despite the risk of being captured, he sneaks into Michitose's room at the Ōguchiya brothel and confesses that he is not the wealthy samurai he once claimed, but a common crook on the run. Michitose swears her love nonetheless and says that she is prepared to kill herself should he be arrested. As the lovers prepare to escape, the authorities burst in, and Michitose takes her own life so that she can be reunited with her lover in the next world. Shunsen's masterful print shows a contemplative Naozamurai out in the cold, his head protected against the falling snow.

74

Natori Shunsen (1886-1960)

"The Actor Ichikawa Kigan V as Otomi in the Play *Yowa nasake ukina yokogushi (The Love Affair of Otomi and Scarface Yosaburō)*," c. 1927

Otomi is the mistress of Akama Genzaemon, the leader of a gang of gamblers. Strolling along the beach one day she falls head over heels in love with a handsome young man named Yosaburō. They begin to meet secretly, but their affair is eventually found out. Yosaburō is severely beaten and disfigured with a knife, and Otomi escapes her pursuers by leaping into the sea. Assuming that his beloved has drowned, Yosaburō – now nicknamed "Kirare Yosa" ("Scarface Yosa") – is heartbroken and earns his living as a petty thief and blackmailer. One day, when he and his sidekick "Kōmori Yasu" ("Yasu the Bat") enter a house in the Genyadana district of Edo to extort money, Yosaburō is surprised to see his former lover Otomi. She had been rescued from the sea by Tazaemon, a merchant who is in reality her brother. Tazaemon decides not to reveal his true identity to Otomi and installs her in a small house. Yosaburō, however, supposes that Tazaemon is her lover and in a long soliloquy he bitterly recalls his and Otomi's past romance.

Shunsen captures the actor Ichikawa Kigan V (1887-1978) in the role of Otomi, just as she is returning from the bathhouse, still unaware of the coming encounter with her former lover. The red bag dangling from her mouth contains ground rice husks (*nuka-bukuro*) used to clean the skin, and it adds a somewhat sensuous air to her portrayal. (*See also above* "The Actor Onoe Matsusuke IV as Kōmori Yasugorō" by Yamamura Kōka.)

75

Natori Shunsen (1886-1960)

"The Actor Ōtani Tomoemon VI as Sugawara no Michizane in the Play *Sugawara denju tenarai kagami (Sugawara's Secrets of Calligraphy)*," c. 1927

Sugawara no Michizane (845-903; also known as Kan Shōjō) was a distinguished poet and calligrapher. In 899 he was promoted to the high-ranking Minister of the Right and became regent for the young emperor Daigo (898-930, *r.* 897-930), much to the annoyance of the then ruling Fujiwara family. The Minister of the Left, Fujiwara no Tokihira (871-909), accused him of conspiracy against the emperor and Michizane was banished for life to Dazaifu on the distant island of Kyūshū. Michizane may have remained an obscure historical figure had not the playwrights Takeda Izumo I (*d.* 1747) and Miyoshi Shōraku (1696-1772), with the assistance of Namiki Senryū (Sōsuke, *d.* 1751) and Takeda Koizumo (Izumo II, 1691-1756), drawn on the story of his life for a puppet play staged in 1746 at the Takemoto puppet theater in Osaka. The play was hugely successful, and in the following year a version adapted for the Kabuki theater was staged concurrently at the Nakamura and Ichimura Theaters in Edo. Ever since, the play has been one of the most popular of the Kabuki repertory. The scene portrayed here shows the actor Ōtani Tomoemon VI (1886-1943) as Michizane in purple court dress decorated with stylized plum blossom motifs. Before going into exile Michizane's daughter Kariya, greatly distressed because her actions contributed in part to the unfortunate course of events, wishes to see her father one last time. Barely able to contain his emotions, Michizane turns away and raises his sleeve to shield his face from her so that she will not see his anguish.

78

Yoshikawa Kanpō (1894-1979)

"The Actor Ichikawa Sadanji II as Hishikawa Gengobei in the Play *Imayō Satsuma uta (The Song of Satsuma in Modern Style)*," 1923, Autumn

Hishikawa Gengobei is an uncouth country samurai from the Satsuma area in Kyūshū. One day he helps his cousin Sasano Sangobei hide Sangobei's paramour Oman because their relationship is frowned on by Sangobei's father, who also happens to be the chief abbot of an important Shinto shrine in Edo. Oman is placed in the care of a widow living in the Meguro district of Edo. Soon after and to everyone's surprise Gengobei, while drunk, declares his love for Oman and secures consent from her parents for their marriage. Sangobei discovers this and a duel follows, in which Sangobei is killed and Oman wounded. Oman then kills herself after delivering the bittersweet words, "Can you cut out love with a sword, can you take it with a sword?," and Gengobei, realizing he cannot receive love through force, also commits suicide. A reworking of the famous play *Godairiki koi no fūjime*, written by Namiki Gohei I (1747-1808) and staged in 1794, *The Song of Satsuma in Modern Style* was first staged in 1920 at the Shintomi Theater in Tokyo. This role of the boorish, inebriated samurai, who falls for his cousin's lover, was one of the greatest for Ichikawa Sadanji II (1880-1940).

79

Yoshikawa Kanpō (1894-1979)

"The Actor Jitsukawa Enjaku II as Igami no Gonta in the Play *Yoshitsune senbonzakura* (*Yoshitsune and the Thousand Cherry Trees*)," 1923

Igami no Gonta figures prominently in the sushi shop scene (Act III) of the famous historical play *Yoshitsune and the Thousand Cherry Trees*, which was originally written for the puppet theater in 1747 by Takeda Izumo II (1691-1756), Namiki Sōsuke (1695-1751) and Miyoshi Shōraku (1696-1772).

Gonta's father, Yaezamon, owns a sushi shop and employs an apprentice named Yasuke. In reality Yasuke is Koremori, a distinguished general of the Taira clan, who is on the run after his clan was defeated by the Minamoto at the Battle of Yashima. Problems arise when the envoy of the shogun, Kajiwara Heizō Kagetoki, arrives and demands Koremori's head. The wicked Gonta, disinherited by his father, has seen through Yasuke's disguise and wants to collect the reward posted for Koremori. He enters, carrying a sushi tub and pulling a bound woman and a child, and presents them as Koremori's wife and child. He then produces a head from the tub which he claims is Koremori's. After the envoy's departure, Gonta's father is so outraged by the horrendous conduct of his son that he stabs him to death. With his dying words Gonta reveals his remorse about his wicked behavior and his change of heart after witnessing Yaezamon's loyalty to Koremori. The head in the tub is actually not that of Koremori but of Kokingo, a retainer killed in an earlier skirmish, and the women and the child are his own wife and child. In his print Kanpō depicts Jitsukawa Enjaku II (1877-1951) as Gonta in his characteristic black (or blue) and white checkered kimono, perhaps as he is considering his evil deeds.

80

Yoshikawa Kanpō (1894-1979)

"The Actor Kataoka Gadō IV as Asagao in the Play *Shō utsushi asagao nikki* (*Diary of the Morning Glory*)," 1924

Miyuki, the daughter of a wealthy samurai, is catching fireflies during an outing on the Uji River. A sudden gust of wind blows off her veil, which lands in another pleasure boat. When the handsome young boat owner, Miyagi Asojirō, returns the veil, Miyuki instantly falls in love with him. As a keepsake of their meeting Asojirō writes a poem about the morning glory (*asagao*) on her fan. That summer they meet once more and Miyuki hands him her fan with the poem as a token of her love. Asojirō subsequently leaves for Kamakura and it is understood that he will not see Miyuki for a long time. When Miyuki's parents decide to marry their love-sick daughter to Komazawa Jirozaemon, she runs away. She becomes blind from her bitter weeping, calls herself Asagao and wanders the countryside as an itinerant musician in search of Asojirō. What she does not know is that Asojirō has changed his name to Komazawa Jirozaemon, and thus the very man her parents had proposed as her future husband. When Jirozaemon, supposing Miyuki had forgotten him, visits an inn in Shimada he sees the poem about the morning glory on a folding screen in his room. The innkeeper tells him the poem is the favorite song of a blind girl named Asagao, who performs for travelers staying at the inn. When Jirozaemon summons the girl to sing for him she plays the *koto* (a type of zither) and recites the tragic story of her life. Jirozaemon recognizes her as Miyuki but he has to depart before he is able to reveal his true identity. Upon leaving he hands the innkeeper the fan with his poem about the morning glory, some money and medicine for Asagao's eyes. In the ensuing turn of events her eyesight is restored so that she can return to Edo.

In this print Kanpō portrays Kataoka Gadō IV (1882-1946) as the blind, dispirited Asagao placing *koto* plectra on her fingers; she is unaware that she is about to perform for her lover. The actor's forehead is covered by a purple crepe band (*murasaki bōshi*). The wearing of the band originated in the early days of Kabuki when young male actors were forced to shave their forelocks and later the practice continued even when wigs were worn. Asagao's robe is decorated with blossoms of the morning glory.

Bibliography

General Bibliography

Bernstein, Gail Lee (ed.). *Recreating Japanese Women, 1600-1945*. Berkeley, Los Angeles and Oxford: University of California Press, 1991.

Conant, Ellen *et al. Nihonga: Transcending the Past*. Saint Louis: Saint Louis Art Museum, 1995.

Editorial Committee for the Dictionary of Classical Japanese Literature [Nihon Koten Bungaku Daijiten Henshū Iinkai] (ed.). *Nihon Koten Bungaku Daijiten* (Dictionary of Classical Japanese Literature). 6 vols. Tokyo: Iwanami Shoten, 1983-85.

Forrer, Matthi (ed.). *Essays on Japanese Art Presented to Jack Hillier*. London: Robert G. Sawers Publishing, 1982.

Lane, Richard. *Images of the Floating World: The Japanese Print*. Fribourg: Office du Livre, 1978.

Leiter, Samuel L. *New Kabuki Encyclopedia: A Revised Adaptation of Kabuki Jiten*. Westport and London: Greenwood Press, 1997.

McClain, James L. *Japan: A Modern History*. New York and London: W.W. Norton & Company, 2002.

Meech, Julia. "The Early Years of Japanese Print Collecting in North America," *Impressions, The Journal of the Ukiyo-e Society of America, Inc.* 25 (2003), 15-54.

Rotondo-McCord, Lisa (ed.). *An Enduring Vision: 17th- to 20th-Century Japanese Painting from the Gitter-Yelen Collection*. New Orleans: New Orleans Museum of Art in association with the University of Washington Press, Seattle, 2002.

Seidensticker, Edward. *Low City, High City: Tokyo from Edo to the Earthquake: How the Shogun's Ancient Capital Became a Great Modern City, 1867-1923*. New York: Knopf, 1983.

Tipton, Elise K., and John Clark (eds.). *Being Modern in Japan: Culture and Society from the 1910s to the 1930s*. Australian Humanities Research Foundation, 2000.

Uhlenbeck, Chris. "Production Constraints in the World of *Ukiyo-e*," 11-22, in Amy Reigle Newland (ed.). *The Commercial and Cultural Climate of Japanese Printmaking*. Amsterdam: Hotei Publishing, 2004.

Volker, Tijs. *Ukiyo-e Quartet: Publisher, Designer, Engraver and Printer*. Leiden, Mededelingen van het Rijksmuseum voor Volkenkunde 5. Leiden: E. J. Brill, 1949.

Annotated Bibliography for Shin-hanga *Studies*

Compiled by Chris Uhlenbeck and Marije Jansen

This bibliography is meant as an introduction to the study of *Shin-hanga* and is not intended as a fully comprehensive collection of sources.

Ajioka, Chiaki *et al. Hanga: Japanese Creative Prints*. Sydney: Art Gallery of New South Wales, 2000.

Exhibition catalogue of works drawn from Japanese and Australian collections, with essays by Ajioka Chiaki, Nishiyama Junko and Kuwahara Noriko covering Sōsaku-hanga *and* dōjin *magazines, and developments in Japanese printmaking from 1904 to the 1950s.*

Blair, Dorothy. *Modern Japanese Prints*. Toledo: The Toledo Museum of Art, 1997 (reprint of the Museum's 1930 and 1936 catalogues).

See below *under The Toledo Museum of Art.*

Blakeney, Ben Bruce. *Yoshida Hiroshi: Printmaker*. Tokyo: The Foreign Affairs Association of Japan, 1953.

Short publication on Yoshida, with a description of his life and work, a listing of his prints and facsimiles of his seals.

Brown, Kendall H. *et al. Light in Darkness. Women in Japanese Prints of Early Showa (1926-1945)*. Los Angeles: Fisher Gallery, University of Southern California, 1996.

Includes seven essays on various aspects of Shin-hanga, *with an emphasis on ideological and political influences on the attitude of artists and publishers toward their subject matter.*

Brown, Kendall H., and Hollis Goodall-Cristante. *Shin-hanga: New Prints in Modern Japan*. Los Angeles: Los Angeles County Museum of Art in conjunction with the University of Washington Press, Seattle, 1996.

Important Shin-hanga *catalogue with a good selection of prints drawn from numerous private collections; two essays offer an in-depth discussion of the historical and social background against which* Shin-hanga *developed, as well as an art historical survey of the movement.*

Brown, Kendall H., and Sharon A. Minichiello. *Taisho Chic: Japanese Modernity, Nostalgia and Deco*. Honolulu: Honolulu Academy of Arts, 2002.

Innovative look at Taishō-period arts, including a number of prints and paintings by Shin-hanga *artists, two background essays and lengthy catalogue descriptions.*

Brown, Kendall H. *et al. Kawase Hasui: The Complete Woodblock Prints*. Amsterdam: Hotei Publishing, 2003.

Bilingual (English and Japanese) catalogue raisonné *of the work of Hasui, with over 600 color illustrations, appendices with seals and signatures, print descriptions, as well as two essays regarding the life and art of Hasui.*

Chiba City Museum of Art [Chiba-shi Bijutsukan] (ed.). *Nihon no hanga I 1900-1910. Han no gatachi hyakusō* (Japanese Prints 1900-1910: One Hundred Views in Print Form). Chiba: Chiba City Museum of Art, 1997.

Informative catalogue of Japanese graphic arts issued between 1900 and 1920. Deals thoroughly with aspects of Sōsaku-hanga *and* Shin-hanga, *as well as including book covers, ex libris, advertisements, etc. In Japanese only.*

Chiba City Museum of Art [Chiba-shi Bijutsukan] (ed.). *Nihon no hanga II 1911-1920. Kizamareta "ko" no kyōen* (Japanese Prints II, 1911-1920: A Carved "Private" Banquet). Chiba: Chiba City Museum of Art, 1999.

The second volume in the above series.

Chiba City Museum of Art [Chiba-shi Bijutsukan] (ed.). *Nihon no hanga III 1921-1930. Toshi to onna to hikari to kage to* (Japanese Prints III, 1921-1930: Cities and Women, Lights and Shadows). Chiba: Chiba City Museum of Art, 2001.

The third volume in the above series.

Chigasaki City Art Museum [Chigasaki-shi Bijutsukan] (ed.). *Tsuchiya Kōitsu ten. Fūkō raisan* (Tsuchiya Kōitsu Exhibition: In the Praise of Natural Scenery). Chigasaki: Chigasaki City Art Museum, 1999.

The only exhibition catalogue to date devoted to Tsuchiya Kōitsu, illustrating his prints and select paintings, works by his teacher Kobayashi Kiyochika and prints by Kawase Hasui. In Japanese only.

Daulte, François, and Chris Uhlenbeck. *La nouvelle vague. L'estampe japonaise de 1868 à 1939 dans la collection Robert O. Muller*. Lausanne/Paris: Bibliotheque des Arts, 1994.

Catalogue published on occasion of the The New Wave *exhibition of prints from the Robert O. Muller collection, which was held at the Musée Marmottan in Paris and the Fondation L'Hermitage in Lausanne in 1994. In French only.*

Edmunds, Will. H. "Modern Japanese Colour Prints," *Apollo* 12 (August 1930), 120-26.

Early critique article in English on a Shin-hanga *exhibition held by Yamanaka & Co. at their New York branch; Edmunds wrote a number of articles on* Shin-hanga *artists.*

Edo-Tokyo Museum [Edo-Tokyo Hakubutsukan] (ed.). *Kindai hanga ni miru Tōkyō – utsuriyuku fūkei* (Tokyo as Depicted in Modern Woodblock Prints – Landscape in Transition). Tokyo: Edo-Tokyo Museum, 1996.
Excellent publication with a fine selection of Shin-hanga *and* Sōsaku-hanga *prints dealing with the city of Tokyo. In Japanese only.*

Freis, Ed. "Seasons of the Pleasure Quarters," *Andon* 48 (1994), 138-39.
Article on Kitano Tsunetomi's series Seasons of the Pleasure Quarters (Kurawa no shunjū) *of 1918.*

Fujikake, Shizuya. *Japanese Wood-block Prints*. Tokyo: Japanese Government Railways, 1949.
A short, but concise guide to the history of Japanese woodblock prints from the eleventh century onward. A remarkably good source of information on twentieth-century Shin-hanga.

Fukumitsu Art Museum [Fukumitsu Bijutsukan] (ed.). *Oda Kazuma ten. Nihon sekibanga no senkusha* (Oda Kazuma Exhibition: A Pioneer of Japanese Lithographs). Fukumitsu: Fukumitsu Art Museum, 1996.
Exhibition catalogue on Oda Kazuma, a leading printmaker in the 1920s and 1930s who worked principally as a lithographer. In Japanese only.

Fukuoka City Art Museum [Fukuoka-shi Bijutsukan] (ed.). *Yoshida Hiroshi ten. Kindai fūkeiga no kyosho* (Hiroshi Yoshida Exhibition: A Master of Modern Landscape Painting). Fukuoka: Fukuoka Art Museum, 1996.
Catalogue devoted primarily to Yoshida's paintings, but over thirty prints in full color are also illustrated. The Japanese text provides a fascinating overview of his life, especially his trips abroad.

Haga, Tōru. *Konetikatto no Taishō hanga: "Midaregami no keifu"* (Taishō-period Prints in Connecticut: "Genealogy of Unkempt Hair"). Tokyo: Bijutsu Kōronsha, 1981.
An account by Professor Haga Tōru of his visits to Robert O. Muller at his home in Connecticut; a similarly titled work entitled "Ikyō no Nihon bijutsu – Konechikatto no Nihon hanga" (Japanese Art Abroad: Japanese Prints in Connecticut) *was published in* Hikaku bungaku kenkyū (Studies on Comparative Literature) *at Tokyo University in June 1977 (pages 103-11).*

Hamada, Taiji, and Hosono Masanobu (eds.). *Itō Shinsui zenshū* (The Complete Works of Itō Shinsui). 6 vols. Tokyo: Shūeisha, 1981-82.
Lavish set illustrating Shinsui's complete oeuvre of prints and paintings. In Japanese only.

Hamanaka, Shinji, and Amy Reigle Newland. *The Female Image: 20th-century Prints of Japanese Beauties*. Tokyo: Abe Publishing and Leiden: Hotei Publishing, 2000.
Comprehensive bilingual (English and Japanese) survey of Shin-hanga *beauties, with images drawn from Japanese, European and American collections.*

Hiraki Ukiyo-e Museum of Art [Hiraki Ukiyoe Bijutsukan] (ed.). *Ohara Koson no sekai. Seiyō de aisareta kachōga* (The World of Ohara Koson: Images of Birds and Flowers Admired in the West). Yokohama: Hiraki Ukiyo-e Museum of Art, 1998.
First catalogue devoted to Koson; it includes 143 prints often accompanied by preparatory drawings, trial prints and paintings. Image captions in Japanese and English.

Iino, Masahito *et al.* (eds.). *Itō Shinsui zen mokuhanga* (Catalogue of the Complete Woodblock Prints of Itō Shinsui). Tokyo: Executive Committee for the Exhibition *The Complete Woodblock Prints of Itō Shinsui*, 1992.
The most comprehensive catalogue to date of Shinsui's prints. Includes an essay in English by Watanabe Tadasu on Shinsui and his working relationship with his father Watanabe Shōzaburō. Image captions in Japanese and English.

Ikeda, Tamio, and Michel Balluteau. *Regards d'acteurs. Natori Shunsen. Estampes de Natori Shunsen (1886-1960) de la seriés des 36 portraits d'acteurs de kabuki.* Paris: Tanakaya, 2001.
Catalogue of an exhibition of Shunsen's famous series of thirty-six actor portraits Shunsen nigao shū *(1925-29), which is illustrated in its entirety. In French only.*

Inoue, Kazuo, and Watanabe Shōzaburō (eds.). *Ukiyo-eshi den* (Discussion of Ukiyo-e Artists). Tokyo: Watanabe Print Shop [Watanabe Hangaten], 1931.
Important, but basic, Japanese text on various aspects of printmaking and Shin-hanga *issues; it contains the critical published writings of Watanabe in an appendix.*

Itabashi Ward Museum of Art [Itabashi Kuritsu Bijutsukan] (ed.). *Taishō ki no hanga ten* (Exhibition of Taishō-period Woodblock Prints). Tokyo: Itabashi Ward Museum of Art, 1988.
General catalogue with short introductory essay relating to Taishō-period prints, including works by Itō Shinsui, Kawase Hasui, Yamamura Kōka (Toyonari), Yoshikawa Kanpō, Yoshida Hiroshi and others. Image captions in Japanese and English.

Jenkins, Donald. *Images of a Changing World: Japanese Prints of the Twentieth Century*. Portland: Portland Art Museum, 1983.
Pioneering American catalogue on the origins of the Sōsaku-hanga *movement.*

Katō, Junzō (ed.). *Kindai Nihon hanga taikei* (An Outline of Modern Japanese Woodblock Prints). 3 vols. Tokyo: Mainichi Shinbunsha, 1975-79.
Comprehensive overview of Shin-hanga *and* Sōsaku-hanga. *Japanese text, with brief captions also in English.*

Kawase, Hasui. "Hangasō zuihitsu" (Miscellaneous Thoughts by Hangasō), *Ukiyo-e geijutsu* 4:3 (March 1935), 63-7.
Personal accounts by the celebrated landscape artist Hasui as relates to his art; Hangasō is a reference to the artist's moniker Hangadō.

Kōno, Minoru. *Hanga: Meiji shōnen kara Shōwa 20nen made* (Prints from the Early Meiji to 1945). 2 vols. Machida: Machida City Museum of International Graphic Arts [Machida Shiritsu Kokusai Hanga Bijutsukan], 1996.
Catalogue of Shin-hanga *and* Sōsaku-hanga *prints, as well as book illustrations. In Japanese only.*

Kōyō Museum, Shōwa Women's University [Shōwa Joshi Daigaku Kōyō Hakubutsukan] (ed.). *Kawase Hasui hanga ten. Sekai de aisareta fūkei hangaka* (Exhibition of Prints by Kawase Hasui: A Landscape Printmaker Admired by the World). Tokyo: Shōwa Women's University, 1997.
A short catalogue illustrating seventy-six prints from all periods of Hasui's career. Image captions in Japanese and English.

Kushigata City Shunsen Museum of Art [Kushigata Chōritsu Shunsen Bijutsukan] (ed.). *Natori Shunsen: Kushigata Chōritsu Shunsen Bijutsukan shozō. Natori Shunzen sakuhin mokuroku* (A Catalogue of the Works of Shunsen Natori: Collection of the Kushigata City Shunsen Museum of Art). Kushigata: Kushigata City Shunsen Museum of Art, 2002.
Catalogue raisonné *of Shunsen's oeuvre, with the inclusion of 148 prints, 286 paintings, and hundreds of drawings and book illustrations. In Japanese only.*

Kuwayama, George (ed.). *Tradition in Transition: Print Masters of the Meiji and Taishō Periods*. Los Angeles: Los Angeles County Museum of Art, 1983.
Small exhibition catalogue with separate sections on Tsukioka Yoshitoshi, Kobayashi Kiyochika, Hashiguchi Goyō and Kawase Hasui.

Machida City Museum of International Graphic Art [Machida Shiritsu Kokusai Hanga Bijutsukan] (ed.). *Taishō jojō – shin-hanga no biten: Watanabe Shōzaburō to shin-hanga undō* (Taishō Lyricism: Exhibition of the Art of *Shin-hanga*, Watanabe Shōzaburō and the *Shin-hanga* Movement). Tokyo: Machida City Museum of International Graphic Art, 1989.
Detailed survey of Shin-hanga *prints from the Taishō period. Includes the prints of Hashiguchi Goyō, Itō Shinsui, Torii Kotondo, Yamamura Kōka (Toyonari), Natori Shunsen and others.*

Machida City Museum of International Graphic Art [Machida Shiritsu Kokusai Hanga Bijutsukan] (ed.). *Oda Kazuma ten. Meiji, Taishō, Shōwa, utsuriyuku fūkei* (Kazuma Oda Exhibition: Meiji, Taishō and Shōwa in Transition). Machida: Machida City Museum of International Graphic Art, 2000.
The most complete catalogue on Oda's lithographs. It also includes a small selection of his watercolors and book illustrations, as well as a chronology of his life with black-and-white photographs. In Japanese only.

MacLean, J. Arthur, and Dorothy Blair. "Two Modern Japanese Print-makers," *The American Magazine of Art* (February 1929), 98-101.

An article inspired by a special exhibition of prints held at the Toledo Museum of Art from November 4 to December 2, 1928.

MacLean, J. Arthur, and Dorothy Blair. "Ten Printmakers of the Last Decade," *The American Magazine of Art* XXI:8 (August 1930), 443-49.

Insightful early article written by two of the organizers of the 1930 and 1936 exhibitions of Japanese prints at the Toledo Museum of Art.

Merritt, Helen. *Modern Japanese Woodblock Prints, The Early Years*. Honolulu: University of Hawaii Press, 1990.

General art historical survey of printmaking in the first decades of the twentieth century, which also includes a discussion of the role of publisher Watanabe Shōzaburō.

Merritt, Helen, and Nanako Yamada. *Guide to Modern Japanese Woodblock Prints 1900-1975*. Honolulu: University of Hawaii Press, 1992.

Indispensable reference work on modern Japanese prints, with facsimiles of signatures and seals, and short biographical notes.

Merritt, Helen, and Nanako Yamada. *Woodblock Kuchi-e Prints. Reflections of Meiji Culture*. Honolulu: Hawaii University Press, 2000.

A study of Meiji-period kuchi-e, *including anecdotal biographies of the artists, facsimiles of signatures and seals, and glossary.*

Minneapolis Institute of Arts (ed.). *A Japanese Legacy: Four Generations of Yoshida Family Artists*. Minneapolis: Art Media Resources, 2002.

A very interesting catalogue on the life and work of the Yoshida family. It discusses the works of Hiroshi, Toshi, Hodaka and three generations of Yoshida women artists.

Mirviss, Joan. "A Tribute to Robert O. Muller (1911-2003)," *Impressions, The Journal of the Ukiyo-e Society of America, Inc.* 25 (2003), 109-15.

Personal tribute to the dealer and collector of Meiji and modern Japanese prints Robert O. Muller.

Mirviss, Joan B., and James Ulak. "Robert O. Muller (1911-2003)," *Orientations*, vol. 34, no. 7 (September 2003), 85-7.

Like the preceding source, a tribute to Robert O. Muller.

Mitchell, C. H. "*Hanshin Meisho Zue*: A Little-known Early *Shin Hanga* Series," 118-24, in Matthi Forrer (ed.). *Essays on Japanese Art Presented to Jack Hillier*. London: Robert G. Sawers Publishing, 1982.

An interesting discussion of an early Shin-hanga *landscape series.*

MOA Museum of Art [MOA Bijutsukan] (ed.). *Kindai Nihon no mokuhanga ten* (Exhibition of Modern Japanese Prints). Atami: MOA Museum of Art, 1983.

Overview of Japanese prints from Kobayashi Kiyochika to Kawase Hasui; short descriptions accompany illustrations, with a brief introduction by Yoshida Susumu. In Japanese only.

MOA Museum of Art [MOA Bijutsukan] (ed.). *Kindai Nihon no mokuhanga ten. Kaiteiban* (Exhibition of Modern Japanese Prints: Revised Edition). Atami: MOA Museum of Art, 1995.

High-quality catalogue tracing the roots of twentieth-century printmaking back to Kobayashi Kiyochika and through to Sōsaku-hanga *and* Shin-hanga. *In Japanese only.*

The Museum of Kyoto [Culture] [Kyoto Bunka Hakubutsukan] (ed.). *Yoshikawa Kanpō to Kyōto bunka. Nihon saidaikyō no fūzoku korekushon* (The Yoshikawa Kanpō Collection and Kyoto Culture: Manners and Customs Seen through Paintings, Costumes and Everyday Objects). Kyoto: The Museum of Kyoto Culture, 2002.

Noteworthy catalogue illustrating Kanpō's own paintings and prints, as well as an enormous selection of over 200 daily objects from his private collection that document Kyoto culture in the Edo and Meiji periods. Introduction and list of exhibits also in English.

Narazaki, Muneshige (ed.). *Kawase Hasui mokuhanga shū* (Collection of Woodblock Prints of Kawase Hasui). Tokyo: Mainichi Shinbunsha, 1979.

The (nearly) complete works of Hasui; all prints published by Watanabe Shōzaburō reproduced in color. Japanese text includes commentaries by Narazaki and Hasui, with extensive annotations based on Hasui's diaries. In Japanese only.

Narazaki, Muneshige (ed.). *Hizō ukiyo-e taikan: Murā korekushon* (*Ukiyo-e* Masterpieces in Western Collections: The Muller Collection). Tokyo: Kodansha, 1990.

Beautiful publication documenting the Robert O. Muller collection of Meiji and Shin-hanga *prints. In Japanese only.*

National Museum of Modern Art [Tōkyō Kokuritsu Kindai Bijutsukan] (ed.). *Kaburaki Kiyokata ten* (Kaburaki Kiyokata Exhibition). Tokyo: Yomiuri Shinbun, 1999.

Fine catalogue of the works of Kiyokata that does much to highlight his pivotal role in the development of twentieth-century painting. A good introduction; image captions in Japanese and English.

Newland, Amy *et al*. *Crows, Cranes & Camellias. The Natural World of Ohara Koson*. Leiden: Hotei Publishing, 2001.

First publication in English on this prolific designer of bird-and-flower prints, including an illustrated checklist in color of Koson's work, as well as an index of seals and signatures.

Nihon Keizai Shinbunsha (ed.). *Kawase Hasui ten* (Kawase Hasui Exhibition). Tokyo: Nihon Keizai Shinbunsha, 1982.

A groundbreaking catalogue, with a valuable explanation of the usage of the Watanabe copyright seals. In Japanese only.

Ogura, Tadao *et al*. *Yoshida Hiroshi zen mokuhanga shū* (The Complete Woodblock Prints of Yoshida Hiroshi). Tokyo: Abe Publishing, 1987.

Bilingual (Japanese and English) catalogue raisonné of the printed works of Yoshida Hiroshi, including an essay on the artist's life, a description of his trip to India and a tribute by his son Yoshida Hodaka.

Okabe, Masayuki (ed.). *Kirameku modan Taishō roman no gakatachi ten* (Modern Glitter: Romantic Artists of the Taishō Period). Osaka: Sankei Shinbun, 1992.

Catalogue of prints and paintings from the Taishō period, including such artists as Takehisa Yumeji and Yamamura Kōka (Toyonari). In Japanese only.

Ono, Tadashige. *Kindai Nihon no hanga* (Modern Japanese Prints). Tokyo: Sansaisha, 1971.

Important treatise on twentieth-century printmaking by one of the foremost postwar Sōsaku-hanga *artists.*

Ono, Tadashige. *Hanga no seishun* (The Heyday of Modern Woodblock Prints). Tokyo: Keishūsha, 1978.

Detailed discussion of the Sōsaku-hanga *movement. In Japanese only.*

Ōta Memorial Museum of Art [Ōta Kinen Bijutsukan] (ed.). *Meiji, Taishō bijin hanga ten* (Prints of Beauties from the Meiji and Taishō Periods). Tokyo: Ōta Memorial Museum of Art, 1993.

Catalogue of a private collection. Includes many examples of prints of beauties from the late Meiji and Taishō periods by such artists as Ogata Gekkō, Mizuno Toshikata and Yamakawa Shūn. In Japanese only.

Ōta Memorial Museum of Art [Ōta Kinen Bijutsukan] (ed.). *Seitan 100nen kinen. Torii Kotondo ten. Hachidaime Torii Kiyotada* (The Centenary of His Birth: Torii Kotondo Exhibition – The Works of Torii Kiyotada VIII). Tokyo: Ōta Memorial Museum of Art, 2000.

Fine exhibition catalogue of the work of Kotondo. Illustrates paintings, drawings, stage designs and painted fans, in addition to his well-known bijin *prints. Essays, a biography of the artist, reproductions of seals and black-and-white photographs of the artist are also included. In Japanese only.*

Ōta Ward Folk Museum [Ōta Kuritsu Kyōdo Hakubutsukan] (ed.). *Ryojō shijin Taishō Shōwa no fūkei hangaka Kawase Hasui* (Traveling Poet: Kawase Hasui, Landscape Print Artist of the Taishō and Shōwa Periods). Tokyo: Ōta Ward Folk Museum, 1990.

Exhibition catalogue illustrating over 200 works of Hasui, including a useful overview of seals and signatures. In Japanese, with catalogue descriptions in Japanese and English.

Ōta Ward Folk Museum [Ōta Kuritsu Kyōdo Hakubutsukan] (ed.). *Hanga ni miru Tōkyō no fūkei: Kantō daijishin kara senzen made* (The Landscape of Tokyo Seen in Prints: From the Great Kantō Earthquake to Prewar). Tokyo: Ōta Ward Folk Museum, 2002.

Catalogue of Shin-hanga *and* Sōsaku-hanga *depicting Tokyo in the period between the Great Kantō Earthquake of September 1923 and World War II. In Japanese only.*

Pachter, Irwin, and Kaneko Takushi. *Kawase Hasui and His Contemporaries: The Shin-hanga Movement in Landscape Art*. Syracuse: Everson Museum of Art, 1986.

Catalogue of an exhibition focusing on Hasui and his contemporaries. The first English publication to attempt a chronological typology of Watanabe publisher seals.

Pinckard, W. H. Jr. *Post-Meiji Japanese Woodblock Prints, 1912-1962*. Oakland: (no publisher), Winter 1983/1984.

Pioneering catalogue which was one of the primary references on Shin-hanga *throughout the 1980s.*

Riccar Art Museum [Riccar Bijutsukan] (ed.). *Taishō no onna. Hashiguchi Goyō ten* (Women of the Taishō Period: Hashiguchi Goyō Exhibition). Tokyo: Riccar Art Museum, 1976.

Catalogue illustrating the prints and drawings of Goyō, with an emphasis on his sketches. In Japanese only.

Riccar Art Museum [Riccar Bijutsukan] (ed.). *Kindai Nihon bijinga ten* (Exhibition of Modern Japanese Beauties). Tokyo: Riccar Art Museum, 1982.

An exhibition of modern prints of beauties from 1877 to 1972, including Shin-hanga. *Japanese text only, but artists' names also appear in romanized script.*

Satō, Mitsunobu *et. al. Hashiguchi Goyō ten* (Hashiguchi Goyō Exhibition). Tokyo: Tōkyō Shinbun, 1995.

Most complete source to date on the prints and drawings of Hashiguchi Goyō. In Japanese only.

Shimizu, Hisao. Ōta Ward Folk Museum 122/123 (2002).

This source is shown on the Shotei website www.shotei.com.

Smith, Henry D. II. *Kiyochika: Artist of Meiji Japan*. Santa Barbara: Santa Barbara Museum of Art, 1988.

A landmark publication on the Meiji-period artist Kobayashi Kiyochika; it did much toward a growing appreciation of Meiji print designers.

Smith, Lawrence. *The Japanese Print Since 1900, Old Dreams and New Visions*. New York: Harper and Row, 1983.

The first survey of modern Japanese prints to be published in Europe. Spans the period from popular prints of the Russo-Japanese War to contemporary Japanese artists.

Smith, Lawrence. *Modern Japanese Prints 1912-1989. Woodblocks and Stencils*. London: British Museum Press, 1994.

Exhibition catalogue based on the holdings of the British Museum and includes Sōsaku-hanga *and* Shin-hanga *with short biographies of all artists.*

Stephens, Amy Reigle (ed.). *The New Wave: Twentieth-century Japanese Prints from the Robert O. Muller Collection*. Leiden: Hotei Prints and London: Bamboo Publishing, 1993.

A groundbreaking and comprehensive book on Shin-hanga. *Essays by Donald Jenkins, Henry D. Smith II and Okamoto Hiromi, and Julia Meech, with 300 prints by more than fifty artists illustrated with accompanying explanatory notes.*

Takamizawa, Tadao. *Meiji Taishō ukiyo eshi: Kiyochika, Goyō, Shinsui hanga ten* (Exhibition of Meiji and Taishō *Ukiyo-e* Artists: Prints by Kiyochika, Goyō and Shinsui). Tokyo: Seibu, 1976.

General exhibition catalogue providing little information. In Japanese only.

Takashima, Masao. *Torii Kotondo. Woodblock Prints and Paintings*. Tokyo: Gallery Beniya, 1995.

Catalogue showing all of Kotondo's prints and a selection of his paintings. Includes an introduction in English and brief captions.

Tokyo Station Gallery [Tōkyō Sutêshon Gyarari] (ed.). *Kitano Tsunetomi ten* (Kitano Tsunetomi Exhibition). Tokyo: Tokyo Station Gallery, 2003.

Catalogue of Tsunetomi's limited print oeuvre, and his paintings of beauties and actors. With seals, signatures and list of exhibits. Preface in English.

The Toledo Museum of Art (ed.). *A Special Exhibition of Modern Japanese Prints*. Toledo: The Toledo Museum of Art, 1930.

The catalogue of the pioneering Toledo exhibition, which was the first systematic catalogue published in the West of Shin-hanga *prints. It includes the work of Hashiguchi Goyō, Itō Shinsui, Kawase Hasui, Miki Suizan, Natori Shunsen, Oda Kazuma, Ohara Shōson, Yamamura Kōka (Toyonari), Yoshida Hiroshi and Yoshikawa Kanpō.*

The Toledo Museum of Art (ed.). *Modern Japanese Prints: Woodblock Prints by Ten Artists. A Retrospective View of Five Years Work by Hakuhō, Hasui, Kiyoshi and others*. Toledo: The Toledo Museum of Art, 1936.

The catalogue of the second show in Toledo exhibiting the work of Kawase Hasui, Kobayakawa Kiyoshi, Torii Kotondo, Itō Shinsui, Kasamatsu Shirō, Ohara Koson, Natori Shunsen, Yoshida Hiroshi and Nomura Yoshimitsu. Of great importance for the development of the interest in modern prints in the United States.

The Ukiyo-e Society of Japan [Nihon Ukiyo-e Kyōkai] (ed.). "Tokushū Taishō ki hanga" (Special Edition: Prints of the Taishō Period), *Ukiyo-e geijutsu* 4 (entire issue) (1963).

Important Japanese source. Entire issue devoted to Shin-hanga *and* Sōsaku-hanga, *with a brief English introduction, short biographies and descriptions of the prints.*

Valentine, E. A. U. "Japan's Color-print Revival," *International Studio* 77 (May 1923), 101-9.

A relatively early article in English on Shin-hanga; *assessment of these prints as revivals of* Ukiyo-e *by early writers like Valentine would color later appraisals.*

Wagōkai (ed.). *Kasamatsu Shirō hanga mokuroku* (A Catalogue of the Prints of Kasamatsu Shirō). Yamanouchi: Shimotakai-gun Yamanouchi-chō Wagōkai, 2002.

Includes one short essay; a chronology of Shirō's works also appears in English.

Watanabe, Shōzaburō. *Sōsaku-hanga mokuroku* (Catalogue of Creative Prints). Tokyo: Watanabe Print Shop [Watanabe Hangaten], 1933.

Japanese-language sales catalogue from Watanabe firm. Published three years prior to the frequently cited 1936 catalogue (see following).

Watanabe, Shōzaburō. *Catalogue of Wood-cut Color Prints of S. Watanabe*. Tokyo: Watanabe Print Shop [Watanabe Hangaten], 1936.

The first Watanabe sales catalogue to be published after the Great Kantō Earthquake of 1923. An important document in the study of Shin-hanga. *It is the English version of the Japanese version of the catalogue,* Watanabe mokuhanga mokuroku, *from 1935.*

Watanabe, Shōzaburō. *Catalogue of Wood-cut Color Prints 2*. Tokyo: Watanabe Color Prints Co., 1951 (reprint 1962).

Watanabe sales catalogue which lists all prints published by the publisher until 1951, including works out of print. Includes a photographic explanation of how prints are made, showing Kawase Hasui at work.

Watanabe, Tadasu (ed.). *Watanabe Shōzaburō*. Tokyo: Watanabe Woodblock Art Gallery [Watanabe Hanga Co.], 1974.

Memorial volume dedicated to the publisher Watanabe Shōzaburō. Includes many photographs of the artists working for the Watanabe studio.

Yamanashi Prefectural Art Museum [Yamanashi Kenritsu Bijutsukan] (ed.). *Natori Shunsen ten* (Natori Shunsen Exhibition). Yamanashi: Yamanashi Prefectural Art Museum, 1981.

The earliest catalogue to gather together works of the artist Shunsen.

Yamanashi Prefectural Art Museum [Yamanashi Kenritsu Bijutsukan] (ed.). *Kawase Hasui: jojō no shi, Taishō . Shōwa no fūkei hangaka* (Kawase Hasui: Lyric Poetry – The Landscape Print Artist of the Taishō and Shōwa Periods). Yamanashi: Yamanashi Prefectural Museum, 1990.

Exhibition catalogue of the works of Hasui, with descriptions in Japanese and English. Only prints published by Watanabe Shōzaburō are illustrated. Reproduces a chronological identification chart of Watanabe publisher's seals.

Yamanashi Prefectural Art Museum [Yamanashi Kenritsu Bijutsukan] (ed.). *Natsukashii fūkei. Itō Takashi mokuhanga ten* (Catalogue of Nostalgic Landscapes: Exhibition of Itō Takashi's Woodblock Prints). Yamanashi: Yamanashi Prefectural Art Museum, 1997.

First and only monograph on Itō Takashi. In Japanese only.

Yui, Kazuto. *Nijū seiki bukko Nihon gaka jiten* (Dictionary of Twentieth-century Japanese Painters). Tokyo: Bijutsu Nenkansha, 1998.

A dictionary of Japanese-style painters – as well as Nanga *and* sumi-e *painters – who died in the twentieth century. In Japanese only; an index of names is included.*

Glossary

bijin ("beautiful person"). Term referring to "beautiful women" (*see also bijinga*).

bijinga ("pictures of beautiful women"). Term referring to one of the major genres in *Ukiyo-e* prints of the Edo and Meiji periods, and in *Shin-hanga*.

bokashi. Printing technique of tonal gradation whereby color is partially wiped off the printing block.

Bunten. Abbreviation for *Monbushō Bijutsu Tenrankai* (Exhibition of Fine Arts by the Ministry of Education), a government-sponsored exhibition (*kanten*) first organized in 1907. In 1919 the *Bunten* was succeeded by the *Teiten*, the government-sponsored exhibition of the *Teikoku Bijutsuin* (Imperial Art Academy; it became the *Teikoku Geijutsuin* or Imperial Art Academy in 1937, *see below*). It exhibited prints as part of the Western-style painting section from 1927. The last *Teiten* exhibition was in 1934, and in 1937 it was replaced by the *Shin-Bunten* (New Bunten) which in 1946 was superseded by the *Nitten*. The *Nitten* (abbreviation for *Nihon Bijutsu Tenrankai* or Japan Art Exhibition) was the annual exhibition of the *Nihon Geijutsuin* (Japan Art Academy), and until 1958 the exhibition was held under the jurisdiction of the Ministry of Education. After this time, it became an incorporated entity.

Chawakai ("Tea Table Talk" Association). Founded in 1918 by the *Nihonga* painter Kitano Tsunetomi (1880-1947; cat. nos. 45-6) in Osaka and paralleled the Kyoto-based *Kokuga Sōsaku-hanga Kyōkai* (National Painting Creation Association).

Dainibukai (The Second Division Society). Group of artists opposing the reorganization of the *Teikoku Bijutsuin* (*see Bunten*).

Edo. Name of present-day capital Tokyo during the Edo or Tokugawa period (1600-1868).

fūkeiga ("landscape pictures"). Print genre that became increasingly popular in the first half of the nineteenth century, especially with the work of Katsushika Hokusai (1760-1849) and Utagawa Hiroshige (1797-1858).

hanshita-e. A preparatory drawing executed in black ink on thin paper, which is used to indicate the outlines of the design in the printmaking process.

Hōsun (*Square Inch*). An influential magazine published from May 1907 to July 1911. Many important print artists such as Ishii Hakutei (1882-1958) and Oda Kazuma (1882-1956; cat. nos. 47-51), as well as pivotal literary figures, were involved in producing its thirty-five issues.

Hototogisu (*Little Cuckoo*). A leading haiku poetry magazine published by Yanagihara Kyokudō (1867-1957) from 1897, which coincided with the haiku reform movement of Masaoka Shiki (1867-1902). From1898 onward, Takahama Kyoshi (1874-1959) oversaw the magazine's publication. After 1915 celebrated poets such as Awano Seiho (1899-1992) and Yamaguchi Seishi (1901-94) became regular contributors.

Inten. *See Nihon Bijutsuin.*

Kabuki. Popular traditional Japanese theater established in the early seventeenth century, its plays and actors providing the mainstay for one of the major genres in *Ukiyo-e* prints and and in *Shin-hanga*. Images of actors are known as *yakusha-e* ("actor pictures").

kachōga ("flower-and-bird pictures"), but often referred to as "bird and flower pictures." Genre that enjoyed increasing popularity in woodblock prints from the nineteenth century onward.

Kano. Academic painting tradition originating in Chinese ink painting and flourishing in Japan from the late fifteenth century onward. The *Kano* school became the official painting school of the Tokugawa shogunate during the Edo period.

Kokumin Bijutsu Kyōkai (People's Art Society). Association that organized exhibitions from the early Meiji period until World War II and aimed at the popularization of arts and conservation of cultural heritage.

kuchi-e ("mouth picture"). Multi-color tipped-in frontispieces in books and magazines popular from the late nineteenth century onward.

Kyōdokai (Homeland Society). Organization of *Nihonga* painters who were students of Kaburagi Kiyokata (1878-1973; cat nos. 5-7).

Kyōto-shi Kaiga Senmon Gakkō (Kyoto Municipal Specialist School of Painting). Formed in 1909 from the *Kyōto-fu Gagakkō* (Kyoto Prefecture Art School); it was revamped after World War II as the *Kyōto shiritsu Bijutsu Daigaku* (Kyoto City Art University). Today it is known as the *Kyōto shiritsu Geijutsu Daigaku* (Kyoto City Fine Arts University).

Maruyama-Shijō. Painting tradition established in Kyoto by Maruyama Ōkyo (1733-95) in the second half of the eighteenth century; it is characterized by an almost "impressionistic" style, combined with the observation and naturalistic treatment of the subject.

Meiji Bijutsukai (Meiji Fine Arts Society). Created in 1888 by *Yōga* painters Asai Chū (1856-1907) and Koyama Shōtarō (1857-1916) as a reaction to the conservative *Nihon Bijutsu Kyōkai* (Japan Fine Arts Association). It staged its first exhibition in 1889, was abolished in 1900 and re-established in 1902 as the *Taiheiyō Gakai* (Pacific Western-style Painting Association) by artist Hiroshi Yoshida (1876-1950; cat. nos. 18-22) and others. Its exhibitions had a *hanga* or "print" section. In 1957 the *Taiheiyō Gakai* became the *Taiheiyō Bijutsukai* (Pacific Western-Style Art Association).

Minogami. A type of paper named after Mino Province (present-day Gifu Prefecture); it is made from *kōzo* (mulberry) fibers.

Nanga ("Southern painting"). Literati or scholar painting tradition that evolved from a renewed interest in Chinese culture in Edo period.

Nihon Bijutsuin (Japan Art Institute). Art school and artists colony founded in 1898 by historian-ideologue Okakura Tenshin (Kakuzō, 1862-1913) to promote an understanding of local traditions and to counter the widespread adoption of Western styles by painters. It was re-organized into the *Saikō Nihon Bijutsuin* (Reorganized Japan Art Institute) in 1914 and has since been revamped on a number of occasions. In its various forms it became and remains the center for *Nihonga* painting (*see following*) and is the organizer of the prestigious annual exhibition *Inten*. From 1898 to 1906, the *Inten* was the annual exhibition of the *Nihon Bijutsuin*, and with its revamping as the *Saikō Nihon Bijutsuin*, it showed both *Nihonga* and *Yōga* (*see below*). The *Yōga* section was discontinued in 1920 and the sculpture section in 1961, after which time the *Inten* only exhibited Japanese-style painting.

Nihonga ("Japanese or Japanese-style painting"). Term appearing in mid-Meiji to differentiate artists working in traditional media from Western-style oil painters (*Yōga*); not a single style, it includes a number of art associations and artists desiring to express an aesthetic believed to be "Japanese" through the use of traditional materials.

Nihon Geijutsuin. *See Teikoku Geijutsuin.*

Nihon Hanga Kyōkai. *See Nihon Sōsaku-hanga Kyōkai.*

Nihon Kaiga Kyōkai. *See Nihon Seinen Kaiga Kyōkai.*

Nihon Seinen Kaiga Kyōkai (Japan Youth Painting

Association). Founded in 1891 by Kajita Hanko (1870-1917) with Okakura Tenshin as president; it became the *Nihon Kaiga Kyōkai* (Japan Painting Society) in 1896.

Nihon Sōsaku-hanga Kyōkai (Society of Japanese Creative Prints). Founded in 1918 by Yamamoto Kanae (1882-1946) and other *Sōsaku-hanga* (*see below*) artists. In 1931 it merged with the *Yōfū Hangakai* (*see below*) to become the *Nihon Hanga Kyōkai* (Japan Print Association), which resulted in the largest group of printmakers and one that is still active today. It holds a competitive annual jury exhibition.

nishiki-e ("brocade pictures"). Term coined for the full-color woodblock prints appearing after 1764-65 that used more advanced printing techniques; so called as they resembled multi-colored brocade silks (*see also Ukiyo-e*).

Nitten. *See Bunten.*

ōban. Print format, approximately 39.0-39.5 x 26.5-27.0 cm.

ōkubi-e ("large-head pictures"). Term describing close-up portraits in which the head and shoulders fill the picture plane.

onnagata ("female person"). Term in Kabuki for actors who perform female roles.

Rinpa. Painting tradition developed by Tawaraya Sōtatsu (c. 1600-40) and Ogata Kōrin (1658-1716) that is characterized by a decorative quality and a delicate style, often using sumptuous colorants like gold and silver. *Rinpa* witnessed several periods of revival, the last being in the late nineteenth and early twentieth centuries with artists like Kamisaka Sekka (1866-1942).

Saikō Nihon Bijutsuin. *See Nihon Bijutsuin.*

Seikinkai (Blue Collar Society). Association of *Nihonga* painters founded in 1939 by Itō Shinsui (1898-1972; cat. nos. 85-101) and Yamakawa Shūhō (1898-1944; cat. no. 84).

sekibanga. Lithography, a type of "stone printing" invented in Munich by Johann Alois Senefelder in around 1800; in Japan it gained widespread use in the later nineteenth century.

Shin-Bunten. *See Bunten.*

Shin-hanga ("New Prints"). Woodblock prints produced for the so-called "movement" initiated by publisher Watanabe Shōzaburō (1885-1962) in the early twentieth century, which sought a new language for the woodblock print medium while also retaining the traditional division of labor in print production as known in *Ukiyo-e*.

Sōsaku-hanga ("Creative Prints"). Prints whose production was, at least in theory, based on Western traditions of printmaking, whereby the artist carried out the entire creative process. *Shin-hanga* works are often discussed in opposition to it.

Taiheiyō Gakai. *See Meiji Bijutsukai.*

Tatsumi Gakai (Southeast Painting Society). Association of *Nihonga* artists founded by Muraoka Tōkō; they held annual exhibitions.

Teikoku Bijutsuin. *See Bunten* and *Teikoku Geijutsuin.*

Teikoku Geijutsuin (Imperial Fine Arts Academy). Founded in 1937 from the *Teikoku Bijutsuin* (Imperial Fine Arts Academy; *see also Bunten*), to whose programs were added music and literature. In 1947 it was reformed into the *Nihon Geijutsuin* (Japan Fine Arts Academy).

Teiten. *See Bunten.*

Tōkyō Bijutsu Gakkō (Tokyo School of Fine Arts). Art school founded in 1887 by the government, teaching Japanese-style arts. In 1896 it was extended with the inclusion of Western-style painting and sculpture. It became the *Tōkyō Bijutsu Daigaku* (Tokyo University of Fine Arts) in 1944.

The Toledo Museum of Art. Located in the US state of Ohio, the museum was the venue of two major exhibitions of *Shin-hanga* in 1930 and 1936; 336 and 289 works were shown in each, respectively.

Ugōkai (Cormorant Society). Founded in 1901 by Kaburagi Kiyokata and other students of Ogata Gekkō (1859-1920) and Mizuno Toshikata (1866-1908) as a society for *Ukiyo-e* and Japanese genre artists; it ceased activity in 1912.

Ukiyo-e ("pictures of the floating world"). Prints and paintings illustrating the "floating world" of the urban population of the Edo and Meiji periods. *Ukiyo-e* includes a broad repertory, including single-sheet prints in different formats, albums, illustrated fiction and paintings. Most early *Ukiyo-e* imagery was drawn from the theater and brothel districts (*see also yakusha-e* and *bijinga*), but over time the subject matter extended to include *kachōga* and *fūkeiga* (*see above*).

yakusha-e. *See* Kabuki *above.*

Yamato-e ("Yamato [Japanese] painting"). Japanese-style painting tradition that developed during the Late Heian (898-1185) and is characterized by the treatment of native subjects in a delicate style.

Yōfū Hangakai (Western-style Print Association). Association of etchers and lithographers founded in 1930. It had one exhibit before joining the *Nihon Sōsaku-hanga Kyōkai* (*see above*) from 1931 onward.

Yōga ("Western or Western-style painting"). Painting tradition strongly influenced by Western artistic trends, with its proponents often using oil paints, watercolors or pastels.

Chronology

Eras (1600-present)

Edo or Tokugawa	1600-1868
Meiji	1868-1912
Taishô	1912-26
Shôwa	1926-89
Heisei	1989-present

Index

The names and terms listed are those that relate to Shin-hanga history, prints and artists discussed in the text.

The Authors

Joan B. Mirviss is an expert and dealer in Japanese art, specializing in prints, paintings and contemporary ceramics. She received her M.A. degree in Japanese art history from Columbia University. She has lectured widely at museums and universities in the United States and Japan, and has contributed scholarly articles to numerous Asian art publications. She has also curated or assisted in the preparation of both international and US exhibitions of Japanese prints. In 2000, she curated an exhibition and authored the accompanying catalogue entitled *Jewels of Japanese Print Making: Surimono of the Bunka and Bunsei Era* for the Ōta Memorial Museum of Art, Tokyo. In 1995 she curated the exhibition of the Frank Lloyd Wright *surimono* collection at the Phoenix Art Museum and the Los Angeles County Museum of Art, and co-authored the accompanying catalogue *The Frank Lloyd Wright Collection of Surimono* (with John Carpenter). In 1984 she collaborated on a book for the Metropolitan Museum titled *Utamaro: Songs of the Garden*. She is currently serving as a consultant to the Freer Gallery of Art and the Arthur M. Sackler Gallery with respect to the Robert O. Muller Collection.

Amy Reigle Newland received her M.A. degree in art history from the University of Washington, Seattle, and for the last twelve years she has worked as a specialist free-lance editor and writer on Japanese woodblock prints. She has been involved in a number of publications, including *The New Wave: Twentieth-century Japanese Prints from the Robert O. Muller Collection* (1993; gen. ed.); *Heroes & Ghosts: Japanese Prints by Kuniyoshi 1797-1861* (1998; ed./co-author); *Time Present and Time Past: Images of a Forgotten Master Toyohara Kunichika 1835-1900* (1999; ed./co-author); *The Ear Catches the Eye: Music in Japanese Prints* (2000; ed.); *Crows, Cranes & Camellias: The Natural World of Ohara Koson 1877-1945* (2001; ed./co-author); *Kawase Hasui: The Complete Woodblock Prints* (2003; ed.) and *A Courtesan's Day: Hour by Hour* (2004; ed./co-author).

Chris Uhlenbeck was educated as an anthropologist at Leiden University, the Netherlands, and since 1982 has been engaged as a Japanese print dealer. He began the specialist bookstore, Ukiyo-e Books, in 1988 and has also been active in publishing books and organizing exhibitions on *Ukiyo-e*, *Shin-hanga* and Japanese photography. The organization of the traveling exhibition of the *Shin-hanga* collection of the late Robert O. Muller and the co-production of the accompanying catalogue, *The New Wave: Twentieth-century Japanese Prints from the Robert O. Muller Collection* (1993), was the springboard for the formation of Hotei Publishing, for which he currently acts as a consultant.

Marije Jansen is a M.A. graduate of Japanese studies from Leiden University. She authored *Hiroshige's Journey in the 60-odd Provinces* (Hotei Publishing, 2004) and is currently working for Hotei Japanese Prints.

Henk Herwig is a connoisseur of Kabuki actor prints. He has been the editor-in-chief of *Andon*, the Journal of the Society of Japanese Arts in the Netherlands, since 1990, and has co-authored a guide to the identification of Kabuki prints entitled *Heroes of the Kabuki Stage* (Hotei Publishing, 2004).